I0605527

Amos
The Genius of Prophetic Rhetoric

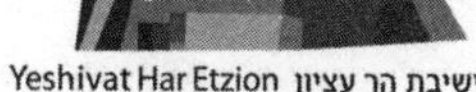

Yitzchak Etshalom

Amos

The Genius of Prophetic Rhetoric

Yeshivat Har Etzion
Maggid Books

Amos
The Genius of Prophetic Rhetoric

First Edition, 2025

Maggid Books
An imprint of Koren Publishers Jerusalem Ltd.

POB 8531, New Milford, CT 06776-8531, USA
& POB 4044, Jerusalem 9104001, Israel
www.korenpub.com

Cover image: Gustave Doré, The Prophet Amos
(engraving, 1865, colorized)

The publication of this book was made possible
through the generous support of *The Jewish Book Trust.*

ISBN 978-1-59264-633-3, *hardcover*

Printed and bound in the United States

In loving memory of Irving and Beatrice Stone,
who dedicated their lives to the
advancement of Jewish education.
We are proud and honored to continue in their legacy.

Their Children, Grandchildren, Great-Grandchildren,
and Great-Great-Grandchildren
Jerusalem, Israel
Cleveland, Ohio USA

In honor of
Rabbi Etshalom

Elayne & Howard Levkowitz

In memory of our grandparents and our parents,
and in honor of our children and grandchildren.

In honor of our friend and teacher, Rabbi Etshalom.

And in memory of those whose lives were lost
defending the State of Israel.

Wendy & Larry Platt
Los Angeles, California

Contents

Preface

Welcome to a stimulating journey to eighth-century BCE Samaria[1] – traveling the roads of the text-study approaches developed by the rabbis of the classical period, with frequent visits to the academies of France, Spain, and Provence, and occasional pit-stops in the halls of modern academia. In our tradition, canonical works are taken to be deeply textured, replete with nuances of language and intertextual allusions. It follows that to recapture the full intent of the text, the reader must be both fluent in the language of that time and also familiar with the geo-political and social realities of the period.

Despite a self-deprecating tendency among some to belittle our current generation's ability to grasp the deepest and broadest meaning of the biblical text – based on the argument that we have become increasingly distanced from the sensitivities and mores that informed the life of the original audience – it may be argued that the opposite is, in fact, more likely. With the development of sophisticated tools of discovery along with the panoramic view afforded by eons of distance, the twenty-

1. In this volume, Samaria and Israel are used interchangeably, both referring to the northern kingdom.

first-century student may be in a better position to fully appreciate the import of the biblical text than his or her forebears.

We generally regard the Tanakh as "written Torah," in apposition to "oral tradition," which ultimately takes shape in the literature of exegetes, sages, and decisors. We are accustomed to approaching the biblical text as a written work, which is appropriate but insufficient. Before the biblical texts were written, in most cases they were orally presented. Note that the single most popular verse in all of Tanakh is "And the Lord spoke to Moses, saying...," which is followed by a command that Moses was to *relay orally* to the people. It was only later that these commands were committed to writing. If this is true about Mosaic commands, it is yet truer for the speeches of the literary prophets of the eighth to fifth centuries BCE. In order to capture the impact of the prophet's words and to understand his lexical choice, we have to put ourselves in the place of the "primary audience," that group of citizens, royalty, or aristocracy who were privy to the "live" version of the speech. This must be done without diminishing by one iota the eternal message of the text, that which we, as the secondary (or "observing") audience, is meant to receive. To "hear with the ears of the primary target group," we have to muster as much information as available about the times – and we are more enabled to do so in the modern era, as noted above. This attempt to listen through ancient ears will be a recurring motif in this book.

The scheme of this book is multi-layered. First and foremost, we will peruse the book of Amos, noting those numerous words and phrases that are abstruse and that have challenged the scholarship and imagination of sages through the ages. We will dive into the seas of interpretation and, along the way, I will sometimes recommend one translation or meaning over the others.

Second, we will integrate information about the "realia" of the period, to the extent that it may shed light on the impact of the text to help us hear the message as the primary audience was meant to experience it.

We will also enter the great academies of rabbinic study throughout the ages, chiefly in the medieval period, and join in the robust debates about the meaning and message implicit in Amos's prophecies. As noted, we will not terminate our journey in the fourteenth century, but will glean from the scholarship of the modern age as well, to the extent that it enlightens us about the text and the world of that text.

Finally, and perhaps most vitally, we will use our study of these nine short chapters of prophetic rhetoric to examine the broad oeuvre of the literary prophets, from Isaiah of Jerusalem to Malachi. This will operate on both a schematic and a methodologic plane. Schematic, insofar as I will identify texts in Amos that appear, in parallel or paraphrase, in the work of Amos's contemporaries as well as his spiritual progeny. Methodologic, as I will use the 146 verses that make up Amos's literary legacy as a starting point to suggest various strategies to studying the larger body of prophetic literature. It is my hope that the reader will come away not only with a deep appreciation for the genius of prophetic rhetoric, but also with a palette of approaches to study the received works of the literary prophets from Isaiah to Zechariah.

I have numerous teachers and colleagues to thank, and have done so in the acknowledgments. However, it is apt to note here those contemporary works that have been constant companions through this long, arduous, and joyful journey.

The *Da'at Mikra* series, which has endeavored to marry traditional approaches to the biblical text with archaeological finds, ancient Near East text studies, and many more disciplines that have taken serious form in the last three centuries, is a marvelous resource. The late, great Amos Hakham produced the *Da'at Mikra* commentary on Amos, and I reference it frequently. The *Mikra leYisrael* series, coming from a less traditional perspective, has much to add to our study of Tanakh. Shalom Paul authored the commentary on Amos, and his brilliant work contributed much to my own understanding of the text and, ergo, to this volume. Both of these masterful series were written in Hebrew. The Anchor Bible series, a compendium of the finest of biblical research, is an excellent resource not only for understanding various textual nuances, but also for integrating numerous ancient Near East textual parallels into our study. Francis I. Andersen and David Noel Freedman authored the hefty Amos volume, and I have referenced it numerous times in this work.

Acknowledgments

This volume is the product of years of study, research, discussions, writing, and rewriting. This adventure began over thirty years ago, when I was asked to teach Amos to a group of high school freshmen and I first fell in love with the Tekoan prophet's brilliant language, imagery, and messages.

Friends, colleagues, teachers, and students have been indispensable to keeping this exciting journey going to its culmination. When Rabbi Reuven Ziegler approached me a few years back and invited me to join the august company of contributors to the Maggid Studies in Tanakh, I accepted all too willingly. When my alma mater, Yeshivat Har Etzion, then invited me to write weekly installments for the Israel Koschitzky Virtual Beit Midrash, it gave me a framework (with that elusive motivator – the deadline) to develop the theses that are core to this work. I have deep and abiding appreciation to Debra Berkowitz and the team of editors at the VBM for their assiduous attention to detail and for faithfully circulating the installments. Numerous readers, along the way, asked questions that helped to distill the presentation.

As heavy as this tome is, the original project was nearly twice its size. The editorial decisions of what to cut, how to refine the presentation for a book, and how to smooth out one hundred installments into one volume were handled capably by Sara Daniel, Ita Olesker, Leah Goldstein, and the team of editors at Koren – and working with Koren has been a joy and an honor. It is a joy, as the folks at Koren are seriously committed to providing stimulating and thought-provoking Torah to as wide a readership as possible; it is an honor, as joining some of my intellectual heroes as an "MST author" is, in every sense, awesome.

I would also like to express gratitude to the Weiss family of Cleveland and Jerusalem, as well as dear friends Elayne and Howard Levkowitz and Wendy and Larry Platt, for their support for this volume.

Along my own path of study, I have been blessed to learn from great teachers, including Rav Yoel Bin-Nun, Prof. Yoel Elitzur, Dr. Leeor Gottlieb, Dr. Yonatan Grossman, Dr. Hagai Misgav, and Rav Elhanan Samet. Each of these scholars has contributed, both explicitly and implicitly, to this Amos study.

Two special friends who, along the way, readily perused my weekly postings (pre-posting) and offered helpful critiques are my long-time *ḥavruta* Dr. Josh Penn and my teacher and colleague Rabbi Avrohom Lieberman. What you are reading is clearer and more precise in large part due to their erstwhile animadversions.

The opportunities that I have had to teach in my home community in Los Angeles, at YULA High School, and at Young Israel of Century City, have afforded me the welcome challenge to refine my teaching and to teach scores of students.

My children have always expressed a genuine interest and taken pride in my work, and have been supportive in more ways than they can imagine. Yossi, Ariella and Yoni, Roni and Ariella, Avi and Yaakov – you are the most amazing support system anyone could ask for. You are, indeed, the נסיך שבכל יום עמנו.

אחרונה אחרונה חביבה. Stefanie, you have been the friendliest critic, reading my work at the craziest hours and offering gentle, insightful suggestions – and always supporting my writing. It is to you that I lovingly dedicate *Amos: The Genius of Prophetic Rhetoric*. שלי ושלכם שלה הוא.

ימי הקציר שנת עז לחמ"י
Los Angeles, Spring 2024

Glossary of Academic Terms

Anaphora: Repetition of the same word or phrase at the beginning of successive clauses

Antiphony: Call-and-response between two groups

Casuistic: The presentation of a law as a case (as opposed to a statute)

Chiasmus: A literary structure in which the components of the text mirror each other in concentric circles. In some cases (e.g., A, B, C, B', A') they include a pivot verse around which the structure revolves.

Epistrophe/Epiphora: Repetition of the same word or phrase at the end of successive clauses

Eschaton: Literally "end," refers to a description of the "end of days"

Gapping: The omission of a key word in one of two related clauses, due to considerations of meter; the omitted word is assumed

Hapax legomenon: A word or phrase that appears only once in the canon

Hei: The letter *hei* functions as a nominal prefix to produce the definite article, or as a verbal prefix to turn the verb into a rhetorical question – this is known as Rhetorical *hei*

Historiosophy: A retelling of history with an ideological agenda

Inclusio: When a passage begins and ends with a similar or parallel phrase – also known as *envelope structure*

Leitwort: A "key word," which appears an inordinate amount of times in a passage

Matres lectiones (lit. "mothers of reading"): Using Hebrew letters (which are fundamentally consonants) as vowels, typically *vav or yod*

***Merismus*:** A rhetorical device (or figure of speech) in which a combination of two contrasting parts of the whole refer to the whole

***Metonymy*:** The substitution of the name of an attribute or adjunct for that of the thing meant

Parallelism: Matching words or phrases in two adjacent clauses of a passage

Plene*/defective** (*ketiv male, ketiv haser*): Hebrew words can be spelled with or without ***matres lectiones – if written with, such as אהרון, that is referred to as *plene* spelling or *ketiv male*; if without, such as אהרן, that is considered *defective* or *ketiv haser*.

Realia: The material world at the setting of a particular narrative

***Sitz im Leben*:** "The setting in life" – the real-world context of a particular narrative

Stich/hemistich: A stich is a measured part of verse; a hemistich is half that measure

***Vav*:** The prefix letter vav has numerous functions, including *vav haḥibur* (conjunctive *vav*), which translates to "and"; *vav hahipukh* (conversive vav), which converts the tense of a verb from past to future and vice versa; *vav habiur* (explicative *vav*), which introduces an explication of the previous clause; and *vav hanigud* (disjunctive *vav*), which is best translated as "but, rather."

***Vorlage*:** The original text from which a given translation or commentary was working

Introduction

The Prophets

Prophecy is as old as humanity. God spoke with Adam and, as such, Adam might be considered a prophet, or *navi*. From another perspective, prophecy only begins with Moses; yet another view is that the onset of the prophetic experience in Israel begins when Samuel anoints Saul. A further approach perceives the prophets of the mid-eighth century BCE – Hosea, Amos, Micah, and Isaiah – as belonging to the first era of prophecy, *nevua*. These claims are all valid and largely depend on our definition of prophecy. To better understand Amos and his fellow prophets, we need to take a moment to explore the meaning of prophecy and the role of the prophet. I will scope out eight definitions of *navi*.

(1) A prophet may be considered anyone with whom God communicates. Maimonides explains that to perceive and receive God's word, the individual must have a sterling intellect and superior morals; then they may be trained in the ways of prophecy.[1] This implies that anyone God speaks with is considered a prophet: Adam, Eve, Noah – even Cain.[2]

1. *Guide for the Perplexed* II:32–46, chiefly in chapter 36.
2. Maimonides is forced, per his approach, to explain God's word manifest in persons

(2) A more stringent definition is that a prophet is a representative of the divine message. The only "prophet" identified as such in Genesis is Abraham (20:7). When Sarah is seized by Abimelech, God appears to the king in a dream (i.e., a prophetic vision)[3] and orders him to return her to Abraham "*because he (Abraham) is a prophet and he will pray for you* and you will be revived." As a prophet, Abraham's prayers will be most effective in healing the king.[4] Alternatively, as a prophet, he knows that Abimelech was innocent of sexual advances.[5] In other words, a *navi* is not only someone who receives divine communication, but also God's representative, whose prayers are accepted and who has supernatural knowledge of events.

(3) Although God speaks with numerous individuals before Moses, none are entrusted with an explicit oratory mission. The words are dictated to them as commands, warnings, chastisements, punishments, promises, exhortations, and covenants – but at no point are these words intended to be transmitted further.

Moses is a "pioneer" from the outset in two ways. He is the first prophet to undergo an inauguration – the scene at the burning bush (Ex. 3:1–4:17). In addition, his first encounter with God is all about a mission. It is his job not only to confront Pharaoh and lead God's people out of Egypt – but also to deliver a specific and explicit divine message to both addressees. He is to tell Israel's elders that God has "remembered" them and will take them out. He is to tell Pharaoh that the God of the Hebrews has sent him with a clear message about His people and His plans for them. Moses's agency is the first time that the formulaic "*ko amar*" (the "messenger formula" – "Thus says") is used in reference to God.[6]

---

of morally dubious character, such as Balaam, Laban – and even the serpent! Nonetheless, when a person would reach a sufficiently sublime level so as to receive divine communication, it may qualify as prophecy.

3. See the discussion of this idea in chapter 9, pp. 285–287.
4. Saadiah, Rashbam, Genesis 20:7.
5. Rashi, Bekhor Shor ad loc.
6. This formula is common in Amos's rhetoric and is discussed in chapter 2.

If we define a prophet as a messenger of God's word, Moses is certainly the first; he is the "father of prophets."[7]

(4) Moses also serves as the first and, arguably, only example of another role of the prophet – the lawgiver. Not only does he transmit God's word about history and destiny, he receives God's eternal law and enforces its integration into the national ethos. Ezekiel and Ezra (and perhaps Samuel and others) institute various reforms, but rabbinic tradition insists that by and large, Moses is the only *meḥokek* (legislator).[8]

In any case, Moses's position in history as "prophet" is assuredly unique and its uniqueness assured (Num. 12:6–8). Intriguingly, Moses is not explicitly called *navi* until his eulogy (Deut. 34:11).

(5) The fifth type of *navi* is the "court prophet." Samuel was arguably a court prophet, as he anointed kings, but David was the first king to have court prophets, even while fleeing Saul. Gad the Seer joined David early and Nathan "haNavi" remained in the court after David's death. They were to keep the king "in check" and ensure that he followed God's word, rather than be blinded by his own power. We will address the role of the court prophet in chapter 9. For now, a brief definition: a "court prophet" is someone employed by the court, who "dines at the king's table" and whose job is advisor to the king. Tragically, most would typically "prophesy" what the king wanted to hear – few of them were true prophets.[9]

(6) With the loss of proper court prophets, a new type of prophet appeared – the "charismatic prophet." The most famous examples are Elijah and his disciple Elisha, who operate outside of the purview of the court and essentially as opponents to the royal house. Ahab and Jezebel detest Elijah; Ahab's son Jehoram hates Elisha and attempts to have him killed in II Kings 6. Along with various anonymous prophets (such as the "man of God" who addresses Jeroboam I on the altar in

---

7. *Av lanevi'im* – Midrash Tehillim 90.
8. See *Sifra,* Leviticus 27:34.
9. See I Kings 12:22 ff for one exception.

Beit El),[10] these charismatic prophets seem to be part of a larger group, "the brotherhood of prophets," who practice prophetic trances and live ascetic lives. Their chief impact on the nation and the leadership is in their miraculous deeds: they effect famines and rain and unexpected military victories, purify the tainted, and revive the dead. This seems to be an exclusively northern phenomenon, as we find no charismatic prophets in Judea. Intriguingly, this regional distinction continued into the rabbinic period: famous charismatics such as Honi and R. Ḥanina b. Dosa were exclusively Galileans.

A panoramic view, thus far, presents a curious and significant omission. When we hear the word *navi,* we think of impressive and impactful orations that inspire, frighten, console, and exhort. Yet such orations are largely absent among these first six categories of prophets. With the exception of Moses – and he will always be the exception – these prophetic leaders accomplish much but say little. The powerful message Samuel delivers to Saul in the aftermath of his Amalek debacle is impressive but brief.[11] That Abraham, Nathan, and Elijah had much to say is likely; little is found in our canon.

The books commonly known as the "Early Prophets" (*Nevi'im Rishonim*) contain scarce prophetic rhetoric. When we think of the prophets as great orators, as the inspiration for generations of preachers and protestors, righteous rebels, and crusading civilians, hardly anyone in Joshua through Kings fits the bill.

One last comment about this period. Prophets consistently appear on the national and regional scene at critical turning points. Samuel oversees the transition from tribalism to monarchy. Which brings us to the divided kingdoms of Israel and Judah.

Global events can sometimes seem unremarkable *in situ,* yet their impact grows with time. After the death of Solomon (c. 930 BCE), the tribes of the north (chiefly Ephraim, Manasseh, and Issachar) engaged in a tax rebellion, throwing off the yoke of the House of David; they appointed Jeroboam b. Nebat of Ephraim to be their king. In order to preempt

10. I Kings 13:2–3.
11. I Samuel 15:22–23.

a return to loyalty to Jerusalem, Jeroboam established worship sites to God at his two border cities, Beit El and Dan; at each one, he erected a golden calf, declaring "this is the God that took you up out of Egypt."

All of these events play a central role in the next stage of prophecy and, most directly, in the prophetic career of Amos.

As the kingdom splits, several "minor" prophets appear; prophetic warnings and/or encouragement are heard before decisive battles; famine is heralded and resolved by the charismatics. Yet only with the impending destruction of the (northern) nation do the literary prophets step onto the biblical stage.

(7) The mid-eighth century BCE brought earth-shattering changes to the region. The Assyrian empire, which had made inroads west but had been rebuffed in the previous century,[12] was rearing its ravenous head toward Egypt – and, as always, the kingdoms of Israel and Judah were in the way. By the middle of the eighth century BCE, the threat was palpable and, as if to underscore the dire times ahead, around 760 BCE a devastating earthquake struck the region.

It was during this period that "literary prophets" first appeared in the streets, palaces, and courts of Israel – orators whose main form of leadership and persuasion was rhetorical. Whether they intended their words to be committed to writing or not is an age-old debate which has not yet been settled. Although we have numerous biographical and autobiographical passages about these prophets, their main impact is through their words. And oh, what amazing words they spoke! Isaiah's rhetorical thunder about the flirtatious women of Jerusalem; Hosea's soothing promise that the people's repentance will be joyfully accepted; Amos's challenge to the complacent, greedy "cows of the Bashan"; Micah's beautiful description of Jacob's travails – all attest to impressive rhetorical mastery.

These "anti-establishment" prophets came in two large waves: one before the northern kingdom of Samaria's demise, the other before the fall of the southern kingdom of Judah. And it is no wonder. Their job – a hopeless and thankless one – was to warn the people in the hope

12. In 853 BCE at Qarqar.

of saving them: only via the rarely traveled road of national repentance would they be spared from impending doom. But, alas, the prophet is heeded only when it is too late – or hundreds of years later by his admirers who, with the safety of time and distance, recognize the truth of his words. During the two centuries from the split of the kingdom until the Assyrian threat, the divine mission to the people shifted from prophetic *leaders*, to charismatics, to powerful orators. It now became the prophet's job to convey God's word to the royal house, the judiciary, the aristocracy, the priestly class, and, occasionally, the people of the Land.

Any assessment of the eighth century BCE in the Levant must consider Assyria. The empire to the east had gone through periods of expansion and conquest, punctuated by lulls when the empire was led by relatively weak rulers. After the demise of Shamshi-Adad V (811 BCE), Assyria entered a "quiet" period, and her potential vassals to the west had a nearly seventy-year respite from active aggression. Along with the weakening of Israel's traditional enemy, Aram, the kingdom of Samaria entered a period of nearly unprecedented growth and prosperity. This wealth was realized exclusively by the ruling classes, creating and exacerbating social and class division. Wealth also prompted military and spiritual complacence.

It was on this stage that Amos, Hosea, Micah, and Isaiah appeared – during a period of national success (so to speak) with dark clouds on the horizon that could only be seen by a prophet. Amos was the earliest of them; his agency was likely completed before the earthquake of 760 BCE. Tiglath-Pilesser III's ascent in 745 BCE reignited Assyria's lust for territory and the empire resumed its westward conquest. This process would culminate, from a biblical perspective, with the decimation of the Israelite kingdom a mere twenty-three years later. In hindsight, this was an era in dire need of the voices of the prophets; but, of course, the audience wasn't listening....

(8) We come to our final category, which we will refer to as "the people's prophet." Once the dust had settled after the destruction of Jerusalem and Judah, prophets were again called by God. This time, instead of rebuke, they were prophets of consolation and rebuilding. This period is known as *Shivat Tziyon* – "The Return to Zion," or the period of national

renaissance. The second half of Isaiah, Zechariah (chapters 1–8), Haggai, and later, Malachi all offer words of encouragement, some chastisement but largely consolation to a battered and exiled people who have been given a chance to return, restore, and rebuild. Although these prophets used the same rhetorical flourishes as their forebears and often referenced the familiar tropes, the message and tone were suited to a nation at a nearly antithetical place in its trajectory. Prophecies usually state the least obvious: in times of plenty, they warn of the corruption of power; in times of sorrow, they express the hope and promise of God's eternal covenant.

With this brief post-destruction period, the age of prophecy came to an end.

This volume will explore the brilliant rhetoric of one of the first of the literary prophets: Amos of Tekoa. We are in for an enchanting, challenging, and uplifting encounter with a monumental figure who spoke harsh words to a soft people and whose words, sadly but predictably, were treasured far more when they mattered far less.

One final note before moving on. Prophecy was always primarily an auditory experience, directed at the present "real-time" audience. Nonetheless, those relatively few prophecies committed to writing and included in the eternal biblical canon have import for generations. "Only prophecies intended for the generations were committed to writing."[13] The words of the prophets speak to two audiences: the prophet's immediate audience and future generations. We will study with an ear attuned to what Amos's contemporary audience heard, yet with an eye open to the eternal messages of this time-bound yet timeless prophetic text.

---

13. Song of Songs Rabba 4:11; Megilla 14a.

Chapter 1

Anthem (1:1–2)

(א) דִּבְרֵי עָמוֹס אֲשֶׁר הָיָה בַנֹּקְדִים מִתְּקוֹעַ אֲשֶׁר חָזָה עַל יִשְׂרָאֵל בִּימֵי עֻזִּיָּה
מֶלֶךְ יְהוּדָה וּבִימֵי יָרָבְעָם בֶּן יוֹאָשׁ מֶלֶךְ יִשְׂרָאֵל שְׁנָתַיִם לִפְנֵי הָרָעַשׁ: (ב) וַיֹּאמַר
ה' מִצִּיּוֹן יִשְׁאָג וּמִירוּשָׁלִַם יִתֵּן קוֹלוֹ וְאָבְלוּ נְאוֹת הָרֹעִים וְיָבֵשׁ רֹאשׁ הַכַּרְמֶל:

1 The words of Amos, who was one of the *nokdim* from Tekoa, who prophesied concerning Israel during the reign of Uziah the king of Judah and during the reign of Jeroboam son of Joash the king of Israel, two years before the earthquake. 2 He would say: "The Lord roars from Zion, and from Jerusalem He sends forth His voice. The pastures of the shepherds will become parched, and the top of the Carmel will wither."

The introductory verse of most prophetic collections presents the prophet's name and select biographical information. This may include his patronym, tribe, hometown, or livelihood, as well as the period of his agency and audience. Amos, a *noked* (see below) hailed from Tekoa. We are told nothing more about him except a time frame for his agency, which approximates the third decade of the eighth century BCE, and his target audience, "Israel."

Amos is the only prophet whose livelihood is explicitly noted; we will explore its significance in chapter 9. Amos's defense of his mission is the source of a well-known aphorism: *Lo navi anokhi velo ven navi* – "I am neither a *navi* nor am I a *ben navi*, rather I am a herdsman (*boker*) and a splicer of sycamore figs" (7:14). Amos never trained or aspired to become a prophet; rather, God plucked him from his regular job to deliver prophecy, and this is essential to understanding his mission.

Amos is a *noked*, a "herdsman" or, alternatively, something to do with tending trees. Classical commentators as well as modern Bible dictionaries direct our attention to II Kings 3:4, where it is clear from context that a *noked* is a shepherd.[1] Amos was likely a seasonal worker who herded sheep and cattle and also worked in sycamore groves. In any case, our prophet is not a "professional" prophet, but rather a farm-worker summoned by God.[2]

Amos prophesied during the reign of Uziah of Judah, who ruled for fifty-two years during the mid-eighth century BCE. Amos is the only one of the four contemporary prophets who prophesied during Uziah's reign alone (the others also prophesied during the reigns of Yotam, Ahaz, and, in the case of Isaiah and Hosea, Hezekiah as well), indicating that his prophetic mission took place during the thirty or so years when both Uziah ruled in Judah and Jeroboam was king of Israel. Although we cannot pinpoint for how long he actively prophesied, I will propose that his career was likely even shorter than that potential window in the biblical text.

Amos's home base is as symbolically significant as his audience: though he hails from the south,[3] his mission is to chastise the northern kingdom – and *only* the northern kingdom. This would be tantamount to a Massachusetts abolitionist coming to preach in antebellum Richmond. As I will soon explore, his anthemic phrase expresses exactly that geographic dissonance; the roaring of God from the south withers the pastures of the north. As such, it is vital that a Judean king be mentioned in his introduction, to generate the association with Jerusalem, the source

1. Radak explains the word as related to *nakud* – spotted; sheep are often spotted (see Gen. 30:32).
2. See Introduction, category 6.
3. Tekoa is a city of Judah and is identified with Khirbet Tuqu', just outside of modern-day Tekoa in Gush Etzion, not to be confused with *Tekoah* (or *Tokea*) in Mishna Menahot 8:3, Eruvin 91a, and elsewhere.

of his (and His) message. The mention of Jeroboam, however, may also serve a purpose beyond framing the date of his prophetic career. In the confrontation at Beit El (7:10–17), Amos is accused of being a troublesome rabble-rouser against Jeroboam; this introductory verse foreshadows the confrontation that will define Amos's agency.

The final phrase in the superscription is also relatively unique: it dates the onset of Amos's career to "two years before the earthquake." Amos is the only prophet introduced by his vocation, and he is the only one whose career is related to a natural event. Some of Jeremiah and Ezekiel's prophecies are dated against the background of political events,[4] whose relevance is self-evident. For instance, Ezekiel's vision about the significance of the tenth day of the tenth month comes with the revelation that on that selfsame day, the king of Babylonia began his siege against Jerusalem. In the case of Amos, however, things are not as clear. We, the long-distance audience,[5] are curious: How is the earthquake related to his prophecy? Is it relevant to the entire collection, which would justify its inclusion in the superscription? If so, what is that relevance? Amos will gradually, brilliantly, reveal its meaning until it fully emerges in his final set of speeches.

We suggest adopting a dating of the earthquake during the fifth decade of the eighth century BCE (between 760 and 750).[6] *Midrash Tanḥuma* (*Tzav*, par. 13) associates the earthquake with Uziah's *tzara'at* (skin-blight).[7] Alternatively, *Midrash Seder Olam* (ch. 20) identifies the earthquake with the description in Isaiah 6. In any case, the earthquake takes on immediate meaning for us in the next verse, and we will experience its aftershocks throughout the work.

---

4. *Inter alii* Jeremiah 24:1, Ezekiel 1:1.
5. Amos's immediate audience, of course, knew nothing about the earthquake until it was, quite literally, too late.
6. See Steven A. Austin, Gordon W. Franz, and Eric G. Frost, "Amos's Earthquake: An Extraordinary Middle East Seismic Event of 750 B.C.," *International Geology Review* 42, no. 7 (2000): 657–671.
7. See II Chronicles 26:16–21.

AMOS'S ANTHEM

And he would say (*Vayomar*):
The Lord roars from Zion,
    And from Jerusalem He sends forth His voice
The pastures of the shepherds will become parched
    And the top of the Carmel will wither

Even though the opening word *Vayomar* is generally read as synonymous with *vayomer*,[8] I have chosen to translate and read it as a refrain – "He would say..." – for two reasons. First of all, had Amos uttered this only once, in advance of the first collection of oracles, it would have read "*vayomer Amos*" or, more likely, "*Ko amar Hashem*," and the description of God's voice would have been presented in the first person. In addition, the verse would have been appended to other prophecies, instead of being juxtaposed to the superscription. More significantly, the image of God's voice emanating from Jerusalem is a subtext throughout Amos's prophecies. The overall messages of Amos's oracles fit this theme, and it is reasonable to call this passage an "anthem."

This tense is one we refer to as the "continuous future," which is expressed in the Bible in the future tense but clearly intended, from context, to be a description of ongoing, regular behavior.[9]

Moreover, a significant number of biblical instances of *vayomar* preface sayings that are either repeated or that seem to be part of a regular prayer tradition. For instance, when Abraham addresses God in his request to spare the cities of Sodom (Gen. 18), the text prefaces his arguments with *vayomar* – and these are repeated, formulaic arguments. When Malkizedek praises God and Abraham (Gen. 14), the text prefaces his blessings with *vayomar* – again, these seem to be somewhat formulaic words, perhaps blessings that the king of Shalem bestowed on special occasions. Most telling is the description of Jonah's declaration in Nineveh, which is prefaced by *vayikra vayomar* (Jonah 3:4). Based

8. The difference usually being a function of syntax, not meaning.
9. The *locus classicus* of this is in Job 1:5 – *Kakha ya'aseh Iyov kol hayamim* – "This is what Job would do all the days."

on the narrative context, it seems clear that the warning "in forty days Nineveh will be overturned" was repeated by the prophet as he walked through the doomed city.

This approach is particularly significant in light of Malbim's claim that the roaring voice of God that would wither the pastures was a poetic reference to that earthquake. This illuminates its mention at the end of the superscription, and perhaps supports the theory that Amos would repeat this anthem before each of his prophecies.

2: The Lord roars from Zion

The lion and its roar as a metaphor for God's voice and God's anger is not unique to Amos. While Isaiah (5:29) uses it to describe Assyria's impending attack, Amos (here and at 3:4, 8) and Hosea (11:10) both use it to describe God's voice. Over a century later, Jeremiah adopts Amos's imagery (25:30); as we will see throughout the book, he was fond of Amos's rhetorical flairs.

The closest parallel to Amos's anthem-phrase is found in Joel 4:16:

> The Lord will roar from Zion and will send forth His voice from Jerusalem; the heavens and earth will shake but the Lord will be a refuge for His people and a stronghold for the children of Israel.

The first two phrases in this verse are a duplicate of Amos's first stich. One would have to surmise that, following nearly all scholars who date Joel later than Amos,[10] this anthem was a well-known prophetic aphorism used by later prophets as well. The significant difference between the usage by Joel and Amos is time frame. If Amos is expressing that his own words represent God's roar, then God's voice is *currently* going forth; it is imminent. In contrast, the last chapter of Joel is eschatological, a terrifying vision of "the day of the Lord."[11] The added phrase, "the heavens and earth will shake" serves to raise Joel's imagery to apocalyptic typology.

10. Exception noted: Abravanel maintains that Joel was much earlier; his overall approach to the chronology of *Trei Asar* is iconoclastic.
11. See chapter 7, "Day of the Lord."

The other clear difference is in the second stich. God's roar in Amos brings Israel's destruction, whereas in Joel it expresses Israel's protection. The critical difference rests in the meaning of the conjunctive *vav*: The *vav* in Amos (*ve'avlu*, "Will become parched") is a conjunction, either the common *vav haḥibur* or perhaps the explanatory *vav habiur*: "God roars, *and as a result* the pastures wither." In contrast, the *vav* in Joel is a *vav hanigud* (disjunctive *vav*): *even though* God's voice will roar from Zion and His voice will go forth from Jerusalem – and the heavens and earth will shake, *nonetheless*, He will protect His nation. Joel inverts Amos's anthem, using it apocalyptically rather than locally, yet presenting it as a source of consolation rather than a threat.

A final word about Amos's "anthem." If, following Malbim, we read this passage as alluding to the earthquake, the imagery of the withering of the mountain tops and the pastures becoming parched, or "mourning," seems forced – the metaphor is somewhat mixed. The withering of lush fields and the subsequent mourning in the pastures is, again, something we find in Joel (chapter 1), where it is explicitly attributed to a plague that destroys the crops. The expected result of an earthquake's devastation, however, is not chiefly agricultural. Per Malbim, we would expect the palaces of the north to be laid waste, not the pastures. This may be why most commentators do not connect this line with the earthquake. What remains to be seen is how figurative this destruction will be. Are God's words going to create a fear and trepidation in the north that will cause mourning? If so, we would interpret God's roaring as the prophet's words carrying the divine messenger to Samaria. If, however, we read the destruction as real, then the roar is not God's word through the prophet. Rather, it foreshadows some natural devastation which will accompany or follow Amos's prophecies.

This anthem is the setting of Amos's first speech-set, the oracles "against the nations." We can envision the Samarian audience tensing for the roar and anxiously waiting for God's words to wither the lush pastures of the Carmel.

Chapter 2

Against the Nations (1:3–2:16)

PART I: THE SET-UP

Amos's prophecies begin with the sequence of eight oracles "against the nations." (The full text is presented below.) Although there are eight different addressees, they were all delivered in Samaria; the "feigned audience" is a common rhetorical tool used by the literary prophets and, as with many such strategies, Amos was likely its inventor.

Amos delivers oracles against Aram, Philistia, Phoenicia, Edom, Ammon, and Moab, then against Judah before zeroing in on Israel. Why these nations? Given the geopolitical realities of his time, we would expect him to indict Assyria, but it is not mentioned at all. Egypt, whose fortunes during this era are perhaps diminished, is nonetheless a consistent, usually problematic presence on Judah's southwest border – why are they similarly omitted? Egypt is certainly the target of prophetic chastisement, included in Isaiah's oracles against the nations (ch. 19) as well as those of Ezekiel (chs. 29–32) and Jeremiah (ch. 46). Why are the two regional superpowers left out of Amos's diatribe?

It may be that this list is not determined by the significance or might of the accused nation, but rather by how they have directly attacked Israel. Damascus (Aram) and Ammon are accused of brutality against the Gileadites (ostensibly the eastern tribes Gad and Reuben); Edom is accused of loathing his "brother" (does this mean Israel?); Gaza (Philistia) and Tyre (Phoenicia) will be punished for handing over exiles to Edom. It is not clear who these refugees or the brothers mentioned in this context are; we might assume that there were Jewish exiles who fled south and north away from Edom, and the accused nation handed them back. We will analyze these individual oracles below; for now, we will point out that none of these crimes is explicated in the Bible. Aram's brutality is foretold by Elisha, but its fulfillment is never described in the text; in fact, it expressly does *not* play out in the fashion envisioned by Elisha (II Kings 8:7–15).

The lack of a corroborating historical record of these crimes leaves us with three choices: (1) these neighbors' brutal behavior may have been acted out toward other nations; (2) they indeed offended Israel, but these acts were not recorded in the biblical narrative; (3) we need to read the oracle in a non-literal sense. For instance, Radak interprets the accusations against Gaza, Tyre, and Edom as prophecies referring to traumatic events nearly a millennium in the future (first century CE). This approach is fraught with difficulties. Not only must we then identify "Philistines" and "Tyrians" during the Roman era, but we must also pinpoint Roman brutality surrounding the destruction of Jerusalem in 70 CE. The greatest difficulty with this interpretation is that it has Amos prophesying destruction in the eighth century BCE for a nation's behavior eight centuries later.

Prefatory Note: Oracles against the Nations

As mentioned earlier, Amos is not the only prophet to deliver God's message regarding the nations. Isaiah, Ezekiel, and Jeremiah all have long series of oracles against the nations. Nahum's entire prophecy is directed toward Assyria, and Obadiah's twenty-one verses all foretell Edom's destruction.[1]

Despite all of these oracles toward and against non-Jewish nations, there are significant indications throughout the Bible that prophets were never *sent* to non-Jewish nations. The one obvious exception is Moses's

1. Jonah is a unique case, which we will address further on in this chapter.

agency to Pharaoh – but that was, of course, *on behalf of* the Hebrews. In other words, prophets were not sent to deliver messages to the non-Jewish nations for their own rehabilitation.[2]

This is implied in Deuteronomy 4 and 18, and by Amos himself in chapter 3: "Only you have I known of all the families of the earth." This statement's context clarifies that God's prophetic agency is only aimed at His people.

If so, how are we to understand the many prophecies against (or regarding) the nations? How are we to interpret God's command to Jeremiah (1:5): "I have made you a prophet to the nations"?

The simplest explanation is that the oracles were presented to an Israelite audience for various reasons, depending on the prophecy's nature and context. Some ridicule the nations' idolatrous practices and beliefs (such as Ezekiel's pronouncement in 29:3 regarding Pharaoh, who claims that "the Nile is mine and I have made it for myself"). These were likely calculated to deter the Israelite audience from such beliefs (when such pagan practices were common) or to give them a sense of intellectual and cultural superiority (when there was need of consolation for a downtrodden people).

Prophecies foretelling a nation's fall likely meant to impress the Israelite audience with God's control over world events and to establish the prophet's *bona fides*. Predictions of nations' short-term success (such as Jeremiah's oracle about Babylonia) were aimed at persuading the audience to accept the divine fiat. In other words, prophecies "addressed" to the nations are for Israel's didactic and soteriological[3] benefit; the nations are used to teach the *real* audience a lesson.

What about Jonah?

While this axiom is expressed by various classical and modern commentators, it faces one daunting challenge: the story of Jonah's mission to Nineveh. God commands Jonah to warn the people of Nineveh that their destruction is imminent if they fail to repent.[4]

2. Again, Jonah is *sui generis*.
3. Relating to salvation.
4. One of the many unnerving features of the book of Jonah is his lack of a call to

The book of Jonah is filled with anomalies. The sailors' atypical sensitivity; Jonah's desperate, enigmatic attempt to flee God; his unprecedented wildly successful mission in Nineveh, and his disconsolate reaction to his own success – all these form a profound biblical conundrum.

This enigmatic core motivates many commentators (including traditional ones such as the Vilna Gaon) to regard the book of Jonah as a figurative work of "prophetic fiction"[5] – as narrative use of a historic figure (from II Kings 14:25) to convey a didactic message (per the Gaon, a metaphysical lesson via a parable). The sailors and people of Nineveh are foils to Jonah, who argues with God about human repentance and divine forgiveness.

The vast majority of traditional commentators, however, read Jonah as a factual account: that the successful mission is an unprecedented event in human history. If so, then just this once, God indeed sends a prophet to rehabilitate a non-Jewish nation (and a sworn enemy of His people, at that). This narrative conveys that individuals and societies are potentially capable of change and are thus worthy of salvation; God holds *all* of his creatures accountable for their actions, yet cares for them and presents them with the chance for salvation. Even if read as a historical event, this would be the exception that proves the rule.

The Purpose of the Oracles

If the oracles were never intended to be communicated to their ostensible addressees, then what is their purpose?

Based on a passage toward the end of Amos, one theory is that the oracles impart a universal message: in spite of Amos's own words at 3:2, not just God's people, but rather all nations are called to account for their moral violations. This, perhaps, might serve to soften Amos's harsh criticism against the Samarian aristocracy: though the impending doom hanging over the northern kingdom is evidence of God's displeasure with them, God is similarly displeased with the behavior of the surrounding

repentance; his entire prophecy of five words: *od arba'im yom veNineveh nehpakhet* – "in forty days Nineveh will be destroyed" – carries no explicit strategic message of how to avoid their fate.

5. Without ceding an inch to Ira Gershwin.

nations, and they, too, will be punished in kind. Thus the decree against Samaria no longer stands as such stark condemnation.

This, however, is not a sustainable approach. First of all, these oracles *precede* Amos's diatribe against Israel, so that an alleviative effect is unlikely. Second, the oracles against Israel – their crime as well as punishment – are far more detailed than the sentence against the nations.

These oracles against the nations do not convey moral equivalence or a common standard; rather, they express that *all* families of the earth are subject to God's judgement. God's baseline rule is that a nation that sins is exiled; whether it actually happens to Aram or Tyre is not the focus of the message to the Israelites. What they need to hear is that even nations that have not had the opportunity to "know God" firsthand are judged.

Written Law Experienced Orally

Although we chiefly experience the Bible as "written Torah" (*Torah she-bikhtav*), many passages were composed to be studied, reviewed, and shared orally, such as Joshua's "song" (Josh. 10:12–14), the Psalms, and many of the songs found in both historic and prophetic books. As a late midrash notes, the book of Lamentations was written as an abecedarian acrostic so it could be chanted easily.[6] Moses's song (Deut. 32) was intended to be memorized and recited by heart.[7]

To properly appreciate the prophet's words, we must not only read them carefully, but also attend to linguistic nuances, geopolitical setting, and imagery. To the extent possible, we must put ourselves in the contemporary audience's position to appreciate the prophecy's potential impact and intended message; that is, to *experience* the words as the prophet's original audience heard them.

How would Amos's intended audience – the royal house and aristocracy of Samaria – have responded to these dire admonitions regarding the surrounding nations? Keep in mind that the addressed nations were or had been enemies of the Israelite kingdom, although some were currently on good terms: for example, Tyre had close economic

6. *Otzar HaMidrashim Pinehas b. Yair*, 17.
7. See Deuteronomy 31:19–21.

ties with Solomon and marital ties with the royal house of Omri; there is no record in biblical narrative of Phoenician aggression against Israel since. Nonetheless, a bordering country is always a potential threat, and news of a neighbor's impending downfall must have had some impact on the Israelites.

A Rhetoric of Illusion – And Entrapment

Hearing that the northern kingdom's perennial enemy Aram would soon fall and be exiled must have brought the Samarian audience a sense of relief and protection – if God is about to destroy their greatest enemy, they have nothing to fear. God is protecting them.

This sequence's geography is informative. Amos begins by denouncing Damascus (northeast of Samaria), moves to Gaza (southwest), then Tyre (northwest), then to Ammon, Edom, and Moab (all in the southeast). The Samarian audience soon realizes that their enemies on every side are about to fall! Even Judah – the southern neighbors who claim sovereignty over the northern kingdom – are slated for punishment.

We can imagine the audience's sense of relief and protection growing with every new pronouncement.

But now Amos's rhetorical sleight-of-hand is revealed. Israel are not being protected – but boxed in! The greatest punishment is waiting for none but Israel.

By contrast, it is possible that the audience wasn't fooled, and knowing that a seer from the south would have nothing positive to report, they could anticipate his message from the beginning. Perhaps rather than growing relief at the news of their enemies' downfall, the Samarian audience experiences mounting dread about what awaits them when he completes his ever-tightening circles of rebuke.

THE ORACLE'S PATTERN

Each of the oracles follows a common pattern – a pattern that is then developed in the final, culminating oracle against Israel:

The pattern:

Ko amar Hashem: "Al shelosha pishei X ve'al arba'a lo ashivenu; al (sin) …"

> Thus says the Lord: "For the three sins of X (= a nation or one of its major city-states) and for a fourth/for four I will not recant. For (sin)…"

Schematically, it looks like this:

1. Messenger Formula: Thus says the Lord (*Ko amar Hashem*)
2. For the three sins of X
   a. And for the fourth I will not recant
3. For Y (the fourth sin)
4. Punishment

This is followed by God's specific punishment(s) for that nation.

There are further nuances to the pattern, but we will begin by analyzing this formula.

"Ko Amar" – The Messenger Formula

The short phrase *ko amar* (כֹּה אָמַר, "thus says") appears nearly five hundred times throughout the Bible, although, predictably, only once in *Ketuvim* (Chronicles aside). The phrase always indicates a message from a superior – a superpower. Although we usually anticipate that the speaker is "the Lord" (*Ko amar Hashem*), this is not always the case, and therein lies the phrase's rhetorical power.

Intriguingly, the first two biblical instances of this phrase, which are its only appearances in Genesis, are exceptions to this rule. When Jacob sends his tribute to Esau, he instructs his messengers to say: *Ko amar avdekha Yaakov* – "Thus says your servant, Jacob" (Gen. 32:4). When Joseph's brothers return to Canaan with the news that he is alive, he tells them to tell his father: *Ko amar binkha Yosef* – "Thus says your son Joseph…" (45:9). We will soon return to these apparent counter-examples.

In Exodus, all but one of the ten instances of *Ko amar Hashem* are presented at critical junctures in Moses's confrontations with Pharaoh: when he first addresses Pharaoh and before plagues preceded by a warning.[8] *Ko amar Pharaoh* (5:10) is used when he increases the labor

8. See Etshalom, *Between the Lines of the Bible*, vol. 2 (Jerusalem: Urim, 2012), ch. 7.

burden on the Hebrew slaves. The phrase appears just twice more in the Torah: in Numbers, when Moses requests passage through Edomite territory, *Ko amar ahikha Yisrael* – "Thus says your brother, Israel..." (20:14); and when Balak sends a second delegation to persuade Balaam to curse Israel, the messengers begin with *Ko amar Balak* (22:16).

This formula occurs fifty-eight times in the historic books of the prophets (Joshua-Kings); some messengers are from Israelite leaders as well as foreign kings at war with Israel.[9]

In the literary prophets, the phrase appears nearly 380 times; outside of Isaiah, it always prefaces God's words, never messages from mere humans. The one exception to this is a single mention in Amos, which has the unprecedented *Ko amar Amos* (7:11) when the Beit El priest Amaziah reports Amos's "treacherous" words to King Jeroboam.

What is the meaning of the (nearly) complete absence of the "messenger formula" in reference to anyone but God after Isaiah? We must note that the use of *ko amar* to introduce a human's words is found again in Chronicles. This, too, requires a solution – if there was some kind of theological development after Isaiah's time that that precluded its use for human words, then why would it return in the Second Temple period in Chronicles?

I would like to propose a solution to the fluctuating pattern of the "messenger formula." First of all, ancient Near Eastern texts show that in the second millennium BCE, similar formulae expressed a "divine" message or a royal edict.

To refer back to *ko amar* in Genesis, both instances of this phrase reflect a certain tension. Jacob seeks to appease Esau and refers to himself as "your servant"; yet by having the messengers introduce it with *ko amar,* he communicates a position of power to his brother. The tension of this "mixed message" is rife throughout their vicarious dialogue (via messengers) and then in their face-to-face meeting. Similarly, when Joseph sends for his father, he is at once a loving son making travel arrangements for his elderly father, and the second most powerful man in Egypt: *Ko amar binkha Yosef.*

9. For example, I Kings 20:3, 5; II Kings 18:19.

The repetition of *Ko amar Hashem* uttered ten times to Pharaoh conveys that Moses is delivering a message to the pseudo-divine king of Egypt from the truly Divine – the God of the Hebrews. The king is, effectively, being put in his place.

The formula was in use for both divine and human messages until near the end of the First Commonwealth. Whether due to a heightened and maturing theological sensitivity or in response to Babylonian claims to royal deification, by the seventh century BCE and throughout the Babylonian exile, the phrase was reserved for God's words. The prophets used it frequently to deliver God's word to the people, aristocracy, and royalty.

This brings us to the formula's use in Second Temple literature. "*Ko amar*" appears once in Ezra: *Ko amar Koresh* (1:2); and again in Chronicles to introduce both Ahab's words as well as Sennacherib's. Why is the phrase demoted to non-divine use?

Theological sensitivity is a product of the *Sitz im Leben*. When Islam accused the Jews of forging the Torah, the historic accuracy and fidelity of every letter in the Torah became a creedal issue. Generations earlier, when the Sadducees denied the notion of resurrection, it became the *cause célèbre* of rabbinic doctrine. In other words, when basic principles or practices are challenged, the traditional community usually closes ranks around what we might call "ideological purity." Once this threat passes, however, the traditional community relaxes its stance and stridency is often replaced by diffidence.[10] This phenomenon has existed since biblical times.

During the First Commonwealth, Ba'al worship in Israel was rampant; Elijah's most famous moment took place at Mount Carmel,

---

10. This is a phenomenon that we have witnessed in the second half of the twentieth century. When surveying the non-Orthodox movements' pronouncements and innovations and how the Orthodox community responded to them, a significant and obvious shift has taken place. "*Teshuvot*" of the 1950s were taken seriously and were seriously attacked. By the 1990s (if not earlier), this was no longer the case, for one simple reason: the chasm separating the non-Orthodox world from the traditional camp became so wide that it was largely felt that rulings issued by a non-Orthodox rabbinic body would have no impact on Orthodox readers. As such, there was no "threat" and no need to respond.

when he challenged, defeated, and slaughtered the Ba'al prophets of Jezebel, and Hosea and Jeremiah both denounce Ba'al worship.[11] As a result, proper names with the theophoric component "Ba'al" are covered with shame. *Meriv-Ba'al* (Jonathan's son) became *Mephibosheth*; *EshBa'al* (Saul's son) is *Ish Bosheth*, and a reference to Gideon's other name, *Yeruba'al*, is modified to *Yerubesheth*.

After the Return to Zion, when Ba'al worship was no longer an active threat, all references to the name were, oddly enough, restored; no longer a threat, it became "safe" to use that name again.[12]

I believe that the phrase *ko amar* underwent a similar process. Though the divinity of kings, a common Near Eastern belief, was never embraced in Israel, it still posed a threat to the extent that biblical authors refrained from using *ko amar* to introduce a human's words. Once that notion was no longer prevalent in Israel (though it certainly persisted in the Persian court), perhaps due to the loss of Israel's sovereignty, it was again safe to use the *ko amar* formula to introduce the words of a human king, of Ahab and even Sennacherib.

"For Three Sins and for Four" – Or Is It "For a Fourth"?

The next part of the rhetorical pattern is *Al shelosha pishei X* (name of the accused nation) *ve'al arba'a lo ashivenu*. Although I presented a rough translation above, this phrase can be rendered several ways; each carries a distinct meaning.

One possible reading is: "I have forgiven/overlooked three sins of this nation, but the fourth one is too grievous to overlook" – meaning, the fourth violation was more heinous than the others.

A slightly different interpretation reads thus: "I have forgiven/overlooked three sins of this nation, but the fourth one is too much to bear." That is, the fourth is not any worse than the first three sins – but it is the proverbial straw that breaks the camel's back. This reading is more

11. Hosea 2:18; Jeremiah 11:6–13.
12. I am indebted to my teacher, colleague, and friend, Prof. Leeor Gottlieb, for bringing this development of the Ba'al usage to my attention.

consistent with the biblical syntax. God was willing to forego three sins, but four was simply too much to overlook.[13]

A third reading is more difficult to support in the first oracles but seems to best fit the final oracle: The Bible makes frequent and consistent use of symbolic numbers. The number 40 (days or years) is often used to symbolize a lengthy time span, whereas 400 represents a *very* long time (Abraham's seed will be subjugated for 400 years). The number 7 represents a complete cycle: 7 days of the week; 7 weeks from harvest festival to harvest festival; 7 years of the Sabbatical cycle, and 7 Sabbatical cycles to the Jubilee.

The Torah repeatedly warns the Israelites that if they abandon God's covenant, they will be punished sevenfold for their sins.[14]

Modern scholars have pointed out that Amos's schema of "for three and for four" is a common biblical rhetorical tool, known as "n/n+1"; "There are three things that are wondrous for me and four things I do not know..." (Prov. 30:18). The formula "n/n+1" implies that any number could represent *n* as long as the pattern is n/n+1 (such as 7/8); nonetheless, I believe that these oracles deliberately employ the numbers three/four because they add up to seven. The prophet is proclaiming that though three sins alone would not stir God's wrath, three plus four – seven – is the limit of God's patience.

This pattern also draws on the Torah: God visits the sins of the parents upon their children "to the third and fourth generations." The numbers three and four in the context of a divine calculus of sin and punishment are anchored in God's own words at Sinai.

This reading does not work well in the case of the first seven (!) oracles, where only one terrible crime is explicated, but this is probably how the final oracle against Israel should be read: as we will see later in this chapter, that oracle lists a few "sevens" – seven crimes, seven divine kindnesses, and seven punishments.

In yet another demonstration of Amos's rhetorical brilliance, the same phrase is used in different ways. Amos indicts the other nations (which

13. This approach is supported by Maimonides's ruling in *Mishneh Torah, Hilkhot Teshuva* 3:5, following Tosefta Yoma 4:13.

14. See, *inter alii*, Leviticus 26.

is, as mentioned, merely a prophetic exposition), with the refrain "for three things I could have overlooked; but the fourth is [either] too heinous [or] too much." When he addresses his real audience in Samaria, the phrase now means "For the three and four [= seven] sins I will not recant…"

Before analyzing each oracle in detail, I wish to consider a panoramic view of the sequence, up to and including Judah. I have listed the cities mentioned in each oracle in parentheses at the header.

The Text (Amos 1:3–2:5)

1. Against Aram (Damascus, Bikat Aven, Beit Eden)

> **3** *Ko amar Hashem*: For the three sins of Damascus, and for four I will not recant: because they have threshed Gilead with sledges of iron. **4** So will I send a fire into the house of Hazael, and it shall devour the palaces of Ben Hadad. **5** And I will break the bar of Damascus, and cut off the inhabitant from Bikat Aven and the one who holds the scepter from Beit Eden; and the people of Aram shall go into captivity unto Kir, *amar Hashem.*

2. Against Philistia (Gaza, Ashdod, Ashkelon, Ekron)

> **6** *Ko amar Hashem*: For the three sins of Gaza, and for four I will not recant: because they carried away captive a whole captivity, to deliver them up to Edom. **7** So will I send a fire on the wall of Gaza, and it will devour her palaces. **8** And I will cut off the inhabitant from Ashdod, and the one who holds the scepter from Ashkelon; and I will turn My hand against Ekron, and the remnant of the Philistines will perish, *amar Hashem Elokim.*

3. Against Phoenicia (Tyre)

> **9** *Ko amar Hashem*: For the three sins of Tyre, and for four I will not recant: because they delivered up a whole captivity to Edom, and did not remember the covenant of brothers. **10** So will I send a fire on the wall of Tyre, and it shall devour her palaces.

4. Against Edom (Teiman, Botzra)

11 *Ko amar Hashem*: For the three sins of Edom, and for four I
will not recant: because he pursued his brother with the sword,
and cast off all of his compassion, and his anger perpetually tore
at him, and he held onto his wrath forever. **12** So will I send a fire
upon Teiman, and it shall devour the palaces of Botzra.

5. Against Ammon (Rabba)

13 *Ko amar Hashem*: For the three sins of the children of Ammon,
and for four I will not recant: because they ripped up the pregnant
women of Gilead, in order to expand their border. **14** So will I
ignite a fire in the wall of Rabba, and it shall devour her palaces,
with shouting in the day of battle, with a tempest in the day of
the whirlwind. **15** And their king shall go into captivity, he and
his princes together, *amar Hashem.*

6. Against Moab (Keriyot)

1 *Ko amar Hashem*: For the three sins of Moab, and for four I will
not recant: because he burned the bones of the king of Edom
into lime. **2** So will I send a fire upon Moab, and it shall devour
the palaces of Keriyot; and Moab will die with tumult, with
shouting, and with the sound of the shofar. **3** And I will cut off
the judge from their midst, and will slay all of their princes with
him, *amar Hashem.*

7. Against Judah (Jerusalem)

4 *Ko amar Hashem*: For the three sins of Judah, and for four
I will not recant: because they have rejected God's Torah,
and have not kept His laws, and their lies have caused them
to err, [those lies] after which their fathers had walked. **5** So
will I send a fire upon Judah, and it shall devour the palaces of
Jerusalem.

The general pattern of the oracles is as follows:

a) Messenger formula (*Ko amar Hashem*)
b) Numeric introduction ("for the three sins of X [I will overlook/forgive] and for four [or for a fourth]) I will not recant")
c) Fourth sin (either the "last straw" or the most egregious act)
   i. Some are presented in a prosaic colon (one phrase).
   ii. Others are presented in a poetic bicolon or couplet (two phrases).
d) Punishment
   i. Always begins with *Veshilaḥti esh* ("I will send a fire") against the palaces or the walls of the city. One subtle variation is in the fifth oracle against Ammon, where the nearly synonymous *Vehitzati esh* ("I will ignite a fire") is used.
   ii. In the third, fourth and seventh oracles, this is the sum of the punishment, which seems to be the utter destruction of the ruling class and capital.
   iii. In the first, second, fifth, and sixth oracles, the punishment is more detailed and explicitly ends with either exile (Aram, Ammon) or genocide (Philistia, Moab).
e) Signature formula (*amar Hashem*)
   i. Does not appear in the third, fourth, or seventh oracles.
   ii. Has a nuanced variant in the second oracle: *"amar Ad-nai Y-H-V-H"* (read "*amar Hashem Elokim*")

Here is a chart to help visualize the pattern and the internal variations:

	Nation	4th Sin	Form	Punishment	Result	Signed
1	Aram	War crimes (excessive destruction?)	Simple	Fire against palaces, shattering city defenses	Exile back to Kir	Yes
2	Philistia	Handing over refugees to Edom	Simple	Fire against palaces, destruction of leadership	Decimation of tribe	Yes – with *Ad-nai* added

3	Phoenicia	Handing refugees over to Edom	Bicolon	Fire against palaces	–	No
4	Edom	Ruthless killing of "brother" (war crimes?)	Double Couplet	Fire against palaces	–	No
5	Ammon	War crimes	Simple (extended)	Fire against palaces	War, king sent into exile	Yes
6	Moab	War crime	Simple	Fire against palaces	War, decimation of ruling class	Yes
7	Judah	Disobedience toward God	Double Couplet	Fire against palaces	–	No

Observation

With the exception of Judah, the nations' crimes are all war-related: Aram and Ammon are accused of brutality in war; Philistia and Tyre are accused of handing over refugees to Edom – this presumably means that the victims believed that they would find sanctuary but were instead handed over to their pursuers. Edom itself is accused of ruthless killing of its "brothers." These are all war crimes.

The Categorical Imperative

The first six nations listed here are not bound by God's covenant; the Noahide laws, even when expounded in rabbinic literature, do not seem to include moral guidelines for wartime. Yet, all these nations face destruction for violating the ethical boundaries of conquest.

It is not at all clear who their victims are. While the pregnant women of Gilead likely belonged to the tribes of Reuben, Gad, and Manasseh, this is not explicit; the identity of the refugees who fled to Philistia and Phoenicia is not mentioned, and it is not clear that they were Israelites. Edom's everlasting hatred and the suppression of fraternal compassion alludes to the Jacob-Esau enmity, but this is not explicit either. The accusation against Moab has nothing to do with Israel. In sum, these nations are incriminated for behavior that did not necessarily affect God's people.

As noted above, these oracles never reached these nations' ears; rather, they are a rhetorical prelude to Israel's indictment. If so, one might argue that there is no need for actual punishment or even real accusations. This, however, is unlikely, given that it would defeat their rhetorical purpose: if the audience realizes that such divine punishment against foreign nations is not "real," then this diatribe loses its impact.

This leads us to a far-reaching conclusion, one which is in dialogue with the early chapters of Genesis. Each individual and every nation is bound by a basic moral code that relies on what Rav Kook would call "natural morality" (*musar tivi*), which is similar if not identical to Kant's Categorical Imperative, and which may be subsumed under the rubric of "Natural Law." God holds all people accountable to a basic moral code, and they are punished for violating it. This is implicit in Cain's punishment for killing Abel and in the destruction decreed for the entire Generation of the Flood. With the exception of the divine edict against eating from the Tree of Knowledge, there are no antediluvian prohibitions. Any consequences before that presume a tacit understanding of right and wrong and acceptance of some culpability for violation.

God will punish these nations for brutality, war crimes, and treachery even though these behaviors have never been explicitly proscribed or warned against.

Crime and Punishment

An interesting and possibly meaningful pattern can be seen in the chart. Four of the nations have committed crimes that are expressed in a single clause. Aram "threshed the Gilead with sledges of iron"; Philistia "carried away captive a whole captivity, to deliver them up to Edom"; Ammon "ripped up the pregnant women of Gilead, in order to expand their border"; Moab "burned the bones of the king of Edom into lime." These four nations' brief crimes are punished with elaborate, lengthy sentences: subjected to war, raucous conquest, decimation of the ruling class, and exile. In contrast, the remaining three nations' sins are described in a more complex and poetic form. Phoenicia "delivered up a whole captivity to Edom, and did not remember the covenant of brothers"; Edom "pursued his brother with the sword, and cast off all of his compassion, and his anger perpetually tore at him, and he held onto his wrath forever"; Judah "rejected the law of the Lord, and have not kept His laws, and their lies have caused them to err, [those lies] after which their fathers had walked." Yet these three nations receive the shortest and least detailed punishment, without divine signature.

This all seems to be part of Amos's rhetorical scheme. The oracles are balanced: a detailed description of the crime is paired with a brief punishment, or the opposite. This creates a rhythm, an essential balance, which speaks to the nature of divine justice in the world.

Significantly, the four oracles with detailed punishments each contain 35 words (except for Moab, which has 32), while the others have 22 (except for Edom, which has 26).

Amos presents two "long" diatribes, with terse accusations and detailed, painful punishments, followed by two "short" oracles, with more developed accusations but a single punishment that hits at the core of that nation's autonomy and power: sending fire against X to consume its palaces. He then continues with two long oracles, with exile and war as the punishments, and concludes with another brief prophecy: the burning of Jerusalem and its palaces, without even using the signature form *amar Hashem*.

This pattern would have Amos's Samarian audience believe that the oracle has reached its end. After these seven prophecies of doom, they might have breathed a sigh of relief and even, perhaps, felt some mean-spirited joy: hearing about the downfall of neighboring enemies is cause enough for celebration, but the final prophecy accusing Judah of infidelity against God's law must have served as a source of vindication for the Samarian aristocracy and throne.

I am not suggesting that the prophet deliberately uses the "three/four" sequence to mis*lead* his listeners, but once that rhetorical pattern is invoked, he employs it to mis*direct* them. The element of surprise may catalyze dismay into horror and perhaps shock his audience into recognizing their grave corruption.

Nonetheless, Amos's "anthem" – "The Lord roars from Zion, and from Jerusalem He sends forth His voice; the pastures of the shepherds will become parched, and the top of the Carmel will wither" – should warn Israel of impending chastisement, but given the pattern, they may be relieved when his seventh prophecy is against Judah. Even when he begins an eighth oracle against his audience, the rhythm of his first seven may have led them to expect a brief indictment and punishment. When his prophecy extends beyond anything they have heard yet, their surprise undoubtedly turns to shock and shame. Perhaps this is his plan; whether it comes to fruition is unclear, as we do not hear of the audience's reaction.

Poetic Justice

Poetic justice, "*midda keneged midda*" (lit. "measure for measure") is a common biblical motif. The first example may be how God covers Adam and Eve's bare bodies after they hide from him, ashamed of their nakedness. A consistent factor in divine punishment and reward, poetic justice is also often seen in human activity that is then interpreted as serving the divine purpose. When Tamar uses the phrase "Recognize this now" (*haker na*) to convey that Judah is the one who has impregnated her, it evokes the same *haker na* that the brothers, presumably led by Judah, used to fool their father into thinking that Joseph was dead.[15]

This series of oracles also seems to be governed by poetic justice. The first six nations are all accused of various war crimes (a relatively uncommon accusation in Tanakh, compared to corruption, perversion of justice, and sexual immorality). Though their punishments vary, as illustrated above, one common feature is clear: the capital city's defenses are destroyed. Damascus's walls will be breached; the walls of Tyre (Phoenicia) and Botzra (Edom) will be burned down. Ammon will suffer war, as will Moab, who will be devastated to the sound of the shofar. We will soon explore the correlation between Judah's crime and its punishment, but the overall spirit of these oracles is, without question, one of poetic justice: *midda keneged midda*.

15. See Genesis Rabba 85:25; also see Genesis 37:32, 38:25.

One Prelude – *"Pesha"*

Amos's oracles are all built on the scheme of *"Al shelosha pishei* X," "For the three sins of X." An analysis of the term *pesha* (singular of *pishei*) can shed light on the nature of these crimes; this, in turn, will shift the spotlight to the real addressee: Israel.

The lexicon of evil in the Bible is understandably varied. Sin has many variants:

1. *Ḥet,* error: a sin generated by neglect or by ignorance of circumstance or law. Judges 20:16 describes an archer's skill with the term *lo yaḥti,* "never missing the mark." When someone violates a ritual law or harms another inadvertently, this is akin to "missing the mark." It is used similarly in modern Hebrew.
2. *Avon,* intentional wrongdoing: a sin of full volition. (Note that it begins with the letter *ayin,* unlike the related word for "sin," *aven,* which begins with an *alef* but has a similar connotation.)
3. *Zadon,* transgression: a sin which expresses inner passion or anger.[16]
4. *Ma'al,* trespass: a sin exclusively associated with sancta: using sanctified materials for mundane purposes or taking an oath to unlawfully acquit oneself of a debt. When Akhan steals the forbidden spoils of Jericho, this is *me'ila.* When a married woman has an affair, this is considered *me'ila* against her husband (Num. 5:12).

Pesha, however, denotes a wrongdoing of a different nature. The four aforementioned terms refer to sins of neglect or appetite, but they are all about the act itself; the term *pesha,* on the other hand, concerns the relationship between the violator and the one whose command is being violated. *Pesha* is used in II Kings 3:1 when the king of Edom stops

16. Cf. Genesis 25:29, in which the term is used for the stew Jacob prepares, as well as the act of preparation. Brown, Driver and Briggs (in the *Brown, Driver and Briggs Hebrew-English Lexicon,* Oxford 1906 – henceforth "BDB") renders the root "seething," which can be used to describe cooking as well as internal passion.

paying tribute to Israel: he is essentially rejecting Samaria's authority.[17] This is why *pesha* is conventionally understood as "rebellion."[18]

What does this mean for Amos? We have seen how the "messenger formula" (*ko amar*), a phrase which has its genesis in liege-vassal relations, is adapted for the Divine. Similarly, rebelling against an overlord or king becomes a model for understanding rebellion against God. *Pesha* is driven less by appetite, ignorance, or lack of awareness than by desire for autonomy and the rejection of external authority.

However, we must consider the first use of *pesha* in biblical law: if an unpaid watcher claims an item has been stolen and the owner disputes the claim, they take the matter to court. Exodus 22:8 presents a general rule: "For all matters of *pesha,* regarding an ox or a donkey… for any case when the court finds him culpable, he shall pay twofold to his fellow." Violation of the contract by a watcher is considered a *pesha*. Although we could probably present a tortured reading to conform to the aforementioned idea of rebellion, this would be contrived. *Pesha* here seems to be the violation of a contract, which adds a fresh wrinkle to our reading of Kings. The vassal relationship so frequently found in ancient Near Eastern texts is about power, but also about a contract. Various contracts from the First Temple Era stipulate what the lord will provide for the vassal and the tribute and fealty the vassal must show in return.

Pesha can be perceived as something more nuanced than mere petulant rebellion. Some violations are generated by a desire to eat something forbidden, to take that which one covets; other violations are driven by a refusal to accept or live by the terms of the contract to which one has (voluntarily or otherwise) become obligated. In the case of divine service, this may mean a sinful act motivated by a refusal to accept the Sinaitic Covenant and all that it implies. A watcher who steals the item is violating the essential contractual understanding and obligations between the guardian and the owner.

Back to Amos: As we have noted, the first six nations are all accused of "war crimes." Beyond the consideration of the "categorical imperative" mentioned earlier, these war crimes are either acts of

17. Cf. II Kings 3:7 and 8:20.
18. See Rashi on Exodus 34:7.

gratuitous brutality on the battlefield or treachery in handing over refugees to the predatory army chasing them. Perhaps Amos's use of *pesha* here indicates an assumed understanding between combatants, a sort of pre-millenial Geneva Convention. That there were rules of war in the ancient world should come as no surprise: Deuteronomy 20–21 presents several restrictions for the Israelite army; similar or parallel restrictions are found in texts from ancient Egypt and Mesopotamia. We might suggest that the brutality of cutting open pregnant women and so on is deemed a violation of the commonly held ethics of warfare. Perhaps Amos is the one who, in God's name, introduces the notion of ethical restraints in war by which even non-Jews must abide. Those acts of treachery easily fall into this category. Whatever understanding Tyre and Philistia had with the refugees that fled to their borders was violated when the respective nation handed them over to Edom.

We will reconsider this nuanced understanding of *pesha* in the context of Judah and Israel's sins; but we will begin with their neighbors.

ARAM

Aram plays a critical and central role in Israel's geopolitical reality during this period. Aram is mentioned first because of its location and because it was Israel's most hostile neighbor at the time. A brief history of Aram and its place in regional warfare from roughly 850 to 750 BCE will help clarify the oracle, their *pesha*, and their punishment.

Aram is placed squarely in Mesopotamia in the postdiluvian Table of Nations (Gen. 10). God bids Abraham the Aramean to go to Canaan. Aram is where Abraham sends his servant to find a wife for Isaac; where Jacob flees to escape Esau; and where Balak sends messengers to fetch Balaam to curse Israel. Biblical and ancient Near Eastern texts imply that for centuries, Aram was a large area made up of warring tribes with no centralized power. Prototypical Arameans are wanderers (Laban a herdsman, Balaam a wizard for hire), and indeed the area is characterized by nomadic life: "My father was a wandering Aramean" (Deut. 26:5). The farmer bringing his first fruits speaks of the long road from the birth of the nation to this point, where he comfortably resides in the Land of Israel and is able to bring his produce to the Temple. Arameans are paradigmatic wanderers. The jubilant farmer, at the moment of his celebration, acknowledges that he used to be a wanderer, without land, and is now landed gentry with the festive basket of fruit as proof.

One thing is clear from the Torah and early post-conquest history: Aram did not have a strong kingdom or army, and David conquered the entire area, maintaining garrisons all the way to the Euphrates.[19]

Significantly, Amos himself mentions Aram's beginnings (9:7):

> Are you not like the children of the Ethiopians unto Me, O children of Israel? says the Lord. Did I not bring up Israel out of the land of Egypt, and the Philistines from Kaftor, and Aram from Kir?

Amos places Aram's beginnings in Kir, which is evidently in northern Mesopotamia. However, since Israel came out of Egypt as a conquering nation, the same may be true of Aram. The Arameans were a wandering people for centuries, but toward the end of the second millennium BCE or later, a population moved south and west from Kir and conquered or consolidated the peoples of Aram, forging the Aramean state. During the period after the united monarchy, when Israel lost control over the region, evidently Aram consolidated power and formed a single kingdom based in Damascus. During Ahab's reign (c. 850 BCE), Aram posed a threat for the first time, with a strong, confident army and a royal line, the house of Ben Hadad and Hazael.

This is anticipated in I Kings 19, when God instructs Elijah to anoint Hazael as king of Aram; Hazael will be the one who will (unwittingly) act as God's executioner, killing those Israelites who worship Ba'al. From this point on, through Elisha's time, Aram is Israel's most significant enemy, and nearly all of Israel's foreign interactions involve Damascus. Ahab wages two great wars against Aram and is killed in the second.[20] The Aramean general Na'aman visits Elisha to be cured of his *tzara'at* (II Kings 5); Elisha visits Aram to anoint Hazael while King Ben

19. See II Samuel 8.
20. Ahab also fought in at least one war *with* Aram, against Assyria, at Qarqar in c. 853 BCE.

Hadad is dying (II Kings 8); Hazael destroys Gilead (see below) – and throughout, Aram poses a constant threat to Samaria.

The Text (Amos 1:3–5)

(ג) כֹּה אָמַר ה׳ עַל שְׁלֹשָׁה פִּשְׁעֵי דַמֶּשֶׂק וְעַל אַרְבָּעָה לֹא אֲשִׁיבֶנּוּ עַל דּוּשָׁם
בַּחֲרֻצוֹת הַבַּרְזֶל אֶת הַגִּלְעָד: (ד) וְשִׁלַּחְתִּי אֵשׁ בְּבֵית חֲזָאֵל וְאָכְלָה אַרְמְנוֹת
בֶּן הֲדָד: (ה) וְשָׁבַרְתִּי בְּרִיחַ דַּמֶּשֶׂק וְהִכְרַתִּי יוֹשֵׁב מִבִּקְעַת אָוֶן וְתוֹמֵךְ שֵׁבֶט
מִבֵּית עֶדֶן וְגָלוּ עַם אֲרָם קִירָה אָמַר ה׳:

3 *Ko amar Hashem*: For the three sins of Damascus, and for four I will not recant: because they have threshed Gilead with sledges of iron. 4 So will I send a fire into the house of Hazael, and it shall devour the palaces of Ben Hadad. 5 And I will break the bar of Damascus, and cut off the inhabitant from Bikat Aven, and the one who holds the scepter from Beit Eden; and the people of Aram shall go into captivity unto Kir, *amar Hashem*.

The Crime

Amos's gravest accusation is that Aram "threshed Gilead with sledges of iron." This certainly refers to their treatment of the people of Gilead, rather than to any agricultural threshing – plowing – of the land itself. This crime seems to reflect an event that took place approximately one hundred years earlier, as recorded in II Kings 13:3–7:

> 3 And the anger of God was enflamed against Israel, and He delivered them into the hand of Hazael king of Aram and into the hand of Ben Hadad the son of Hazael continually. 4 And Jehoahaz besought God, and God listened to him; for He saw the oppression of Israel, how the king of Aram oppressed them. 5 And God gave Israel a deliverer, so that they went out from under the hand of the Arameans; and the children of Israel dwelt in their tents, as beforetime. 6 Nevertheless, they did not depart from the sins of the house of Jeroboam, of which he made Israel sin, but walked in those ways; and there remained the Ashera also in Samaria.

> 7 For there was not left to Jehoahaz of the people only fifty horsemen, and ten chariots, and ten thousand footmen; for the king of Aram destroyed them *and made them like the dust in threshing.*

This brutal simile is picked up by Amos as he describes Aram's fourth sin. At this point, it seems that the crime was unnecessarily brutal treatment of their Israelite enemy.

Yet, perhaps something even uglier lurks behind this description.

In II Kings 8, Elisha visits Damascus, capital of Aram, when King Ben Hadad lies ill.

> 9 So Hazael went to meet him, and took a present with him, even of every good thing of Damascus, forty camels' burden, and came and stood before him, and said: "Your son Ben Hadad, king of Aram, has sent me to you, saying: 'Shall I recover of this sickness?'" **10** And Elisha said to him: "Go, say to him: 'You will surely recover'; however in reality God has shown me that he will surely die." **11** And he settled his countenance steadfastly upon him, until he was ashamed; and the man of God wept. **12** And Hazael said: "Why are you weeping my lord?" And he answered: "Because I know the evil that you will do to the Israelites: you will set their strongholds on fire, and you will slay their young men with the sword, and you will dash their little ones to pieces and rip up their pregnant women." **13** And Hazael said: "But what is your servant, who is but a dog, that he should do this great thing?" And Elisha answered: "God has shown me that you will be king over Aram."

Since we never hear an explicit report of the Aramean king committing such atrocities, it is tempting to believe that Elisha's tears are an overreaction – or are, perhaps, calculated to keep Hazael in check when he successfully invades Samaria.

However, the description of the conquest belies this understanding: "... for the king of Aram destroyed them and made them like the dust in threshing."

Does this describe the fate of the Israelite soldiers, or does it perhaps allude to Elisha's terrifying vision of Hazael and its realization? Amos's prophecy may tip the scales in favor of an uglier reality.

The Punishment

The punishment is made up of three components:

1. **Destruction of the royal houses by fire:** So will I send a fire into the house of Hazael, and it shall devour the palaces of Ben Hadad
2. **Desolation of major cities:** And I will break the bar of Damascus, and cut off the inhabitant from Bikat Aven, and the one who holds the scepter from Beit Eden
3. **Exile of the population:** and the people of Aram shall go into captivity unto Kir.

Fire is a common biblical motif in war, both in war imagery and actual warfare. The burning of the fortresses and royal houses is the first step toward a kingdom's destruction. Although the king involved in this crime was likely the Hazael of Elisha's time, the Ben Hadad royal name remains; thus, we find the parallelism of Hazael and Ben Hadad.

The city of Damascus was a well-fortified walled city; breaking the bolt (another common biblical image) represents a breakdown of the capital's defenses. The "one who sits" and the "one who holds the scepter" refer to leaders, and the cities mentioned are royal cities or provincial capitals. Bikat Aven literally means "vale of iniquity" (and is similar to "Beit Aven," the derogatory term used by Amos and others for the northern royal sanctuary at Beit El). The reference is likely to the Beqaa valley in southern Lebanon, at the southwestern reaches of the Aramean kingdom. Beit Eden has been identified with Tel Ahmar, which is approximately 320 kilometers northeast of Damascus. Bikat Aven and Beit Eden form a *merismus* encapsulating the entire Aramean empire – an Aramean version of "from sea to shining sea" or the biblical "from Dan to Be'er Sheva."

The final step in the punishment is a complete erasure of Aram's evolution when they are sent back to their point of origin, "unto Kir."

PHILISTIA

We are familiar with the Philistines from narratives in Genesis, Judges, and Samuel; they are also mentioned in Exodus (geographically)[21] and Joshua,[22] and they appear in the oracular sequences of the Major Prophets.[23]

Like Aram, Philistia's earliest mention is in the postdiluvian genealogy: they are descended from Ham's second son Mitzrayim (Egypt):

> Mitzrayim gave birth to Ludim and Anamim and Lehavim and Naftuḥim and Patrusim and Kasluḥim, from whence emerged the Philistines and Kaftorim. (Gen. 10:13–14)

Traditional scholarship maintains that "Kaftor" is Crete. Philistia is juxtaposed with Kaftor elsewhere in the canon.[24]

Jeremiah pronounces that Philistia will be conquered by Egypt. During the same period, Zephaniah (2:3–7) includes the Philistines in his dire prophecy about the impending day of God's anger:

> **3** Seek *Hashem,* all you humble of the earth, who have executed His ordinance; seek righteousness, seek humility. It may be that you will be hidden in the day of the Lord's anger. **4** For Gaza will be forsaken, and Ashkelon a desolation; they shall drive out Ashdod at the noonday, and Ekron shall be rooted up. **5** Woe to the inhabitants of the seacoast, nation of Keretim (*goy Keretim*)! The word of the Lord is against you, O Canaan, the land of the Philistines; I will even destroy you, that there will be no inhabitant. **6** And the seacoast shall be pastures, even meadows for shepherds (*kerot ro'im*) and folds for flocks.

"Keretim" here is likely a reference to Cretans, which, as noted above, is synonymous with Kaftor. "*Goy Keretim*" could be (loosely) translated

21. Exodus 13:17, 23:31.
22. Joshua 13:2–3.
23. Isaiah 14:29–32; Jeremiah 47; Ezekiel 28:15–17.
24. Jeremiah ibid.

as "nation about to be cut off," a play on words; this root is used again in "meadows for shepherds," *kerot ro'im*.

Ezekiel, in his screed against the neighboring nations, declaims:

> Thus says the Lord God: Because the Philistines have dealt by revenge and have taken vengeance with disdain of soul to destroy, for the old hatred; therefore, thus says the Lord God: Behold, I will stretch out My hand upon the Philistines, and I will cut off Keretim, and destroy the remnant of the seacoast. And I will execute great vengeance on them with furious rebukes; and they shall know that I am God, when I shall lay My vengeance on them. (Ezek. 25:15–17)

Here, the wordplay which is hinted at in Zephaniah is explicit: "*vehikhrati et Keretim.*"

Philistia of the Patriarchs

The Philistines' early appearance in the Patriarchs' time poses several problems that may be related. First, the historical records of the "sea-peoples" who migrate to Canaan from the Mediterranean islands and who fight with Egypt are the earliest extra-biblical testimony of the Philistines' existence. These records, however, date from the mid-twelfth century BCE (c. 1180), which is significantly later than the era of the Patriarchs. The lack of extra-biblical evidence of the Philistines during this period is immaterial: absence of evidence is hardly evidence of absence. However, external evidence indicates that the Philistines migrated to the south Israelite coast during the period of Egyptian servitude, long after the Patriarchs.

Second, the "sea-peoples" Ramesses III mentions are organized into military units and have no political governing system: the various Philistine cities are governed by military leaders, not kings. However, the interactions with the Philistines in Genesis all revolve around their king. Abimelech is not only a king, but also bears a royal titular name (evidently there were several kings of this dynasty with that name; Abraham and Isaac both form covenants with "Abimelech").

Finally, the Philistines of the late Bronze/Early Iron Age (identified as the "sea-peoples") settled in five coastal cities. They lived in Gaza,

Ashdod, Ashkelon, Ekron, and Gath. The Philistines of Abraham's time lived in one city – Gerar – which is inland and south of Be'er Sheva.

Devotees of the Documentary Hypothesis, who posit that Genesis is a combination of traditions from the first half of the first millennium BCE, maintain that any mention of Philistines in Genesis is anachronistic. The difficulties with this approach are clear. Why would a later author introduce a "current" nation but give it such wildly divergent characteristics?

The common approach of those who accept Genesis's historicity[25] is that "*Pelishti*" and "land of the *Pelishtim*" may be generic terms for any non-Canaanite residents of the Land of Israel, specifically migrants from eastern Mediterranean islands. Some suggest that Abimelech's Philistines are migrants from Phoenician Tyre and its environs. Both nations hail originally from the islands of Greece; perhaps, they argue, these early Philistines moved south along the coast and then migrated inland.

Philistia at Its Peak

Curiously, although Philistia is mentioned in the Song at the Sea as one of the nations terrified by God's power, Joshua does not fight them in his war of conquest; nor are the Israelites commanded to wage war against Philistines as they are regarding the seven Canaanite nations. These Philistines seem to occupy some sort of protected space.

In Judges, Philistines are Samson's primary antagonists, but otherwise they appear only briefly. They are listed among the unconquered ethnicities at the beginning of Judges and are the Ammonites' allies against Manasseh in Judges 10. At the end of Judges 3, Shamgar ben Anat is credited with killing six hundred of them with a cattle prod. Some suggest that Shamgar was a Canaanite; both his non-Israelite name as well as his father's idolatrous name are strong clues to his Canaanite identity. This implies that the Philistines were not beloved by their Canaanite hosts and that, in an ancient version of "the enemy of my enemy is my friend," the Canaanites and Israelites may have been allied against them.

25. For instance, Y. M. Grintz, in his *The Book of Genesis, Its Uniqueness and Antiquity* [Heb.] (Jerusalem: Magnes Press, 1983), and Kenneth Kitchen in his *On the Reliability of the Old Testament* (Cambridge: Eerdmans, 2005).

The Samson cycle (Judges 13–16) is a dramatic story of spiraling vengeance – motivated by personal insult rather than national salvation. We learn much about Philistine customs, less about their pagan worship, and very little about their military tactics and ethics.

The Philistines may have reached the peak of their power and impact just prior to the establishment of the united monarchy; indeed, one chief motivation for its establishment may have been the constant Philistine threat. During Samuel's time, the Israelites were constantly at war with the Philistines.

As Saul's reign began, Philistine garrisons in some Israelite cities[26] had sufficient control over Israel to prevent them from developing Iron Age technology, forcing them to come to the Philistines to sharpen their tools.[27]

At *Efes Damim*, young David defeated the Philistine warrior Goliath and the Israelites chased the fleeing Philistine army back to Ekron.[28] During the subsequent era (c. 1000 BCE) as David fled from and eventually succeeded Saul, the Philistines remained central antagonists, as evidenced by their pillaging the granaries of Ke'ila.[29]

Although David led the charge to save Ke'ila from the Philistines, he eventually fled *to* Philistia for refuge.[30] By this time, the Philistines have (again?) a unified capital, Gath, ruled by a king, Achish, although the *seranim* (lords?) continue to lead them into battle.[31] David swore "loyalty" to Achish and was granted a Gazan city (Ziklag), which he and his band of desperados used as their base for raiding other desert tribes.

Even with Saul's death and David's return to Judea to become king in Hebron,[32] the Philistines only truly perceived David as an enemy after he conquered Jerusalem[33] and they were defeated by him at Ba'al

26. See I Samuel 10:5.
27. I Samuel 13:19–21.
28. Ibid. 17:52 ff.
29. Ibid. ch. 23.
30. Fleeing to Gath happens again when two of Shimi's slaves seek refuge there (I Kings 2:39).
31. I Samuel 29:2.
32. II Samuel 2:1 ff.
33. Ibid. ch. 5.

Peratzim and at Emek Refa'im.[34] At this point, we sense the beginning of the Philistine decline. At the beginning of the brief recap of David's conquests in II Samuel 8:1, the text records that David "smote the Philistines and subdued them, and he took *meteg ha'ama* from the hands of the Philistines." Based on the parallel verse in Chronicles, most regard this as a reference to the Philistine town of Gath. II Samuel 21:15–22 reports several battles between David (or his men) and the Philistines, and in 23:13–17 we learn of the famous battle against the Philistine stronghold at Bethlehem.

There is no further mention of the Philistines in Early Prophets, except for a brief mention of Hezekiah's conquest of the Philistines at the end of the eighth century BCE.[35] Nevertheless, their regular appearances in the oracles against the nations by Isaiah, Jeremiah, and Ezekiel, along with mentions by Amos and Zephaniah, show that the Philistines remained hostile throughout the pre-Babylonian period.

The book of Chronicles gives us a broader picture with two later mentions. In the mid-ninth century BCE – over a hundred years after David – we are told about Jehoshaphat's strong rule over Judah:

> And a terror from God fell upon all the kingdoms of the lands that were round about Judah, so that they made no war against Jehoshaphat. And some of the Philistines brought Jehoshaphat presents, and silver for tribute; the Arvi'im also brought him flocks, seven thousand and seven hundred rams, and seven thousand and seven hundred he-goats. (II Chr. 17:10–11)

Nearly a hundred years later, during Uziah's long, successful realm:

> And he went forth and warred against the Philistines, and broke down the wall of Gath, and the wall of Yavneh, and the wall of Ashdod; and he built cities in [the country of] Ashdod, and among the Philistines. And God helped him against the Philistines,

34. Ibid. vv. 17–27.
35. II Kings 18:8.

> and against the Aravim of Gur Ba'al, and the Me'unim. (II Chr. 26:6–7)

The Philistines apparently endured throughout the First Commonwealth, had to be subdued – and had enough wealth to bring tribute to the king.

The Philistines of Amos

By Amos's time, the Philistines are bit players in the drama of Israelite history. This prompts the question asked by most commentators – what were the circumstances of "a whole captivity" that the Philistines "handed over" to Edom?[36]

Many commentators, modern as well as medieval, assume that these were Israelite refugees. Grintz[37] suggests that the Philistines would take people who fled from Assyria and sell them as slaves to the Mediterranean islands. He then suggests a novel understanding of who Edom might be,[38] in order to have it all fall into place.

There is no need to start with this assumption. After all, if the common denominator of the war crimes in the first six oracles is violation of an assumed code of ethics in war, it hardly matters who the victims of this treachery may have been. Indeed, the point may be even considered stronger if the victims were not our brothers, but rather another nation that fled from the Edomites to the west (as we see David's flight from Moab to Gath, and Shimi's slaves' fleeing from Jerusalem to Gath), who had some sort of a treaty with the Gazans upon which they relied. The Philistines violated this understanding and handed them over to their pursuers – and this treachery and violation of trust is the crime that sealed Philistia's fate.

---

36. We might similarly ask why they are so prominently castigated in the other prophecies of the time and even later – but that may be more historic reflection, as even Sodom is mentioned in the same chapter in Ezekiel.
37. Y. M. Grintz, "Because They Carried Away Captive a Whole Captivity, to Deliver Them Up to Edom," [Heb.], *Bet Mikra* 13, no. 1 (1968): 24–26.
38. He suggests either "Aram" or "Aden."

The Text (Amos 1:6–8)

(ו) כֹּה אָמַר ה׳ עַל שְׁלֹשָׁה פִּשְׁעֵי עַזָּה וְעַל אַרְבָּעָה לֹא אֲשִׁיבֶנּוּ עַל הַגְלוֹתָם
גָּלוּת שְׁלֵמָה לְהַסְגִּיר לֶאֱדוֹם: (ז) וְשִׁלַּחְתִּי אֵשׁ בְּחוֹמַת עַזָּה וְאָכְלָה אַרְמְנֹתֶיהָ:
(ח) וְהִכְרַתִּי יוֹשֵׁב מֵאַשְׁדּוֹד וְתוֹמֵךְ שֵׁבֶט מֵאַשְׁקְלוֹן וַהֲשִׁיבוֹתִי יָדִי עַל עֶקְרוֹן
וְאָבְדוּ שְׁאֵרִית פְּלִשְׁתִּים אָמַר אֲדֹנָי ה׳:

6 *Ko amar Hashem*: For three transgressions of Gaza, indeed, for four, I will not recant: because they carried away captive a whole captivity, to deliver them up to Edom. **7** So will I send a fire on the wall of Gaza, and it will devour her palaces. **8** And I will cut off the inhabitant from Ashdod, and the one who holds the scepter from Ashkelon; and I will turn My hand against Ekron, and the remnant of the Philistines will perish, *amar Hashem Elokim*.

Just like Aram, the primary punishment is destruction of Philistia's capital cities and leaders, which ultimately results in its complete annihilation. This prophecy was presumably fulfilled soon afterward, as there is no further mention of the Philistines after the First Commonwealth.

PHOENICIA

Unlike Philistia, Phoenicia remains in the background for most of Israelite history. The Phoenicians never went to war against Israel; in fact, they even married into Israelite monarchy (Jezebel – although we all know how well *that* turned out), and long before, both David and Solomon formed warm alliances with King Hiram of Tyre, the Phoenician capital. Not only did the Tyrians provide wood, lumberjacks, and carpenters for Solomon's Temple, but Hiram also considered Solomon a "brother," and praised God for having chosen such a wise son to succeed David.[39] In addition, the Phoenicians provided the Israelites with one

39. I Kings 5:15–25; for "brother," cf. ibid. 9:13.

of their greatest gifts – the alphabet. By the ninth century BCE, ancient Hebrew script (Paleo-Hebrew) had integrated Phoenician pictogram stylings into their alphabet.

Given this harmonious history, it is hard to fathom Israelite exiles fleeing to Phoenicia and being turned away. Moreover, geographically, why and how would northern Phoenicia traverse Judea or Samaria to betray refugees to southern Edom?

Similar to the Philistines' crime, we must assume that the refugees are not Israelites, but rather a different people who fled from Edom, whose trust the Tyrians betrayed: instead of honoring their assumed alliance, they handed them over to their pursuers.

The Text (Amos 1:9–10)

(ט) כֹּה אָמַר ה׳ עַל שְׁלֹשָׁה פִּשְׁעֵי צֹר וְעַל אַרְבָּעָה לֹא אֲשִׁיבֶנּוּ עַל הַסְגִּירָם
גָּלוּת שְׁלֵמָה לֶאֱדוֹם וְלֹא זָכְרוּ בְּרִית אַחִים: (י) וְשִׁלַּחְתִּי אֵשׁ בְּחוֹמַת צֹר
וְאָכְלָה אַרְמְנֹתֶיהָ:

9 *Ko amar Hashem*: For three transgressions of Tyre, indeed, for four, I will not recant: because they delivered up a whole captivity to Edom and did not remember the covenant of brothers. **10** So will I send a fire on the wall of Tyre, and it shall devour her palaces.

Note that this oracle shifts to the "short form" with just one stage of punishment. This thus adheres to the aforementioned literary pattern of "long-long-short-short"; conveniently, the Phoenicians apparently have only one major city (Tyre/Tzor) to rhetorically attack – although why Sidon is spared is unclear.

Again, the geographical and rhetorical "convenience" of aligning Philistines with Phoenicians may have historic roots: the first wave of "sea-peoples" invading (Heb. "*poleshim*") Canaan may have been Phoenicians who migrated south.

EDOM-ESAU

Israel's relationship with Edom is rooted in the story of Jacob and Esau, beginning with the prophecy Rebecca hears when they are *in utero*:[40]

> And the Lord said to her: "There are two nations in your womb and two peoples will separate from your insides; people will strive against people and the older will serve the younger" (Gen. 25:23)

This prophecy is made up of four distinct and sequenced stages:

1. "There are two nations (*goyim*) in your womb." Each twin will found his own nation.
2. "Two peoples (*le'umim*) will separate from your insides." Though this line implies that the difference between the twins will be evident from birth (as emphasized in their birth narrative), nothing in these two lines implies contention or discord between the brothers; indeed; their differences could have resulted in a broader base of leadership of the two nations.
3. "People will struggle with people." This relates to the brothers' descendants. Somewhere down the annals of history, these two distinct nations will confront each other.
4. "The older will serve the younger." This phrase, "*verav ya'avod tza'ir*," can be parsed in two opposite ways. The traditional reading "and the older will serve the younger" is countered by the parsing indicated by the trope marks – "*verav, ya'avod tza'ir*" – which means "the older will the younger serve." This ambiguity hints to perpetual tension between them; one will always subdue the other. Neither will ever fully triumph; either could be master at any time.

The brothers, different from birth, choose livelihoods that hark back to the primordial fratricidal tension between Cain and Abel; between the man of the field, Esau, and the shepherd, Jacob. Esau's ruddiness

40. Although it can be posited that it begins with God's blessing to Abraham that Sarah "will become *nations*, kings of peoples will emanate from her" (Gen. 17:16).

and his rash demand for "that red stuff" to be "stuffed down my throat" contribute to the etiology of his tribal name – Edom ("red"). From this moment, their relationship is characterized by deception by Jacob and murderous outrage by Esau, anticipating the future tension between their descendants.

Nonetheless, it is not clear that Esau truly means Jacob harm, and his angry outburst may merely reflect his rash temper. Though Jacob still fears Esau over twenty years later,[41] their reunion ultimately seems warm, although Jacob shrewdly cuts it short with a promise to "catch up later." This is the brothers' last detailed encounter. Esau's impressive genealogy is presented just as he disappears; ominously, the hated Amalek is introduced as his grandson.

We next meet Edom during our travels in the desert:

> Moses sent messengers from Kadesh to the king of Edom: "So says your brother (!) Israel: You know the afflictions that have found us. Our ancestors descended to Egypt and we settled in Egypt for many years and the Egyptians dealt badly with us and oppressed us… behold we are now at Kadesh, the city on your border." (Num. 20:14–16)

This passage echoes Jacob's message to Esau after *his* oppressive years with Laban:

> Jacob sent messengers to Esau his brother: "So says your servant Jacob: I sojourned with Laban and was delayed until now." (Gen. 32:4)

This intertextuality implies that Israel and Edom's relationship should be filtered through Jacob and Esau's, grounded in that timeless prophecy communicated to Rebecca.

Edom's refusal to allow Israel passage notwithstanding, the nation was commanded to avoid war with Edom and allow Esau's descendants

41. At least twenty years, but maybe many more; cf. Etshalom, *Between the Lines of the Bible,* vol. 1 (revised) (Jerusalem: Urim, 2016), ch. 16.

to inherit Mount Se'ir, similar to the ordained respect for Moab and Ammon's inheritance. Coupled with a prohibition against "despising Edom" (Deut. 23:8), the paradigm seems to be one of guarded distance and respect for boundaries – a "cold brotherhood" with Edom.

Edom only made an active appearance in biblical history in David's time,[42] when he conquered Edom as part of his broad conquest of the eastern lands up to the Euphrates.[43] The next mention of Edom is as the birthplace of Solomon's "adversary," Hadad, who fled to Egypt when David conquered Edom; upon the death of David and his general Yoav, he returns to Edom.[44] The kingdom is hardly mentioned until Judah, Israel, and Edom form an unlikely alliance to punish rebellious Moab, who ceased paying tribute to Samaria after Ahab's death.[45]

From a broad historical perspective, this quiet on the southeastern front is somewhat unsettling – Rebecca's prophecy anticipates ongoing tension between Israel and Edom.

The first biblical record of Edom challenging Israel/Judah is c. 840 BCE, when they rebel against Judah in Jehoram's time: that is, when Amos delivers his diatribe against Edom, they had been independent of Judah for less than a century. Edom's lowly status is apparent from its next mention in Kings: when Amaziah of Judah defeats Edom in the "Salton Vale," he then challenges Joash of Israel, who contemptuously replies: "You smote Edom and your heart became haughty; keep your honor and stay in your home. Why should you provoke evil such that you will fall (in war) and Judah right along with you?" (II Kings 14:10). This implies that defeating Edom is not an impressive military feat; Amaziah should not let it "go to his head."

Here is where things get interesting. Though Edom is not included in Isaiah's sequence of oracles against the nations (chapters 14–22), it is threatened in a separate prophecy in chapter 34. In Joel 4 (dating undetermined), God promises vengeance against Edom for the Judean blood

---

42. "Edom" is mentioned briefly in Joshua as a geographical marker, in Judges (as it was earlier in Exodus) in war poetry, and in I Samuel in the brief summary of Saul's wars (I Sam. 14:47).
43. II Samuel 8:14.
44. I Kings 11:14–22.
45. II Kings 3:5.

it spilled. One thing is clear from several texts: Edom played a central role in Jerusalem's destruction in 586 BCE. The psalmist calls on God to remember what "the daughter of Edom" did on the day of the destruction (Ps. 137:7); Lamentations 4 ends with a promise of God's punishment against Edom (4:22). Yet there is no biblical evidence of any heinous offenses by Edom against Israel that predate Amos's time – Joel and Obadiah may be later, and destruction-era texts tell us nothing about Edom's behavior prior to the Assyrian conquest. The oracles against Edom in Jeremiah (chapter 49) and Ezekiel (25:12–14) also reflect the destruction era, by which time Edom had become an active and brutal enemy to Judah.

Significantly, a number of these prophecies include a component unmatched in oracles against other nations – the promise that Israel/Judah will conquer Edom's land and dispossess Esau from there. This is the ultimate verse in Obadiah and a quote from Amos:

> And saviors shall go up to Mount Zion to judge the mountain of Esau (*lishpot et Har Esav*), and dominion shall be the Lord's. (Ob. 21)

> On that day I will raise up David's fallen tabernacle ... in order that they may possess the remnant of Edom, and all the nations upon whom My name is called. (Amos 9:11–12)

A careful reading of Amos's oracle against Edom may shed some light on this mystery.

The Text (Amos 1:11–12)

(יא) כֹּה אָמַר ה׳ עַל שְׁלֹשָׁה פִּשְׁעֵי אֱדוֹם וְעַל אַרְבָּעָה לֹא אֲשִׁיבֶנּוּ עַל רָדְפוֹ
בַחֶרֶב אָחִיו וְשִׁחֵת רַחֲמָיו וַיִּטְרֹף לָעַד אַפּוֹ וְעֶבְרָתוֹ שְׁמָרָה נֶצַח: (יב) וְשִׁלַּחְתִּי
אֵשׁ בְּתֵימָן וְאָכְלָה אַרְמְנוֹת בָּצְרָה:

11 *Ko amar Hashem*: For three transgressions of Edom, and for four, I will not recant: because he pursued his brother with the

> sword, and cast off all of his compassion, and his anger perpetually tore at him, and he held onto his wrath forever. **12** So will I send a fire upon Teiman, and it shall devour the palaces of Botzra.

Botzra and Teimah-Teiman are cities in Edom. Note that the accusation is the longest and most detailed so far, while the punishment is brief. Surprisingly, unlike the other accused nations, Edom does not stand accused of *doing* anything. Their offense is their attitude – they deliberately suppress their instinctive brotherly compassion. The assumption is that in Amos's time – perhaps since the beginning of the monarchy or even Israel's conquest and settlement – they have maintained an inherited enmity for their Israelite brothers. In Amos's eyes, whether they actually chased Israelites with the sword pales in comparison to the offense of suppressing any brotherly compassion and consciously stirring the embers of hatred glowing inside.

Instead of actual historic precedents (as seen with Aram, Philistia, and Phoenicia), perhaps the prophet is opening our eyes to something too abstract to document in a historical record.

Edom has spent centuries stoking hatred for their brother Israel; years after Amos is no more, this anger will erupt in a gush of enmity and a dance of joy at Jerusalem's destruction. Condemning not war crimes and brutality, but rather poisonous, corrosive attitudes, this prophecy may have an even more profound impact on the audience in Samaria. Israel are not accused of brutality, of "threshing the pregnant women" of their enemies, but the notion that God holds people accountable for harboring malice *does* resonate with their own spiritual failings.

It is as if the ancient prophecy about Edom/Israel is awaiting resolution, with the reading of *verav ya'avod tza'ir* – and the older will serve the younger – the desired and anticipated final state – *lishpot et Har Esav*.

AMMON AND MOAB

Ammon and Moab are Israel's difficult neighbors on the east bank of the Jordan. Both terrorize certain tribes during the period of the Judges: Moab oppresses Benjamin (Judges 3); Ammon oppresses Manasseh in Gideon's time (ibid. 6) and in Jepthtah's name (ibid. 11).

Both of them are subjugated by David during his great eastward expansion (II Sam. 8).

They are grouped together in the Deuteronomic intermarriage prohibitions (23:4–7):

> Neither an Ammonite nor a Moabite shall enter God's congregation; even to the tenth generation shall none of them enter into God's congregation forever. For they did not greet you with bread and with water on the way, when you came forth out of Egypt; and because they hired Balaam, the son of Be'or from Petor of Aram Naharayim, against you to curse you… You shall not seek their peace nor their prosperity, all of your days forever.

Ammon and Moab are also grouped together earlier in Deuteronomy (2:8–9, 18–19) when Moses recounts the divine directives affecting the Jews' circuitous route to the Land:

> And we turned and passed by the way of the Wilderness of Moab. And God said to me: "Neither act as an enemy against Moab, nor contend with them in battle; for I will not give you of his land for a possession; because I have given Ar to the children of Lot for a possession…You are passing this day over the border of Moab, even Ar; and when you come nigh over against the Ammonites, neither harass them nor contend with them; for I will not give you of the Ammonites' land for a possession; because I have given it to the children of Lot as a possession."

Both of these East Bank neighbors were given a "divine pass," keeping their territory without being threatened by Israel's sword, both for the same reason: "I have given it to the children of Lot as a possession."

To fully understand this complex relationship, we must go back to the genesis of the Jewish nation.

Ammon and Moab: Beginnings

God bids Abram: "Go by yourself from your land" (Gen. 12:1). He is apparently to leave on his own, but he brings his nephew Lot. Subsequent events suggest that this was a mistake, and they soon part ways. Abram proposes their separation with a curious phrase: "If you choose the left, I will go to the right; and if you choose the right, I will go to the left" (Gen. 13:9). This unusual wording is best understood against the backdrop of the biblical compass: the biblical assumption is that one is facing east, so that "in front" (*kedem*) is another way of saying east and "in back" (*aḥor*) is another word for west. Thus, "left" is north and "right" is south (viz. 14:15). Abram offers Lot two options: go north (Shechem) and I will go south (Hebron) or vice versa. Leaving the hill country is not on the table, but Lot chooses exactly that, turning east and down into the lush Jordan Valley, despite the depravity of its denizens in Sodom.

When God seeks Sodom's destruction, Lot is to be saved in Abraham's merit, but the only members of Lot's family who agree to go with him are his wife and his two unmarried daughters; his wife violates the angels' command, looks back, and becomes a pillar of salt.[46] Lot and his two daughters flee to a cave near the town of Zoar; the daughters, convinced that they are the last people on earth (or that no man will agree to mate with them), get him drunk and have relations with him on subsequent nights (19:36–38):

> And the two daughters of Lot became pregnant from their father. The elder gave birth to a son and she called him Moab (lit. "from father"); he is the father of Moab until this very day. And the younger also gave birth to a son and she called him Ben Ammi (lit. "son of my people"); he is the father of the Ammonites until this very day.

This etiological tale, distasteful as it is, establishes Ammon and Moab as distant relatives of Israel. On the one hand, they are kin and are accorded special status as such. According to the Mekhilta,[47] before God offered the Torah to Israel, He approached other Abrahamic nations: the progeny of Esau, Lot, and Ishmael. Ammon and Moab balk at the prohibition of adultery, saying "We are all born of incest!" Nonetheless, their

46. However, cf. Ralbag on Genesis 19:26.
47. *Yitro, BaḤodesh* 5.

aggadic presence indicates their status as part of Abraham's family, and the concept of Lot's divine inheritance seems to reflect the same idea.

The flipside is that their callous inhospitality to their cousins in the desert (first failing to offer them bread and water, then actively hiring Balaam to curse them – not to mention, one suspects, their ignominious beginnings) puts them permanently at arm's length. Only through Ruth's persistence (and the delicate parsing of "a Moabite, but not a Moabitess") is Moab admitted into God's congregation.

The Text – Ammon (Amos 1:13–15)

(יג) כֹּה אָמַר ה׳ עַל שְׁלֹשָׁה פִּשְׁעֵי בְנֵי עַמּוֹן וְעַל אַרְבָּעָה לֹא אֲשִׁיבֶנּוּ עַל
בִּקְעָם הָרוֹת הַגִּלְעָד לְמַעַן הַרְחִיב אֶת גְּבוּלָם: (יד) וְהִצַּתִּי אֵשׁ בְּחוֹמַת רַבָּה
וְאָכְלָה אַרְמְנוֹתֶיהָ בִּתְרוּעָה בְּיוֹם מִלְחָמָה בְּסַעַר בְּיוֹם סוּפָה: (טו) וְהָלַךְ
מַלְכָּם בַּגּוֹלָה הוּא וְשָׂרָיו יַחְדָּו אָמַר ה׳:

13 *Ko amar Hashem*: For the three sins of the children of Ammon, and for four I will not recant: because they ripped up the pregnant women of Gilead, in order to expand their border. **14** So will I ignite a fire in the wall of Rabba, and it shall devour her palaces, with shouting in the day of battle, with a tempest in the day of the whirlwind. **15** And their king shall go into captivity, he and his princes together, *amar Hashem.*

Note that unlike the other nations listed in this series, the Ammonites are called "*Bnei Ammon*" – even Israel is not called "*Bnei Yisrael.*"[48] This name is supported by the foundational story where Lot's younger daughter calls her son Ben Ammi. It is also supported by external texts. An inscription discovered on an ancient bottle in Tel Siran (in 1972, on the grounds of the University of Jordan in Amman) mentions King Amminadav of "*Bnei Ammon*"; similarly, a shard found in an ancient theater in Amman

48. One might argue that "*Bnei Yisrael*" would not be a fitting cognomen for the northern kingdom, as they are only part of the Jewish people, and never its heart.

mentions "*Bnei Ammon.*" Significantly, in both cases, it is one word, "*bn'mn.*"

The Ammonites are accused of a more explicit version of the Arameans' crime (v. 3). The earlier accusation could be read as the offense of "scorching earth" (although we rejected this interpretation), but this horrific crime cannot be interpreted in any but the most horrific way. Though there is intentional wordplay between *harot* (pregnant women) and the mountainous terrain of Gilead (*harim*), the Ammonites clearly attack the people of Gilead, not the mountains themselves. This oracle may be in dialogue with the demands of Nahash of Ammon, in the eleventh century BCE, who will only accept the Israelites' surrender if they poke out their right eyes. In response, Saul attacks them and achieves his first military victory (I Samuel 11).

One of the fragments of Samuel found at Qumran contains a significant addition. In 4QSama, written c. 50 BCE, the following text bridges the end of chapter 10 to the beginning of chapter 11 (supplemental text in bold):

> But some worthless fellows said, "How can this man save us?" And they despised him and brought him no present. But he held his peace. **Now Nahash, king of the Ammonites, had been grievously oppressing the Gadites and the Reubenites. He would gouge out the right eye of each of them and would not grant Israel a deliverer. No one was left of the Israelites across the Jordan whose right eye Nahash, king of the Ammonites, had not gouged out. But there were seven thousand men who had escaped from the Ammonites and had entered Yavesh Gilad.** About a month later, Nahash the Ammonite went up and besieged Yavesh Gilad; and all the men of Yavesh said to Nahash, "Make a treaty with us, and we will serve you." But Nahash the Ammonite said to them, "On this condition I will make a treaty with you, namely that I gouge out everyone's right eye, and thus put disgrace upon all Israel."

Whether this is an aggadic addendum or a variant *vorlage* (always a question in Qumran research) is unclear. Nonetheless, there was certainly a tradition – written or oral – that the Ammonites had indeed committed such atrocities against the eastern Israelite tribes, more than just the unrealized threat recorded in the Masoretic text (MT). Perhaps Amos's indictment here supports this expanded version of I Samuel, and his Samarian audience is familiar with such Ammonite brutality. The hyperbolic image of ripping open the bellies of pregnant women (which may have been Aram's crime) would serve to exacerbate the audience's revulsion.

This rhetorical flourish accomplishes yet another literary aim. As we have pointed out along the way, the eight indictments are structured as long-long-short-short, and this pattern repeats right up to the denouement. This deliberately misleads the audience into a more relaxed attitude so that even when they hear that Israel is the "next" nation to be named, they anticipate a short and relatively mild punishment. The abrupt shift serves to surprise and hopefully shock them into repenting and mending their ways.

Ammon is the fifth nation and the long-long-short-short pattern begins again in this oracle. Its crime recalls the offense of the first nation, and the punishment awaiting Ammon begins like the rest, with a variant verb used for lighting the fire against the city. Instead of the usual *veshilaḥti esh,* here we have *vehitzati esh,* "So will I ignite a fire." Most scholars believe that this is simply driven by literary considerations, with no difference in meaning or import.

Once the city of Rabba is burned, the punishment moves into "new territory." Ammon stands accused of a war crime, and their punishment is to be defeated in war; the blasts of a shofar or screaming (*terua*) and the terror of storms and hurricanes are metaphors for the horrors of war.

The final step is that the king will be exiled – perhaps. The text reads "*malkam,*" "their king," but this may be a variation of the name *Milkom,*[49] the Ammonite god, in which case "his princes" would refer to the priests of the cult.

49. This clever play on Milkom is attested to elsewhere (for example, II Sam. 12:30).

The Text – Moab (Amos 2:1–3)

(א) כֹּה אָמַר ה׳ עַל שְׁלֹשָׁה פִּשְׁעֵי מוֹאָב וְעַל אַרְבָּעָה לֹא אֲשִׁיבֶנּוּ עַל שָׂרְפוֹ
עַצְמוֹת מֶלֶךְ אֱדוֹם לַשִּׂיד: (ב) וְשִׁלַּחְתִּי אֵשׁ בְּמוֹאָב וְאָכְלָה אַרְמְנוֹת הַקְּרִיּוֹת
וּמֵת בְּשָׁאוֹן מוֹאָב בִּתְרוּעָה בְּקוֹל שׁוֹפָר: (ג) וְהִכְרַתִּי שׁוֹפֵט מִקִּרְבָּהּ וְכָל
שָׂרֶיהָ אֶהֱרוֹג עִמּוֹ אָמַר ה׳:

1 *Ko amar Hashem*: For the three sins of Moab, and for four I will not recant: because he burned the bones of the king of Edom into lime. 2 So will I send a fire upon Moab, and it shall devour the palaces of Keriyot; and Moab will die with tumult, with shouting, and with the sound of the shofar. 3 And I will cut off the judge from their midst, and will slay all of their princes with him, *amar Hashem.*

The Crime

Moab is accused of a curious, anomalous crime. Most critically, this is the only crime that cannot possibly involve Israel – God is not just acting vengefully against those who harm His people; He also holds all nations accountable for their deeds.

Like most of these offenses, their specific crime is not easily detected in biblical history. The closest we come is the king of Moab's bizarre and ruthless act against *his own son* – sacrificing him as a burnt offering on the city wall, which somehow ends Israel, Judah, and Edom's attack on Moab (II Kings 3). It is unlikely that this act is the referent here, as Moab is accused of acting against another king.

The end of v. 1, "into lime" (*lasid*), might imply that he burned the bones of the king to use the ashes as plaster. This would be technically difficult; a more likely interpretation is that he burned the bones and used that fire to make plaster.

The dominant motif is, once again, war: for this war crime, Moab will burn down, its fortresses at Keriyot (situated between Divon and Medba) devoured, and they will suffer as Ammon, to the blasting of the war shofar. Their leaders, too, will be targeted, both judge and princes, who were presumably the instigators or supporters of Moab's terrible offense.

INTERIM SUMMARY – THE SIX ACCUSED NATIONS

As outlined above, the oracle series follows this rhythm:

> *Al shelosha pishei* [nation] *ve'al arba'a lo ashivenu; al* [crime]
> *Veshilaḥti/ vehitzati esh be-*[nation/city]
> [General or detailed punishment]

What is the larger pattern? We have identified the consistent and internal pattern of each oracle. What is the series' panoramic scheme?

First Proposal: The Chiasmus

One common biblical structural model is the chiasmus. The word comes from the Greek letter X ("chi") and is defined by the shape of that letter. A text begins with a particular idea or keyword, moves on to a second idea and so forth – and then begins doubling back on itself, such that it ends with the same keyword or theme as the beginning. There are two general types of *chiasma*: A-B-B'-A' and A-B-C-B'-A'. Neither of these models is limited to two or three themes; some chiastic structures involve up to, or even more than, a dozen themes.[50] The difference between the two models is the presence of a "pivot verse," a center at which point the structure turns back.

A simple example of the first kind is the description of Elkana's two wives (I Sam. 1:2):

> Elkana had two wives:
> A: one named Hanna,
> B: the other named Penina;
> B': and Penina had children
> A': while Hanna had no children.

50. See, *inter alia*, Etshalom, *Between the Lines of the Bible*, vol. 2, chs. 5, 10.

An example of the pivot-chiasmus is Genesis 28:10–32:3 (all of *Parashat Vayetze*). These nearly four chapters are all one single Masoretic paragraph. The story of Jacob's sojourn in Haran begins with:

A: Jacob having a vision, seeing angels and naming the location (*Beit El*) in honor of that vision,
  B: Jacob erecting a commemorative stele
    C: Jacob negotiating with Laban,
      D: Jacob interacting with Rachel and Leah (note the order),
        E: Jacob and his wives bearing children,
      D': Jacob interacting with Leah and Rachel,
    C': Jacob negotiating with Laban,
  B': Jacob erecting a commemorative stele and
A': Jacob having a vision, seeing angels and naming the location (*Maḥanayim*) in honor of that vision.

If we were to propose a chiastic structure for the oracle series (the first six[51]), we would likely suggest a non-pivot model, as follows:

A: Aram
  B: Philistia
    C: Tyre
    C': Edom
  B': Ammon
A': Moab

The argument in favor of this structure is historical, not literary. Moab and Aram (A and A') are both active enemies of the monarchy; Philistia and Ammon (B and B') are only active enemies during the Davidic era; and Tyre and Edom (C and C') are never direct enemies of Israel

51. We will not consider a chiastic or any other type of envelope structure involving the first seven oracles exclusively, as that would include Judah with the foreign nations. That would be a highly unlikely rhetorical move on the part of a prophet hailing from Judah.

during the First Commonwealth – in fact, as mentioned, they are sometimes allies.

This is an interesting consideration, but not a very compelling proposal. A chiasmus is a literary structure. As such, it should be parsed in literary terms, not geopolitical ones.[52]

Second Proposal: The Reverse Historical Chain

Israel's oldest enemies in the region are Moab and Ammon, the former acting more heinously with the hiring of Balaam. Hence, the final enemy in the series is the oldest (Moab), preceded by the next oldest (Ammon). This even fits their birth order (per Gen. 19). Edom, which is not an enemy during this period (and, unlike Ammon and Moab, is not barred from entering "God's congregation"),[53] becomes an enemy at a later point (perhaps when Hadad the Edomite becomes Solomon's *satan*).[54] We do not know when Tyre became Israel's adversary (if ever). The Philistines, unpleasant neighbors from Samson's time and throughout Saul's and David's reigns, may continue to cause trouble after Solomon's reign.

In any case, as mentioned at the beginning of this chapter, it is clear that Aram is the "newest" enemy on the block. If so, we find an intriguing and unprecedented rationale behind the sequence of oracles: they are presented in reverse historical order, beginning with the current enemy, Aram, and moving backwards in Israelite history to the oldest enemies, with whom we share a complex family history and relationship.

As noted, however, the analysis rests on several unsubstantiated premises. To posit that the "friendly disagreement" between Hiram and Solomon constitutes a state of enmity is somewhat contrived; suggesting that tension with the Philistines continued after Solomon's time requires more substantial textual support. All of this leads us to a third proposal, and even to a fourth.

---

52. Geographic considerations might be taken into account in reckoning the literary structure, as we saw in the introductory chapters to this section.
53. Deuteronomy 23:4–9.
54. I Kings 11.

Third Proposal: *Al Shelosha…Ve'al Shelosha*

We have already addressed the opening refrain of the oracles and its contribution to both the poetic rhythm of the oracle sequence as well as, possibly, a metaphysical lesson about God's grace. Might this anaphora also allude to the series' structure?

At first glance, we are tempted to read the opening segment, *Al shelosha,* as numbering not only the "minor" violations that lead up to the cataclysmic "fourth," but also as setting out the pattern. There are two sets of three nations here: (a) Aram, (b) Philistia, and (c) Tyre; and in the parallel set, (a) Edom, (b) Ammon, and (c) Moab. What is particularly attractive about this schema is that the first three were all "foreigners" who came to the region from distant areas. The Philistines and Phoenicians were "sea-peoples" who came from the northern Mediterranean. Aram, as we see in both our chapter and Amos's eschatology (chapter 9), comes from Kir, near the headwaters of the Euphrates in Asia Minor. On the other hand, Edom, Ammon, and Moab are all "locals," whose roots were right where they lived at this time. As Jeremiah states (48:11):

> Moab has been at ease from his youth, and he has settled on his lees, and has not been emptied from vessel to vessel, neither has he gone into captivity; therefore his taste remains in him, and his scent is not changed.

Moreover, the first "set" of nations are not part of the extended Abrahamic clan, with no family ties with Israel. In contrast, Edom, Ammon, and Moab are distant relations, and Israel must avoid conquering their territory – while Aramean, Philistine, and Phoenician lands are all theirs for the taking.

This, too, is a tempting structural scheme, but it fails on its own literary and structural terms. Structurally, the first two oracles (Aram and Philistia) are similar; the next two (Tyre and Edom) are both briefer; Ammon and Moab then resemble the first pair. From a literary perspective, neither the crimes nor the punishments match up on the three-to-three model. The brutal crime of "threshing the (pregnant woman of) the Gilead" (Aram) is not comparable to "chased his brother with the sword" and "crushed his own compassion" (Edom). The punishment of destruction and ultimate exile to one's birthplace (Aram to Kir) is unmatched in Edom's fate.

Fourth Proposal: *Al Arba'a...Ve'al Arba'a*

Having suggested that series' anaphora may hold the key to understanding the structure, we now turn to the number four. In each case, it is the alleged fourth crime that generates the harsh divine sentence. As we have already noted, the "For the three sins of X, and for four I will not recant" formula should not be taken as an exact reckoning of moral violations, but rather as a poetic and literary convention. Nonetheless, the numbers utilized in that convention are three and four. Perhaps considering our sequence as two sets of four will help decipher its structure and underlying messages. That would match (a) Aram with (aa) Ammon; (b) Philistia with (bb) Moab; (c) Tyre with (cc) Judah (see below), and (d) Edom with (dd) Israel. Let's examine this proposal and see if it fits.

Aram's fourth and unpardonable crime is "*al dusham beḥarutzot barzel et haGilad*" (1:3), threshing the Gilead with threshing sledges of iron. Ammon's violation is "*al bikam harot haGilad*" (1:13), slicing open the pregnant women of the Gilead (in order to expand their border). The affinity between the two crimes is quite clear; indeed, both LXX[55] and one of the Amos fragments from Qumran (5QAm [4]1) read *harot haGilad* in Aram's indictment. The Gilead is positioned directly between Aram to the north and Ammon to the south; in David's battle for Rabbat Ammon, his armies are attacked from the south by Ammon and from the north by Aram (II Sam. 10).

Aram's punishment, following the burning of major cities which is common to all seven oracles, ends with its leaders' destruction and its people's exile; Ammon's punishment is similar.

Philistia is paired with Moab; significantly, both of them played a central role in David's life. David's great-grandmother Ruth is from Moab; when fleeing Saul, his first haven is Moab. He later moves across Judea and finally "immigrates" to Philistia. Philistia is accused of treachery: of handing over refugees to Edom (presumably despite some kind of alliance). Moab is accused of an act of brutality against the king of Edom.

55. The Greek translation of the Bible, c. second century BCE.

Philistia and Moab are to suffer the same consequence – their cities will be burned and their leaders destroyed, but there is no mention of exile.

This theory pairs Tyre with Judah. Significantly, Tyre's most prominent biblical role is their alliance with Israel (Hiram calls Solomon "my brother" – I Kings 9:13). Tyre's crime was the same as Philistia's, but v. 9 adds "*velo zakhru berit aḥim*," "They did not remember the covenant of brothers." This presumably refers to the treaty binding Solomon and Hiram. Judah stands accused of rejecting God's Torah and failing to keep His laws, "and their lies have caused them to err, [those lies] after which their fathers had walked." Tyre and Judah are the only ones accused of forgetting a covenant. Tyre did not honor its covenant with the people it handed over; Judah did not stay true to its covenant with God.

Amos condemns both Phoenicia and Judah to a single punishment: their capital will be burned down (Tyre, Jerusalem).

Edom, the final oracle in the first set, is accused of harboring spite toward their brother. When we study the culminating oracle against Israel, it will emerge that Samaria's web of sin is woven with corruption that impacts, above all, their relationship with their own people, their poor and destitute brothers – much as Edom destroyed their own natural compassion for their brothers and deliberately fanned the flames of their hatred.

This is the *coup de grâce* of the "rhetorical entrapment." If the listeners have been entranced by the rhythm of the oracle sequence, they expect their own kingdom to be accused of a "milder" crime – a problematic attitude – and to hear of a brutal but brief punishment. This, as we will soon see, is the greatest surprise awaiting the Samarian audience.

This final proposal – arranging the oracles in two parallel sets of four – is thus the most compelling structural interpretation.

And Therefore...

Why attempt to discover the underlying literary structure of the oracles – or, for that matter, any biblical passage? How does it impact our understanding of the text or its import for us?

In some cases, defining or discovering the structure helps uncover its meaning. Since a chiasmus generally highlights the center, we can comfortably assume, for example, that the birth of Jacob's children is the pinnacle of his sojourn in Haran. The problem with this is that we *already* believe these to be true before looking at the text, and use our "discovery" to support our preconception. Sometimes, however, identifying a chiastic structure can help lead us in a new direction. For instance,[56] the long chiastic structure stretching from the Israel's departure from the border of Egypt to their arrival at edge of Sinai helps identify the *manna* episode as central to that narrative.

Similarly, a parallel structure (either two sets of three or two sets of four), helps us glean information from one oracle to its parallel; precisely this consideration compels us to abandon the three-to-three model in favor of the four-to-four structure.

This structure thus illuminates our understanding of Aram's crime. The Masoretic text merely expresses that they threshed the mountains of Gilead, but the parallel with the more detailed account of Ammon's offense helps us understand this expression as a pithy way of describing their brutality. Moreover, it may point to Aram's motivation; just as Ammon sought to expand their territory, the same may apply to Aram.

Identifying the parallel pattern also underscores the precise nature of the Samarian audience's anticipation. The offenses of the first set – Aram, Philistia, Phoenicia, Edom – decrease in severity from the most brutal crime imaginable, to being an accessory to war crimes, to a having a problematic attitude. When the second set begins, there is a sense of déjà vu – Ammon is accused of the same war crime as Aram, then both Moab and Judah are accused of crimes of treachery against treaty partners – and when they hear "*Al shelosha pishei Yisrael*," they (correctly) anticipate condemnation of criminal thoughts and attitudes.

There is much to be gained from discovering the underlying literary structure of any biblical passage. Not only does it help us uncover additional meanings and read in between the lines – it also may help us glimpse what the impact on the original audience might have been.

56. See Etshalom, *Between the Lines of the Bible*, vol. 2, ch. 10.

Judah: The Final "Set-Up"

Perhaps the biggest surprise is that Judah is included in this series. Keep in mind that Amos himself is from Judah and his anthemic refrain (1:2) describes God's voice roaring *from* Jerusalem – a roar that withers the lush north.

The inclusion of Judah – similar to Isaiah's contemporary prophecies[57] – serves two nearly opposite rhetorical purposes. On one hand, it clarifies that *no one* is exempt from accountability to God: neither foreign nations; nor those descended from Abraham; nor even His chosen people, Israel. On the other hand, this mention of Judah here might lull the Samarian audience into a false sense that they are being spared, which makes the final oracle in this sequence all the more powerful. Contrasting Judah's crimes with the detailed list of Israel's failings should profoundly shock the audience. Hearing the "short-form" punishment awaiting their neighbors (and brothers) to the south, followed by the much longer and detailed punishment awaiting them, should ideally jolt them into a state of repentance. But alas, the audience's moral state is far from ideal.

The Text (Amos 2:4–6)

(ד) כֹּה אָמַר ה׳ עַל שְׁלֹשָׁה פִּשְׁעֵי יְהוּדָה וְעַל אַרְבָּעָה לֹא אֲשִׁיבֶנּוּ עַל מָאֳסָם
אֶת תּוֹרַת ה׳ וְחֻקָּיו לֹא שָׁמָרוּ וַיַּתְעוּם כִּזְבֵיהֶם אֲשֶׁר הָלְכוּ אֲבוֹתָם אַחֲרֵיהֶם:
(ה) וְשִׁלַּחְתִּי אֵשׁ בִּיהוּדָה וְאָכְלָה אַרְמְנוֹת יְרוּשָׁלִָם:

> 4 *Ko amar Hashem*: For the three sins of Judah, and for four I will not recant: because they have rejected God's Torah and have not kept His laws, and their lies have caused them to err, [those lies] after which their fathers had walked. 5 So will I send a fire upon Judah and it shall devour the palaces of Jerusalem.

Note that Judah's punishment is less severe in three ways: it does not end with exile; there is no mention of their leaders' death; and there is no

57. See, *inter alii*, chapters 1–5.

signature of "*Ani Hashem.*" Their crime is clearly of a different nature: one related to God's unique, intimate relationship with the people of Judah.

And when the audience hears "*Al shelosha pishei Yisrael,*" what do they expect to hear next? Of what crimes will they be accused? What punishment awaits them? That is the anxious anticipation Amos seeks to generate among his listeners. We have but to read on…

PART II: BULLS-EYE

The entire series culminates with Amos's oracle against Israel, which is the longest by far. Sixteen verses long, it brings us to the end of chapter 2. Like the other oracles, it comprises an accusation and a punishment; however, two significant expansions make it exceptional. First, it also contains a mini-historiosophy of God's great kindnesses for Israel; second, both indictment and punishment are expanded. The accusation is not limited to a single crime (the "fourth"), nor is the punishment as monochromatic as the earlier ones.

The Text (Amos 2:6–16)

(ו) כֹּה אָמַר ה׳ עַל שְׁלֹשָׁה פִּשְׁעֵי יִשְׂרָאֵל וְעַל אַרְבָּעָה לֹא אֲשִׁיבֶנּוּ עַל מִכְרָם
בַּכֶּסֶף צַדִּיק וְאֶבְיוֹן בַּעֲבוּר נַעֲלָיִם: (ז) הַשֹּׁאֲפִים עַל עֲפַר אֶרֶץ בְּרֹאשׁ דַּלִּים
וְדֶרֶךְ עֲנָוִים יַטּוּ וְאִישׁ וְאָבִיו יֵלְכוּ אֶל הַנַּעֲרָה לְמַעַן חַלֵּל אֶת שֵׁם קָדְשִׁי:
(ח) וְעַל בְּגָדִים חֲבֻלִים יַטּוּ אֵצֶל כָּל מִזְבֵּחַ וְיֵין עֲנוּשִׁים יִשְׁתּוּ בֵּית אֱלֹהֵיהֶם:
(ט) וְאָנֹכִי הִשְׁמַדְתִּי אֶת הָאֱמֹרִי מִפְּנֵיהֶם אֲשֶׁר כְּגֹבַהּ אֲרָזִים גָּבְהוֹ וְחָסֹן הוּא
כָּאַלּוֹנִים וָאַשְׁמִיד פִּרְיוֹ מִמַּעַל וְשָׁרָשָׁיו מִתָּחַת: (י) וְאָנֹכִי הֶעֱלֵיתִי אֶתְכֶם
מֵאֶרֶץ מִצְרָיִם וָאוֹלֵךְ אֶתְכֶם בַּמִּדְבָּר אַרְבָּעִים שָׁנָה לָרֶשֶׁת אֶת אֶרֶץ הָאֱמֹרִי:
(יא) וָאָקִים מִבְּנֵיכֶם לִנְבִיאִים וּמִבַּחוּרֵיכֶם לִנְזִרִים הַאַף אֵין זֹאת בְּנֵי יִשְׂרָאֵל
נְאֻם ה׳: (יב) וַתַּשְׁקוּ אֶת הַנְּזִרִים יָיִן וְעַל הַנְּבִיאִים צִוִּיתֶם לֵאמֹר לֹא תִּנָּבְאוּ:
(יג) הִנֵּה אָנֹכִי מֵעִיק תַּחְתֵּיכֶם כַּאֲשֶׁר תָּעִיק הָעֲגָלָה הַמְלֵאָה לָהּ עָמִיר:
(יד) וְאָבַד מָנוֹס מִקָּל וְחָזָק לֹא יְאַמֵּץ כֹּחוֹ וְגִבּוֹר לֹא יְמַלֵּט נַפְשׁוֹ:
(טו) וְתֹפֵשׂ הַקֶּשֶׁת לֹא יַעֲמֹד וְקַל בְּרַגְלָיו לֹא יְמַלֵּט וְרֹכֵב הַסּוּס לֹא יְמַלֵּט נַפְשׁוֹ:
(טז) וְאַמִּיץ לִבּוֹ בַּגִּבּוֹרִים עָרוֹם יָנוּס בַּיּוֹם הַהוּא נְאֻם ה׳:

> 6 *Ko amar Hashem*: For the three sins of Israel, and for four, I will not recant:
>
> For their selling a *tzaddik* for silver, and the needy for (a pair of) shoes; 7 that pant after the dust of the earth on the head of the poor, and turn aside the way of the humble. And a man and his father go unto the same girl, in order to profane My holy name. 8 And they lay themselves down beside every altar, upon clothes taken in pledge, and in the house of their god they drink the wine of them that have been fined.
>
> 9 Yet I destroyed the Amorite from before them, whose height was like the height of the cedars, and he was as strong as the oaks. Yet I destroyed his fruit from above, and his roots from beneath. 10 Also I brought you up out of the land of Egypt, and led you for forty years in the wilderness, to possess the land of the Amorites. 11 And I raised up your sons for prophets, and your young men for Nazirites. Is it not even thus, children of Israel? Says the Lord. 12 But you gave the Nazirites wine to drink, and commanded the prophets, saying "Prophesy not."
>
> 13 Behold, I will make it creak under you, as a cart creaks that is full of sheaves. 14 And flight shall fail the swift, and the strong shall not exert his strength, neither shall the mighty deliver himself; 15 neither shall he stand that handles the bow; and he that is swift of foot shall not deliver himself; neither shall he that rides the horse deliver himself; 16 and he that is courageous among the mighty shall flee away naked in that day, says the Lord.

This oracle comprises a list of accusations (vv. 6–8), a "historiosophical" list of God's kindnesses for Israel (vv. 9–11), and a detailed punishment (vv. 13–16), discussed in Part III below, concluding with the army in utter flight (this summary skips verse 12, which we will address later).

The Structure of the Oracle

Israel is accused of the following crimes, which we can number thus (vv. 6–8):

1. They sell the righteous for silver

2. (they sell) the needy for a pair of shoes
3. That trample the ground on the heads of the destitute
4. (they) turn aside the way of the humble
5. A man and his father go unto the same girl in order to profane My holy name
6. They lay themselves down beside every altar upon clothes taken in pledge
7. In the house of their god (or is it God?) they drink the wine of them that have been fined.

Until now, we have read the refrain "*Al shelosha…ve'al arba'a*" as a literary cliché, not necessarily three specific sins that lead up to a fourth. We also read the numeric sequence as ordinal (even though the form is cardinal) – i.e., for the fourth, not "for four."

Here, however, the refrain takes on a literal meaning, and the numbers "three" and "four" are cumulative. Amos has brilliantly turned the literary trope on its head and counted out 3 + 4 sins = 7 specific transgressions in all.

Perhaps this is why Amos uses this refrain in the first seven oracles: to set up his audience for a rhetorical shock. Hearing "*Al shelosha pishei Yisrael ve'al arba'a lo ashivenu*," the audience likely anticipates being accused of a single crime…but hearing *one crime after another* might just break through their complacency and move the aristocrats to reflect on their behavior.

After reading their detailed indictment, the prophet interrupts the seven-time repeated pattern with a list of seven kindnesses God has done for the people (vv. 7–9):

1. I destroyed the Amorite from before them, whose height was like the height of the cedars and he was as strong as the oaks
2. Yet I destroyed his fruit from above and his roots from beneath
3. Also, I brought you up out of the land of Egypt
4. And led you for forty years in the wilderness
5. To possess the land of the Amorites
6. And I raised up your sons for prophets
7. And your young men for Nazirites

The prophet masterfully matches seven kindnesses to seven alleged crimes. This pattern is seen in Judges 10, where seven idolatrous cults the people worshipped are followed by a list of seven nations from which God had delivered them.

The final segment of the oracle presents Israel's detailed punishment. This third section more closely resembles the punishments in the other oracles, as opposed to the sins, which are significantly different (and the list of divine kindnesses is completely absent in the earlier prophecies). "Long" oracles (against Aram, Philistia, Ammon, and Moab) detail destruction of military prowess, death of the leadership, and some form of exile or subjugation. While each is accused of a single crime, the punishments include a sequence of calamities. Israel's punishments are similar (vv. 13–16):

> Behold, I will make it creak under you, as a cart creaks that is full of sheaves.
>
> 1) And flight shall fail the swift,
> 2) And the strong shall not exert his strength,
> 3) Neither shall the mighty deliver himself;
> 4) Neither shall he stand that handles the bow;
> 5) And he that is swift of foot shall not deliver himself;
> 6) Neither shall he that rides the horse deliver himself;
> 7) And he that is courageous among the mighty shall flee away naked in that day.

One note about the opening line, "Behold I will make it creak under you," which I have excluded from this heptad. Some analysis is required to determine its function – it is not strictly part of the punishment, but rather seems to introduce the punishments, as I will elaborate below.

This oracle comprises seven crimes, seven divine kindnesses and seven punishments – or, more accurately: *in spite of* seven divine kindnesses, we have seven sins and, *thus*, seven punishments.

This pattern echoes the rhetorical rhythms of the curses in Leviticus 26: "And if you will not heed Me after all these things, then I will chastise you seven times for your sins" (v. 18). This sentiment is repeated, nearly verbatim, three more times (vv. 21, 24, 28). As the *Sifra* observes: "You committed seven sins before Me; come and accept upon yourselves seven punishments."[58]

Typologically, seven represents a complete natural cycle.[59] This paradigm of seven sins is established in the Covenant at Sinai and is evident from the dawn of biblical history through the end of the First Commonwealth: in Judges (cited above) and in our text. Jeremiah explains that seventy years of Babylonian exile are punishment for seventy violated sabbatical years.[60]

Assessing the Structure

The oracle is made up of three clearly demarcated units; each is three verses long and contains seven items.

The structure may be understood as *linear*: rebellion, in spite of divine benevolence, leads to punishment. Alternatively, the first two units may be read as cyclical or symmetrical. They committed sin X despite gift A, sin Y despite gift B, etc. This sevenfold pattern of ingratitude is repaid with seven punishments. The two verses between God's kindnesses and Israel's punishment distinguish between this perpetual symbiosis and its resolution through punishment.

A different understanding of the relationship between these three units, however, also takes the two "stray" verses into account.

First, we must consider the middle unit – the praise for God's kindnesses – and its purpose.

Historiosophic speech is didactic and exhortative, not (merely) informational;[61] similarly, Amos's purpose is *not* merely to read the people their sentence, but also to persuade them to mend their ways. If they never again "sell the righteous for silver and the needy for a pair of shoes," if they never again "drink the wine of them that have been fined," then his goal will have been accomplished. There are two ways

58. *Sifra, Beḥukotai* 2:5.
59. Creation lasts seven days, and *Shabbat* is later extended to cycles of seven years; in addition, various formulae for ritual purity depend on cycles of seven.
60. II Chronicles 36:21.
61. See Joshua 24; I Samuel 12; we might include Judges 11 as well.

to move people to change: the fear of consequence or the call to duty. If they cannot imagine their once-mighty army fleeing in impotent terror as described in the punishment, then perhaps a sense of loyalty, obligation, and gratitude might sway them. Thus, the middle unit serves as an alternate motivator for the final unit.

A different perspective is that the middle unit informs both other units. The God who forbids such behavior is the same God who has done so many astounding kindnesses for them. The people's crimes are all the fouler in contrast with God's kindnesses. These kind acts are then reversed in the punishments that God will mete out to the people.

In this scheme, the entire oracle should be viewed as a triangle, as follows:

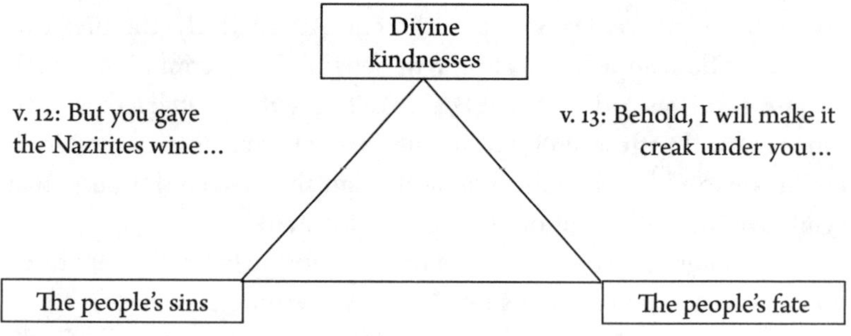

Thus, verse 12 and verse 13 each become a bridge between the axis and its offshoots.

God dealt kindly with His people – He redeemed them *and* gave them the opportunity to become holy. Yet they spurned this offer and acted to profane the holy ones among them. This is the ultimate rejection of divine kindness, which explains the direct relationship between God's accusations and kindnesses.

God's withdrawal upon this rejection explains why the military loses its power – He is no longer there to carry their weight. The people have forgotten that their military success and prowess is a divine gift – without God's presence and support, their armies will be useless.

According to this reading of the final oracle, Amos warns that if the people do not change their attitude toward God, Samaria will be rendered powerless.

Section I – The Indictment (2:6–8)

> **6** *Ko amar Hashem*: For the three sins of Israel, and for four, I will not recant. For their selling a *tzaddik* for silver and the needy for (a pair of) shoes. **7** That pant after the dust of the earth on the head of the poor, and turn aside the way of the humble. And a man and his father go unto the same girl, in order to profane My holy name. **8** And they lay themselves down beside every altar, upon clothes taken in pledge, and in the house of their god they drink the wine of them that have been fined.

These 3 verses include the refrain and seven accusations: two in the first and last verse, while the middle verse, v. 7, contains three. We will revisit this pattern below.

6a: For the three sins of Israel, and for (the) four (th), I will not recant
6b: For their selling a *tzaddik* for silver

The meaning of the word *tzaddik* has evolved over time. The Hebrew language, like all living languages, is dynamic: as Bendavid comprehensively demonstrates,[62] the Sages' Hebrew during the classical era differed from biblical Hebrew. The Torah's *etz* (tree), for example, became the Mishnah's *ilan* (see Mishna Berakhot 6:1); the biblical *shemesh* (sun) became *ḥama* (as in *henetz haḥama, birkat haḥama*); there are hundreds of examples, which comprise a nearly distinct subset of the language.

Beyond substitutions, the meaning of phrases also evolves. The phrase *am ha'aretz,* which first appears in Genesis 23, was a laudatory term and referred to the landed gentry and members of the town council; this meaning was retained through the First Commonwealth. By

62. Abba Bendavid, *Lashon Mikra VeLashon Hakhamim* (Tel Aviv: Dvir, 1967); see also R. Yohanan's observation in Avoda Zara 58b (also Hullin 137b).

mishnaic times, however, it began to refer to people who are lax in some areas of observance; by the pre-modern era, it had become synonymous with "ignoramus."

The word *tzaddik* has experienced a similar metamorphosis. The biblical word *tzaddik*, in reference to humans, simply means "innocent" – Abraham challenges God that if there are fifty *tzaddikim* in Sedom, He "may not" destroy the town. Abraham was not asking for *righteous people*, but for people *innocent of the crime* for which the city was sentenced. The Torah discusses punitive lashes in court and refers to two litigants: *vehitzdiku et hatzaddik vehirshi'u et harasha* – they shall clear the innocent and render the wicked one guilty. Various biblical examples substantiate this meaning of the word.[63]

In the rabbinic period, *tzaddik* took on a different meaning: not absence of guilt, but rather affirmative righteousness. The phrase *tzaddik gamur* – a complete *tzaddik* – is a rabbinic term. (At the beginning of the modern era with the advent of Hassidut, the word took on a further meaning.)

Here, the people of Samaria stand accused of selling *innocent* people for silver. Why are they selling them, and to whom are they selling them? How are they even able to do this? Were they sold *for* silver, or *on account of* silver? This will be easier to determine after looking at the next passage.

6b: and the needy for (a pair of) shoes

Again, does this mean that the accused "sold" poor people in exchange for shoes? Or were the destitute sold because they owed a meager sum ("shoes") and couldn't repay it? This sad phenomenon is rife throughout human history – there are even examples in the Bible: the widow of one of Elisha's acolytes is about to lose her sons as slaves to her creditor before Elisha miraculously helps her pay off her loan (II Kings 4:1–7).

---

63. See, *inter alii*, II Samuel 4:11.

A parallel phrase later on in Amos (8:6) implies that the poor *are exchanged for* silver:

> **…That we may buy the poor for silver, and the needy for a pair of shoes** (*liknot bekesef dalim ve'evyon ba'avur na'alayim*) and sell the refuse of the corn?

This is an inverted version of the crime. Instead of selling poor people, the accused buy them as slaves. The parallel clause therefore means that the poor can be purchased for a meager price – (a pair of) shoes. Thus the first two crimes in the indictment refer to selling people as slaves for *silver* or *shoes*. Although *kesef* is often understood as something of value in the Bible,[64] the parallel with "shoes" seems to relegate *kesef* here to a meager amount, implying that not only are the accused selling people as slaves, but they are also doing so for little profit.

This is an odd accusation. Is it aimed at debt-collectors who sell their debtors as slaves due to their inability to repay their loans? If so, why mention the meager price – wouldn't the accusation be all the sharper if the profit were greater? Others suggest that the accused are judges who are willing to take meager bribes to sentence innocent people to slavery, but if so, the verb "selling" (*mikhram*) is ill-suited; we would expect language expressing a perversion of justice (*al ḥatotam mishpat* or similar).

The solution may lie in ancient Near Eastern texts. Hittite law 22a states:

> If a male slave shall run away, and someone brings him back, if he captures him nearby, he shall give him (i.e., the finder) *a pair of shoes* (the law, in 22b–c, continues to grant greater bounty if found farther from the master).[65]

64. See, *inter alii*, Exodus 22:6, 16.
65. Selling the poor for shoes: Avi Shveka, "For a Pair of Shoes: A New Light on an Obscure Verse in Amos's Prophecy," *Vetus Testamentum* 62 (2012): 95–114. The translation here follows Hoffner, *op. cit.*

The code of Hammurabi has a similar law:

> If anyone finds runaway male or female slaves in the open country and brings them to their masters, the master of the slaves shall pay him two shekels of *silver*.[66]
> (The same law appears in the laws of Ur-Namma, LU 17.)

The common practice in the Near East, during the First Commonwealth, was to claim a bounty for returning fleeing slaves to their masters. This explains the parallel of *kesef* ("silver") with *na'alayim* ("[a pair of] shoes"), reflecting both Mesopotamian practices that undoubtedly had parallels throughout the Levant; but this practice was prohibited in the Torah:

> Do not deliver to his master a slave that has run away to you from his master. He shall live with you, in your midst, in one of your gates that is to his benefit; you shall not oppress him. (Deut. 23:16–17)

Amos condemns this practice and describes the slave as "innocent" (*tzaddik*) and "destitute" (*evyon*). The second term is easily understood and needs no elaboration. Why, however, describe the slave as *tzaddik*? The biblical meaning of *tzaddik,* "innocent," clarifies his accusation. People were wrongfully taken as slaves in adjacent regions and would flee their unjust oppression. Perhaps some fled to the Samarian kingdom, having heard that Israelite leadership was more kindhearted[67] – only to be handed over to their masters for a small bounty. The coldhearted practice of handing poor innocents back to oppressive masters – and to do so for such a small profit – was the first nail in their proverbial coffin. Although this is a single indictment, Amos divides it into two. Perhaps this reflects the two kinds of bounty deals mentioned above; another

66. Retrieved from http://avalon.law.yale.edu/ancient/hamframe.asp, on January 7, 2018.
67. I Kings 20:31.

possibility is that this division helps him reach the "three/four" pattern to complement the seven divine kindnesses and the seven punishments.

We cannot move on without mentioning this passage's famous midrashic association with the Joseph narrative in the midrashic work known as "The Ten Martyrs" (*Asara Harugei Malkhut*).

The northern kingdom theoretically included ten of the Israelite tribes, as per Ahijah's symbolic gesture to Jeroboam ben Nebat.[68] The northern kingdom's original capital was Shechem.[69] The combination of the location, the ten tribes of the north, and the phrase "selling the innocent for silver" created a strong association with the sale of Joseph. Although Joseph was sold in Dotan, over twenty miles to the north, he was originally sent to Shechem to find his brothers;[70] so this became the site connected with his sale in the midrashic imagination:

> [Commenting on Rehoboam's going to Shechem for his coronation]: It was taught in R. Yose's name: Shechem is a hazardous place. It was in Shechem that Dinah was raped; it was in Shechem that Joseph was sold by his brothers; and it was in Shechem that the Davidic kingdom was divided.[71]

These many associations led the homilists to interpret verse 6b – the first indictment – as an allusion to the sale of Joseph. This association led to the rabbinic epithet "*Yosef haTzaddik*," which is unattested in the canon yet ubiquitous in midrashic literature.[72] Several midrashim claim that the brothers used the proceeds to purchase – shoes.[73] This association also resulted in the universal custom to read this passage in Amos as the *Haftarah* for *Vayeshev*, the section in Genesis (chapters 37–40) that contains the story of the sale of Joseph.

---

68. Ibid. 11:30–31.
69. It was subsequently moved to Tirzah and then, following Omri's purchase of a mountain from Shemer, moved to that mountain, which was renamed Shomron (Samaria) in honor of Shemer (I Kings 16:24).
70. Genesis 37:12.
71. Sanhedrin 102a.
72. See, *inter alia*, Yoma 35b, *Seder Olam* 30.
73. See *Pirkei deRabbi Eliezer*, ch. 37.

In the midrashic development of the narrative, the Roman governor invites the "ten sages"[74] into his offices to ostensibly pose a halakhic question – what is the punishment for a Jew who sells another Jew as a slave? The sages arrived to find the rooms filled with shoes – hinting to our passage and to the punishment they would soon receive as retribution for the sale of Joseph "for a pair of shoes."

Moving on to the next indictment:

7a: That pant after the dust of the earth on the head of the poor

The first word, *hasho'afim,* seems to come from the root *sh-a-f,* "to breathe,"[75] but this does not make much sense here. I have adopted Paul's proposal[76] that this is a secondary root of *sh-a-f* – an alternate form of *sh-v-f,* meaning "to trample."[77] Biblical lexicons recognize this secondary root as well. Hence: "... who trample the ground on the heads of the destitute" refers to those who "walk all over them," either figuratively or literally.[78] The rich treat the poor like the dust of the earth, trampling over them to fulfill their venal ambitions.

This imagery and root appear again in 8:4: *Shimu zot hasho'afim evyon.* "Hear this, you who trample the poor one."

And turn aside the way of the humble

Here, *anavim* is translated in its usual sense, "humble," also it often functions as an alternate version of *aniyim* – the poor. For example, in Isaiah 11:4, *anvei aretz* means "the poor of the land," as it stands in parallel with *dalim,* "the destitute." Indeed, the same parallel in our verse militates in favor of understanding the word as "the poor." Some biblical dictionaries conflate the two, reading the word as "poor, humble, meek," but the

74. The ten sages mentioned in the various martyrologies did not live at the same time and were not executed in one period.
75. As in Jeremiah 2:24.
76. Shalom Paul, *Mikra leYisrael, Amos* (Tel Aviv: Am Oved, 1994) (henceforth "Paul"), 49.
77. As in *hu yeshufkha rosh ve'ata teshufenu akev,* in Genesis 3:15.
78. See also Sanhedrin 7b; cf. Yevamot 105b.

two roots, although related, are distinct. Some modern English translations render the word as "needy" or "destitute," or even take it in a third direction and translate it as "oppressed," reading the root as *a-n-y*.

The Samarian aristocracy is accused of "perverting" or "pushing away" the path of the needy. The verb used here, *yatu*, from the root *n-t-h*, means to incline, stretch out, or bend: they are "bending the path of the poor." This can be explained with the help of I Samuel 8:3, where we learn that Samuel's sons "inclined (*vayitu*) after graft" and "bent (*vayatu*) justice." The verb also appears in the context of warning judges not to pervert justice,[79] and as one of the curses pronounced at Gerizim and Eval.[80] The apparent meaning of this crime is that the accused "bend" (pervert) justice to the disfavor of the lowly.

The first four accusations are apparently directed at Samaria's wealthy and/or judiciary. The opening pair of accusations allude to the slave trade. This could be something of which the wealthy populace is guilty – or a crime that corrupts the judicial system. Debt sales, as we see in II Kings 4, were common in the region, and the judges may have been complicit in allowing or promoting such sales. Alternatively, as I posited above, the first crimes listed may have been engaged in by citizen "bounty-hunters" who (immorally) returned slaves to their "owners." The next two accusations also describe ill-treatment of the poor. Again, they may be aimed at the wealthy citizenry who oppress the poor or, as the verb used in the second clause indicates, to the judges who pervert cases against the poor.

7b: And a man and his father go unto the same girl, in order to profane My holy name

This fifth accusation is enigmatic in several ways. First of all, it is by far the longest,[81] which gives the impression that it is more depraved than

79. Exodus 23:6; Deuteronomy 16:19, 24:17.
80. Deuteronomy 27:19.
81. The first two indictments are three words each, the third is four words and the fourth is, again, three words. Our accusation is eight words long. The final two accusations are five words each. We are reckoning multi-word phrases that are connected via *makaf* as one word.

the rest – or, perhaps, that it holds the key to the attitude behind the other crimes.

The meaning of the words is clear, but the context is anything but. In what situation does "a man and his father go unto the same girl, in order to profane My holy name"? I will analyze each individual phrase before offering an explanation of its context and meaning.

"A man and his father" is a unique and unmatched biblical phrase. A far more common biblical motif is fathers *leading* their sons – toward righteousness[82] or perdition.[83]

"Go unto the same girl" – although "go" does not usually have sexual connotations, this is the accepted reading among traditional and modern scholars, due to the accompanying preposition *el* ("to" or "unto"). Who is this girl, and what is the context of their sexual congress with her?

Some traditional commentators interpret the girl as a "betrothed maiden" (*na'ara me'orasa*): she is betrothed to a third man, and both son and father are committing adultery with her. But is this a case of rape, where the girl is blameless, or is she complicit in the adultery? Adultery is grave enough – to read that the son and father are committing adultery with the same girl seems like overkill.

Others, chiefly modern scholars, read this as a cultic offense, based on the two crimes that follow: that is, father and son engage in fertility rites with the cult prostitute, which surely raises the stakes from sexual immorality to full-blown idolatry. If so, however, why is the girl referred to as *na'ara* as opposed to a cult prostitute, *kedesha*? Moreover, why would this involve a father and son going together? Radak takes a different approach, which is embraced by more recent commentators. He notes the son-father connection does not ascribe any special feature (betrothed or ritual prostitute) to the girl herself, and rather points to the general indecency of a father and son sharing a sexual partner: this in itself serves to "profane My holy name," and defiles the sanctity of Israel who are commanded to "be holy as I, the Lord who sanctifies you, am holy" (Lev. 19:2). Referring to an act that is not illegal, albeit

82. Genesis 18:18–19.
83. Numbers 32:14.

frowned upon, as a grave offense that "profanes My holy name" is surprising. After surveying the rest of the accusations, we will return to this thorny passage and reassess it.

One final, more technical explanation before moving to the next accusation, regarding the phrase *lema'an: "In order to* profane My holy name." As opposed to the usual sense of *lema'an* – "in order that" – here, it seems to mean "which results in." When "a man and his father go unto the same girl, *it results in* a profaning of My holy name." This sense of *lema'an* is supported by Leviticus 20:3:

> And I will turn My face toward that man and will cut him off from the midst of his nation, for he gave of his seed to the Molekh *which results in* (*lema'an*) profaning my sancta and defiling My holy name.

8a: And they lay themselves down beside every altar upon clothes taken in pledge

In biblical times, it was common to seize clothing and nightwear from the poor as a pledge or collateral for a loan.[84] The Torah forbids seizing a widow's garment.[85] The prohibition in Exodus is poignant:

> If you lend money to any of My people, even to the poor with you, you shall not be as a creditor to him; neither shall you put interest on him. If you take your neighbor's garment at all as a pledge, you shall restore it to him by the time that the sun goes down; for that is his only covering, it is his garment for his skin; wherein will he sleep? And it shall come to pass, when he cries to Me, that I will hear; for I am gracious. (Ex. 22:24–26)

84. Exodus 22:25.
85. Deuteronomy 24:17. See the halakhic discussion regarding the parameters of legitimate seizure in the ninth chapter of Bava Metzia. Note the well-known dispute regarding the application of this law to the wealthy widow in Tosefta Bava Metzia 10:3.

The image of the poor shivering without the bedclothes that now rest in the wealthy money-lender's house is abhorrent. A pledge comes with clear limitations that allow the poor to continue living with minimal decency – in fact, the concept of the collateral is only permitted to ensure that the rich will continue lending money, as the rabbis express their concern: *shelo tin'ol delet bifnei lovin* – not to shut the door in the face of borrowers. *Sifri Re'eh*[86] brings a dispute between R. Judah and the Sages regarding the phrase *ha'avet ta'avitenu* – "you shall surely take a pledge from him" (Deut. 15:8). R. Judah maintains that this repetition indicates that the lender may take a pledge and, after returning, re-take the pledge. The Sages disagree, and explain that this repetition expresses a sense of coercion: the poor person must bring a pledge for their own sake, to prevent their own sense of shame! If so, the entire system of pledges is for the ultimate (and immediate) *benefit of the poor* – yet the wealthy ignore the poor's actual needs and use their clothes to lie upon. I will address the end of the clause – *etzel kol mizbe'aḥ* – below. For now, it seems that the wealthy money-lenders stand as the accused.

8b: And in the house of their god they drink the wine of them that have been fined

Israel's final crime is "drinking the wine of punished people." *Anushim* is broadly understood as those who were (perhaps wrongly) fined in court – the accusation is that those fines were used to purchase wine.

This reading supports the claims of R. Joseph Kara and others (perhaps Ibn Ezra) that the "punished" were poor people oppressed by the wealthy.[87]

Nonetheless, the use of *anushim* here seems in line with the mainstream approach, which compels us to reexamine who is taking the pledged garments in the first half of the verse. I believe that in both cases, the Samarian judges stand accused of exploiting their position for their own benefit: of using the money from fines, and of seizing pledges for

86. *Sifri* on Deuteronomy 116:7.
87. This approach is supported by the passage in 4:1, ahead; see our discussion in chapter 4.

loans (pledges were not necessarily in the lender's purview) and using them rather than safeguarding them to ensure the loan's proper repayment. If so, then three of these crimes are committed by the corrupt judiciary, given that *derekh anavim yatu* is clearly aimed at the perversion of justice in the wealthy's favor, and the continuum is clear: the poor come to court, are judged unfairly and assessed a debt, for which a pledge is taken; when a fine is imposed upon them (perhaps in a different type of case or for defaulting on the loan), the judges use the money to buy wine for themselves.

Both halves of the verse imply a cultic setting, which leads most commentators to augment the accusation with an aspect of idolatry – these corrupt scoundrels abuse the poor and use their ill-gotten gains to throw an idolatrous feast! This, in turn, invites the reading of the "man and his father" crime as an act of ritual prostitution or the like.

The difficulty with all of this is that Amos's emphasis is on abuse of the disadvantaged. He does address idolatry in various places (for example, 4:4–5, 5:5); but I believe that this oracle is not one of them. There is no direct attack on paganism or its practices; if the "girl" in v. 8, "every altar," or "the house of their god" were references to idolatry, we would expect a more direct attack.

Rather, the prophet seems to be utilizing familiar biblical images for rhetorical advantage. The "place of justice" is adjacent to the Sanctuary. When the Torah commands (lower courts or citizens) to seek legal instruction, they are told to "Arise and go up to the place that the Lord, your God, chooses" (Deut. 17:8). The Torah juxtaposes the establishment of just courts with laws relating to the altar (ibid. 16:21–17:1). When Isaiah envisions Jerusalem in its redeemed state, he promises it will be known once more as "the city of justice" (*ir hatzedek* – Is. 1:26).

Here, I believe, Amos is inverting this connection. A place of corrupt judgment is considered idolatrous; if a judge extorts money from the poor for his own home, then that home is like an idolatrous temple. When he lies down on the pledges of the poor, he is essentially lying beside an idolatrous altar; when he imbibes the wine bought with ill-gained fines, it is as offensive as a libation to foreign gods.

"A Man and His Father" Reexamined

As mentioned, the crime of "the man and his father" is fraught with difficulties:

1. Why is there an emphasis on the man and his father going together – or both going?
2. Why is the order presented as "a man and his father" and not "a man and his son"?
3. Who is the *na'ara* with whom they are engaging in sexual congress?
4. Why is this act, of all the crimes listed, considered a *ḥillul Hashem*?
5. Finally, why is this accusation twice as long as the other six crimes listed?

Essentially, this crime exemplifies the corruption behind all seven indictments. The aristocracy (and perhaps royalty) stand accused of the first three crimes; the judiciary of three others. All six crimes constitute terrible abuse of the poor – within ostensibly legitimate parameters. But how should we define this specific offense?

In nearly all ancient societies, including Amos's, slavery was a central component of the economy. Strange as it sounds to modern ears, in some ways slavery was a safety net for the slave (and often, his family), a guarantee of room and board for the destitute. Therefore, the Torah legislated slavery and instituted guidelines intended to ensure minimal abuse of slaves. This was especially true in the case of Israelite slavery. The Israelite slave, *eved ivri,* could only work for six years, was necessarily freed at the Jubilee, and had to be provided for by his master. Additionally, an Israelite man had the right to sell his daughter into slavery (Ex. 21:7–11) – once again, though it sounds heinous to modern readers, this often promised her a secure future. Stipulated therein was the rule that when the girl reached maturity, the master had three choices – to marry her himself, to marry her off to his son, or to free her (ibid.).

Unsurprisingly, slaves were always an underclass, had few advocates, and their rights were easily abused. Jeremiah famously accuses

Judean slave-owners of retaining their slaves beyond the six-year maximum (Jer. 34).

I propose that the *na'ara* in question is a slave-girl, sold by her father as a minor. Keeping in mind that the master *or his son* may marry her when she reaches majority, here we have a case of a man *or*[88] his father (the slave-owner himself) having relations with her. If so, there is nothing wrong with this behavior – why is it even listed here?

The operative word here is *na'ara*. Although the masculine *na'ar* has various meanings,[89] *na'ara* usually refers to a girl who has reached physical maturity and is ready for marriage – that is, a girl *who should already have been freed*. In other words, the master has held onto this Jewish slave-girl beyond the legal limit, and now wishes to exercise his (formerly) legal right to cohabit with her. This also explains the unusual wording *yelkhu el hana'ara* – she has theoretically left his domain, but the master is following her, staking his "claim" on her. It is even possible to read "a man" as being the slave-owner and/or "his father" – that the owner exploits his rights and invites his *father* to take the girl, rather than limiting her to himself or his son.

Herein lies the *ḥillul Hashem* in this oracle: the essential offense of all seven accusations is the wealthy and powerful classes' exploitation of the underprivileged. These laws exist to protect the downtrodden, but the powerful are twisting these very laws of protection for their own benefit, and *this* is a desecration of God's name. The courts, the legal system, and God's laws themselves have become instruments of oppression instead of safeguards of protection. The Torah constantly emphasizes the need to protect and care for the widow, the orphan, and other vulnerable members of society – but these are the very people who are exploited in Samaria.

The father and son do not go to the girl "together" (the word *yaḥdav* is not used). The order is "a man and his father" because the slave-girl would more likely marry the son, who is probably closer to her in age. The *na'ara* is an Israelite slave-girl who has not been freed,

88. Reading *ish ve'aviv* as "a man *or* his father," following R. Yonatan at *Mekhilta Mishpatim, Nezikin* 5.

89. Cf. Ramban on Genesis 37:2.

even though her time to leave has come. This accusation carries with it the strongest sense of *ḥillul Hashem* – and is thus twice the length of the other crimes – because it underscores how wealthy socialites are exploiting the very laws that are meant to help impoverished, struggling families – and abusing them for their own benefit.

Section II: The Kindnesses (2:9–12)

God's kindnesses are presented in three distinct rhetorical styles and contexts in the canon: in purely liturgical form as songs of praise;[90] as a historiosophy calculated to inspire praise of God;[91] or as here: juxtaposed with a description of the people's rebellious behavior. Rather than being devotional or exhortative, this last one is a special form of chastening, as we will see.

All three forms of praise present events differently than the biblical narrative. They are all selective: when Joshua mentions the Exodus in his final address to the people, he completely omits any mention of Pharaoh, and the sequence he describes differs from the narrative record.[92] Similarly, events are often fused together. In Judges 2:1–5, the angel speaks to the people at Bokhim and implies that they entered the Land at the same time (or even before) they are warned against forming a covenant with the Canaanites, whereas this prohibition is in fact issued a full generation before they enter the Land.

As discussed earlier, historiosophy differs from history: while not inaccurate, its goal is to evoke a particular reaction from its audience. It is therefore no surprise when Amos's chastising historiosophy is not fully consistent with the narrative account of Israel's history of conquest and settlement.

---

90. For example, Psalms 78, 105, 136; Exodus 15; Judges 5; Isaiah 12; I Chronicles 29; Nehemiah 9.
91. Deuteronomy 4; Joshua 24; Judges 2, 10; I Samuel 12; among others.
92. For example, in Nehemiah 9, Abraham's name change is presented before the covenant; in Joshua 24, the battle against Sihon and Og are presented *after* entering the Land.

This section, too, can be presented as a numbered list:

1. Yet I destroyed the Amorite from before them, whose height was like the height of the cedars and he was as strong as the oaks
2. Yet I destroyed his fruit from above and his roots from beneath
3. Also, I brought you up out of the land of Egypt
4. And led you for forty years in the wilderness
5. To possess the land of the Amorites
6. And I raised up your sons for prophets
7. And your young men for Nazirites

The Structure of the Liturgical Recitation

Like the accusations, this section is divided into three parts: the first and last verse each contain one clause and the middle verse contains three, as is clear from the verses' syntax, themes, and content:

a) Destruction of the Amorite nations
b) (1) Exodus →(2) wanderings →(3) conquest
c) Sanctification of the people

As mentioned, this historiosophy alters the narrative sequence: the destruction of the Amorite nations (a) happened within the context of the conquest (b3). The final segment is not at all clear, nor does it seem to fit within the scope of these "kindnesses." The first five are all great, wondrous acts that clearly express God's power and favor toward His people, but the final two seem to be personal choices perhaps more accurately classified as acts of free will. How should we understand God's election of prophets and Nazirites? To what degree are these roles assigned by God, and how much do we credit these young men (and their parents, teachers, extended family, and environment)? I will address this after our analysis of this praise.

From a thematic perspective, these three sections can be read as a mini-chiasmus, or perhaps, more accurately, as a complex *inclusio*. The hemistiches that frame the segment form an inverted parallel: God destroyed the Amorites and raised up the young men of Israel. The

Amorites are described as tall (as cedars) and strong (as oaks); young men (*baḥureikhem*) are also depicted thus, as saplings that grow strong and tall.[93] Moreover, the destruction of the Amorites is depicted using imagery of "roots" and "fruit" – both are common biblical metaphors for genealogical relationships: roots refer to ancestors and fruit to offspring.

Analysis of the Text

9: Yet I destroyed the Amorite from before them, whose height was like the height of the cedars and he was as strong as the oaks

What is the meaning of the opening *vav* here ("yet")? A *vav* is usually read as the conjunction "and," but it has various meanings, especially in biblical Hebrew. The well-known *vav hahipukh*, the conversive *vav,* changes verb tense: for instance, the word *yelekh* means "he will go," whereas *vayelekh* in the Bible means "he went." The *vav habiur* (explicative *vav* or *vav* of clarification) serves to clarify: in Genesis 4:4, "And Abel also brought from the finest of his flock, and [*vav*] from their fat," the *vav* conveys that the "finest of his flock" *means* "from their fat." Another common use is *vav hanigud* (*vav* of opposition), which expresses contrast: in Ruth 1:14, "Orpah kissed her mother-in-law, but [*vav*] Ruth cleaved to her."

The *vav* in Amos 2:9 seems to function as a *vav hanigud*: God declares that *despite* Israel's sinfulness, He showed them great kindnesses.

If so, however, the chronological sequence is problematic. These offenses are taking place in Amos's own time, so we would expect the *vav hanigud* to introduce an opposite action taken by God *in spite of* their behavior – not to recall something that He did hundreds of years earlier.

Rather, the *nigud* – contrast – here can be explained by pointing out that God's statement "I destroyed" should be read as the past-perfect tense, to mean: "Though I had *already* destroyed the Amorites." In other words, the *vav hanigud* does not introduce a divine *reaction* to Israel's wayward behavior; rather, it reflects the tragic disconnect between God's beneficence to His people and their behavior toward Him, to His law, and to the lowly and downtrodden among them.

---

93. See, *inter alia*, Psalm 127 and the definition of *baḥur* in I Samuel 10:23–24.

This supports our earlier perception of this oracle as "triangular" in form, with the paean to God's kindnesses forming the opening and central theme, while the accusations (on one side) and the punishments (on the other) express the tragic disparity between what *should have been* and what *was*.

One small anomaly in the opening clause is God's declaration that He had already destroyed the Amorites "from before them," not "from before you": that is, the nation who benefited from God's destruction of the Amorites is in the third person, not the second. This subtly conveys a sense of *hester panim*, of God's turning away from the people and regarding them as "not My people" (to borrow from Hosea 1). This tension cannot be alleviated by positing that the entire praise-psalm is presented to Israel in the third person because the next verse uses the second person ("I brought *you* up out of Egypt").

One final issue remains before moving on. Why should we consider this as an ode at all, when it is not being sung or recited by the people, but rather by God Himself? The answer, I believe, increases the entire oracle's harsh impact. God speaks of the glorious relationship He once had with His people – in contrast to the current state of affairs – and expresses to them: Be aware that your once-secure status in the Land was due to none but My kindness; this is the song you *ought to be singing*.

...Whose height was like the height of the cedars, and he was as strong as the oaks

The Land's former inhabitants are described as tall as the cedars and strong as the oaks. This combination of trees in this simile pair, I believe, imparts a special message.

Trees are a common biblical metaphor: Jotham likens the ruthless Abimelech who craves power to a lowly, useless thorn bush (Judges 9); the psalmist declares that the righteous will flourish like the date-palm and will grow tall like the cedar (Ps. 92:13); Jeremiah compares the righteous to a tree planted by the waters (Jer. 17:8) – there are countless examples of the metaphorical use of trees in the canon. The righteous are characterized as well-planted trees, offering constant nourishment, bearing fruit like the date-palm, and standing tall like the cedar; the wicked are rootless and wither away like desert tumbleweed. These metaphors may all be rooted in this passage:

> When you besiege a city for a long time, in making war against it to take it, you shall not destroy the trees thereof by wielding an axe against them; for you may eat of them, but you shall not cut them down; *for is the tree of the field man* (*ki ha'adam etz hasadeh*), that it should be besieged of you? Only the trees that you know are not trees for food, those you may destroy and cut down, that you may build bulwarks against the city that makes war with you, until it falls. (Deut. 20:19–20)

"Ki ha'adam etz hasadeh" has been variously interpreted as a declarative statement or a rhetorical question. If we read it as a declarative, then the metaphor, identifying humankind as a tree, has firm roots in the Torah and its legislative prose.

It is no surprise that Amos uses tree similes to describe the mighty nations that God defeated during the Israelite conquest. What is unusual is his juxtaposition of the mighty cedar (*erez*) with the oak (*alon*). Usually, the *erez* either stands alone, as in Ezekiel's beautiful description of Assyria (Ezek. 31:3–5), or is paired with a tree that provides that which the cedar cannot: the date-palm, known for its fruit and shade; or the cypress, known for its fragrance. Here, however, the tall, stately cedar is matched with the mighty oak; the cedar is "high" whereas the oak is sturdy and strong. Even more enigmatic is the description of God's deed: "I destroyed his fruit from above and his roots from beneath." Neither of these trees bears fruit. If fruit is so crucial to the *navi*'s description of the Canaanites' destruction, why not pick a fruit-bearing tree – like the cedar's common counterpart, the date-palm?

I believe that the solution lies in Israel's historic memory.

Back to the Exodus

When the Israelites left Egypt, their destination was unclear; all evidence indicates that the people believed they were leaving for a three-day festival before returning to slavery in Egypt. Only after they crossed the Reed Sea did they realize that they were continuing to a journey through the desert to conquer the Land. The powerful promise at Sinai of divine protection and military support[94] implies that these redeemed slaves would have been unable to defeat the mighty Canaanite nations without divine help.

Thus, the image of the Canaanites as strong and well-rooted in the Land is firmly planted in the nation's psyche; it is imprinted even further by the scouts' report of "people of unnatural measure. And there we saw the Nephilim, a giant's sons from the Nephilim. We were as grasshoppers in our own eyes, as we were in their eyes" (Num. 13:32–33). The notion of giants inhabiting the Land is further described in Joshua 11:21–22, indicating that this report was not hyperbolic:

> And Joshua came at that time and smote the giants from the mountain, from Hebron, from Debir, from Anav, from all of the Judean mountains and from all of the mountains of Israel; he destroyed them along with their cities. There were no giants remaining in the Land of the Israelites; only in Gaza, Gath,[95] and Ashdod did they remain.

Hence, when God describes the mighty enemies He defeated in the Land on Israel's behalf, He uses the image of trees both tall (cedar, representing the giants) and strong (oak, representing the deeply rooted peoples). Who are these nations?

The Amorites

In this description, the dispossessed natives are called "the Amorite(s)" (*HaEmori*). This tribal-national name is used in three ways: as the name of one of the seven Canaanite tribes of the Land (for example, Ex. 3:8); as a generic name for the hill tribes, as opposed to those in the plains and by the sea, for example, "All of the Amorite kings on the other side

94. Exodus 23:23, 27–31.

95. This likely means that the giants fled from the hill country, which was completely seized by Joshua's army, and ran to the Philistine territory, which was not conquered during that era. This may explain how a giant like Goliath – and others identified in II Samuel 21:15–22 – become fighters (mercenaries?) for the Philistines.

of the Jordan and the kings of the Canaanites living by the sea heard that God had dried up the waters of the Jordan" (Josh. 5:1); and finally, "the Amorite" also seems to be synonymous with Canaan: the Land's nations are sometimes called "Canaanites" and sometimes "Amorite." In the Covenant Between the Pieces, Abraham is promised: "The fourth generation will return here, for the sin of the *Amorites* has not yet reached its fullness" (Gen. 15:16).

The text in Amos seems to refer to all the conquered Canaanite tribes; so why call them "Amorites"? Hakham[96] suggests that since treetops are known as *amir* in biblical Hebrew,[97] the name "Amorites" alludes to the (tall) tree imagery. Alternatively, it may generate dialogue with Joshua's final address to Israel: "Choose whom you will worship...whether the gods of the Amorites (*elohei haEmori*)" (Josh. 24:15), although this is unlikely, as Amos is not accusing Israel of idolatry in this context.

I believe that the use of *Emori* here evokes a different scene. According to the beginning of Joshua, Israel wins the psychological war against Canaan long before any sword is drawn, as Rahab tells the two spies (Josh. 2:10):

> For we have heard how God dried up the water of the Reed Sea before you, when you came out of Egypt; and what you did to the two kings of the Amorites, that were beyond the Jordan, to Sihon and to Og, whom you utterly destroyed. (Josh. 2:10)

One of these kings made a fateful incursion into the east bank of the Jordan that ultimately led to the Israelite conquest of that side of the river; the other intervened in that war. Both are referred to as "Amorites," even though Sihon seems to be the only one to have originated on the Jordan's west bank. Sihon was considered a local superpower; Israel's victory over them terrified the local population. Og is the first of the giants the Israelites defeat. Thus, "destroying the Amorites" can be read

96. Amos Hakham, *Da'at Mikra, Trei Asar*, vol. 1 (Jerusalem: Mossad Harav Kook, 1990) (henceforth "Hakham"), 13.
97. Isaiah 17:6–9.

as the defeat of Sihon and Og. This, in true historiosophic style, evolves into a reference to the entire conquest of the Land.

His Fruit Above and His Roots Below

The Canaanites are likened to deciduous trees: fruit symbolizes continuity. God destroys the Canaanites' roots – their past – and they are fruitless – they have no future in the Land. It is the Israelites themselves who fail to complete their destruction (see Judges 1–3).[98] These are God's first two kindnesses for Israel, who, had they taken advantage, could have remained sovereign and empowered forever. Alas.

The Exodus

The next three components of praise reflect the stages of the Exodus – leaving Egypt, wandering through the desert, and conquering the Land. Amos's threefold presentation of God's kindnesses during that epoch follows the arc presented in the divine promise, the biblical narrative, and the commands of commemoration.

But there is far more to this trajectory. The entire oracle is moving toward a threat, as seen seven times in the buildup. The pattern introduced in the first seven oracles is the threat of military destruction, decimation of cities and the leadership, and, ultimately, exile. With that in mind, we must return to Israel's original entry into the Land (from which they stand to be exiled) and the constant reminder that their right of possession rests on one premise – moral superiority.[99]

Although the proximate context of that warning is sexual immorality, there are other behaviors that the Torah describes as "abominations," including numerous idolatrous practices but also extending to business fraud.[100] This last behavior certainly hits home in the list of accusations against Israel; moreover, "a man and his father go unto the same girl," may certainly be read as sexual perversion, along with our "slave-girl" proposal above.

98. Otherwise, the Canaanites would never have been able to rise up and oppress Israel.
99. Most notably in Leviticus 18 and Deuteronomy 18.
100. Corrupt weights and measures are called an abomination in Deuteronomy 25:16.

Thus, we may read this praise section as teleological: the ultimate goal of God's kindnesses was to uproot the immoral Canaanites and their culture and bring Israel to the Land to build a holy nation, a kingdom of priests (Ex. 19:6) whose moral beacon would shine for the world and become a blessing for all families of the earth.[101]

This illuminates why this historiosophy does not follow the chronological sequence of events. The goal of this hymn is not merely to recount them, but rather to prepare an argument in favor of the impending punishment and exile of the northern kingdom. The Canaanites were uprooted because of their moral depravity, but despite God's love and kindness, Israel have strayed from the moral path and have thus lost their right to the Land.

10a: I brought you up out of the land of Egypt

One final note about Amos's invocation of the Exodus. The Exodus is sometimes referred to as "taking out," (the root *y-tz-a*) as in "I am The Lord your God who *took you out* of the land of Egypt" (Ex. 20:2); here and elsewhere, it is described as "bringing up," with the root *a-l-h* (Ex. 3:8). "Taking out" relates to relief from the servitude of Egypt; for example, "you shall guard the *matzot,* for on this very same day *I have taken out your hosts* from the land of Egypt..." (Ex. 12:17). "Bringing up" seems to express a broader national spiritual mission, as in "I am the Lord your God *who brought you up* out of the land of Egypt, open your mouth that I may fill it" (Ps. 81:11). God seems to be seeking a deeper relationship with Israel, beyond the political and geographic movement of taking them out.

Here, Amos is expressing that the people have failed in the spiritual mission that began with the Exodus; thus he speaks of God bringing them "up" from Egypt.[102]

101. Genesis 12:3; see how that phrase is ironically invoked below in Amos 3:2.
102. See R. Joseph Kara on our verse.

10b: And led you for forty years in the wilderness

While various literary prophets use the wilderness motif,[103] only Amos explicitly mentions the forty years of wandering – twice: here and in 5:25, in a critique of the sacrificial cult. This trope – "forty years of wandering" – is used frequently in Numbers (after the decree in Num. 14), throughout Deuteronomy, and sparingly in Joshua – but it does not appear elsewhere in the prophetic canon except for these two occurrences in Amos. I will discuss this further in the context of Amos 5:25, but one specific aspect may inform our understanding of this passage.

Although the forty years of wandering is generally perceived as a punishment (which is the decree's original context), these forty years also functioned as proof of the people's loyalty to God and as a crucible of their commitment to Him (Deut. 8:1–10). As Amos implies, these years in the wilderness were a period of growth and appreciation for Israel's divine gifts, and helped forge Israel's identity as a nation.

10c: To possess the land of the Amorites

Unlike the first two clauses, this is not a distinct act of kindness, but rather seems to be the goal of the Exodus, the sojourn through the desert, or both. Its interpretation depends on whether we read its precedent as "And I took you up out of Egypt (and led you forty years through the wilderness) to possess the land of the Amorite" – that is, that the years in the desert were an unavoidable step between the Exodus and the Land's conquest – or as: "I led you forty years through the wilderness *to* possess the land of the Amorite": that the main purpose of the wilderness years was to prepare the people for the Land's conquest. Radak reads it this way in his first approach:

> Before I brought you to the Land, I brought you out from the land of Egypt, from the house of slaves, and I led you forty years through the wilderness, as you lacked for nothing. I accustomed you to My laws so that you would not learn the customs of the Amorite land when you came to inherit it.

---

103. Hosea 2; Jeremiah 2:1.

Ibn Ezra states this even more clearly:

> "And I…" the meaning is as follows: I guided you for forty years, until you learned My laws, so that afterwards you would disinherit the Amorites.

Each approach leaves us with a different emphasis in Amos's oracle, each resulting in a slightly different message. If we read it the first way, the message seems to be as follows: "You were in exile, I brought you up out of there to this Land – and now, due to failing to fulfill the mission of your Exodus, you will be re-exiled." If we read it the second way, the text conveys disappointment more than threat: "All those years of guiding you, teaching you, and refining you in the desert were apparently a waste of time," with tragic results: divine disappointment leads to divine abandonment.

But if Amos is in fact deftly expressing that both the Exodus and the years in the desert were necessary prerequisites to conquering and possessing the Land, then Israel has failed even more miserably. In the astute words of R. Eliezer of Beaugency:[104]

> Behold *I destroyed the Amorite from before them, whose height was like the height of the cedars,* and they would steal and act violently against those who were lower and smaller than they. They should have remembered *that I took you up out of the land of Egypt* from the house of slaves, from those who stole from them and oppressed them; therefore, they should not have defrauded and oppressed orphans and widows. *And I led you forty years through the wilderness,* so you should have had compassion and taken care of the poor as I did for you. For I took care of you *for forty years* until I dispossessed for you *the land of the Amorite* so you

104. Twelfth-century France, from the *peshat* school of Rashi. He may have been a student of Rashbam. For a biographic snapshot along with a description of R. Eliezer's place within the development of *peshat* exegesis in twelfth-century France, see Robert A. Harris, *Rabbi Eliezer of Beaugency, Commentaries on Amos and Jonah (With Selections from Isaiah and Ezekiel)* (Medieval Institute Publications, 2018).

should not have dispossessed and driven the poor and orphans from their ancestral inheritance.

The Prophet and the Nazirite

> **11** And I raised up your sons for prophets, and your young men for Nazirites. Is it not even thus, children of Israel? says the Lord.
> **12** But you gave the Nazirites wine to drink, and commanded the prophets, saying "Prophesy not."

The ultimate goal of the Jewish nation is to channel blessing for all the families of the earth. It all begins with Abraham's journey, Genesis 12:1–3 (and is reiterated after the Binding of Isaac):

> Go by yourself from your land, your family,[105] and your father's house, to the Land that I will show you. I will make you into a great nation; I will bless you and make your name famous; and you will be a blessing. I will bless those who bless you and curse the one who curses you; and through you, all families of the earth will be blessed.

The subtext of the moral high road as a justification for Israel's elevated status and successful conquest of the Land courses through the Covenant Between the Pieces, where Abraham is told that his seed may not conquer the Land until the "sin of the Amorite" is "complete" – that is, until their depravity goes beyond redemption, thus justifying their expulsion from the Land (Gen. 15:13–16).

The Torah warns that the Land will not tolerate sin and will "vomit out" violators who defile it;[106] this implies that Israel's political independence and sovereignty in the Land is contingent on their morality and capacity to inspire and bless other nations. This is further alluded at the beginning of Joshua, when Rahab of Jericho acknowledges God

---

105. *Moledet* in modern Hebrew is commonly understood as "birthplace." In biblical Hebrew, however, it is most accurately rendered as "family."
106. Leviticus 18:24–30; see Ramban's comments at v. 25 ad loc.

as the one all-powerful deity (2:9–11), but is not mentioned again until the advent of the literary prophets. The historical books focus solely on the nation of Israel. Only beginning with Isaiah of Jerusalem (2:1–4) and Micah (4:1–5) do we again hear universal messages; Deutero-Isaiah refers to the Temple as "a house of prayer for all of the nations" (Is. 56:7). Even Joel's bloody apocalypse (Joel 4) and Obadiah's visions of Edom's day of reckoning (Ob. 1) – echoed at the end of Jeremiah – are universal in scope. In general, while their specific perspectives differ, nearly all share the vision that God's plan includes all of humanity, and that Israel's role is to act as teacher[107] and model.[108]

Amos deftly shifts from the national landscape of Exodus and conquest to Israel's ultimate goal: to raise spiritual guides and models. The Land's sanctity, the people's glamorous and challenging historical epic, and the divine law which frames their lives all contribute to an environment that produces exceptional youth. Commenting on our verse, Ibn Ezra notes that God puts His spirit in the young men, turning them into prophets and inspiring them to teach His laws to the people.[109] Radak notes that God inspires young men with His spirit, showing the people that such special and lofty communion is possible.

Indeed, God Himself raises some of the young men to become prophets or Nazirites:

11a: And I raised up your sons for prophets

As noted in the introduction, a prophet is not only a vehicle for God's word to humankind, but is also a spiritual person who "resides in the shadow of God." From the conquest to the end of the monarchy, there were guilds of prophets who trained to be receptive to God's word. Their "rapture" exercises and spiritual experiences are noted in I Samuel 10 and 19. Raising young men and training them to forsake the pursuit

107. Isaiah 61:6.
108. Zechariah 8:23.
109. R. Eliezer of Beaugency and R. Joseph Kara take a similar approach.

of material wealth for spiritual riches should be the task of the nation itself – but as Amos testifies, it is God who raises them to be *nevi'im.*[110]

There are two salient points in this phrase. First of all, the fact that it is God, rather than the *people,* who is raising the young men to a life of prophecy, suggests subtle rebuke, though it is part of the praise section. Second, this phrase alludes to the prophetic guild (*bnei hanevi'im*), the group with which Amos is *not* associated.

11b: And your young men for Nazirites

Rather than read *nezirim* (lit. "those who are set apart") as those who take a formal vow of *nezirut* – who avoid contact with the dead, abstain from wine, and let their hair grow – Rashi, following Targum Yonatan, suggests that the *nezirim* here are teachers (*malfin*).[111] Radak reads *nezirim* as per the halakhic definition, but only mentions their abstinence from wine, implying that instead of material pleasures, these young men aspire to spiritual greatness.

These two spiritual models – *nevi'im* and *nezirim* – serve God differently. The *navi* is trained to be a worthy recipient of God's word; the *nazir* has trained himself to live a life of sanctity by virtue of restraint. One inspires others to listen to God, while the other inspires others with their potential for individual holiness. These two exemplars serve as the nexus for the "holy nation," whose vocation is to teach the world about God and model a holy society.

12: But you gave the Nazirites wine to drink, and commanded the prophets, saying "Prophesy not"

As mentioned, this verse does not seem to fall under the category of accusation (vv. 6–8), praise-hymn (vv. 9–11), or punishment (vv. 14–16); if so, what *is* its purpose and place within the oracle?

110. II Kings 4:1–6; 38–43.
111. R. Joseph Kara concurs.

I believe that this verse functions as a Janus parallelism within the section (named for the Roman god Janus, who had two faces, one looking to the past and the other to the future). In the words of Cyrus Gordon:

> [A Janus parallelism has] two entirely different meanings: one meaning paralleling what precedes, and the other meaning, what follows. *Song of Songs* 2:12 reads: "The blossoms appear in the land | the time of the *zamir* has arrived | and the song of the turtle-dove is heard on our land." *Zamir* means either the "pruning season" or "music." The commentators insist that while either meaning is conceivable, the author could have intended only one or the other. But this misses the point. The poet knew how to exploit the double meaning of *zamir*. Retrospectively it parallels the first member of the tristich pertaining to the growth of the soil; proleptically it parallels the final members pertaining to song. The skillful exploitation of twin meanings, providing through a single word twofold parallelism, is artistry of a high order.[112]

This concept has been embraced and developed by scholars since, and I believe that the principle can be applied to phrases and whole verses, not just words.[113] Here, it may hold the key to the purpose and place of v. 12.

On one hand, v. 12 is a direct – chiastic – response to v. 11 – the young prophets and *nezirim* were forced away from their sanctified drives. On the other hand, the tone of v. 12 fits the mood of vv. 6–8, the accusations against the people. If we were to read vv. 6–8 and then 12, without the praise-hymn, what would we have? Being ever mindful of the typological number seven, we will recast the seven accusations as follows:

112. Cyrus Gordon, "New Directions," *Bulletin of the American Society of Papyrologists* 15, 1–2 (1978): 59–66.

113. An excellent example of this is in Psalms 48, where the psalmist sets up Jerusalem in apposition both to the cultic centers of Tzafon and Nof (biblical Memphis, in Egypt), which it supersedes, as well as against the beauty of the land, being the chief source of joy – *mesos kol ha'aretz*.

1. Because they sell the righteous for silver, and the needy for a pair of shoes.
2. That pant after the dust of the earth on the head of the poor,
3. And turn aside the way of the humble.
4. And a man and his father go unto the same girl to profane My holy name.
5. And they lay themselves down beside every altar upon clothes taken in pledge, and in the house of their God they drink the wine of them that have been fined....
6. But you gave the Nazirites wine to drink
7. And commanded the prophets, saying "Prophesy not."

In this reckoning (which, admittedly, reflect an alternative reading of some of the divisions suggested earlier), the aristocracy's sins move in a curious direction. First, those in power (slave-owners) sell the poor because they have power over them. They then act arrogantly toward those who are below them ("on the head of the poor"), who are, nonetheless, not fully subjugated to them. They then "turn aside the way of the humble," seemingly taking those whose financial status does not put them at any disadvantage, but whose station in life may subject them to some power of the judges or of the wealthy. We have already considered the middle passage and its implications for taking advantage of slaves who are (in a limited sense) part of the household. Moving away from personal abuse, they take items legally – but wrongfully – seized from the poor and use them for their own purposes. Finally, they intoxicate and poison the pure young men of society. After pushing down those beneath them, they pull down those above them – the spiritually elite and morally sensitive – to their own depraved level.

This is a familiar emotional strategy of the prurient when faced with their morally superior peers. Instead of humbling themselves and being inspired by the enlightened, the morally bankrupt citizens of the north seek to corrupt any model of holiness among them so that they may continue their spiritually defective lives without the hindrance of conscience.

We have considered vv. 6–8 as an independent indictment, but our Janus structure suggests that a second look may be worthwhile, perhaps inspiring a reevaluation of the entire line of accusation.

Now, we may ask the following question: Which of these is the intended meaning of the diatribe? Is v. 12 to be read in concert with and in apposition to v. 11, or as the direct continuation of v. 8? I would like to suggest that Amos deliberately and brilliantly intends both, enhancing his message and giving it greater impact for all generations.

At this point, Amos's assemblage expects the hammer to fall and are anxiously prepared to hear what punishment awaits Samaria.

To the audience's surprise, perhaps, Amos prefaces the punishment with another "bridge verse." We will analyze the entire section and its structure before turning our attention to this prefatory verse.

PART III: ISRAEL'S PUNISHMENT

The Text (Amos 2:13–16)

(יג) הִנֵּה אָנֹכִי מֵעִיק תַּחְתֵּיכֶם כַּאֲשֶׁר תָּעִיק הָעֲגָלָה הַמְלֵאָה לָהּ עָמִיר:
(יד) וְאָבַד מָנוֹס מִקָּל וְחָזָק לֹא יְאַמֵּץ כֹּחוֹ וְגִבּוֹר לֹא יְמַלֵּט נַפְשׁוֹ:
(טו) וְתֹפֵשׂ הַקֶּשֶׁת לֹא יַעֲמֹד וְקַל בְּרַגְלָיו לֹא יְמַלֵּט וְרֹכֵב הַסּוּס לֹא יְמַלֵּט נַפְשׁוֹ:
(טז) וְאַמִּיץ לִבּוֹ בַּגִּבּוֹרִים עָרוֹם יָנוּס בַּיּוֹם הַהוּא נְאֻם ה':

13 Behold, I will make it creak[114] under you, as a cart creaks that is full of sheaves. **14** And flight shall fail the swift, and the strong shall not exert his strength, neither shall the mighty deliver himself; **15** neither shall he stand that handles the bow; and he that is swift of foot shall not deliver himself; neither shall he that rides the horse deliver himself; **16** and he that is courageous among the mighty shall flee away naked in that day, says the Lord.

114. This is one possible translation – see below for a range of possible meanings.

One prefatory note regarding the oracle's "signature": the first two oracles (Aram and Philistia) have a signature ("*amar Hashem*"); the next two (Tyre and Edom) do not; the next two (Ammon and Moab) do. Judah has no signature, while Israel does: "*ne'um Hashem*."

Having placed our oracle into its structural context within the larger series, let's attend to the chastisement-consequences.

The introductory transitional verse is followed by seven consequences:

1. Flight shall fail the swift
2. And the strong shall not exert his strength
3. Neither shall the mighty deliver himself
4. Neither shall he stand that handles the bow
5. And he that is swift of foot shall not deliver himself
6. Neither shall he that rides the horse deliver himself
7. And he that is courageous among the mighty shall flee away naked in that day

War is the context of the entire sequence of punishments: the fourth ("he that handles the bow") and sixth ("he that rides the horse") are explicit references to military positions. The other five (fleet,[115] strong,[116] mighty,[117] fleet [again], and courageous) are all common biblical military references.

Considering the long history of biblical chastisements and warnings we might have expected a different or broader context. Exile, famine, plagues, destitution, loss of sovereignty, and much more can be found in

115. Cf. II Samuel 2:18: Asa'el, the first person described as "fleet of foot" in the Bible, is characterized that way in a clearly military context; similarly, Ahimaaz (II Sam. 18:23), who famously "overtakes the Cushite," is delivering news from the war to David.
116. The phrase that Moshe uses to encourage Joshua throughout Deuteronomy and which makes up the *leitmotif* of God's investiture of Joshua (ch. 1) is "*Ḥazak ve'ematz*" ("Be strong and courageous"), both of which are found in the second punishment (which literally reads "the strong will not encourage his power"). *Amitz* appears as the final item on our list too.
117. See, for instance, the list of David's "mighty ones" in II Samuel 23:8. They constitute the upper echelon of David's army.

the Sinai covenant (Lev. 26) and the re-covenant in the plains of Moab (Deut. 28), as well as the (relatively) minor admonitions of (*inter alia*) Joshua 23–24, I Samuel 12, and I Kings 9. Why, then, is this sequence limited to military failure? Parenthetically, if all of these dire threats are realized, all that we have is a vanquished army. True, this is never good news; but within the broader scope of Israelite history, it seems to fall short of the terrifying messages we have come to expect.

Deciphering the "Light" Punishment

This unexpectedly "light" sentence may be explained in one of three ways.

First, the punishment may be far worse than we imagine. If Israel's military loses its power, they will certainly be subject to all the devastation their neighbors are accused of in these oracles.

Second, perhaps the punishment is indeed less severe because Israel's offenses, at this point, are less severe. Perhaps the destruction and exile of its cities are worse fates than Israel currently deserves.

Finally, we have to look at the literary context. Israel's punishment stands in stark contrast to the nations' aforementioned punishments, as listed above.

All seven nations' major cities will be burned down; their leaders will perish; some nations will be cast into exile. Although the context is a military defeat/conquest, none of this action takes place on a battlefield; the setting, rather, is the targeted kingdom's cities. Our final oracle, on the other hand, takes place entirely on the battlefield and does not mention Samaria or any of its cities at all. This anomaly may be interpreted in two ways.

1. Distinction: The simplest way to read it is as a clear distinction. Whereas the other nations will suffer devastation in their palaces and cities, Israel will suffer defeat after defeat on the battlefield, with their army rendered useless. The first six oracles (excluding Judah) can be read as sharing one overall theme, with similar crimes and punishments, whereas Israel's crimes and therefore punishments are of a different nature. This is a tempting direction to take, but it seems inadequate. If the nations' crimes are, as described, *war crimes*, why should they be "spared" punishments on the battlefield? Moreover, Israel's offenses are *not* war crimes, but it is the only nation whose punishment is confined to the battlefield. This implies that analyzing this pattern as mere distinction does not resolve its anomaly. Therefore, we may wish to take the opposite approach, seeing Israel's punishment as *completing the picture* of all of the oracles. This would take us on the interpretive road of clarification, utilizing the rabbinic maxim that "the words of Torah are poor in one place, yet rich elsewhere."[118] In other words, what the text omits in one place may be filled in from a related passage.

2. Clarification: The earlier, much briefer oracles all end with destruction of the major cities of the targeted kingdoms. Perhaps our longer oracle serves to complete the picture in each of those earlier ones. How will Damascus, say, be defeated? Its warriors will cease to be fleet and their archers will no longer be able to control the bow.

According to this reading, the final oracle and the first seven speak to each other, filling in the gaps in each other's message, warning that the cities of Israel will suffer the same fate of fire and destruction of its palaces. This conflagration will begin with a measured disabling of the army.

13: Behold, I will make it creak under you…

As mentioned above, another "transition verse" precedes the threat of the sevenfold punishment: "Behold, I will make it creak (*mei'ik*) under you, as a cart creaks (*ta'ik*) that is full of sheaves."

Mei'ik/ta'ik, as a verb, is a *hapax legomenon* – its only biblical appearance is in our verse (twice). It is commonly rendered as "creak" (or "totter"). Koehler-Baumgartner also suggests "hinder," "roar," or "split open."[119]

---

118. The earliest authority credited with this maxim is Rabbi Neḥemya (*Mishnat Rabbi Eliezer*, end of *Parasha* no. 1), specifically as a method for deciphering unclear nonlegal statements (Aggada). His application of this notion is exactly on point for us: "They require substantiation to be brought from another place (i.e., text)." Rabbi Yoḥanan is quoted as deriving this maxim from the verse praising the woman of valor: "She is like a merchant ship, bringing her bread from afar" (Prov. 31:14).

119. Ludwig Koehler, Walter Baumgartner, and Johann J. Stamm, *The Hebrew and*

Regardless of its meaning, the image is powerful. God is hindered/overburdened/ roaring due to the tremendous weight of Israel on His back. This image has roots as early as Cain's words to God: "Is my sin to great (for You) to bear?" (Gen. 4:13). God describes Himself as "One who carries sins" (Ex. 34:7) – He assumes the weight of sin from humanity's shoulders. The image of a forgiving God is not usually one of "cleaning the slate,"[120] but rather of acknowledging that the sins exist, the burden is heavy, and it is God's compassion that lifts humanity's burden.

In our case, it is as if the burden is so heavy that God is (as it were) incapable of bearing it. Poignantly, it is grain – the plenty with which God has blessed His people – that becomes a metaphor for their sins, hinting that it is a surfeit of blessing that has led to the people's corruption: "Yeshurun became fat and rebelled" (Deut. 32:15).

This verse seems to serve as a transition from the praise-hymn to the punishments. It does not list punishments, nor does it fit with the military images used in the seven punishments outlined in the next passage. Moreover, the overall seven-fold scheme of the entire oracle frames vv. 14–16 separately and presents this "tottering" verse as independent.

Rather than a transition, Paul suggests that this verse is a topic sentence describing the punishment in general terms: [121]

> The armies of Israel will be stopped and will stand in their places as if paralyzed, like a wagon which is stopped because of the weight of the straw... the image, taken from the world of agriculture, Amos's world, is paradoxical. The wagon is stopped due to the weight of the straw, which testifies to great bounty, the same bounty which Amos himself degrades in other prophecies.

I would argue, rather, that this verse is a preface, a divine cry that expresses the pain God "feels" when He decides to mete out punishment

Aramaic Lexicon of the Old Testament, trans. and ed. under the supervision of Mervyn E. J. Richardson, vol. 1 (Leiden: Brill, 2001) (henceforth "Koehler-Baumgartner"), 802.

120. One famous exception is "I have blotted out your transgression like a cloud" (Is. 44:22).

121. Paul, 54 (translation mine).

to His own people: to still the "armies of God" and paralyze their defenses. The image of the wagon is not the armies themselves stopped in their tracks; rather, it is God Himself who is frozen, so to speak, due to their overwhelming sins. We might almost be tempted to then read the description of the Israelite army's paralysis not as an active punishment, but rather as an inevitable weakening of divine support for the Israelite warriors, as He is "burdened down" and "cannot move" to help them.

Indeed, a careful reading of the next three verses carefully reveals this subtle image shadowing the descriptions of the weakened forces. God does not declare that He will slow down the fleet or rob the hero of his courage; rather, "Flight shall fail the swift." Without God's support and help, the warriors are powerless. God is anticipating the question that will be asked on the day of defeat: "Where is God?" The answer to the people is that He is burdened with their sins – incapable, so to speak, of intervening on their behalf and giving them the necessary strength to stand and fight.

Here are the seven retributive phrases:

1. Flight shall fail the swift
2. And the strong shall not exert his strength
3. Neither shall the mighty deliver himself
4. Neither shall he stand that handles the bow
5. And he that is swift of foot shall not deliver himself
6. Neither shall he that rides the horse deliver himself
7. And he that is courageous among the mighty shall flee away naked in that day

The Punishment: Where Is the Enemy?

Before dissecting each of these curses on its own terms, it must be noted that these punishments are missing a key factor. Each of them reflects weakness, incompetence, or faintheartedness on the battlefield. At no point, however, is there any mention of an enemy, much less a description of their victory or their brutality after conquest. How can we explain this surprising omission?

Is omission of the human agent calculated to emphasize the divine hand? With just a cursory look through the Bible, this theory is immediately refuted. Abraham is told at the Covenant Between the Pieces that his seed "will be a stranger in a foreign land and *they will enslave and oppress them for four hundred years.* Indeed, I will judge *the nation for whom they toiled*" (Gen. 15:13–14). God's human agent is immediately introduced; what is more, they will be punished for their oppression. The covenants at Sinai and at the plains of Moab both mention that Israel will be punished by enemies. Isaiah, Jeremiah, and other literary prophets explore how God sends punishment through human agents that will be punished in turn, in due course. There is no need to omit the human hand in order to emphasize God's hand.

Could the enemy's absence be read literally? Could the curse be that the Israelite army will run from its own shadow, and no enemy is mentioned because there is no enemy at all?! The wild scenario of armies defeating themselves in fact takes place in several biblical scenes: Leviticus describes how "they will stumble, each over his fellow" (26:37); Gideon attacks the Midianites with just 300 soldiers, who frighten the 135,000-strong enemy into destroying themselves (Judges 7); the Assyrian army flees before attacking Jerusalem (II Kings 19:35–36).

In contrast, Amos explicitly describes Israelite soldiers under attack, but the focus is on their failure to respond to the unmentioned enemy.

Rather, perhaps, the significance of this scene can be derived from the words of a younger contemporary of Amos. When Sennacherib of Assyria threatens to invade Judah, Isaiah rebukes those who advocate seeking military protection from Egypt (Is. 30:12–18):

> **12** Wherefore thus says the Holy One of Israel: because you despise this word, and trust in oppression and perverseness, and stay thereon; **13** therefore this iniquity shall be to you as a breach ready to fall, swelling out in a high wall, whose breaking comes suddenly at an instant…
>
> **15** For thus said the Lord God, the Holy One of Israel: in sitting still and rest shall you be saved, in quietness and in confidence shall be your strength; and you would not. **16** But you said: "No, for we will flee upon horses"; therefore will you flee; and: "We

> will ride upon the swift"; therefore will they that pursue you be swift. 17 One thousand will flee at the rebuke of one, at the rebuke of five will you flee... for the Lord is a God of justice; happy are all they that wait for Him.

An important exegetical note: the prophet paraphrases the people's crooked intent as *"Al sus nanus* (or *nanos*)" – which is translated by some: "We will flee upon horses." This translation makes little sense in light of the divine "comeuppance" for this plan, *"Al ken tenusun,"* which would affirm their plan's success! This is not much of a warning or punishment. More convincing is the interpretation of Ibn Janach, quoted by Ibn Ezra:[122] he reads *nanus* as anchored, not in the root *n-w-s* (to flee), rather in the root *n-s-s,* a banner to be lifted high: the people take pride in their horses, but, ironically, they will have to flee from their enemies (perhaps on those very horses). This interpretation is recommended by v. 16, the second hemistich, *"Ve'al kal nirkav, al ken yikalu rodfeikhem"*: "You were saying 'we will ride' – not flee! – 'on a swift animal,' but (instead) your enemies will be swift (to chase you)."

Isaiah's oracle mentions issues of injustice and corruption, though they are not his central point of chastisement. The core message of *"Beshuva vanaḥat tivashe'un,"* "In sitting still and rest shall you be saved," suggests a passive foreign policy platform, "allowing" God to step in and defeat Assyria. Nonetheless, Isaiah does not fail to mention Judah's corruption (as discussed extensively in the opening chapter of Isaiah); indeed, he presents them as the breach in their walls, leading to their incompetence on the battlefield and ironic downfall.

The equation is aptly illustrated by the Talmud Yerushalmi:

> Rabbi Abba bar Kahana said: David's generation were all righteous, yet because they had *dilatorim,* they would go out to war and suffer casualties, as David says (Ps. 57:5): "I am in the midst of lions; I am forced to dwell among ravenous beasts – men whose teeth are spears and arrows, whose tongues are sharp swords..."

122. Ad loc. v. 16; see Shadal ad loc., who develops it further, suggesting that the root may be related to *naso,* to be lifted.

> The generation of Ahab were idolaters; but because they had no *dilatorin,* they would go out to war and win.[123]

Most dictionaries render *dilatorin* (from the Greek *dylatir*[124]) as "informers, sycophants" – this highlights the *aggada*'s underlying message. Regardless of spiritual and ritual impiety, when the troops are a cohesive, loyal unit on a unified mission, the army stands a much greater chance of success; conversely, the best-trained, most well-equipped military that suffers from internal strife and mistrust cannot emerge victorious amidst its own divisiveness. This is a universal and eternal truism.

Isaiah's message is two-fold, and he weaves it together masterfully. First of all, a society whose leadership is tainted by corruption will fail on the battlefield. Second, the particular foreign policy sought out by the court is doomed to fail and the monarchy should adopt a passive approach, trusting that God will defeat Assyria. The first point is eternally true and applies broadly; the second is a local directive, specifically addressing the Assyrian threat. The second message is not relevant to our passage, but the first speaks volumes.

As mentioned, biblical punishments of death in battle or oppression usually involve an active enemy. However, these punishments are all in response to ritual sins, typically idolatry: as illustrated repeatedly through the "Shoftim-cycle,"[125] we stray from God and He sells us to a foreign oppressor. This oppressor is God's agent of discipline[126] against the Israelites, His wayward children.

However, when Israel's sin is moral and social corruption, a depraved gap between those in power and those trampled underfoot, then that society is its own worst enemy. This is the point that Isaiah makes – and this is the point that Amos masterfully communicates here.

---

123. Y. Peah 1:1.
124. English also has "delator" (an informer).
125. See Judges 2:11–20. The general scheme of the cycle is (1) idolatry → (2) foreign oppressor → (3) oppression → (4) crying out (not necessarily in prayer) → (5) God sending a *shofet* to redeem them → (6) they reform their behavior for the duration of the *shofet*'s life (at most).
126. Or anger – see Isaiah 10:5.

This is not to suggest that Amos focuses solely on Samaria's corrupt "justice" and the elite's oppression of the poor; he will yet address their idolatry and related sins. In this first prophecy, however, Amos casts the spotlight on the sickness which pervades the societal structure in Israel. Earlier, I suggested that Israel's seven offenses should be read in this vein, and the mentions of "every altar" and "the houses of their gods" are incidental rather than central to the rebuke.

Chiasmus… or a Different Type of Literary Structure?

We have discussed chiastic structures several times so far. A different biblical structure, however, comprises chiastic elements, but gains momentum toward the end of the passage and climaxes in a resounding crescendo of ideas, in which smaller elements strewn along the way join to create a more powerful and impactful message.

This structure is evident, for example, in the well-known narrative of the covenant at Sinai (Ex. 19–24).[127] The sequence begins with God's summoning Moses to the top of the mountain and is neatly bookended by Moses's ascent into the fire atop the mountain at the end of chapter 24. At the beginning, Moses ascends the mountain to commune with God and is given a message for the people. Though the narrative's final chapter echoes this pattern, its conclusion is a fiery, terrifying amplification of the first summons. Moreover, while hints of Moses's role as agent (*malakh*) of God, emissary between God and the people (*shaliaḥ*), lawgiver (*meḥokek*), and officiant (*kohen*) are strewn throughout the narrative, these four roles are condensed into the final, epic description of Moses's ascent to the smoking, fiery peak of Divine Presence. Thus the elements softly echoed in the first part of the narrative, combined with elements scattered throughout, come together in a powerful interwoven crescendo at its end.

Let's explore how this structure functions in Amos 2:14–16.

1. Flight shall fail the swift (*Ve'avad manos mikal*)

127. See a more developed analysis of this structure in Etshalom, *Between the Lines of the Bible*, vol. 2, ch. 10.

2. And the strong shall not exert his strength (*Veḥazak lo ye'ametz koḥo*)
3. Neither shall the mighty deliver himself (*Ve'gibbor lo yemalet nafsho*)
4. Neither shall he stand that handles the bow (*Vetofes hakeshet lo ya'amod*)
5. And he that is swift of foot shall not deliver himself (*Vekal beraglav lo yemalet*)
6. Neither shall he that rides the horse deliver himself (*Verokhev hasus lo yemalet nafsho*)
7. And he that is courageous among the mighty shall flee away naked in that day (*Ve'amitz libbo bagibborim arom yanus bayom hahu*)

At first glance, this heptad seems to follow a chiastic structure. The first and seventh punishments alone lack the key word *lo* but include the root *n-w-s*, to flee. In the first stage the nominal form *manos* is used, which means "ability to flee" (or "speed"). In the final line, the verbal form *yanus* ("will flee") is used. The irony stretching across the "envelope structure" is clear: those who normally flee will lose their ability to do so in the face of the enemy, while one who would normally stand and courageously face their adversary "will flee away naked in that day." In lines 3, 5, and 6, the hero cannot save himself. The implication is clear: the one who was charged with saving many others cannot even save himself. These observations seem to place the fourth line (the only one to mention a specific type of fighter, the archer) at the axis of the chiasmus. This is far from perfect (line 2 does not match up with line 6 and seems to feed directly into the last line), but it is an appealing proposal.[128]

Yet the claim that this is a chiasmus poses several difficulties. The one fleeing in line 1 is unable to escape the enemy, an idea mentioned again in line 5. The courageous one who will not be able to stand his ground, who eventually flees in shame, echoes the incompetence expressed in line 2. The deeper the analysis, the less these lines seem to

128. Paul (*Mikra leYisrael*, 54) assumes the structure to be chiastic.

form a chiasmus. With this in mind, we can now reevaluate the structure and meaning of our passage.

Kal (fleet of foot) appears in line 1 and then line 5 – but with a slightly different meaning. In the first, he is incapable of fleeing; but in line 5, he does not escape. These are related but not identical. Flight, however, appears as well in the last line: not as something which the (speedy) soldiers are incapable of, but rather as something that the mighty *will* do (which is *his* failure) on that day. The *gibbor* of line 3 does not save himself; in line 7, the most courageous of the *gibborim does* flee, unclad and disgraced.

In other words, our three verses are an interwoven crescendo, in which the various arms of the military are deprived of their particular abilities – while ultimately, these "abilities" are adopted, desperately and without dignity, by the other forces. Those who would stand their ground and fight adopt the flight of the fleet; those who are fleet of foot can only fall. The horseman who should be able to escape cannot do so (line 6), while the archer who should be able to stand his ground and take aim, must flee (line 4). The crescendo is, as expected, in the final line: the most powerful, who should be advancing on the enemy without fear, ultimately flee without dignity.

The various components of the ultimate failure – the mightiest and most courageous of the combat soldiers fleeing in disgrace – are strewn among the previous lines and brought together for the powerful climax: "And he that is courageous among the mighty will flee away naked in that day."

To conclude this chapter and our analysis of Amos's first oracle against Israel, I will step back and consider the entire series with two questions in mind: Why does Amos precede his main message to Samaria with seven oracles, and why does the book begin in this manner?

It is difficult to resolve the second question by claiming that this was Amos's first prophecy; though chronological markers appear in narrative contexts in some prophetic books[129] or date specific prophecies,[130] they are clearly not the basis for organizing such works. Unless specified

129. Including Isaiah, Jeremiah, Ezekiel, Haggai, Zechariah – and Amos.

130. Isaiah 6; Jeremiah 25; Ezekiel 1; among others.

(for example, "When the Lord spoke at first with Hosea"; Hos. 1:2), there is no reason to assume that a prophetic book's opening passage was the prophet's first oracle. We might expect that the book's first oracle would be addressed directly to Israel, rather than moving from nation to nation before finally speaking to the royal house of Samaria.

In addition, as stated, I believe that Amos's "anthem" (1:2) is a repeated formula.

If so, these two questions stand, and we will soon see that their answers are intertwined.

Overall Themes

Longer prophetic collections often have many themes. Isaiah 40–55 carries a consistent theme of return and consolation; chapters 56–66 are messianic in nature; his "oracles against the nations" (14–24) also share a theme, as do Jeremiah's prophecies against the nations at the end of his collection.

Shorter prophetic works, including most of *Trei Asar* (Twelve Prophets) generally have one main theme (Zechariah is a notable exception). Joel's focus is apocalyptic, from his description of the devastating locust plague (or military invasion?) to the Day of Judgement in the Valley of Jehoshaphat. Jonah's book concerns his struggle with God's compassion. Haggai explores the challenge of convincing the people to rebuild the Temple. Obadiah's one prophecy is aimed at Edom, and Nahum's at Assyria.

If we were pressed to identify a single, unifying theme in Amos, it would be the ideal of justice: "Let justice well up as waters and righteousness as a mighty stream" (5:24). We might even argue that Amos's repeated denouncement of the people's engagement in idolatry emphasizes the devastating social consequences that this lifestyle has brought to Samaria.

One of the Bible's central ideas is that all of humanity is ultimately accountable to God. The bar is set significantly higher for Israel, but all people must have basic morality and justice. Moral rot of the social fabric is disastrous for all families on God's earth.

Amos's core mission is to convey this message to Samaria's royalty and aristocracy. God is angry when *any* people mistreat their poor and abuse their power; this is even true of nations who were not fathered by Abraham, taught by Moses, or ruled by David. God's anger is ever greater when the nation riddled with corruption has been miraculously redeemed, brought to the canopy of Sinai, encountered the Divine face-to-face, cared for like a little child through the desert, and led triumphantly to the Promised Land!

This is expressed in Amos's introduction to the next section (3:1–2):

> Hear this word that Hashem has spoken against you, O children of Israel, against the whole family which I brought up out of the land of Egypt, saying: You only have I known of all the families of the earth; therefore I will visit upon you all your iniquities...

It is God's exclusively intimate relationship with Israel that raises the bar and demands a higher caliber of justice from Israel. Hence the divine justice to be meted out against the nations God did not "know" pales next to Israel's looming consequences.

The Oracles Revisited

Whether or not this set was Amos's first prophecy, its placement sets the tone for his career.

Using the "*Ko amar... ashivenu*" pattern, he builds a rhetorical rhythm, binding all neighboring nations into one common indictment. Even though their crimes are not identical, he poetically draws them together, underscoring their ruthlessness and lack of moral compass.

Amos rhetorically creates a geographic box, starting with Aram (northeast), then Philistia (southwest), followed by Tyre (northwest) and then Edom, Ammon and Moab (southeast). The seventh nation is none other than his own, Judah. The inescapable message is the God's judgment will be visited on *any* nation that fails His moral expectations.

Amos's oracle does not actually reach these nations (not even Judah). His target audience is Samaria, and he deftly draws them in by beginning with God's anger at their neighbors and rivals. Intelligent listeners might be apprehensive nonetheless, anticipating that the hammer swinging to their north, south, east, and west is merely gathering momentum before it strikes the center; this is confirmed when Amos finally declares *"Al shelosha pishei Yisrael,"* followed by the most detailed, crushing blow of them all.

* * *

ADDENDUM: ON BIBLICAL POETRY

Structure and Meaning: Introduction

A fundamental feature of biblical poetry is parallelism; i.e., that the composite parts of a line (usually a verse, but not always) "speak" to each other in either synonymous or antonymous ways.

Let us examine, for example, the opening line of Moses's Song (Deut. 32):

Ha'azinu hashamayim va'adabera	*vetishma ha'aretz imrei fi*
Give ear, O heavens, and I will speak	Let the earth hear the words of my mouth

This is straight-up parallelism, where the words are aligned perfectly. "Give ear" is synonymous with "let... hear"; "heavens" stands in relation to "the earth" (more on this below); and "I will speak" is expressed in the nominal form, "the words of my mouth."

As mentioned above, the heaven-earth pair doesn't seem to be a synonymous parallel; indeed, the two are not the same. Nevertheless, in the poetic language of the Bible, the two are often matched; sometimes, this is because they are perceived and depicted as a pair that comprises known creation.[131] In other contexts, we read the heaven-earth pair as a *merismus,* a poetic device whereby the two extremes are invoked as if to include all points in between. Similarly, in Psalms 148:12, "Young men as well as maidens, elders with the young" is a poetic way of referring to everyone, *including* men and women, *from* the old *to* the young. In this case, heaven and earth would be understood as "*from* the heavens *to* the earth" – i.e., all of creation.

---

131. Genesis 1:1, 2:4.

Synonymous parallelism, while enhancing the *beauty* of the text and possibly expanding the imagery of the poem, generally does not per se broaden our *understanding* of the text.

A less common form is antithetical parallelism, wherein the two halves of the verse speak in contrast. For example, Isaiah 65:13:[132]

Hinei avadai yokhelu	*ve'atem tiravu*
Hinei avadai yishtu	*ve'atem titzma'u*
Hinei avadai yismaḥu	*ve'atem tevoshu*
Behold my servants will eat,	yet you will be hungry;
Behold my servants will drink,	yet you will be thirsty;
Behold my servants will rejoice,	yet you will be shamed.

Whereas the stark differences serve to deepen our understanding of God's love for His loyalists, the structure does not, on its own, do anything to give us a deeper understanding of the intent of the text. While the structure makes us *feel* something, it doesn't help us *understand* anything more than its own words.

There are, on the other hand, several uniquely identifiable forms of parallelism, some of which have structural variations that (potentially) inform and enhance meaning. A common form is inverted parallelism (also known as a chiasmus), wherein the words paralleling each other are presented in reverse order. For instance, in the third verse of Moses's Song, we find:

Ki shem Hashem ekra,	*havu godel lelokeinu*
When the name of the Lord I invoke	grant greatness to our God

(The translation is awkward, but I wanted to maintain the syntactical sequence of the original.)

Here, the parallel names for God are at the poles of the verse; the inside positions are taken by the verbs, "I invoke" and "[you] grant." Note that this places the interaction between the speaker and the audience at the core of this verse; God's name, as it were, serves to envelope them.

132. This verse consistently employs the *vav hanigud*, disjunctive *vav*, presented above.

Returning (briefly) to Amos, we have a clear example of a chiasmus (2:11–12):

Va'akim mibeneikhem linvi'im	*umibaḥureikhem linzirim...*
	Vatashku et hanezirim yayin
V'al henevi'im tzivitem leimor – lo tinavu	

I raised up your sons for prophets	and your young men for Nazirites...
	But you gave the Nazirites wine to drink;
And commanded the prophets, saying "Prophesy not!"	

Within the context of these two verses alone, the Providential raising of Nazirites from among the young men and the disgraceful (coerced?) profaning of their sanctified status by the aristocracy of Samaria sit at the core of this couplet. The raising of prophets from among their sons and their vile response ("Prophesy not!") form the bookends of this couplet. Shocking as this behavior might be, it seems to take a backseat to the people's actions toward their own Nazirite sons. Perhaps it is the act of having them take drink, seen as more forceful than merely directing a prophet to cease prophesying, which earns this gift and its spurning center stage.

However, we understand the relative greatness of becoming prophets versus becoming Nazirites – and the criminality of forcing or goading Nazirites to drink wine versus silencing prophets – the internal structure within these two verses is clear.

All of this brings us back to our original question: What is the role of v. 12 within the larger pericope?

Before answering that – and to do so more effectively – we will revisit our discussion of the Janus parallelism (see above, pp. 91–92).

Since Cyrus Gordon's modest but innovative categorization, other scholars have identified examples of Janus parallels, such that it seems to be a valid and particular type of parallelism that deliberately plays off of the equivocal meaning of words to generate multiple parallels. It is, if nothing else, a paragon of verbal efficiency, creating two separate and distinct parallels with only three (instead of four) words. Another delightful example, in Jacob's deathbed blessing of Joseph, is proposed by Rendsburg.[133]

> *Birkot* ***avikha***
> The blessings of your father
> *Gavru al birkot* ***horai ad***
> Have overcome the blessings of my parents (*horai*), to (*ad*)...
> *ta'avat* ***givot*** *olam*
> ...the delight of the eternal hills. (Gen. 49:26)

Rendsburg suggests that the verse be read (against the MT version) as *horai ad*, either "parents" or "eternal mountains." He cites *Rishonim* and other texts that come down on either side of the equation, demonstrating that the pregnant term *horai* (*ad*) is sufficiently equivocal as to serve as an excellent pivot for a Janus parallel. Thus it can be paired with "your father" or "eternal hills."

133. Gary Rendsburg, "Janus Parallelism in Gen. 49:26," *Journal of Biblical Literature* 99, no. 2 (1980): 291–293.

Chapter 3

The Inevitability of Prophecy (3:1–8)

Verses 3:1–8 make up a series of "causal riddles" that argue for the inevitability of prophecy; that passage is, in turn, the apologia-preface to the "Hearken" sequence that follows.[1] The two-verse introduction also serves to affirm Israel's special relationship with God, which sets a higher standard of societal ethics – not to mention theological fidelity. This "raised bar" was the subtext of Amos's first oracle, as discussed in the previous chapter.

The Text (Amos 3:1–8)

(א) שִׁמְעוּ אֶת הַדָּבָר הַזֶּה אֲשֶׁר דִּבֶּר ה׳ עֲלֵיכֶם בְּנֵי יִשְׂרָאֵל עַל כָּל הַמִּשְׁפָּחָה
אֲשֶׁר הֶעֱלֵיתִי מֵאֶרֶץ מִצְרַיִם לֵאמֹר: (ב) רַק אֶתְכֶם יָדַעְתִּי מִכֹּל מִשְׁפְּחוֹת
הָאֲדָמָה עַל כֵּן אֶפְקֹד עֲלֵיכֶם אֵת כָּל עֲוֹנֹתֵיכֶם: (ג) הֲיֵלְכוּ שְׁנַיִם יַחְדָּו בִּלְתִּי
אִם נוֹעָדוּ: (ד) הֲיִשְׁאַג אַרְיֵה בַּיַּעַר וְטֶרֶף אֵין לוֹ הֲיִתֵּן כְּפִיר קוֹלוֹ מִמְּעֹנָתוֹ
בִּלְתִּי אִם לָכָד: (ה) הֲתִפֹּל צִפּוֹר עַל פַּח הָאָרֶץ וּמוֹקֵשׁ אֵין לָהּ הֲיַעֲלֶה פַּח

1. See chapter 5.

מִן הָאֲדָמָה וְלָכוֹד לֹא יִלְכּוֹד: (ו) אִם יִתָּקַע שׁוֹפָר בְּעִיר וְעָם לֹא יֶחֱרָדוּ אִם
תִּהְיֶה רָעָה בְּעִיר וַה' לֹא עָשָׂה: (ז) כִּי לֹא יַעֲשֶׂה אֲדֹנָי ה' דָּבָר כִּי אִם גָּלָה סוֹדוֹ
אֶל עֲבָדָיו הַנְּבִיאִים: (ח) אַרְיֵה שָׁאָג מִי לֹא יִירָא אֲדֹנָי ה׳ דִּבֶּר מִי לֹא יִנָּבֵא:

1 Hear this word that the Lord has spoken to you, O children of
Israel, regarding the whole family that I brought up out of the
land of Egypt, saying: 2 You only have I known of all the families of the earth; therefore I will visit upon you all your iniquities.
3 Will two walk together, unless they have agreed? 4 Will a lion
roar in the forest, if he has no prey? Will a young lion raise his
voice from his den, if he hasn't taken anything? 5 Will a bird fall in
a snare upon the earth, where there is no lure for it? Will a snare
spring up from the ground, and have taken nothing at all? 6 Shall
the shofar be blown in a city, and the people not tremble? Shall
evil befall a city, and the Lord has not done it? 7 For the Lord
God will do nothing, if He has not revealed His counsel to His
servants the prophets. 8 The lion has roared, who will not fear?
The Lord God has spoken, who can but prophesy?[2]

These verses are followed by two sets of prophecies, each beginning with the same *leitwort* – *shimu* ("hear" or "hearken") – as our opening verse. *Shimu* is used in the earlier biblical books (Torah and the Early Prophets) in two nearly antithetical contexts. On one hand, figures of authority and high power employ it to express a threat to their subjects;[3] conversely, individuals use it to preface their pleas.[4]

---

2. Paul suggests that vv. 3–8 follow vv. 1–2, as the latter describe the divine selection of Israel, and the former the selection and appointment of the prophet. A careful look at the text indicates that the first two verses are not operating on the same plane as the next six; the first two verses speak of a history between God and His people that has raised them to an august position, which carries greater responsibility and moral accountability. What I call "the inevitability of prophecy" speaks to the nature of things – that just as anything that happens in the natural world has its cause, similarly, when grander events take place, God is the power behind them; and He always notifies His prophets of this.
3. Numbers 12:6, 16:8; II Kings 18:28.
4. Genesis 37:6; Judges 9:7; I Samuel 22:7; II Samuel 20:16.

Moses does not use the *shimu* introduction when presenting law or prophecy, while speaking to Korah's group or the "rebels" at Kadesh (Num. 20:10). Neither Samuel nor Elijah rebuke the people with this word; Elisha only uses it once, when foretelling of Samaria's miraculous salvation from siege and famine (II Kings 7:1).

All this changes with the advent of literary prophecy. Amos and his contemporaries (Hosea, Isaiah, and Micah) use the phrase with a singular purpose: neither royal fiat nor plea, *shimu* always functions as a preface to the prophetic word.[5] In a sense, this prophetic formula combines *both* royal edict and plea, for the prophet transmits God's word, yet finds himself pleading with his audience to listen to it.

After Amos concludes his "oracles against the nations," which culminate in Samaria's military downfall, he turns to his audience with *shimu*, broadcasting the voice of authority yet fearfully pleading for their attention.

This second section of Amos's prophecies may be dubbed the "hearken" (or *shimu*) section: the repetition of this word helps define his stance vis-à-vis his audience and the tone of these prophecies.

To You

Whereas a conventional translation of the word *aleikhem* would be rendered "against you" or "about you," we may have to be more flexible in our reading here. The prepositions *al* (with an *ayin*) and *el* (with an *alef*), which usually means "to" or "toward," are used somewhat interchangeably in the Tanakh.[6] Consequently, we have adopted the reading: "Hear this word that the Lord has spoken *to* you…"

One might ask why the text does not use *eileikhem*? Although we've already seen the versatility of these two prepositions, the use of *aleikhem* gives his message an additional layer of meaning: he also implies that this declaration is directed "against you." God spoke *about* you, selecting you from all the families of the earth; at the same time, these selfsame words operate *against* you, as they attest to the special

5. It appears seventeen times in Isaiah, six times in Micah, twice in Hosea, and in five instances in Amos.
6. I Samuel 2:11; II Kings 24:12; Jeremiah 23:35, and, perhaps, Numbers 20:8.

relationship you have been granted with God – which comes with a stricter measure of justice, as the prophet lays out in the next verse.

Regarding the Whole Family

The term *mishpaḥa* ("family"),[7] which is used over 170 times in Tanakh, nearly always connotes a clan, such as the subdivisions of the tribes[8] or even an entire tribe; occasionally, in rare poetic flourishes,[9] the word refers to specific clans or sub-clans.[10] I will refer back to this later.

1: That I brought up out of the land of Egypt

The mention of the Exodus in 3:1 is not only surprising, it is also (and this may be a bigger surprise to us) relatively rare in the rhetoric of this first generation of literary prophets. As mentioned, Amos alone among the literary prophets refers to the Exodus theme as an explicit historic event that carries implications for the present nation and their moral standing before God.[11]

Here, Amos references the Exodus as an expression of God's special relationship with His people – a relationship that exacts higher, unique moral standards the nation has miserably failed to meet.

2: You only have I known

The verb "*yadoa*'" ("know") in Tanakh sometimes refers to awareness,[12] but may also express intimacy; the most famous example of this sense

7. Koehler-Baumgartner, 1620–1621, mentions a tentative association of *shifeḥa* (maidservant) with *mishpaḥa*, based on the Ugaritic and Punic *sh-ph-h*.
8. Deuteronomy 29:17; Joshua 7:16–17.
9. For example, Psalms 96:7, 22:28; in Genesis (exclusively) the word is used to connote an entire nation. Curiously, the first appearance of the word in the Bible (Gen. 8:19) refers to animals.
10. One curious adaptation of the word is found in Jeremiah 15:3, where he refers to four types of divine judgment as *mishpaḥot*.
11. See above, commentary on 2:10, and in his eschaton at 9:7.
12. For example, Genesis 19:33.

is to have[13] (typically consensual) sexual relations.[14] Such "knowing" implies an exclusive merging, which not only binds two together but also inherently excludes all others. Buber, in his *Darko Shel Mikra*, suggests that the essential meaning of the word in biblical Hebrew is not "to know," as in cogitation; rather, it means "contact":

> In the language of the Bible ... it refers to the contact between him (the "knower") and the object which is "known"... however, this notion of the contact of the "knower" is elevated to a unique and sublime level without parallel when referring to the relationship between God and His creatures: with His prophets, whom He intends to dispatch (Ex. 33:12, Jer. 1:5); to Israel, when preparing them for His mission (Amos 3:2, Hos. 13:5); or to "regular" people who are wholehearted and trusting, who take their refuge in Him (Nahum 1:7, Ps. 31:8, 37:8).[15]

The Exodus was the great act that generated that special relationship between God and His people. The first statement of the Decalogue states as much: "I am the Lord your God who took you out of the land of Egypt, from the house of slavery." As Rashi notes,[16] the import of the declaration is that God is "your God" because of the Exodus – it is His claim on the people: "They are My slaves" (Lev. 25:55).

Israel's connection with the Divine imbues them with greater spiritual potential, but failure to fulfill this potential is punished.

Back to the *Mishpaḥa*

Amos's second mention of *mishpaḥa* is used in the sense of "nation" for the first time since Genesis. More significantly, he makes nearly explicit reference to the covenant with Abraham, who was charged to be the source of blessing for "all families of the earth." The phrase *mishpeḥot*

---

13. Usually consensually, but see Judges 19:25.
14. Beginning with Genesis 4:1.
15. Buber, *Darko Shel Mikra*, 142.
16. Ad loc.; see also Ibn Ezra's "Long" Commentary on Exodus at 20:2, and his response to R. Yehuda Halevi's question.

ha'adama appears only three times in the canon. Two of them are in the patriarchal narratives,[17] and the final mention is ours. Why does Amos, of all prophets, allusively bring us back to Abraham with the use of *mishpaḥa*?

A careful look at Abraham's career reflects someone with a strong sense of loyalty to his family[18] – both new and old. This includes his nephew/adopted son Lot, his ultimately exiled son Ishmael, and his treaty partners, Aner, Eshkol, and Mamre.[19] Abraham will be a blessing to all of the "families" of the earth because he demonstrates the proper way that family ought to operate – fierce protection of family members and steadfast refusal to "give up" on them. His ethical majesty is informed by his commitment to kin. He is deeply committed to Sarah, in spite of her barrenness; he only agrees to take a concubine to fulfill the divine mandate of bearing a great nation after Sarah asks him to.[20] He continues to watch over Lot even after they part ways;[21] he insists on Isaac marrying within the family.[22]

Perhaps this is why Amos, of all prophets, uses *mishpaḥa* to describe the nation. The nation that came out together from Egypt, forged as one in the crucible of slavery, should hold the welfare of each member of the nation as a core priority. When we read about the abuse of power, the gouging of the poor and trampling of the downtrodden, we see that the *mishpaḥa* has forgotten not only their mission, but also their common history and essential responsibility toward each other.

First Structural Consideration – The Sequence

The argument for the inevitability of prophecy serves two functions in Amos's speech. First, it *explains* why he must repeat God's prophecies and that there is no escaping them. Second, it operates as a type of *apologia* before he utters such harsh imprecations.

17. Genesis 12:3, 28:14.
18. Abraham's intense devotion to monotheism is far less prominent in the text, although it is front and center in midrashic literature.
19. Genesis 14:24.
20. Ibid. 16:1–4.
21. Ibid. 14:13–16; 18:23–33.
22. Ibid. 24:1–9.

His argument is presented as a series of rhetorical questions. In order to decipher the structure of this passage – which holds the key to understanding his message – we need to consider the dichotomy between the eternal opportunity of *reading* prophecy and the one-time event of *hearing* prophecy, experienced only by the immediate audience.[23]

From the perspective of an oral presentation, the structure of these riddles follows a variation on the numerical scheme Amos used before – seven plus one.

The Oral Presentation: Amos's Septad Plus One Model

1. Will two walk together, unless they have agreed?
2. Will a lion roar in the forest, if he has no prey?
3. Will a young lion give forth his voice out of his den, if he hasn't taken anything?
4. Will a bird fall in a snare upon the earth, where there is no lure for it?
5. Will a snare spring up from the ground, and have taken nothing at all?
6. Shall the shofar be blown in a city, and the people not tremble?
7. Shall evil befall a city, and Hashem has not done it?
   For the Lord God will do nothing, if he has not revealed His counsel to His servants the prophets.
8. The lion has roared, who will not fear?
   The Lord God has spoken, who can but prophesy?

His opening oracles present seven prophecies against the other nations and then hit home with the ultimate eighth; here, too, he follows a similar structure. Seven riddles echo the causal relationship between known events, while the line beginning "For the Lord God will do nothing…" is a continued explanation of God's role in human affairs. The crescendo eighth is of a different tone, where the question is not the *cause* but the

23. See Introduction, p. xxiii.

inevitable *effect*; the final line: "the Lord God has spoken…" echoes the eighth line and brings the message home.

Note that both of the "non-enumerated" lines begin the same way and are the only explicit mentions of God in the passage.[24]

Experiencing the prophecy as a *written record* reveals a different scheme:

The Written Presentation: Ten Steps from Collegiality to Dominion

1. Will two walk together, unless they have agreed?
2. Will a lion roar in the forest, if he has no prey?
3. Will a young lion give forth his voice out of his den, if he hasn't taken anything?
4. Will a bird fall in a snare upon the earth, where there is no lure for it?
5. Will a snare spring up from the ground, and have taken nothing at all?
6. Shall the shofar be blown in a city, and the people not tremble?
7. Shall evil befall a city, and Hashem has not done it?
8. For the Lord God will do nothing, if he has not revealed His counsel to His servants the prophets.
9. The lion has roared, who will not fear?
10. The Lord God has spoken, who can but prophesy?

This sequence functions differently as a written record rather than an oration, forming a perfect whole, as I will demonstrate.

24. One might tenuously suggest that these lines were a well-known refrain, and that the audience was expected to respond in kind. The prophet would say, "The lion has roared, who will not fear?" and the people would respond, "The Lord, God, has spoken, who can but prophesy?"

The Riddles

3: Will two walk together, unless they have agreed?

Who are these "two"? Friends, colleagues, parent and child, master and servant? The reader's initial assumption is that they are equals: unlike the following riddles, there is no subject/object relationship. It is a fully "I-Thou" partnership here. Yet Amos's audience – and we, his later readers – might recognize this evocative phrase from an archetypal narrative: this phrase twice appears in the story of Isaac's Binding (Gen. 22:6, 8). Not only are the two of unequal status, but also one is (in the eyes of reader) marked for life, and the other for death.

Nonetheless, note that unlike the rest of the sequence, this first pair walks together with "agreement" – with mutual consent. This is certainly not the case with the bird and its trap, nor the lion and its prey.

The verb used for "agreement" is also laden with meaning. *No'adu*, meaning "set an appointment," evokes the Tabernacle, the *Ohel Mo'ed*: that set place, those set times (*Mo'adei Hashem*) of the human's encounter with the Divine. Perhaps the two walking together are prophet and God – who "meet" and commune. This is in dialogue with the last of the ten riddles and brings the reader full circle – perhaps the first riddle is not about people, but about Man and God.

4a: Will a lion roar in the forest, if he has no prey?

4b: Will a young lion raise his voice from his den, if he hasn't taken anything?

This couplet – two separate lines that seem to be the same riddle – moves away from the mutuality of the first line to the subject-object causal relationship. The two lines form a parallelism:[25] lion::young lion; roar::raise voice; forest::den; no prey::if he hasn't taken anything.

Although this couplet is removed contextually and stylistically from the first line, the prophet deftly connects them through the common

25. See the addendum to chapter 2: "On Biblical Poetry."

word *bilti* (each of the negations literally means "without"): as if the prey "agrees" to be hunted as the partner "agrees" to meet his friend.

From the neutral image of two people meeting, the rhetoric shifts sharply to a violent setting of death and prey. Yet both images – consensual journey and non-consensual hunt – share the feature that at least one of each pair made a decision to act.

The image of a lion roaring harks back to Amos's anthem (1:2), which contains the same parallelism of *yishag* and *yiten kolo*. God is speaking: Will the audience be willing participants, as Isaac was when climbing the mountain? Or will they be merely prey, caught in the divine trap?

5a: Will a bird fall in a snare upon the earth,
where there is no lure for it?

5b: Will a snare spring up from the ground,
and have taken nothing at all?

These next lines shift focus again – from the predator's perspective to that of the prey. The ornithological motif is not incidental: birds sometimes represent Israel in prophetic and poetic literature.[26]

If the use of the lion in the previous couplet is intended to remind the audience of the "roaring lion" of Amos's anthem, then the evocation of the trapped bird may complete the picture. God roars (through His prophets? through His punishments?) and the bird (Israel) is subsequently trapped without hope of escape.

As before, these two lines form a parallelism. Yet by now, the causal relationships in each pair seem to be getting weaker. Two people walking together presumably arranged to meet, but lions roar even without prey, birds sometimes fall into a trap without bait, and traps sometimes spring shut by mistake.

26. Isaiah 31:8; Lamentations 3:52; Psalms 124:6–8.

6a: Shall the shofar be blown in a city, and the people not tremble?

In this sixth segment of the series, the prophet apparently reverses syntax. He first presents the cause (the sounding of the shofar) and follows it with the effect (people trembling). What is the rhetorical strategy operating here?

It may be that he is *not* switching the pattern. The shofar may be sounded as the effect of an unstated cause – and the subsequent effect of the sound (and what it represents) causes the people to tremble. This is another example of Amos's rhetorical flair. By omitting the reason why the shofar is sounded, the town's imminent doom is a mystery, which generates terror and suspense – the unknown is far more frightening than the known.[27] The sound of the shofar portends disaster, and the people tremble for what it represents.

This thus forms a smooth transition with the next line, and the two may also be read as a parallelism:

6b: Shall evil befall a city, and the Lord has not done it?

In response to the nameless evil about to befall this paradigmatic city, the shofar has been sounded. This evil, of course, is God's doing, and that is why the people are trembling.

Once again, the parallels are clear:

Im yitaka shofar be'ir	*Im tihyeh ra'a be'ir*
Shall the shofar be blown in a city	Shall evil befall a city

Both lines begin with the conditional "*im*" followed by a passive participle – *yitaka; tihyeh*. The shofar is parallel to *ra'ah* – evil. This seems like an odd pairing, but once we consider that the shofar is a response to the "evil," it fits well. Each hemistich ends with *be'ir*, forming a perfect

27. As authors like Shirley Jackson and directors like Alfred Hitchcock well understood, the subconscious can create horrors far worse than can be described or shown on film. The creaking door that never fully opens is far more threatening than the door that swings wide to show a gory scene. The imagination can summon much worse scenes than the printed page or the screen.

match in the first halves. The second halves, however, form a parallel of contrast (*"tikbolet nigudit"*) – the people who quake in fear are contrasted with God who has chosen to bring this (unnamed) disaster to the city. When people hear the shofar, they obviously tremble; when evil comes about, it obviously came from God.

This concludes the heptad. To the listener, most likely, this is a non-threatening treatise on relationships of various degrees of cause and effect.

7: For the Lord God will do nothing, if He has not revealed His counsel to His servants the prophets.

Unlike the first seven, this line is a statement rather than a rhetorical question.

Moreover, moving away from the rhetorical shift, the earlier statements/riddles are all demonstrable and, while arguable (it is *possible* for a trap to be sprung without prey having been caught), are inherent in the relationship between the subject and object. A predator yells in triumph when it catches prey; a bird is lured by bait; a trap springs up when something falls in. Even the providential premise that if evil occurs it is God's doing is presumably shared by both prophet and audience.

This statement, however, is neither obvious nor assumed. Is it at all axiomatic that God will only act if He has first revealed His plans to the prophets? Does this mean that prophets are bound to broadcast these plans in advance? If not, then what advantage would this statement have?

This complex declaration comprises several components.

First, God speaks to His prophets. This is, contextually, a safe assumption to make and thus a valid point of argument.

Second, God reveals His plans to the prophets: when God is prepared to act in this world, He first notifies His servants. This is a further assumption that does not follow from the first: although God communicates with prophets, this does not imply that the content is necessarily predictive.

These two assumptions sit at the heart of the prophetic mission, and the latter is the prophet's *raison d'être.* As such, there is nothing remarkable here; we might even ask what the purpose of this self-referential claim might be. We are left with one answer – it is the final implication to which all of this leads – and that is where our difficulties begin.

The most radical implication of the statement is that God will *not* act in this world *unless* He has first informed His prophets and, we further assume (as above), they fulfill their task to declaim the message to the public. This is surprising and theologically troubling on two counts. First of all, are God's hands really tied thus? If so, doesn't this effectively put the prophet in charge of God's actions in the world – if the prophet does not deliver the message, is God held back from executing it?

Second, this statement implies that with the cessation of prophecy, God ceases to act in the world – a problematic assertion that attacks some basic tenets of religion.

We might overcome the second implication by proposing that this divine "rule" only applied when prophecy was an active and regular phenomenon in society. If people were used to hearing such warnings and were familiar with the rhythms of living in a society modified and defined by prophecy, then it would be "only fair" to withhold punishment until the people have been made aware of the dire consequences of their behavior and what awaits them unless they correct their course.

The first surprising implication, however, is far more problematic. If the text is to be understood in a literal sense, then God has "tied His own hands" and kept Himself from acting in any significant way in the world before his prophets have been notified and have broadcast His intentions. We might soften the statement by positing that this only refers to divine punishment on a grand scale. God will certainly continue to bless or punish individuals or groups according to their actions.[28]

Yet when we step back and consider the biblical history of God's interactions with His people, we see this principle borne out with consistency. Since Noah's time, "major" divine punishments are meted out only after God has notified *someone* about the impending calamity. Moreover, since Moses's time, this became the most vital role of the *navi*: to warn the people that God finds their behavior unacceptable, and that a specific, catastrophic consequence "crouches at the door."

28. For example, II Samuel 6:11; I Chronicles 13:14; Amos 4:7.

Thus this statement, which initially seems theologically outrageous, is nonetheless substantiated, and we can now explore its place as the conclusion of these seven riddles.

We pointed out that though these questions are phrased rhetorically, the causal relationship of each riddle is not necessarily inevitable: two people may meet by chance and choose to walk together; a lion may roar for reasons other than having captured prey; a trap sometimes snaps shut without having secured a victim. Nonetheless, probability prevails: if we lived in an environment of bird traps and lion's lairs, we would probably learn to expect the results presented here. These are not *necessary* effects and therefore not *inevitable* causes; they are, rather, anticipated effects and, therefore, *reasonable* causes.

One final note on this verse. Amos asserts that God will not act without first informing "His servants, the prophets." Why use the honorific "servants"? Perhaps this phrase serves to emphasize that the prophet always does what his Master directs him to do. God's agents do not seek to manipulate the course of events; they are purely servants that channel His will. Against all sociological barriers and challenges, prophets – by definition – fulfill their prophetic missions.[29] Similarly, based on Israel's history, God will not punish His people without a prophetic warning: "For the Lord God will do nothing if he has not revealed his counsel to His servants the prophets."

One final verse precedes the next section: "The lion has roared, who will not fear? The Lord God has spoken, who can but prophesy?"

The Coda: The Rhetorical Riddles Become the Message

Until now, Amos has drawn in his audience with an engaging academic exercise. His riddles may hint to ominous messages – lions catch their prey and birds are ensnared by traps – but this introduction is more inviting than threatening. We might even imagine a dialogue, with the audience responding to his questions or completing his statements (if these were familiar riddles).

29. This, of course, brings us to the case of Jonah, which we might argue is an exploration of whether a prophet is in fact capable of refusing their mission – and the book's famous conclusion is that they cannot do so.

Even the last line can be read in this light. God's word to His prophets does not yet pose a direct threat; it is, rather, part of the sequence of cause and effect.

Amos uses the lion motif skillfully here. Is this the lion he just mentioned, or the lion of his anthem? Does this lion roar because it has just caught its prey (which, perhaps, would generate relief – they are safe for the meantime), or is this the beast whose roar withers the pastures and scorches the peak of the Carmel?

This lion, it seems, is Amos's "anthemic lion." Amos coyly mentions a lion we need not fear – and then circles back to the divine roar that animates his prophecies of doom.

God roars from Zion and gives forth voice from Jerusalem – all who hear Him are wise to fear and tremble! The lion's roar is God's voice, roaring through the words of the prophet. If so, how do we understand the second half of the verse – "the Lord God has spoken, who can but prophesy?" Is it a clarifying parallelism (*tikbolet meva'eret*),[30] where the second half of the verse explicates the first half? The "lion" in the first half is really God's voice, but this does not comport with the rest of the parallel:

Aryeh	← →	*Hashem Elokim*
sha'ag	← →	*dibber*
mi lo	← →	*mi lo*
yira?	← →	*yinavei?*

or

The lion	← →	The Lord God
has roared	← →	has spoken
who can but	← →	who can but
fear?	← →	prophesy?

30. This is not to be confused with *tikbolet mashlima* (synthetic parallelism), in which the second stich clarifies or completes the first; in this case, the second stich *reveals* what the first stich means.

The fear, which is the reaction in 8a, is not parallel to prophesying in 8b. If the lion's roar is God's voice, why are there two distinct and irreconcilable reactions to it?

The sequence of this verse is rather unusual: the parallelism represents two elements that are clearly linked and, in some sense, one and the same. God's voice is the lion's roar but the reactions vary, depending on reference point. God's words induce fear in the people and stir the prophet to prophesy. Of course, it is his prophecy that finally brings the divine roar to the people, so that the causal relationship here is complex and multi-staged:

The lion roars → the prophet must speak → the people must tremble.

Bringing It All Together

At this point, the curious audience, intrigued by the prophet's riddles, is once again stunned when these theoretical, detached examples of cause and effect hit home. God's voice is about to ring out, moving prophets to speak and their audiences to tremble.

While we questioned whether these oracles are presented in their chronological order, this is hardly relevant from a literary perspective: in its final form, the first two chapters of Amos lead beautifully and smoothly to this next step. After beginning with seven oracles about the surrounding nations before attacking Israel with an eighth, Amos's audience (both contemporary and eternal) have learned to brace themselves for a stinging blow after seemingly unthreatening rhetoric. His next words, we realize, will echo the lion's roar from Zion, spoken through the prophet who has no choice but to deliver these words.

Chapter 4

Warnings Issued (3:9–4:5)

THE FIRST WARNING: *HASHMIU… SHIMU* – PROCLAIM… HEARKEN

The Text (Amos 3:9–15)

(ט) הַשְׁמִיעוּ עַל אַרְמְנוֹת בְּאַשְׁדּוֹד וְעַל אַרְמְנוֹת בְּאֶרֶץ מִצְרָיִם וְאִמְרוּ הֵאָסְפוּ
עַל הָרֵי שֹׁמְרוֹן וּרְאוּ מְהוּמֹת רַבּוֹת בְּתוֹכָהּ וַעֲשׁוּקִים בְּקִרְבָּהּ: (י) וְלֹא יָדְעוּ
עֲשׂוֹת נְכֹחָה נְאֻם ה׳ הָאוֹצְרִים חָמָס וָשֹׁד בְּאַרְמְנוֹתֵיהֶם: פ (יא) לָכֵן כֹּה אָמַר
אֲדֹנָי ה׳ צַר וּסְבִיב הָאָרֶץ וְהוֹרִד מִמֵּךְ עֻזֵּךְ וְנָבֹזּוּ אַרְמְנוֹתָיִךְ: (יב) כֹּה אָמַר ה׳
כַּאֲשֶׁר יַצִּיל הָרֹעֶה מִפִּי הָאֲרִי שְׁתֵּי כְרָעַיִם אוֹ בְדַל אֹזֶן כֵּן יִנָּצְלוּ בְּנֵי יִשְׂרָאֵל
הַיֹּשְׁבִים בְּשֹׁמְרוֹן בִּפְאַת מִטָּה וּבִדְמֶשֶׁק עָרֶשׂ: (יג) שִׁמְעוּ וְהָעִידוּ בְּבֵית יַעֲקֹב
נְאֻם אֲדֹנָי ה׳ אֱלֹהֵי הַצְּבָאוֹת: (יד) כִּי בְּיוֹם פָּקְדִי פִשְׁעֵי יִשְׂרָאֵל עָלָיו וּפָקַדְתִּי
עַל מִזְבְּחוֹת בֵּית אֵל וְנִגְדְּעוּ קַרְנוֹת הַמִּזְבֵּחַ וְנָפְלוּ לָאָרֶץ: (טו) וְהִכֵּיתִי בֵית
הַחֹרֶף עַל בֵּית הַקָּיִץ וְאָבְדוּ בָּתֵּי הַשֵּׁן וְסָפוּ בָּתִּים רַבִּים נְאֻם ה׳:

9 Proclaim (*Hashmiu*) it upon the palaces in Ashdod, and upon the palaces in the land of Egypt, and say: Assemble yourselves upon the mountains of Samaria, and behold the great confusions therein, and the oppressions in the midst thereof. 10 For they know not to do right, says the Lord, [they] who store up

violence and robbery in their palaces. **11** Therefore, thus says the Lord *Hashem*: An adversary, even round about the land! And he shall take down your strength from you, and your palaces shall be despoiled. **12** Thus says the Lord: As the shepherd rescues out of the mouth of the lion two legs, or a piece of an ear, so shall the children of Israel that dwell in Samaria escape with the corner of a couch, and the leg of a bed. **13** Hearken (*shimu*), and testify against the house of Jacob, says the Lord God, the God of Hosts. **14** For in the day that I shall visit the transgressions of Israel upon him, I will also punish the altars of Beit El, and the horns of the altar shall be cut off and fall to the ground. **15** And I will smite the winter house with the summer house; and the houses of ivory shall perish, and the great houses shall have an end, says the Lord.

The Indictment (Verses 9–10)

Verses 9–10 present Samaria's indictment; the rest of the chapter describes their impending punishment.

Parallelism

To maintain the meter, the word *hashmiu* is omitted from the second hemistich, but is assumed,[1] so that the verse can be read thus:

> Proclaim it upon the palaces in Ashdod
> and [proclaim it] upon the palaces in the land of Egypt

The first half of the verse presents an unlikely pairing: Ashdod (one of the chief Philistine cities) and Egypt. Throughout the Bible, Egypt is nearly always presented as the great foreign power to the south, and in such parallelisms, is usually matched with a superpower in Mesopotamia – Assyria or Babylonia.[2] This is such a common parallel that the Septuagint renders our text as: "Proclaim it upon the palaces of *Assyria* and upon the palaces of the land of Egypt." This is most likely erroneous,

1. This phenomenon is known as "forward gapping" (see Glossary of Academic Terms, p. xv).
2. For example, Isaiah 19:23–25, 27:13.

however: Assyria was not a superpower in Amos's time. Moreover, following the text-criticism principle of *lectio difficilior potior* (Latin – "the more difficult reading is the stronger"), when manuscripts conflict, we usually prefer the *less likely* reading.[3] Thus, Ashdod, the MT version, is more likely.[4]

Amos summons the princes of the southern kingdoms – Philistia and Egypt – to testify about Samaria's sins. Presumably this is not an earnest invitation, but rather a rhetorical device expressing the extent of Samaria's corruption. Not only is it unlikely that these kingdoms would respond to such an invitation, but it also stands to reason that Amos is not really interested in Israel's enemies witnessing Samaria's social and moral decay, since his true goal is to effect their repentance and salvation.

Amos's speech is punctuated with rhetorical flairs, for example, *Ve'imru,* "And say." To whom are these words addressed? Who should "say"? Is Amos challenging his audience to call their enemies to witness their corruption? Once again, Amos does not expect (nor likely wish) his Samarian audience to summon their enemies; rather, his ironic language forces them to confront their own failings.

Amos cajoles his audience to invite their enemies to assemble on the mountains *surrounding* Samaria, to gather around the city from this vantage point.[5]

The second half of verse 9 presents a synthetic parallelism, in which the second phrase completes the parallelism by explaining the first phrase. We understand that the nations are being "summoned" to the mountains around Samaria to witness what is happening there: the *mehuma,* "confusion," in the city, which is the result of the upper class's oppression of the lower classes. The word *mehuma* appears several times

3. Based on the following reasoning: Why would a scribe deliberately or inadvertently change an expected reading to an unusual one?
4. See the end of this discussion, p. 132, for another argument in favor of reading "Ashdod."
5. See Isaiah 31:4. The Septuagint reads "mountain (instead of "mountains") of Samaria," likely influenced by the later occurrence of *har Shomeron* (4:1; 6:1). Note that beside Jerimiah 31:5 and the mountain's original naming by Omri in I Kings 16:24, Amos is the only book that uses the term "mountain(s) of Samaria."

in Tanakh, always in the context of military defeat.[6] A *mehuma* is an unspecified confusion, which is usually then explicated in the text: "see the great confusion therein / [see] the oppressions in her midst" – hence, a "synthetic parallelism."[7]

This brings us to the first critical point of information in this oracle. We have heard about the inevitability of prophecy; the prophet has urged the Samarian elite to invite their neighbors to testify against them; now we see where this is all leading. Once again, Amos is pointing to the oppression of the poor in Israelite society.

The word *ashukim* refers to the various aspects of this oppression. Though its form suggests it is a passive verbal form, "those who are oppressed," it seems clear from Ecclesiastes 4:1 that it means "acts of oppression." Based on its appearances in Leviticus, *ashak* seems to be either ill-gotten gains or money owed.[8] Most commentators read this prohibition as withholding wages.[9] This is consistent with Amos's first portrait of a society that abuses the poor and whose justice system fails to provide relief for the disadvantaged; rather, this system is abused and manipulated for the benefit of those in power.

Verse 10 completes the city's indictment. Its opening clause simultaneously defends and further incriminates the people. If they no longer know how to behave justly, are they truly culpable? On the other hand, this implies even greater guilt: they have slipped to a level of depravity beyond mere crime. How is the audience intended to hear this line? One attuned to the moral message may hear the deeper crime; one hoping for relief from the prophet will likely latch on to the "lenient" reading.

The invocation of God's name mid-verse seems to signal the end of one rhetorical section, or even a pause, giving the people a chance to reflect on Amos's words; it may also serve to build up some expectation (terror?) about what is to come.

---

6. For example, Deuteronomy 7:23; I Samuel 5:9, 14:20.
7. The Hebrew term for this is *tikbolet mashlima* – lit. "complementing parallelism" (see Glossary of Academic Terms, p. xv).
8. Leviticus 5:20–26, 19:13.
9. See Shadal's proposal for the meaning of the root in Leviticus 19:13.

Ḥamas in the final clause retains its usual biblical meaning: the resultant illicit or immoral gains from violence;[10] this is supported by the parallel *shod*, "plunder." Note that the words *shod* and *otzerim* generate alliteration with the names Ashdod and Mitzrayim (Egypt) – this, too, supports the MT version, as opposed to the Septuagint's "Assyria" (noted above).

The Punishment (Verses 11–12)

The people's crime is followed by their punishment, which is described in two halves: vv. 11–12 and then vv. 13–15. Verse 13 begins with the introductory *shimu* and describes the punishment in a different context; I will discuss these sections separately.

The word *lakhen* frequently marks the transition from accusation to consequence in prophetic literature.[11] Here, anomalously, the messenger formula *ko amar* is used mid-speech; even though Amos has already begun pronouncing "sentence" on Samaria, he underscores the punishment that he is about to describe by using a formal introduction (it is used again in 12a – see further below), followed by the fuller Divine Name, *A-D-N-Y Elokim* (as above, 1:8). It may be significant that of Amos's eight oracles against the nations, three conclude with the formula *"amar Hashem,"* but the only one that concludes with *"amar A-D-N-Y Elokim"* is Philistia (Ashdod), one of the two nations "invited" to witness Samaria's sins.

An unnamed enemy (*tzar*) will mete out God's punishment against Samaria; its anonymity may serve to frighten the audience further – from where will the attack come? Alternatively, it may be that Amos is also unaware of its identity (perhaps the enemy will be a resurgent Assyria, who is currently dealing with internal turmoil and rebuilding their empire).

Just as *otzerim* and *shod* in v. 10 allude to *Mitzrayim* and *Ashdod*, the word *tzar* (instead of the expected *oyev*) may allude to *Tzor* (Tyre), the Phoenician capital and the third neighbor in Amos's opening series

10. Unlike its first appearance in Genesis 6, where it refers to the violent method for gaining another's property.
11. Including Amos 4:12; 5:11, 15, 16; 6:7; 7:17.

of oracles. Note that the first three nations listed are Aram (Damascus), Philistia (Ashdod), and Phoenicia (Tyre). All three are alluded to in our section,[12] further supporting the sequence of the text and the notion that both sets of oracles were delivered to the same audience.

The word *usviv* is problematic: after the introduction of the enemy (*tzar*), we would expect a predicate.[13] The classic commentators read it as if there were a missing word – *yaḥaneh*, i.e., the enemy will come and (encamp) around Samaria.[14] Ibn Ezra, perhaps bothered by the odd *usviv*, reads *tzar* not as an enemy (or, not exclusively as an enemy), but rather as the verb "to besiege," and understands that *usviv* modifies that verb: they will set up a siege all around the city.

Hakham suggests that the *vav* before *usviv* establishes a new clause,[15] which makes *tzar* an independent statement: "the enemy will come," and then *usviv* modifies where they will be – all around the land. He further notes that the use of *ha'aretz* means that the enemy will not limit their encampment to Samaria, but rather will encircle the entire land. The latter theory is not convincing, as *ha'aretz* can be a reference to one city;[16] moreover, v. 9 describes how enemies are invited to witness the evils of the city from *harei Samaria* – from the hills surrounding Samaria. Here, *aretz* likely means the area surrounding Samaria, not the entire northern kingdom.

The *etnaḥta* (Masoretic punctuation mark indicating the verse's logical midpoint) rests under *ha'aretz*; the verse seems to mean that the enemy will come and surround the land, and the verse's second half describes what the enemy will do there.

I would like to suggest that both opening words *tzar* and *seviv* (or *tzar usviv*) should be read as imperatives: that God calls on these nations to besiege (per Ibn Ezra) and surround the city. This is more consistent with the previous verses: God Himself summons Israel's enemies as

12. With regard to Damascus, see our discussion of the word *demeshek/demesek* in v. 12 below.
13. For this reason, text critics suggest emendations of the phrase; for instance, Paul proposes *sovev*.
14. Rashi, R. Joseph Kara, Radak.
15. Hakham, 23.
16. For example, Joshua 2:1.

witnesses and executioners, as described in Deuteronomy: "The hands of the witnesses shall be upon [the guilty one] first..." (17:7).

The Breach of Samaria (Verse 11b)

The second part of v. 11 also comprises a synthetic parallelism:

Vehorid mimekh uzekh	*venavozu armenotayikh*
He (they) will take down from you	they will be despoiled
your strength	your palaces/ fortresses

The second half of the parallel, unlike the first, uses the passive voice (*venavozu*), likely for purposes of variation. Note that the final word is *armenotayikh*, which serves not only as a *leitwort,*[17] but also as a *leitmotif* in this entire speech.

In the first half, the enemy will "take down from you your strength." The word *oz* has two common meanings in biblical poetry: "strength,"[18] and when juxtaposed with *kavod* or *hadar,*[19] "honor" or "glory." In this context, without any modifying juxtaposition, we will read "*oz*" as "strength": the witness-nations will besiege the city and take down her strength, i.e., her walls.

The use of the second person, "from you," renders this destruction more personal, reminding us of the Edomites's cry "Strip her naked, down to the foundation" (Ps. 137:7) during Jerusalem's destruction.

As mentioned, "palaces" are a *leitwort* in this section: the "*armenot*" of Ashdod and Egypt are invited to come see the ill-gotten loot hoarded in the *armenot* of Samaria. In a clear example of poetic justice, these *armenot* – symbols of the Samarian aristocracy's greed – will fall, and that wealth will be plundered by outsiders.

The use of the passive voice in this last phrase (*venavozu*) opens up the frightening possibility that not only will the fortresses be despoiled by the besieging enemy, but they will also be laid open for all to plunder.

---

17. "Key word" – see Glossary of Academic Terms, p. xv.
18. Exodus 15:3; Psalms 29:11.
19. Proverbs 31:25.

Surprisingly, *ko amar* appears *again* in v. 12, as if to reiterate that this is God's word. This time, God's name is simply *Hashem,* so that the full sequence echoes the rabbinic formula for *berakhot*: a proper, full address to God at the introduction (*petiḥa*), i.e., "*Hashem, Elokeinu Melekh Ha'olam* – Lord, our God, King of the Universe," which then ends with the brief signature of *Hashem* – as in "*Barukh Ata Hashem, mekadesh haShabbat.*" Similarly, this creates a parallel *petiḥa/ḥatima* relationship between the opening introductory pronouncement of punishment (summoning the besieging army to tear down Samaria's walls and fortresses) and the resultant pillaging described with terrifying imagery in this verse.

The pronouncement is presented as an analogous parallel, using the formulaic *ka'asher/kein* ("as.../so...") pair, which appears numerous times throughout the canon, albeit almost always in a different format. Usually, the *ka'sher/kein* pair expresses how the order is executed as directed. In none of these cases, however, is the *ka'asher/kein* pair a bridge from analogy to referent. Here, however, Amos uses a familiar image from the animal kingdom to illustrate the terror that awaits them. This type of *ka'asher/kein* pairing appears in only two other places in the Bible,[20] both at least a century after Amos's time. Intriguingly, both instances are prefaced with "*Ko amar Hashem.*"

Verse 12: The Analogy

Part 1: The Index[21]

12: As (*ka'asher*) the shepherd rescues (*yatzil*) out of the mouth of the lion two legs, or a piece of an ear (*bedal ozen*)

Amos has already used lion imagery: in his anthem, to illustrate the fearful roar of God's rebuke and punishment; in his "inevitability of prophecy" section, the lion and its prey are part of the cause-effect set, leading up to: "When the lion roars, who fears not?" Here, the lion represents the enemy, while Israel is its victim.

20. Jeremiah 13:11; Ezekiel 15:6.

21. An analogy is made up of an *index* (the already known) and a *target* (that which is informed by the index).

The shepherd is virtually helpless; at most, he manages to save remnants of a lamb's flesh. Although it seems that the shepherd is trying to save what he can, Ibn Ezra and R. Joseph Kara suggest another motivation: the shepherd grabs the animal's remains to testify that it has been killed by a predator, to exempt himself from payment to the rancher.[22]

The word *bedal* (the nominal form is a *badal;* due to the construct state, the opening *kamatz* becomes a *sheva*) is a *hapax legomenon,* a word that appears only once in the canon. Its root suggests that it means "separate," or "a distinct part." *Bedal ozen* therefore means a separated piece of the ear. The *Targum,* quoted by Rashi, Radak, and others, reads *bedal ozen* as *ḥasḥos de'odan* (the ear's cartilage). Radak suggests that the hind legs and ear cartilage are the last thing the lion would eat, which is why the shepherd is able to rescue them.

In any case, Amos portrays a shepherd who is either so devoted to his flock that he will save what he can (too little, too late), or who is so concerned with his liability that he will risk life and limb to bring evidence of his diligence. In this metaphor, the lion is clearly the enemy, while Israel is the flock. But who is the shepherd? It seems unlikely that it is God, as the shepherd is powerless, able to save just a remnant. Is the shepherd the prophet?[23] This is a frightening possibly: If so, is Amos warning Israel so he can later bring evidence to God of his loyalty and diligence, as if saying: "But there was nothing I could do"?

Part 2: The Target

The analogy's meaning (the "target") is introduced with *kein* ("similarly").

In v. 11, the active voice (*vehorid*) in the first hemistich is offset by the passive voice (*venavozu*) in the second hemistich. Similarly, here, the active verb describing the shepherd saving the carcass remnants (*yatzil*) is matched in the verse's second half with the same root in the passive voice (*yinatzelu*). This pattern may serve more than a poetic advantage;

22. See Exodus 22:12.
23. See Jeremiah 23:1 and (*pseudo-*) Rashbam to Cant. 1:8.

the shift from active to passive may reflect Samaria's loss of power in the face of their enemy.

The above translation – that the people of Samaria will escape, but with little furniture – seems inaccurate and anticlimactic. For this reason, perhaps, Ibn Ezra explains that phrase means that only "those who lie on the bed in the corner" – that is, those who are too sick to fight – will survive the onslaught. He explains that the word *pe'ah*, which means "corner," refers not to the corner of the bed, but rather to a sick-bed, which is placed out of view, in the corner of the house. Although syntactically unusual, this is a more palatable translation and consistent with the analogy.

The most challenging word in this verse is *demeshek* (or is it *demesek?*). To begin with, the word *eres* is parallel with *mita;* both mean "bed" or "couch." It stands to reason that the word before *mita* would mean something like "corner." But what is that word? If it is *demesek*, is it an allusion to the ancient city of Damascus? If so, what does it have to do with the edge of a couch?

The commentators present a wide range of approaches – but first, let us consider the text itself. R. Yedidya Norzi, the sixteenth-century Mantuan Masorete, in his monumental *Minḥat Shai*, records that the Targum and *Midrash Seder Olam* seem to read it with a "left *sin*" (*demesek*) but he points out that all the best Masoretic manuscripts have a "right *shin*" (*demeshek*). If so, it is another *hapax legomenon*, which, based on the parallel, can be read as "corner" or "edge." Paul reads it as the leg of a bed, and *pe'at mita* as its head. This fits the metaphor well: only the lamb's extremities can be salvaged, and all that can be saved are the two ends of the bed.

I would like to propose a further reading: Amos has summoned Egypt and Philistia to witness the evils of Samarian society; God then invites them to besiege the city. The word for "siege" here is *tzar*, which hints to the northern neighbor Tyre/Phoenicia. Perhaps the unusual word *demeshek* is used here to evoke wordplay with the capital of Israel's contemporary enemy, Aram.[24] Aram/Damascus is the first nation to

---

24. The LXX has an entirely different reading of the end of the verse and certainly has a "left *shin*," and reads it as Damascus.

stand accused in the oracles of the nations. By now, Amos has mentioned or alluded to the first three nations of this oracle, along with Egypt, the cradle of Israelite history. These nations, first accused by Amos, may now serve as God's rod of wrath against His people.

Verse 13: Introduction

Even though this verse begins with another *shimu,* I read it as the previous passage's conclusion for two reasons. First of all, there is no new indictment here. The punishment is apparently an expansion on the punishment in vv. 11–12, which is the divine response to the accusation in vv. 9–10. Furthermore, "the day that I shall visit the transgressions of Israel upon him (Israel)" (v. 14) refers back to the previous verses.

Furthermore, although the opening imperative *shimu* is likely directed to the audience, to whom is the subsequent directive of *veha'idu* addressed? Witnesses (whether real, as in legal texts, or imagined, as in many prophetic texts) are rarely the subject of the given testimony. For the aristocracy and monarchy in Samaria to testify here is odd, unless they are testifying to their own sins (i.e., confessing).

Perhaps the terms are distributive: *shimu* is addressed to the real Israelite audience, whereas *ha'idu* is addressed to the Philistines and Egyptians that Amos "summons" as witnesses. It is instructive to note that the root *a-d-h* (*ayin-daled-hei*), which usually means "testify," means "warn" in Akkadian.[25] This introduction to the intensified stage of punishment takes on a new meaning: not only will these neighbors witness Samaria's corruption (and perhaps execute God's punishment) – they will also warn them of this punishment.

In any case, these summonses, as before, are merely a rhetorical device – it is most pronounced here. This new stage of punishment includes the destruction of idolatrous sites, which would be an unlikely warning to come from idolatrous nations. Nonetheless, the image is powerful: enemies from whom God has saved His people come to see

25. Hence the clever wordplay in Genesis 4:23, in which Lemekh is *warning* his two wives, appropriately named Ada (warning) and Tzila (ringing sound [in the ears of someone hearing a threat; see, for example, I Sam. 3:11]). See also Genesis 43:3.

their sins and then act as God's agents, delivering the warning of His intended punishment.

The "house of Jacob" is a relatively rare term; it appears roughly twenty times in the canon, usually in the literary prophets. Amos uses it twice; why here, instead of his usual "Samaria" or "Israel"?

I would like to propose two theories. First, continuing the ongoing theme of social corruption and oppression, Amos is hinting that his audience are all descendants of Jacob and as such, the wealthy ought to help support their less fortunate brothers – subjugation and exploitation essentially denies their shared history.[26]

Second, for the first time, in v. 14 Amos addresses the northern kingdom's worship practices. Jeroboam built sites in Beit El and Dan to allow the people to worship God without going to Jerusalem, violating the "single-nation, single-Temple" commandment in Deuteronomy 12.[27] Amos frequently refers to the northern kingdom as "Jacob" (especially in chapter 7), but the addition of "House" here serves at least two purposes. First, as above, it serves as a reminder of *Beit Yaakov* who descend to Egypt together[28] (their common history) as well as *Beit Yaakov* who accepted the Sinai covenant together[29] (their common mission). Second, the word *bayit* (house) is a *leitwort* in this passage, appearing six times within just three verses.

Finally, this expression might generate a different association for the audience. Amos's contemporary Isaiah refers to the Temple as *Beit Elokei Yaakov* (2:2). Jacob alone among the Patriarchs refers to a sanctified place as a "house": he renames Luz "Beit El" and promises to make the place a "*Beit Elokim*" (Gen. 28:22). When Amos denounces the idolatrous altars at "Beit El," he reminds his audience that they are all *Beit Yaakov*. How ironic! Jacob recognized God's presence there and named the site; now his descendants are using the same site for pagan worship.

---

26. See, for instance, Y. Nedarim 9:4, where the prohibitions of revenge and holding a grudge are explained with an analogy to the ludicrous image of one part of the body taking "revenge" on another limb that inadvertently caused it pain.
27. And re-stressed in Joshua 22.
28. Genesis 46:27.
29. Exodus 19:3.

Verse 13 concludes with the longest name Amos uses for God. The cognomen *tzeva'ot* is difficult to translate. It may mean "Who rules the heavens" (*tzivot hashamayim,* the hosts of the heavens), or "Who leads the camp of Israel" (the Israelites are led out from Egypt *al tzivotam,* "by their hosts," in Ex. 12:51), or "Who wages war" (Num. 1:3). In any case, the commentators do not address why this lengthy and somewhat opaque Divine Name appears here – and nowhere else in the canon. I would like to suggest that this long name sequence reflects the moment when Amos expands his focus from purely social criticism to religious criticism as well.

Verse 14: Destruction of the Idolatrous Sites

Often (mis)translated as "because," the opening word, *Ki,* is best read as "for." Rather than justify the coming punishment (which would be "because"), it emphasizes the warning (*ha'idu*) of what is to come.

The biblical concept of "visiting sins" refers to God's account of humanity's sins. It first appears after the sin of the Golden Calf (Ex. 32:34):

> *Uveyom pokdi, ufakadti aleihem ḥatatam.*
> And on the day that I remember (?), I will visit their sin upon them.

Thus Amos's use of this phrase in regard to forbidden worship at Beit El and Jeroboam's golden calf deliberately evokes Israel's first offense of idolatry.

However, unlike the first mention of a "day of reckoning" in Exodus, which clearly expresses that punishment will be postponed, Amos's reproach implies that this day of reckoning is imminent.

Yet another critical difference between Amos's warning and the sin in Exodus spells greater doom for his audience. In context, the Golden Calf in Exodus is referred to as a *ḥeit* (lit. "error"), but Amos says God will hold Israel accountable for their *pesha'im*. As noted in chapter 2, *pesha* means "deliberate crime" and "rebellion" against authority. God may have perceived Israel's offense in the wilderness as an "error," but now Israel's behavior is considered rebellious, and judgment will be swift and harsh.

The second half of the verse defines what the *pekida* will be. Its structure is triangular parallelism, with each of the A and B clauses matched by the C clause: the altars and their horns are both modified by the phrase "fall to the ground," while the "horns" of the B clause also define the altars in "A." In this eloquent rhetorical flourish, Amos brings the idolatrous altars of Beit El crashing down.

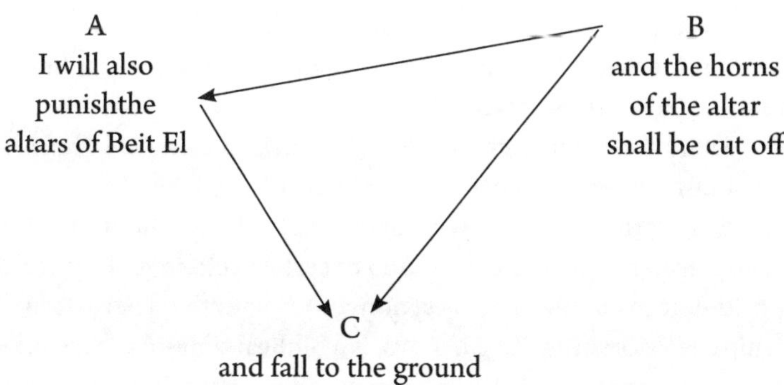

Several aspects are worth noting: firstly, Amos focuses solely on Beit El, without mention of the parallel site in Dan. This can be explained through the narrative in I Kings 13: an unnamed prophet (who seems to foreshadow Amos; more on that in chapter 9) comes to Beit El, witnesses Jeroboam's offering on the altar, and declares a scion of David will one day cut down this altar and its priests. Beit El, it seems, was the central worship site, associated with the royal house – a "Royal Sanctuary," as the cult priest Amaziah admonishes Amos.

Abraham and Jacob both recognized Beit El's special nature. It is first acknowledged in the Early Prophets, when Samuel tells Saul he will meet three men "going up to God at Beit El" (I Sam. 10:3–4). Between Shiloh's destruction (in Samuel's youth) and Solomon's Temple, when *bamot* (altars outside the Tabernacle or Temple) were still permitted, Beit El was a national center of worship, and a logical location for Jeroboam's cultic center when he decides to establish religious alternatives in the northern kingdom.

The plural form "altars," however, is unexpected. All the Beit El narratives mention a single altar.[30] The possibility that there were ancillary altars is challenged by the second clause's emphasis that "the horns *of the altar* will be broken off," which again refers to a single altar.

I believe that through this, Amos is equating the northern cultic center in Beit El to idolatry: an altar that stands anywhere but Jerusalem is considered as idolatrous as if the worshipper is serving many gods at many altars. This is not to suggest that the two are *halakhically* equivalent, but that worshipping God anywhere but Jerusalem stems from the same mindset that drives idolatrous religions – the belief that humans can set the parameters of worship.

Altars throughout the ancient Levant typically had "horns," a small abutment at each corner; in ancient times, including in Israel, grasping these horns was a symbolic act of taking sanctuary. Horns were also used for receiving the blood of certain offerings. Thus tearing down "the horns of the altar" is synonymous with the destruction of a worship site. Moreover, "*keren*," horn, is a biblical symbol of power,[31] so the audience understands this phrase as a deliberate double entendre. Not only will the altars be destroyed, Amos hints – the whole kingdom will be rendered powerless.

One final point about this verse. As we have seen several times, Amos likes to alternate between the active and passive voice. Here, God promises to "punish/call to account" the altars, and then the horns "will be cut off." *Venigde'u* is a passive verb. This may be a case of rhetorical variation for its own sake, or it may convey a more powerful message: once God attacks the altars, their horns (their power) will fall to the ground *of their own accord.*

Verse 15: The Destruction of the Palaces

The final verse of this oracle returns to Samaria's yawning gap between poor and rich: the destitute are so severely oppressed that God will punish the city on their behalf, while the powerful have multiple palaces. To this day, the wealthy sometimes have two homes, in a warmer

30. I Kings 13:2 and its resolution in II Kings 23:15.
31. For example, I Samuel 2:10.

climate for the winter, and a cooler "summer home." Jeremiah mentions Jehoiakim's winter home. A famous post-biblical example is Herod, whose summer home was Herodium, near Amos's hometown, Tekoa. God will punish the wealthy until they experience the same destitution as those they oppress.

15: The houses of ivory shall perish and the great houses shall have an end

This next stich (*ve'avdu… rabim*) is presented in the passive voice, as if once God initiates the winter houses' destruction, the rest of the infrastructure will come tumbling down on its own.

Ivory has always been considered a luxury.[32] Solomon's throne is made of ivory (I Kings 10:8) and an "ivory house" is mentioned in Ahab's eulogy (I Kings 22:39). Rashi and R. Joseph Kara read *shen* here as "ivory," but R. Eliezer of Beaugency reads it as "promontory"[33] – as luxury homes built on their own sprawling promontories.

In conclusion, the destruction will begin with the idolatrous altars of Beit El until it reaches the palaces of the wealthy.

This oracle concludes with the signature *ne'um Hashem,* which clearly marks its end. The next oracle is the famous "cows of Bashan" address.

THE SECOND WARNING: THE COWS OF THE BASHAN

The Text (Amos 4:1–5)

א) שִׁמְעוּ הַדָּבָר הַזֶּה פָּרוֹת הַבָּשָׁן אֲשֶׁר בְּהַר שֹׁמְרוֹן הָעֹשְׁקוֹת דַּלִּים הָרֹצְצוֹת
אֶבְיוֹנִים הָאֹמְרֹת לַאֲדֹנֵיהֶם הָבִיאָה וְנִשְׁתֶּה: (ב) נִשְׁבַּע אֲדֹנָי ה׳ בְּקָדְשׁוֹ
כִּי הִנֵּה יָמִים בָּאִים עֲלֵיכֶם וְנִשָּׂא אֶתְכֶם בְּצִנּוֹת וְאַחֲרִיתְכֶן בְּסִירוֹת דּוּגָה:
(ג) וּפְרָצִים תֵּצֶאנָה אִשָּׁה נֶגְדָּהּ וְהִשְׁלַכְתֶּנָה הַהַרְמוֹנָה נְאֻם ה׳: (ד) בֹּאוּ
בֵית אֵל וּפִשְׁעוּ הַגִּלְגָּל הַרְבּוּ לִפְשֹׁעַ וְהָבִיאוּ לַבֹּקֶר זִבְחֵיכֶם לִשְׁלֹשֶׁת יָמִים

32. See our discussion in chapter 8.
33. As in I Samuel 14:4.

מַעְשְׂרֹתֵיכֶם: (ה) וְקַטֵּר מֵחָמֵץ תּוֹדָה וְקִרְאוּ נְדָבוֹת הַשְׁמִיעוּ כִּי כֵן אֲהַבְתֶּם
בְּנֵי יִשְׂרָאֵל נְאֻם אֲדֹנָי ה׳:

> 1 Hear this word, you cows of Bashan, who are in the mountain of Samaria, who oppress the poor, who crush the needy, who say to their masters, "Bring, that we may drink!" 2 The Lord God has sworn by his holiness that, behold, the days are coming upon you, when you will be carried away with hooks, even the last of you with fishhooks. 3 And you shall go out through the breaches, everyone straight before her; and you shall be cast forth into Harmon, says the Lord. 4 Come to Beit El, and transgress; to Gilgal, and multiply transgression; bring your sacrifices every morning, your tithes every three days; 5 offer a sacrifice of thanksgiving of that which is leavened, and proclaim freewill offerings, publish them; for so you love to do, O people of Israel! says the Lord God.

Though v. 5 is not marked off with a Masoretic paragraph, the signature formula, *ne'um Hashem Elokim*, "says the Lord God," signifies the end of this section. Moreover, this brief passage focuses on these "cows of the Bashan." The accusation against them is followed by a vivid description of their punishment, whereas the following verses shift to the worship sites at Beit El and Gilgal, accusing the men who officiate and participate in that worship.

Verse 1: Indictment

The indictment is made up of two sections: the prophet identifies a specific audience, and then names their crime.

The introductory *Shimu*, perhaps, tells the audience to focus on the prophet's specific choice of words, rather than the general thrust of the rebuke and threatened punishment. We will do the same.

As before, Amos employs familiar farm imagery, from his own livelihood and background. The "cows" he addresses are the wealthy women of Samaria; a prophecy addressed specifically to women is a rare phenomenon in prophetic literature.[34] "Cows of Bashan" suggests

34. See Isaiah 2:16–23, although the prophet does not address the women of Zion

indolent beasts who graze (on others' land) and spend their days growing fat, of no benefit to anyone else.

The Bashan, captured from Og and given to Manasseh, is on the eastern slopes of the Golan, part of the northern kingdom. While not near Samaria, the area is close enough for the audience to be familiar with its lush pastures. Although the image of cows grazing in the Bashan is pastoral and serene, that serenity is shattered when we learn where the "grass" upon which they graze comes from.

The apparent contradiction between *parot haBashan* and *asher behar Shomeron* is worth noting. This underscores their greed: not only are they feeding off of the misfortunes of others, but they are also in entirely the wrong place! Bear in mind that Samaria suffered drought just before Amos's time (II Kings 8), and the green pastures of Bashan may be foreign to the Samarian landscape. This underscores the class divide in Samaria – while most of the people are starving and oppressed, the despicable bovine women of the Samarian aristocracy are growing fat at the lower classes' expense.

A brief prefatory comment about the verse's cantillation marks. The Masoretic pause (*etnaḥta*), which indicates the verse's halfway mark, appears under the word *evyonim*. The *etnaḥta* usually appears at the end of a clause or idea; in this verse, we would expect the *etnaḥta* to appear under the word *Shomeron*, the end of the addressees' description, to be followed by *ha'oshekot dalim* – the beginning of the indictment. The fact that the description "who oppress the needy, who crush the poor" is read as part of the first half exacerbates Amos's reproach. Their oppressive behavior is so pervasive that it has become part of their identity: they are now defined as "oppressors of the poor," as "crushers of the destitute." Who is Amos's audience? Those "cows of the Bashan," residents of Samaria, oppressors of the disenfranchised and crushers of the indigent! To be accused of a crime is one thing; to be rebuked as a chronic offender is worse. But to be *defined* by your corruption is most piercing of all.

Ashuk and *ratzutz* are a common word pair. This verse in Hosea 5:11 seems to be a double-edged reference to the verse from the covenantal

---

directly in that passage.

curse in Deuteronomy:[35] "*Ashuk Efrayim, retzutz mishpat,*" which either means "Ephraim [Samaria] is oppressed, its judgment crushed," or "Ephraim oppresses and its judgment [on behalf of the oppressed] is crushed." This ambiguity is likely deliberate, hinting that as a *result* of the oppression of the poor in Ephraim, that kingdom *will then be* oppressed and crushed by the outside enemy. In other words, the text's plain meaning describes Samaria's corruption, but the use of the passive participle of *ashuk* (instead of the active *oshek,* as our passage) hints to the poetic justice (*midda keneged midda*) awaiting Ephraim.[36]

Note that these two contemporaries, Amos and Hosea, utilize Deuteronomy's description of Israel being oppressed to describe Israel's oppression of their own poor. This poignant inversion generates a powerful sense of rebuke: God warned you of terrible punishment – but that is how *you* are treating *your own*!

In Amos 4:1, the use of the "ongoing present" (*oshekot* and *rotzetzot*) in the description hints that this oppression is an integral part of life in Samaria, not an occasional lapse or abuse of power.

The second half of the verse comprises four simple words, but there is nothing simple about the phrase they form: [The "cows"] who say to their masters: "Bring and we will drink!"

The continued use of the ongoing present (*ha'omerot* instead of, for example, *she'ameru*) again indicates that such behavior has become the norm. This half of the verse details *how* and *why* the rich oppress the poor and crush the destitute: these pampered women speak "to their masters." The context indicates that this refers to their husbands, who are generally called *ish* or *ba'al.* Although it is not unheard of for a woman to refer to her husband as "master" (Sarah says of Abraham, "My master is old" – Gen. 18:12), it is unusual in narrative. This odd word choice may be hinting to yet another sinful aspect of their behavior. Give that the next indictment is aimed at the idolatrous worship in Beit El and Gilgal, it may be that these "cows" are urging their husbands to partake in feasts of an idolatrous nature. Amos has already accused Israel of a

35. Deuteronomy 28:33: *Vehayita rak ashuk veratzutz kol hayamim,* "You will be oppressed and crushed all of your days."
36. Yehuda Kil, *Da'at Mikra, Trei Asar,* vol. 1, 42.

perditious combination of moral oppression and idolatry (2:8); perhaps the unusual use of *adoneihem* here suggests these women seek to serve their new master, Ba'al.

These women's two-word command, *"Havia*[37] *venishteh!"* seems like a simple request for wine – or for a feast, but this forces their husbands to further oppress and drain the poor to cater to their excessive appetites (for idolatry?). Amos's vivid language further heightens our sense of horror at the miscarriage of justice and abuse of the downtrodden in Samaria, all the while increasing our appreciation for his rhetorical skill.

Verse 2: Punishment

The punishment pronounced against the *parot haBashan* is punctuated with a divine oath, God swearing "by His holiness,"[38] which suggests that the oath is to be taken with the utmost gravity. Evidently, these "cows of the Bashan" and the severe toll their insatiable appetites take on the poor is seen as most grievous on high. The image of these pampered women cajoling their husbands into further abuse and oppression is part of the tragic portrait Amos paints of Samarian society. Perhaps it is their extreme depravity and utter lack of empathy that moves Amos to punctuate their description with such a serious oath.

2: Behold, the days are coming *(Hinei yamim ba'im)*

Amos seems to have coined the eschatological introduction "*hinei yamim ba'im*" (besides for one mention in pre-monarchic literature [I Sam. 2:31]

37. A fragment from cave 4 in Qumran renders it *haviu* in the plural. LXX renders it that way; however, our received text seems more likely, as it is quoting what each woman says to her "master" – in the singular, of course.
38. This specific formulation is unique in the Bible, although similar variations (all in the literary Prophets) include divine oaths in which God swears "by His X" (X being "Himself" – Amos 6:8; "the pride of Jacob" – 8:7). R. Eliezer of Beaugency suggests that "the pride of Jacob" refers to the Temple. Although he does not comment here, this verse could also be read thus, consistent with the meaning of *kodsho* used throughout the Psalter. These may be poetic expansions of "I have sworn by Myself" (*bi nishbati*), or *"Ḥai ani."*

and a single mention by his later contemporary Isaiah[39]). Amos uses the phrase three times.[40] In his wake, Jeremiah uses the phrase fifteen times, but it is not used by any other prophet! This cannot be attributed to theme, given that most prophets engage in some form of eschatological speculation or prophecy; rather, this is another demonstration of Jeremiah's dependence on Amos's rhetorical style.

Amos emphasizes that punishment will soon strike these wealthy, pampered women. The first half of the verse consists entirely of strong prophetic formulae that warn of the punishment's imminence and severity.

You will be carried away with hooks

Venisa etkhem betzinot	*ve'aḥaritkhen besirot duga*
You will be carried away (?) with hooks	and your residue (?) with fishhooks(?)

This translation is tentative – several phrases are not easily understood, let alone translated.

The verb *(ve)nisa* is fairly straightforward; meaning "to carry/ lift up," with the root *n-s-a*. In passive form, it becomes: "You will be lifted up by."

The word *tzinot* (singular *tzina*) is more challenging. BDB suggests three meanings: "coolness," "shield,"[41] and "hook" or "barb." The third meaning seems the most likely, as the first two do not fit the context.[42]

39. 39:6 (= II Kings 20:17).
40. The other two instances form the "envelope" around his eschaton which starts at 8:11.
41. I Samuel 17:12; I Kings 10:16; Jeremiah 46:3; Ezekiel 23:24.
42. How one arrives at this meaning is unclear, except perhaps by arguing that *tzinot* is a variation on the masculine plural *tzinim* in the famous passage *tzinim paḥim bederekh ikesh* (Prov. 22:5), which is rendered as "Thorns and snares are in the crooked path" or "…in the path of the crooked." This is further informed by the second half of our phrase, which references some fishing setting. Hence, *tzinot* become "fishhooks." The image of these women being hoisted up and away by fishhooks is a reasonable one and a powerful punishment.

Koehler-Baumgartner make four suggestions, each with its own advantage:[43] "prickles," related to fishhooks, as BDB; "rope, cord" based on an Akkadian cognate, which certainly fits the context; "shield," which is the most common biblical meaning; and finally, "basket," based on the parallel *sirot* [*duga*] which, in most contexts, means "pots." Additionally, "*tzana*" is "basket" in Aramaic, as pointed out by Paul,[44] based on Ibn Janah, Ibn Balaam, and R. Eliezer of Beaugency.[45]

In Zechariah 5:6–7, the prophet envisions a woman carried away in a basket – the woman represents evil leaving Jerusalem. The similarity to Amos's vision raises the possibility that Zechariah is drawing on Amos. If so, these women are also likely being taken away in baskets.

What about *aḥaritekhen*? The literal translation is "your residue," in feminine plural form, but what does that mean? Rashi reads *aḥaritekhen* as "your children."[46] R. Eliezer of Beaugency interprets *aḥaritekhen* as "your end" – your destiny.

Whomever or whatever *aḥaritekhen* are, they are destined to end up in *sirot duga*. Most *Rishonim* associate *duga* with fishing and assume that *sirot duga* are small fishing vessels, shaped like pots (to keep the fish inside). Ibn Ezra and R. Eliezer of Beaugency, in contrast, interpret *sira* as another form of barbs,[47] and connect *duga* to the verb *yidgu,* to take possession: these women will be dragged away by thorns and their children will end up skewered by thorns.

Verse 3: A Challenging Text

Not only are the words themselves hard to translate, but the syntax is equally challenging. The general image is of a city with breached walls, and the women must leave through these gaping holes (taken by force,

43. Koehler-Baumgartner, 1037.
44. Paul, 73.
45. R. Eliezer of Beaugency associates it with the word *tzintzenet* (Ex. 16:33).
46. And, following him, R. Joseph Kara, Ibn Ezra, and Radak. He bases this interpretation on Dunash b. Labrat's rendering of Daniel 11:4.
47. Per Nachum 1:10.

or fleeing of their own accord?). The walls will be so riddled with holes that every woman will have a "ready-made exit" *negdah,* right next to her, and she will leave the city through there.

The kingdom will be crushed by the conquering, pillaging enemy. This scene recalls Israel's conquest of Jericho: "Each man entered the city from where he stood" (Josh. 6:20). The fact that the women of Samaria will be dragged away through its breached walls so easily points to a painful reversal of Israel's fortunes.

Moreover, the unusual syntax, "*Ufratzim teitzena*" (instead of the expected *veteitzena baperatzim,* they will go out through the breaches) hints to a deeper message. The breaches in the city walls reflect the breaches that these women have created in society. The breachers will go out through the breaches effected by their own corruption.

3: And you shall be cast forth (?) into Harmon (?)

The first of these two difficult words is a *hapax legomenon,* but its meaning is accessible. The root *sh-l-kh* in the causative (*hifil*) means "to cast" and appears dozens of times in the canon (for instance, when Joseph is "cast" into the pit, or when Pharaoh orders that the Hebrew babies be "cast" into the Nile). Ending with the relatively rare feminine plural imperfect, its meaning is "you (feminine plural) will cast them (feminine plural) out/ down." Who will cast out whom? This is likely why the Septuagint renders it in the passive voice, as if it were written *vehoshlakhtena*; i.e., "you (feminine plural) will be cast out." Possible meanings include a literal reading: the women will be "cast" down the mountain of Samaria;[48] or a figurative one: they will become outcasts, rejected from society;[49] they may be cast into exile; or their dead bodies will be cast outside the city.[50]

48. R. Eiezer of Beaugency.

49. Rashi.

50. As Amos himself states (8:3): *Rav hapeger, bekhol makom hishlikh, has,* "The dead bodies shall be many; in every place [they are] cast down – silence!"

"HaHarmona"

The final word in this set is practically inscrutable. Some suggest the word is a variation of *armon* (palace). Most likely, following Ibn Ezra, "Harmon" is a location outside of Samaria where these women will be exiled (or their bodies cast). R. Joseph Kara posits that *harmona* is an unusual variation of *harim*: they will be cast down the mountains, which recalls Eliezer of Beaugency's interpretation of *vehishlakhtena,* above.

This sub-oracle addressed to the "cows of the Bashan," has its own signature. Thus this three-verse passage stands as a semi-independent prophecy, intensified by an opening divine oath, a threatening apocalyptic introduction "*hinei yamim ba'im,*" and a signature.

The Oracle's Structure

The first three verses of chapter 4 address the "cows of the Bashan" and conclude with *ne'um Hashem*. The final two verses diverge thematically and neatly conclude the chapter with a "creation hymn." Verses 6, 8, 9, 10, and 11 have the same epistrophic refrain: "*Velo shavtem adai, ne'um Hashem* – You have not [yet] returned to Me, says the Lord," marking each separate segment.

Three short prefaces are necessary before analyzing this "creation hymn."

Preface 1: Worship at Beit El and Gilgal

The medieval commentators unanimously explain that this worship is idolatrous, or at the very least, violates the prohibition of cultic worship (of Hashem) outside Jerusalem. Modern scholars read Amos's rebuke as criticism that the people focus on sacrificial worship, but are socially and morally corrupt – in fact, some claim that Amos does not reproach the people for idolatry at all, but rather emphasizes that justice is far more important than sacrifice.

While Amos certainly emphasizes justice, it is simplistic to view his condemnation of worship at these two sites as a mere polemic against offerings in general or misplaced priorities. Worship at Beit El is challenged as early as Jeroboam's time. The one narrative section in Amos describes his confrontation with the priest in Beit El, who refers to the site as a "royal sanctuary." While overemphasis of offerings at the expense of obeisance to God's word is an old problem,[51] nowhere in *Nevi'im* is the sacrificial order rejected in itself. The *Rishonim*'s approach is more compelling: here, Amos is expressing that worship at Beit El and Gilgal is inherently evil.

Preface 2: The Location of Gilgal

Many commentators assume that this is Joshua's Gilgal,[52] where the people offered up their first public sacrifice: the Passover offering brought upon their entry into the Land.[53]

There is, however, at least one other location known as Gilgal (likely named for an abundance of roundish rocks) in the mountainous region near Shechem. In Deuteronomy 11:30, the mountains of Ebal and Gerizim are identified as *mul haGilgal* (at the foothills of Gilgal) – this cannot be Joshua's Gilgal, which is a few miles northeast of Jericho.

There is likely a third "Gilgal," which is also considered a holy place. Before he ascends to heaven, Elijah goes to Gilgal, then to Beit El (!), then Jericho before crossing the Jordan and rising up to heaven (II Kings 2). He takes leave of his disciples of the "brotherhood of prophets" at each stop, which suggests that each place was considered a holy site. Although this Gilgal may have been the same one mentioned in Deuteronomy 11, many scholars identify Elijah's Gilgal as the town of Jiljilyya, approximately 15 miles north of Beitin, the site of biblical Beit El. If so, this third Gilgal is a good 25 miles south of Gerizim and cannot be the Gilgal mentioned in Deuteronomy.

Saul's third coronation probably took place at Joshua's Gilgal,[54] but there is no mention of that Gilgal after his defeat of Amalek,[55] and no further evidence of any cultic activity there.[56] The Gilgal mentioned

51. See I Samuel 15:22.
52. Joshua 4:19–20, 5:9–10.
53. Ibid. 5:9–10.
54. I Samuel 11:14–15.
55. Ibid. 15:12–21.
56. Gilgal is mentioned in David's return after Avshalom's death (II Sam. 19:41 is almost assuredly Joshua's Gilgal), but there is no cultic reference there.

by Amos and Hosea[57] is in Samaria and can be identified with Elijah's Gilgal. This is the position we will adopt in our discussions.

Preface 3: The Cows Redux

As mentioned, the first three verses in the chapter are addressed to the "cows of the Bashan." While this is a distinct oracle, it may nonetheless extend and be linked to the entire chapter. Klaus Koch suggests:

> Perhaps the comparison [of the wealthy women to cows] is not the work of Amos's own outraged imagination. He may be mockingly picking up a cultic name the women gave themselves, since they imagined themselves to be the worshippers of the mighty bull of Samaria (Hosea 8:5f).[58]

Jacobs embraces this suggestion, noting several archeological finds from the Israelite monarchic period: bovine figures (in wall drawings) identified with divine names.[59] Additionally, the odd use of *la'adoneihem* mentioned earlier may relate to cult worship.

If so, the epithet "cows of the Bashan" may have bearing on the rest of this oracle. While the first three verses are specifically addressed to these women, their sin may extend beyond their exploitation of the poor. Similar to Amos's first oracle, where corruption and idolatry intersect ("reclining on pledged clothes near every altar" – 2:8), these women may also be held accountable for the cultic activity at Beit El and Gilgal.

The Text: Verse 4

Bo'u Beit El ufishu	*haGilgal harbu lifshoa*
Come to Beit El and rebel[60]	to Gilgal and multiply rebelliousness

57. 4:15, 9:15, 12:12.
58. Klaus Koch, *The Prophets: The Assyrian Period,* Fortress (Philadelphia: 1983), 46.
59. Paul Jacobs, "'Cows of Bashan' – A Note on the Interpretation of Amos 4:1," *Journal of Biblical Literature* 104, no. 1 (March 1985): 109–110.
60. We use "rebel" to represent *pesha,* as explained in the shiurim on the first chapter; reiterated below.

Beit El and Gilgal are presented here and later in Amos as a pair of problematic worship sites. Whether associated with Ba'al worship, or merely sites outside of Jerusalem, they are considered sinful. Medieval commentators all read the worship as idolatrous – that Amos condemns the "leniencies" offered by the pagan priests instead of the "stringencies" of proper divine worship.

While Amos "invites" his audience to come and sin in Beit El, he is obviously not encouraging them to sin further. Rashi explains: "This is similar to a man saying to his wayward son: 'Keep doing that until your measure (of sin) is full.'"

R. Joseph Kara is more emphatic: "This is not a command, rather it is like a man saying to his fellow: 'Do all of the bad things you are able to do now; the day will come when your evil acts will be accounted for.'"

Amos repeats the root *p-sh-a* – rebel – in his pseudo-invitation. Going to Beit El or Gilgal is an act of rebellion against God. Modern scholars read these lines as reproach against proper divine worship eclipsing justice: "Go to Beit El yet continue to rebel (when you return from worship)." In contrast, traditional commentators see the act of going to these sites as rebellion against God.

4: Bring your sacrifices every morning and your tithes every three days

Rashi and other *Rishonim* read these lines as criticism of lenient pagan practices, as opposed to the "stringent" rules of God's altar: whereas Torah laws dictate that an offering cannot lay on the altar overnight (Ex. 23:19), or that it cannot be eaten beyond the second day, the pagan priests allow this. This interpretation, however, seems somewhat forced.

Others, including Radak and R. Eliezer of Beaugency, read Amos's words as a lament that these people are offering *proper* sacrifices to pagan gods instead of to the true Lord: that bringing offerings first thing in the morning reflects enthusiasm and fervent devotion. He then reads the "three days" in our verse as "three years" (*yamim* does mean "years" in some contexts). This is, again, proper service, as commanded in Deuteronomy 14:28–29 – Amos's despair is that the people show such devotion at pagan sites rather than in worship of God.

The Text: Verse 5

The first half of v. 5 forms a parallel and matches both halves of the previous verse. In these three hemistichs, Amos uses some of his favorite numerical patterns, with the numbers 3 and 7. Here, the three days of the tithes are followed by seven verbs: *bo'u* (come), *ufishu* (rebel), *lifshoa* (to rebel), *haviu* (bring), *kater* (burn), *kiru* (call out), and *hashmiu* (sound out, publicize). These two verses comprise, as mentioned, a tightly crafted mini-oracle.

5a: Offer a sacrifice of thanksgiving of that which is leavened

5b: And proclaim freewill offerings, publish them

The thanksgiving offering (*toda*) consists of forty loaves, including ten that are leavened, which is consistent with "proper" worship. The question is, once again, whether Amos is criticizing improper worship of God or forbidden Ba'al worship. R. Eliezer of Beaugency reads the word *meḥametz* as "without *ḥametz*" – Israel are so eager to worship Ba'al that they bring their offerings without waiting.

What is Amos criticizing in the second half of the verse? Rashi suggests they are bragging about how this offering is accepted; Radak explains that they are publicly appealing to the people to bring such offerings. Either way, the line is not entirely clear.

5c: For so you love to do, O people of Israel
Says the Lord God.

This mini-oracle, too, ends with its own signature. Perhaps this is the most painful phrase of all. Whether they are engaging in the leniencies of pagan worship or passionately, stringently serving other gods, what enrages the prophet is their deep love and devotion. Does this similarly move his audience? In the next chapter, we will discover how the people respond to these threats and to actual consequences, and whether this inspires them to correct their ways.

Chapter 5

“Hearken”: The Call to Return (4:6–13)

(ו) וְגַם אֲנִי נָתַתִּי לָכֶם נִקְיוֹן שִׁנַּיִם בְּכָל עָרֵיכֶם וְחֹסֶר לֶחֶם בְּכֹל מְקוֹמֹתֵיכֶם
וְלֹא שַׁבְתֶּם עָדַי נְאֻם ה׳: (ז) וְגַם אָנֹכִי מָנַעְתִּי מִכֶּם אֶת הַגֶּשֶׁם בְּעוֹד שְׁלֹשָׁה
חֳדָשִׁים לַקָּצִיר וְהִמְטַרְתִּי עַל עִיר אֶחָת וְעַל עִיר אַחַת לֹא אַמְטִיר חֶלְקָה
אַחַת תִּמָּטֵר וְחֶלְקָה אֲשֶׁר לֹא תַמְטִיר עָלֶיהָ תִּיבָשׁ: (ח) וְנָעוּ שְׁתַּיִם שָׁלֹשׁ
עָרִים אֶל עִיר אַחַת לִשְׁתּוֹת מַיִם וְלֹא יִשְׂבָּעוּ וְלֹא שַׁבְתֶּם עָדַי נְאֻם ה׳:
(ט) הִכֵּיתִי אֶתְכֶם בַּשִּׁדָּפוֹן וּבַיֵּרָקוֹן הַרְבּוֹת גַּנּוֹתֵיכֶם וְכַרְמֵיכֶם וּתְאֵנֵיכֶם וְזֵיתֵיכֶם
יֹאכַל הַגָּזָם וְלֹא שַׁבְתֶּם עָדַי נְאֻם ה׳: (י) שִׁלַּחְתִּי בָכֶם דֶּבֶר בְּדֶרֶךְ מִצְרַיִם
הָרַגְתִּי בַחֶרֶב בַּחוּרֵיכֶם עִם שְׁבִי סוּסֵיכֶם וָאַעֲלֶה בְּאֹשׁ מַחֲנֵיכֶם וּבְאַפְּכֶם וְלֹא
שַׁבְתֶּם עָדַי נְאֻם ה׳: (יא) הָפַכְתִּי בָכֶם כְּמַהְפֵּכַת אֱלֹהִים אֶת סְדֹם וְאֶת עֲמֹרָה
וַתִּהְיוּ כְּאוּד מֻצָּל מִשְּׂרֵפָה וְלֹא שַׁבְתֶּם עָדַי נְאֻם ה׳: (יב) לָכֵן כֹּה אֶעֱשֶׂה לְּךָ
יִשְׂרָאֵל עֵקֶב כִּי זֹאת אֶעֱשֶׂה לָּךְ הִכּוֹן לִקְרַאת אֱלֹהֶיךָ יִשְׂרָאֵל: (יג) כִּי הִנֵּה
יוֹצֵר הָרִים וּבֹרֵא רוּחַ וּמַגִּיד לְאָדָם מַה שֵּׂחוֹ עֹשֵׂה שַׁחַר עֵיפָה וְדֹרֵךְ עַל בָּמֳתֵי
אָרֶץ ה׳ אֱלֹהֵי צְבָאוֹת שְׁמוֹ:

6 I gave you cleanness of teeth in all your cities, and lack of bread in all your places, yet you did not return to me, says the Lord.
7 And I also withheld the rain from you when there were yet three months to the harvest; I made it rain upon one city, and upon one city I did not make it rain; one plot will be rained upon, and

> one in which there will be no rain will wither away; **8** so two or three cities wandered to one city to drink water, and were not sated; yet you did not return to me, says the Lord. **9** I smote you with blight and mildew; I laid waste your many gardens and your vineyards; your fig trees and your olive trees the locust devoured; yet you did not return to me, says the Lord. **10** I sent among you a pestilence after the manner of Egypt; I slew your young men with the sword; I carried away your horses; and I have raised up the stench of your camp into your nostrils; yet you did not return to me, says the Lord. **11** I overthrew some of you, as when God overthrew Sodom and Gomorah, and you were as a brand plucked out of the fire; yet you did not return to me, says the Lord. **12** Therefore thus will I do to you, O Israel; because I will do this unto you, prepare to meet your God, O Israel! **13** For lo, behold, He who fashions mountains and creates the wind, and informs man of his words; who makes the morning darkness, and treads on the high places of the earth – the Lord, the God of Hosts, is His name!

In the previous chapter, we analyzed the prophet's facetious invitation (read: "accusation") against the worshippers of Beit El and Gilgal and their offensive offerings. These lines are followed by five passages, each ending with the epistrophe *"Velo shavtem adai, ne'um Hashem,"* "[Still and all] you have not [yet] returned to Me, says the Lord."

Epistrophes

An epistrophe (or epiphora) is the repetition of the same word or phrase at the end of successive phrases or passages. Used in biblical poetry,[1] it adds impact to group recital; moreover, the rhetorical rhythm it generates sometimes serves to underscore the passage's message.[2] This

1. An example of this is Psalm 136, which has 26 lines, each of which is made up of two even hemistichs. In all 26 lines, the second hemistich is *"Ki le'olam hasdo,"* "For His kindness endures forever," and it is clearly intended to be recited antiphonally (call-and-response).
2. See Psalms 24:7–10, 118:10–12.

repetition allows the group to chant the refrain together, creating a sense of community and helping them internalize its idea.[3]

In this passage, Amos uses epistrophe to convey his sense of desperation and doom at the people's imminent fate. "You did not return to Me... and you still did not return to Me... and after all of that, you *still* have not returned to Me..."

In these five passages, the prophet recounts seven disasters that have befallen the people:[4] famine (v. 6), drought (v. 8), plant-blight (v. 9a), locusts (v. 9b), plague (v. 10a), war (v. 10b), and the earthquake (v. 11) mentioned at the start of the book ("two years before the earthquake"). The first five gravely affected national agriculture and recall the plagues against Egypt.

Amos interprets these misfortunes as divine punishments calculated to bring the people back to God – to no avail. Even if the people experienced them as punishment, Amos attempts to explain that they were meant to be instructive, not punishment for their sins. If so, they should be read as events that have already happened, which should therefore resonate with the audience.

THE FIRST DISASTER: FAMINE (VERSE 6)

God has given the people

> cleanness of teeth in all your cities
> and lack of bread in all your places

The famine the people have already suffered is explained here not as divine punishment, but rather as divine motivation to bring the people back to God.

3. Consider the many medieval liturgical poems (*piyyutim*) that utilize this tool; we are most familiar with them from *Seliḥot*, the *Kinot* of Tisha B'Av, and *piyyutim* added into the service of Rosh HaShana and Yom Kippur.
4. Yet another example of Amos's use of the typological number seven as part of his rhetorical strategy.

The meaning of "cleanness of teeth" (*nikyon shinayim*) is contextually clear here, even though the phrase is a *hapax legomenon* and an unusual way to describe a famine. Why does Amos use this phrase?

This particular construct form of *nikyon* appears in only one other context. When Abimelech takes Sarah into his palace, he claims innocence: "I did this with an innocent heart and cleanness of hands (*venikyon kapay*)" – without evil intention or knowledge of her marital status. This, in turn, recalls the Psalmist's description of who may ascend to the mountain of God: "one who is clean of hands (*neki khapayim*) and pure of heart" (Ps. 24:4). Amos describes the famine they have just experienced using this hauntingly familiar phrase, *nikyon shinayim*. The people of Samaria cannot claim such "cleanness of hands," and the divine response to this lack of cleanness of hands (*nikyon kapayim*) is cleanness of teeth (*nikyon shinayim*). Keep in mind that Amos's voice is the "roar" from the same holy mountain (1:2), the mountain that is reserved for those with *nikyon kapayim*.

Amos's rhetorical strategy in this first of five passages seems clear. He points out that the people's own moral failings are the root cause of the famine they suffered. He then makes it clear that they have not responded as they should have:

> Yet you did not return to Me, says the Lord

The biblical preposition used to modify the verb *shuv* is always *el*, best translated as "toward." The preposition *ad*, which means "up to," is only used in the context of returning to God. Perhaps the difference between returning *ad Hashem* and returning *el Hashem* is exactly that: are we returning *ad*, all the way to God, or are we merely turning toward Him, with a long way to go before we reach this lofty destination?

In later biblical books, the use of *el* when returning to God often refers to the beginning of the process: the people must turn away from their sins and chart out a new direction – toward God. Whether coming from exile (as in Zechariah and Malachi, or as foretold in Deuteronomy), from defeat and captivity (Solomon's prayer),[5] or eschewing idolatry as Samuel

5. I Kings 8.

encourages,[6] the nation must change orientation and direction. This in no way implies an achievement of that goal, but rather a shift in direction. That is, perhaps, why the preposition *el* is more common in exilic and post-exilic texts – much of the nation is outside of the Land.

The call to return *ad Hashem* means "to return *all the way* to the Lord": beyond this initial change of heart, the people must "arrive" at the proper relationship. Amos expresses hope that, motivated by their suffering, the people will come all the way back to God – but these disasters do not bring them back.

THE SECOND DISASTER: DROUGHT (VERSES 7–8)

And I also withheld the rain from you
When there were yet three months to the harvest

These phrases serve as a topic sentence, introducing God's role in the drought. The rest of the verses describe its selective nature and how the people attempt to survive it. Once again, the people are not inspired to reform their ways.

A Word about *Vegam*

The opening word *vegam* can be rendered several ways, and its interpretation impacts our understanding of how the Samarian audience is to understand this drought.

The word *gam*, typically translated as "as well" or "also," appears over 600 times in the canon. In some cases, however, it seems to carry a more intense and nuanced meaning.[7]

One such example is in I Kings 21:19. God tells Elijah to reproach Ahab for having Nabot killed so that he can seize his vineyard:

6. I Samuel 7:3.
7. Joshua 9:4; see Ibn Kaspi and R. Joseph Kara ad loc., compared with Rashi and Radak ad loc.; both understand the *vegam* as alluding to some measure of poetic justice.

> And you shall speak to him, saying: "Thus says God: 'Have you murdered **and also** (***vegam***) inherited?'"

> And you shall speak to him saying, "Thus says God: 'In the place where the dogs lapped up Nabot's blood, the dogs will lap up your blood **as well** (***gam ata***).'"

Here, *gam* firsts underscores the extent of Ahab's evil and bloodguilt; the second instance reflects poetic justice.

By introducing the drought with *vegam*, Amos points to its deeper message. Not only does this drought demonstrate God's ultimate control over life, death, and the market – as biblical droughts always do[8] – but this particular drought in Samaria is also an agent of divine justice. Just as the aristocracy, judiciary, and monarchy withhold sustenance from the poor, God withholds rain from the land.

The explicitly spelled-out timing of this drought, three months before the harvest, is a clear statement of providential disapproval. Three months before the harvest is the middle of the winter, when the spring grains are germinating and require significant rainfall for a healthy crop.

Note that Amos emphasizes that God both "withholds" rain and "sends" rain. Though rain in the winter is considered a "natural" occurrence, Amos implies that rainfall is always a gift from God and a sign of Providence: God is in control and nothing is to be assumed or taken for granted. If there is no rain, then God is withholding it; if it does rain, God is sending it. This is a variation of Isaiah's powerful declaration: "I am God and there is no other. Who forms light and creates dark" (45:6–7).[9] Neither light nor dark is the "default" state – both are the result of God's will.

8. See Amos 8:11–14.
9. Isaiah 45:6–7. In the case of deutero-Isaiah, we assume this to be an anti-dualist polemic, likely responding to the cult of Zoroaster. This is unlikely in the case of Amos.

7: I made it rain upon one city, and upon one city I did not make it rain

The parallelism and chiasmus in this stich is clear:

> *Vehimtarti*
> *Al ir eḥat*
> *Ve'al ir aḥat*
> *Lo amtir*

The heart of the chiasm emphasizes that it is God who determines which city gets water and which does not. Is this phenomenon, certainly familiar to the herdsman from Tekoa (where such rain-patterns are common), a sign of God's favor for one city and disfavor for the other? In this tale of two cities, will it be the best of times for one, and the worst of times for the other? We will yet see that Amos turns *both of them* into warning signs.

We will also discuss the prophet's shrewd use of the verb *matar* (rain) in four different forms in a single verse.

One plot will be rained upon, and one in which there will be no rain will wither away

While this phrase seems to be another example of the previous selection, a certain element invites attention. The first half of this clause mirrors the first half of the previous phrase (*ir eḥat/ ḥelka aḥat*), but the second adds the assumed consequence. The plot of field that gets no rain dries out. Why isn't this consequence mentioned in the context of the cities?

In the ancient world, there was no simple way to share rain with neighboring cities. In the case of adjacent fields, however, it is relatively easy to dig trenches or use some other method to bring water from one field to another. These two *ḥelkot* presumably belong to different people, for why would someone fail to water his dry field if they have water to spare elsewhere?

A more likely reading is that these two fields are owned by two people, but the one with plenty does not share with his neighbor. Hence, this verse stresses that the field that has not received plenty "from heaven" withers, because the farmer refuses to help his neighbor.

Even when God blesses some and withholds from others, the people do not help each other.

Note that the next verse only mentions the inter-city requests for water, but does not mention any fields – were these requests made, only to be refused?

8: So two or three cities wandered to one city to drink water and were not sated

Perhaps a more accurate breakdown is:

Vena'u shetayim veshalosh arim *el ir aḥat*
Lishtot mayim velo yisba'u

Situated in the middle of our structure is the same *ir aḥat* from the previous verse, the one blessed with water. On the outside are the deprived cities, who are "not sated." Do the blessed cities refuse to share, or is there simply not enough to go around? The second reading seems more consistent with the verb *yisba'u*.

R. Joseph Kara, however, suggests a different approach: rainfall or no rainfall, both cities are cursed.[10] One city suffers from drought, while one receives too much rain, no sunshine, and their crops rot. As a result, neither city can be sated.

Yet you did not return to Me, says the Lord

In spite of all of this, with the manifest providence of God, you have still not returned.

10. Following Rashi, per Ta'anit 6b. It seems that Rav's statement is in reference to the second half: the field that gets rain is also cursed. This is borne out by Rav Ashi's support ad loc.

THE THIRD DISASTER: AGRICULTURAL RUIN (VERSE 9)

The opening *Hikeiti* (stress on the penultimate: *hi-KEI-ti*) is best translated in the pluperfect: "I had smitten you." These events have already taken place, but, as the prophet points out, these "disciplinary measures" accomplished nothing.

In contrast, three familiar instances of *hikeiti* in the Torah, in which the ultimate syllable is stressed (*hi-kei-TI*), indicating future tense, are all divine threats.[11] Elsewhere, Amos also uses *hikeiti* in the future tense as a threat (3:7).

Besides our text, there are only two instances where the Tanakh uses the word in this form;[12] not surprisingly, both are uttered with a sense of frustration, as if this "smiting" was an unfulfilled opportunity for reflection, repentance, and change. Jeremiah bemoans: "I smote your sons for naught"(2:30). Much later, Haggai castigates the priests of the impending Second Temple for their ignorance of the law and disrespect for the holy despite God's punishment:

> **I smote you** with blight and with mildew and with hail in all the work of your hands, yet you did not turn to Me, says the Lord. (2:17)

The similarity to Amos is more than coincidental – Haggai deliberately borrows Amos's words, which were likely known to the priests of Jerusalem over two centuries later. Evidently, plagues struck Judah's fragile agricultural infrastructure at the beginning of the Persian era, and Haggai interprets them as God's response to the people's estrangement from His Torah. The details of this verse reflect a concrete event of his time, rather than something of the distant past, but his use of Amos's language suggests that he is equating the people's estrangement from God with the corruption of the Samarian court and aristocracy in Amos's time.

---

11. Exodus 3:20, 12:12; Leviticus 26:24.
12. A third may be Ezekiel 22:13. I have deliberately omitted Jeremiah 33:5 as that seems to be, per Shadal, a parenthetic statement.

In any case, the use of *hikeiti* in the pluperfect is rare in Tanakh,[13] especially when spoken with God's voice.[14]

Shidafon and *Yerakon*

Plagues of blight (*shidafon*) and mildew (*yerakon*) are a familiar biblical pair;[15] in fact, they never appear independent of each other.[16] "Blight" means that the plant tissue is browning and dying; although *yerakon* suggests the word "green," it is a whitish growth that indicates that the plant is starved of nutrients and will have stunted growth. While unrelated, these conditions are both serious agricultural crises. "Blight and mildew," therefore, seem to be a blanket phrase for the loss of an entire year's yield. This crisis naturally recalls the year of plagues that struck the Egyptians. Hence, the Deuteronomic series of curses that culminates with Israel's return to slavery in Egypt (28:68) begins with a list of threats that recalls the Egyptian plagues, of Egypt's destruction before Israel's salvation.

When Solomon describes calamities that evoke prayer, he mentions this pair of agricultural crises – which are events that ought to stir the nation to turn to God in prayer. When Israel suffers from plagues similar to those that struck the Egyptians, they ought to reflect on how far they have strayed from God, and whether He is now tormenting them with the same measures that once preceded their deliverance.[17] This alone should have brought them back to God.

Your Many (Gardens...)

There are only six biblical instances of the infinitive form *harbot* (assumed to be equivalent to *leharbot* or *lema'an harbot*; see below). A brief perusal

13. There is one instance where a human makes this statement about himself: Samson, regarding his slaughtering the thousand Philistines, boasts that *hikeiti elef ish* (Judges 15:16).
14. It is fair to assume that once God has smitten, there isn't much of an audience to address.
15. Deuteronomy 28:22; I Kings 8:37 (= II Chronicles 6:28).
16. The one exception isn't really an exception, as Jeremiah 30:6 describes tormented human faces.
17. Amos will build on this image in the next rebuke.

of these six instances reveals an interesting pattern. When this infinitive is associated with human endeavor,[18] it is associated with problematic excess; but when associated with divine action,[19] it refers to blessing.

Humans who seek excess always do so, it seems, at terrible cost. Even the two instances where God increases the nation's population are presented within a negative context. This suggests that the word *harbot* connotes problematic excess. Thus Amos's use of this rare infinitive clearly condemns the greed of the Samarian elite, whose wealth is gained by exploiting the oppressed members of society – Amos's constant refrain.

One final note about *harbot*. The greedy acquisition of *ganot* and *keramim*, of gardens and vineyards, finds its starkest biblical expression in the story of Nabot of Jezreel,[20] which epitomizes the corruption of the Samarian monarchy. The word *harbot* should instantly remind the Samarian audience of the sinful reign of Ahab and Jezebel, only a few generations back.

9: Your many gardens and your vineyards; your fig trees and your olive trees

The cantillation marks split the four nouns in this phrase into two pairs: *ganot* (gardens) with *keramim* (vineyards), and *te'einim* (figs) with *zeitim* (olives), which means "fig orchards" and "olive groves." Do they usually appear together? Should they indeed be categorized as two pairs, or are they a general term (gardens) followed by three specific types? This largely depends on how we read the word *gan*.

Gan in Tanakh

Gan (and its alternative form, *gina*) appears over 50 times in biblical narrative, poetic, and prophetic literature. BDB considers the root of *gan* to be *g-n-n* (to protect)[21] and reads it as "enclosure." Indeed, a *gan*,

18. Deuteronomy 17:16; Proverbs 22:16, 25:27.
19. Deuteronomy 28:63; I Chronicles 27:23.
20. I Kings 21.
21. See, *inter alia*, Isaiah 31:5; this is the root of *hagana* and *magen*.

a garden, is nature enclosed and protected. God places Adam inside the "Gan" of Eden to tend it; when Adam is exiled from the *gan*, he is kept out of this enclosure. The lovers of the Song of Songs long to be alone together, secluded in the garden.[22]

Amos himself uses this word in parallel to "vineyards": one day, Israel will return to the Land and "will (re)build desolate cities / They will plant vineyards and drink of their wine / They will make gardens and eat of their fruit" (9:14).[23]

Thus, in line with the cantillation marks, this phrase can be read as two pairs, one generic, and one specific: *ganot* and *keramim*, with the second half detailing the meaning of *ganot*: gardens of figs and olives.

While figs and vineyards are a common biblical pair,[24] and these fruits are included in the "seven species,"[25] the particular triad of grapevine, fig, and olive only appears elsewhere in the context of Jotham's parable,[26] where each of these trees are invited to become "the king of the trees." It may be that owning all these was considered a status symbol in the Samarian aristocracy, and that this is the focus of Amos's diatribe.

In any case, all of these trees have been devoured by locusts. *Gazam*, a species of locust most well-known from Joel's prophecy,[27] again evokes the plagues of Egypt and the particular message this imparts.

Yet you did not return to Me, says the Lord.

22. For example, 5:1.
23. Jeremiah, again building on Amos, uses this meaning for *gan* in his epistle to the exiles in chapter 29 and in his elegant prophecy about the return to Zion in chapter 31.
24. For example, I Kings 5:5; Jeremiah 8:13.
25. Deuteronomy 8:8.
26. Judges 9.
27. Joel 1:4, 2:25.

THE FOURTH DISASTER: DEVASTATING PLAGUE (VERSE 10)

This plague is described as having been "sent" (*sh-l-ḥ*). This root has various related meanings: it may refer to sending things[28] or people;[29] with the *lamed* prefix or the preposition *el*, it means to "summon"[30] or " exile."[31]

Sometimes, however, it expresses destructive or even murderous intent. The moment before Abraham slaughters Isaac upon the altar, God's angel cries out, "Do not send (*tishlaḥ*) your hand against the boy" (Gen. 22:12). To declare innocence regarding theft, a person must swear that "he did not send his hand (*lo shalaḥ yado*) upon his friend's property" (Ex. 22:7).

This root may also express divine punishment:

> I will send (*veshilaḥti*) pestilence (*dever*) among you[32]

The Exodus process, beginning with the requisite punishment of the Egyptians, is foretold with the words:

> I will send (*veshilaḥti*) My hand and strike Egypt… [33]

This root appears in the context of pestilence, the fifth Egyptian plague, *dever*.

> I sent My hand (*shalaḥti et yadi*), and I smote you and your nation with pestilence… [34]

This is immediately prefaced by His promise to Pharaoh:

---

28. Genesis 37:32.
29. Ibid. 32:3–4.
30. I Samuel 11:6; Numbers 22:37.
31. Deuteronomy 24:1, paralleled in Jeremiah 3:1.
32. Leviticus 26:25; see also Ezekiel 28:23.
33. Exodus 3:20.
34. Ibid. 9:15.

> This time, I will send (*shole'aḥ*) all of my plagues to your heart ...[35]

Amos also uses this root to describe God's punishment of pestilence against His people.

The more difficult clause in this verse is *bederekh Mitzrayim* – what is the meaning of this phrase? Will God plague them as He did the Egyptians? Or does it mean that, more recently, a certain plague struck the people on the road to Egypt? The subsequent mention of "young men" (soldiers?) and "horses" suggests that this refers to some sort of military campaign involving Egypt. How do the *Rishonim* interpret this phrase?

Bederekh Mitzrayim: A Survey of the *Rishonim*

R. Eliezer of Beaugency suggests that the people went to Egypt for help, without clarifying what sort of aid they sought. R. Yosef ibn Kaspi suggests that this refers to Hosea ben Ela (mid-eighth-century BCE), who turned to Egypt for military assistance; we will discuss this reading below. Radak, in contrast, surmises they were going to Egypt for provisions instead of turning to God: "And you did not think that I was the one who brought the famine upon you that you should return to Me."[36]

Rashi interprets that "*bederekh Mitzrayim*" refers to a plague that afflicted the Israelites on their way out of Egypt. R. Joseph Kara, however, interprets *bederekh Mitzrayim* as those "who died during the three days of darkness."[37] Thus he links this plague to the plagues of Egypt – albeit to the plague of darkness, not *dever.*[38]

35. Ibid. 9:14.
36. Metzudat David concurs.
37. This is a surprising comment, considering that there is no textual basis for claiming a pestilence during the plague of darkness. It is likely rooted in the midrashic tradition that the plague of darkness was effected in order to stealthily kill off those Hebrews who were reluctant to participate in the Exodus.
38. Paul (p. 80) makes a similar claim that *bederekh Mitzrayim* (here and in Isaiah 10:24, 26 should be understood as "in the manner that I did to Egypt" – a direct allusion to the plague of pestilence.

The Sword and the Horses

Is this a separate event, or part of the plague that took place *bederekh Mitzrayim*? Is the death of the young men slain by the sword the plague itself?

Medieval commentators generally read them as part of the same crisis; Radak perceives them as two distinct tragedies that take place within one event: "You went to Egypt and I sent against you pestilence and the sword of the enemy on the road." R. Eliezer of Beaugency sees it as a double blow: they are afflicted with pestilence on the way to Egypt and attacked by the sword on their way back.

Modern scholars tend to see them as separate attacks. Hakham reads it as a skirmish with Aram (the prominent enemy of that time) with unusually high casualties.[39] Paul, in contrast, counts the punishments in this entire sequence differently, numbering the pestilence as the fifth attack and the sword as the sixth.[40] He concedes, following an earlier biblical trope,[41] that this is a series of catastrophes, rather than one continuous event.

Nonetheless, all agree that the third clause is linked to the second clause: that the horses are ridden by the "young men," who are either taken captive while their horses are slaughtered, or they themselves are slaughtered while their horses are seized.

If we read "*bederekh Mitzrayim*" as "*on* the way to Egypt," as Radak and others do, then the prophet is reminding them of a recent incursion (or mission) to Egypt that ended in unmitigated disaster. If we favor Rashi, reading *bederekh Mitzrayim* as "*in* the way of Egypt," as referring to some element of the Exodus narrative, then this may simply be referring to some sort of a military skirmish – most likely, as mentioned, a violent conflict with Aram.

Either way, horses are historically associated with Egypt. Egyptian military power is associated with horses: at the Song of the Sea: "He

39. Hakham, 32. Andersen and Freedman, *Amos*, Anchor Bible 24A (New York: 1989) (henceforth "AB"), 443, raise the proposal that it may be referring to the events recounted in II Kings 13:7, but then reject it on the grounds that these events seem to be of recent vintage and fresh in the memory of Amos's audience.

40. Paul, 80; see also AB, 447.

41. For example, Leviticus 26:25.

cast the horse and its rider into the sea." Kings of Israel are prohibited from acquiring too many horses to prevent the inevitable formation of ties with Egypt (Deut. 17:16). Perhaps "the way of Egypt" also hints to exactly that: Samaria's materialistic obsessions have led to their corruption and thus their devastation.

I have raised up the stench of your camp into your nostrils

The use of the opening phrase, *A'aleh* (lit. "I have raised up"), creates an ironic, devastating rhetorical twist. The verb first appears in God's promise to Jacob just before his descent to Egypt: "I will go down with you to Egypt, and I will indeed make you also to come up (*a'alkha gam alo*)" (Gen. 46:4). Centuries later, God tells Moses: "I declare: I will raise you up (*a'aleh*) out of the oppression of Egypt" (Ex. 3:17). God uses this form of the verb once more, in the context of bringing the people out of Egypt (Judges 2:1).

Rather than an expression of redemption, however, here Amos wields *A'aleh* in God's voice, to describe how God raises up the foul stench of plague-driven death – still associated with the Exodus, but as an expression of Israel's suffering.

The terrible stench of death is *be'osh*, which appears in noun form only three times in prophetic literature.[42] In Joel and Isaiah, it describes God's victory over Israel's enemies and the stench of their carcasses. Here, however, Amos uses it to depict the stench of Israel's own dead.

This stink rises from "your camp" – not on the battlefield, but rather within the camp itself. Perhaps this alludes to the stench of Israel's own corruption – to how their greed and excess (like the king with too many horses?) has led to this death "*bederekh Mitzrayim*." Note that the stench does not rise on its own – God Himself "raises it" so that the living will smell it and take it to heart.

Devastatingly, even so,
Yet you did not (yet) return unto Me, says the Lord.

42. Isaiah 34:3; Joel 2:20; and, of course, Amos 4:10.

THE FIFTH DISASTER: DESTRUCTION AND SURVIVAL (VERSE 11)

The invocation of Sodom and Gomorra here seem to speak more to the justification for God's punishment than the actual event (which, of course, no one present could have experienced – a Sodom-like devastation leaves no survivors).

And you were as a brand plucked out of the fire

This recalls a later verse in Zechariah, where the High Priest of the Second Temple is a "brand plucked from the fire" (3:2); the unique phrase is clearly borrowed from Amos. Zechariah uses it favorably, in defending Yehoshua, the High Priest, against the Adversary's accusations. Amos, however, uses it ironically: the survivors are like Lot, who is saved, but not by his own merit (Gen. 19:29). Those who have survived the disaster have nothing to be proud of and no merits upon which to rest; rather, they serve as living testimony to the destruction their immorality has wrought.

Alas – Yet you (still) did not return to Me, says the Lord.

MAKING SENSE OF THE "DISASTERS"

The divine attacks are, in order, famine, drought, agricultural blight, pestilence, and destruction. The first two, famine and drought, are prefaced with the introductory "*Vegam ani/anokhi*," an expression of poetic justice. The first three – famine, drought, and agricultural blight – are all contained in the same Masoretic paragraph, together with the preceding passage, whereas pestilence and destruction each have their own paragraph. This hints, perhaps, to various layers of division within these five rebukes.

Although each rebuke is distinct, the first two can be grouped together in what we might refer to as the "*gam* unit." Another possible division is to group the first *three* together in the "bread-and-water unit."

The first plague, famine, is described as *ḥoser leḥem*. *Leḥem* can mean food or bread; here famine is most acutely felt in the area of grain production and consumption. The second plague focuses exclusively on water: rain for agriculture and drinking water. Pestilence and plant blight, described in the third disaster, further threaten food production. Although all three disasters could easily be read as allusive to the plagues of Egypt, Amos does not employ any familiar terminology to this end. As such, these rebukes stand on their own, creating their own context.

In contrast, the final two disasters are in clear dialogue with major historic events, and their language is undoubtedly familiar to the audience: they evoke the Exodus narrative[43] and the destruction of Sodom and Gomorra, which was well known at this time and used by various literary prophets as examples of utter destruction.

Thus, this sequence of disasters progresses from threats to daily existence to meta-historical, epic catastrophes. Regardless of the sequence of events in actual history, which we cannot know, Amos presents them in this order for his own rhetorical purposes, moving from "regular" threats like famine and drought to more calamitous, devastating destruction.

STRUCTURAL CONSIDERATIONS

Beyond the order of these disasters, their general structure also serves Amos's suasive purpose.[44]

The disasters may be read chiastically in several ways:

A) If we look at the *impact*:
   1. Famine in "all of your cities"
      2. Drought in "two or three cities"
      3. Pestilence and the sword in "your camp"
   4. Complete destruction (such that the survivors are a "brand plucked from the fire")

B) The information provided can also be arranged as a chiasmus:
   1. Result of the disaster (famine)

43. Amos already referenced it twice, in 2:10 and 3:2.

44. See Meir Weiss, *Sefer Amos*, vol. 1 (Jerusalem: 1992), 121.

2. The disaster (drought) and its consequences (migration, etc.)
    3. The disaster (locusts)
4. The disaster (pestilence, the sword) and its consequences (the camp's stench)
5. Result of the disaster (devastation)

The first and final disasters' mechanisms are not described; only their results. The second and fourth describe both vehicle of destruction (drought, pestilence / the sword) and its results (having to migrate from drought-stricken city to rain-blessed city, the stench from the camp). The middle disaster, the peak of the chiasmus, tells only of the disaster itself (the locusts), leaving the awful impact of this plague to the imagination (or for Amos's contemporary audience, to their memories).

One further structural observation:[45] Amos vacillates between describing how these disasters affect the people and how they affect their environment. The first disaster results in "cleanness of teeth" – that is, he describes human suffering; the next describes the disaster's effect on the city ("I will cause it to rain on one city..."); then on the field ("one field will get rain"); back to people; and so forth, in the following pattern:

1) People
    2) City
        3) Field
4) People
        5) Field
6) People
    7) City
8) People

Analysis of the Structure

A straightforward reading of this sequence reflects how the nation stubbornly refuses to repent, despite the rising severity of these disasters. Drawing upon these chiastic elements, however, we are able to detect a

45. Weiss, loc. cit.

more complex message. There are inner connections between the first and last disasters, as well as the second and the penultimate; other disasters are linked by their direct impact on people.

I believe that this complex, multi-layered interlocking rhetoric, punctuated by the epistrophic refrain "Yet you have not [yet] returned to Me," takes us back to the opening word of the series. The introductory *vegam* underscores how these disasters from God serve poetic justice.

Merely reading the series in order, we might apply this only to the first two disasters, which both begin with *gam*. If we were to be satisfied with reading the series in a linear fashion, then only the first two attacks would be understood that way. The Samarian audience would accept the famine and drought as direct punishments for their reluctance to feed and support the poor – but they might perceive the other disasters as divine anger without cause or as a sign of God's abandonment of His people, rather than as the result of their own behavior. But this intricate, complex rhetorical structure ties all five disasters together and presents the whole series in one light, as five tragedies that all stem from Israel's corruption.

Famine: The people are reluctant to provide for the poor and hungry, thus in response – *vegam* – God makes them suffer from hunger.

Drought: As described by Moses (Deut. 11:10–12), in the Promised Land, the most vital and basic of resources – water – depends entirely on God. Drought is always an expression of divine disapproval and is the central motivation for public fasting and prayer.[46] When the people refuse to provide basic sustenance to the poor, they are thus denied of such sustenance. They dwelled in their palaces, "reclining next to every altar" (Amos 2:11), so now they must wander as nomads, looking for water – but there will not be enough to slake their thirst.

Blight: The Land's great blessing of agricultural bounty – "grain, wine, and oil" and "flowing milk and honey" – is predicated on the people's

---

46. Mishna Ta'anit, chapters 1–2.

morality.[47] These plagues, as described in such warnings, increase famine, render rainfall futile, and undermine the economic infrastructure of this entire corrupt society.

Read in light of *vegam,* as poetic justice, these disasters emerge as the sevenfold result of Samaria's unwillingness to feed the poor.

Pestilence and the Sword: The Exodus carried with it an implicit danger: those who had been enslaved for several generations would, when opportunity presented itself, become slave-owners themselves instead of identifying with the isolation, humiliation, and rootlessness of the slave class. The beginning of the Law Code given at Sinai is about proper treatment of a fellow Hebrew who has been forced to sell himself as a servant.[48]

The Samarian upper class has forgotten that core lesson and have enslaved their fellows, at least figuratively: they oppress the lower class and abuse the judicial system, if not enslaving them outright. The plague of *dever,* so reminiscent of the plagues against Egypt, is most telling. The phrases "the way to Egypt" and the Egyptian trope "horses" further underscore the message that they have turned their backs on the Exodus, both in returning to Egypt and in assuming the position of "taskmaster" over their fellows.

Destruction: The mention of Sodom and Gomorra notes not only what happened to them but, more critically, also why they deserved it. As Ezekiel points out, Sodom's sin was the wealthy's refusal to help the poor (16:49). Though God had blessed Sodom – with "plenty of food" (*sivat leḥem*), "they did not support the hand of the poor and destitute." If we perceive the recent disaster as reminiscent of the destruction of Sodom and Gomorra – aware that this, too, is a case of divine poetic justice – the message clearly emerges.

Tragically, even so, "*velo shavtem adai, ne'um Hashem.*"

This unit concludes with God's response to the people's unwillingness to repent, which begins with the causal *lakhen* (therefore).

---

47. As delineated in Leviticus 26 and, more devastatingly, in Deuteronomy 28.
48. The *eved ivri* – Exodus 21:1–6.

This coda is a frightening yet majestic crescendo in two verses. Though v. 12 initially seems repetitive and empty, we will see that appearances are most deceiving.

The common "therefore" (*lakhen*) appears two hundred times in the canon; with one exception[49] in dialogue. It is usually, but not always, spoken in God's name. Although the word is inherently neutral, it expresses consequence: sometimes reward,[50] more often punishment:[51] "on account of the aforementioned, therefore the following will happen."

12a: Therefore thus will I do to you, O Israel

Some have interpreted the opening *Ko,* along with the *zot* in the next clause, as indicative that the prophet is gesticulating to emphasize his point.[52] Others suggest that *ko* is a shortened form of the oath-formula "*Ko ya'aseh vekho yosif.*"[53] A third suggestion posits that the word *ko* (thus) means that as a result, God will inflict these same punishments on you once more.[54]

Despite their merits, all three suggestions are unlikely. Although some sort of theatrical component sometimes accompanied prophetic declarations,[55] these gestures are invariably described or more than implicit in the text, and the lack of any such description is telling. While the oath-formula *"Ko ya'aseh… vekho yosif"* is common and has several variations, it is always presented in God's name, at the very least with God mentioned in the third person. "*Ko e'eseh* – Thus will I do" does not fit this model. Nonetheless, a certain aspect of biblical oath-formula *is* utilized in this passage, as we will see below. The argument that *ko* means that God will punish the people with these disasters again is the least likely reading. If after all these, "you have not returned to Me," then

49. I Samuel 27:6.
50. Numbers 25:12.
51. Numbers 20:12; Judges 10:13; and in prophetic rhetoric, Jeremiah 5:14, 7:32, 8:10.
52. Shalom Paul, *Mikra LeYisrael: Yoel and Amos* (Am Oved, 1994), 81.
53. *Inter alii,* I Samuel 3:17.
54. Hakham, 33.
55. This is the case especially in some of the more unusual scenes involving Jeremiah and Ezekiel, such as the breaking of the yoke on Jeremiah's neck in Jeremiah 28.

what would be the point of using the same tactics? Perhaps this would be a more convincing reading if the language were slightly different, something along the lines of *Ki khein e'eseh lakhem sheinit*: Thus will I do to you again. However, without a clear, explicit indication of intent to repeat these plagues again (and why would that help?), this reading is not compelling.

In this context, it is worth noting that R. Eliezer of Beaugency reads that God will finish the destruction that He started. This presents two problems: It assumes that the destruction "like the overturn of Sodom and Gomorra" of the fifth and final rebuke is only partial, and there is no evidence in the text for this. Additionally, it presumes that God has moved from punishment as a corrective measure to punishment as divine rage, but again, this is unsupported by the text.

One final note on this phrase. Although we have translated *e'eseh* as "I will do," both in this phrase and the next, there is room to read it as the pluperfect "I have done," which dramatically transforms the line from a foreboding warning of doom to a summary of the disasters before reaching his conclusion. This is how Andersen and Freedman[56] read it, based on Amos's use of the word *zot* as a reference to past events or something present before the people:

> [*Zot*] is never used [in Amos] as an adjective, but rather always as the independent pronoun, so it stands alone. It has a specific theological sense: it always refers to something or, more specifically, to the thing that [God] has done, is doing, or will do, or has said, or has revealed in a vision.[57]

Nonetheless, nearly all versions and translations (including the Targum, Septuagint, and Vulgate) read *e'eseh* as future tense, "I will do."

56. Anchor Bible, 450–452.
57. Ibid. 452.

12b: Because I will do this unto you

Together with the previous clause, this statement seems circular and deliberately vague: What is the anticipated punishment? What will God do to His obstinate and recalcitrant people?[58]

The opening word *Eikev* appears a total of fifteen times in the Bible: six in wisdom literature, five in narrative, and four times in oratory. These last nine are all used by God or His prophet.

All five narrative occurrences promise divine reward for loyalty (Abraham,[59] Caleb[60]) or punishment for disloyalty (David[61]). The term is used at a turning point in Moses's speech;[62] Moses may have been alluding to Abraham's blessings. The word appears just once in oratory (besides here): in Isaiah, the *eikev* consequence is not divine (5:23); rather, human corruptibility leads *eikev* to the perversion of justice. The relatively rare use of *eikev* lends it specific connotations. Starting with Abraham, it seems to reflect the rewards of loyalty and the consequences of treachery. When corrupt judges accept bribery, it is a deep betrayal of the power granted to leadership.

Here, *eikev* comes with divine punishment after the people have failed to repent. Once again, these five disasters are manifestations of poetic justice, and the use of *eikev* may convey two messages. First, the people bring these disasters on themselves with their own unethical behavior. Second, more profoundly, the upper classes' corruption is not merely an injustice; it is also a betrayal of the national and institutional raison d'être of the people and their institutions (specifically, the court).

---

58. One brief interjection is called for here. We have assumed that these two verses are threatening and foreboding for the people, and have interpreted the words as such. This is, however, not a matter of consensus among the *Rishonim*. Ibn Ezra (second commentary) informs us that "some interpret it negatively, *some interpret it positively*," and he goes on to present the "negative" (i.e., punitive) take on the verse. Later on he presents the positive understanding, which is oriented toward driving the people to repent, rather than destroying them. He is, however, alone among traditional commentators. Moreover, he doesn't present it as his own take, but rather as "some interpret it positively."
59. Genesis 22:18, 26:5.
60. Numbers 14:24.
61. II Samuel 12:6, 10.
62. Deuteronomy 7:12, 8:20.

The phrase "*zot e'eseh lakh*" is opaque and seemingly redundant: "Therefore, I will do this to you, because I will do this to you…" This repetition only amplifies the obscurity of *ko* and *zot*. We will need to look further in the text to decipher the import of these enigmatic words.

12c: Prepare to meet your God, O Israel

Is this the long-awaited resolution of *ko* and *zot*? Does a direct encounter with God mean further punishment? Most commentators, medieval and modern, read this passage as threatening; they are divided as to whether the threat is the punishment that awaits them upon meeting, or that the encounter itself inspires dread. Either suits the tone of the text; neither is more compelling than the other.[63]

THE WORDS BEHIND THE SILENCE

Verbal taboos are as old as human civilization. People avoid discussing intimate details of their lives, or mask private or distasteful subjects with euphemism; instead of "dying," for example, we speak of someone "passing away."[64]

Occasionally, overly upsetting biblical words or phrases are substituted with milder versions; these emendations are known as *tikkunei soferim*.[65] There is, however, a more intense textual silence, not replaced with protective niceties, in biblical rhetoric: the oath-formula used in *Tanakh* often omits the consequence for breaking its terms.[66] There are dozens of examples of this "protective silence," and two possible reasons

63. Curiously, the Sages use this phrase – and it is adopted and extended by later Halakhic decisors – in a prescriptive manner. For instance, the practice of the Babylonians to put on a belt before praying (Shabbat 9b–10a) is associated with this verse, as if to say, "when you are going to encounter God, preparation is appropriate." This is not an unusual move on the part of the Sages, taking phrases from *Tanakh* out of their context and eisegetically reading norms into them. This is commonly referred to as *asmakhta*.
64. See Pesaḥim 2a–3a.
65. See, *inter alia*, I Samuel 5:6, 9, 12 and II Kings 18:27 (= Isaiah 36:12).
66. For example, Genesis 31:52; I Samuel 3:17; Psalms 27:13 should be read this way as well.

for such omissions: either the listener is being protected from hearing a terrible and terrifying divine punishment, or the speaker prefers to leave it to the imagination. Great novelists, directors, and other artists have long understood that the imagination is far more powerful than any lexicon. The unseen or unknown is exponentially more frightening than anything actually shown or described.[67] This principle is liberally employed in biblical narrative. I believe that this is Amos's approach in this oracle. The *ko* and *zeh* are ominous; the audience waits, with bated breath, to hear what punishment awaits them. The silence that follows is deafening and, hopefully, terrifying enough to scare them into reflection and repentance. (Spoiler alert: it doesn't work.) Instead of hearing the painful details, they are told to prepare to meet God – though they are given neither preparation nor foreknowledge of what they will meet. This brings us to the crescendo and coda of this sequence.

This beautiful paean is inherently related to Israel's crime and punishment;[68] these dramatic lines are a sublime crescendo to the overall message and the mysterious epilogue that precedes it.

Verse 13

For lo (*Ki*)

The meaning of the word *ki* here is difficult. Many translations render it as "for," which is somewhat obscure in context; others entirely omit it. Paul reads it as a "connecting word" that bridges the threat of v. 12 to this verse's hymn.[69] Hakham offers two possible explanations:[70] that it connects to the ominous "Prepare to encounter your God, Israel," in the previous verse, explaining why that encounter demands preparation;[71]

67. Hitchcock understood this well; note also Stephen King's paean to Shirley Jackson, in reference to her classic *The Haunting of Hill House*: "She never had to raise her voice."
68. *Contra* Freedman and Andersen, who see this as a "cosmic hymn" with no association to the proximate verses.
69. Paul, 81.
70. Hakham, 33.
71. Ibn Ezra ad loc. makes a similar proposal.

alternatively, the phrase *ki hinei* is a poetic opening, as seen in the popular Yom Kippur *piyut "Ki hinei kaḥomer beyad hayotzer."*[72]

Behold (*hinei*)

This may be read with *ki* as an opening phrase. If, however, *ki* stands alone, then *hinei* requires explanation. The word *hinei*, archaically translated as "behold," usually introduces something unexpected.[73] But how is the description of God as the supreme and ongoing Creator surprising? Perhaps a different reading of *ki* will illuminate the "surprise" of *hinei*, as we will explore below.

He who fashions mountains and creates the wind

With these powerful words, Amos begins his praise of God. But why is there a hymn here at all, and why does it include these surprising elements – as opposed to, say, the more common motif of God's role in history?

These first two phrases contain a rare pair of verbs (rare in the Bible, yet familiar to many from daily prayers): *yotzer* (forms) and *borei* (creates); they appear in tandem just three other times, all in Isaiah.[74] The verb *bara* consistently describes God's role in creation (beginning with Gen. 1:1), but *yatzar* is rarely used; it is associated, rather, with the world of craftsmanship, specifically pottery, and expresses how the world is clay for God's hands.[75]

Nevertheless, this is still unusual imagery. Mountains are typically matched with the sea or hills,[76] not wind.

72. Note, however, that in the original source of that phrase, Jeremiah 18:6, the word *ki* does not appear and the passage begins with *hinei*.
73. For example, Genesis 22:13, 41:3.
74. Isaiah 43:7, 45:7, 18.
75. Jeremiah's visit to the potter is a classic example of *yotzer* as "potter" (Jer. 18:1–4, 6); indeed, we have reason to suspect that Jeremiah builds his entire presentation there on Amos's use of *yotzer* to describe God.
76. For example, Psalms 114; Isaiah 54:10.

Traditional commentators explain that this unlikely pair serves to define the range of God's control and power: He creates the firm, constant pillars of the earth (mountains), as well as the unseen and changing (wind).[77] But, again, why these specific examples?

And informs man of his words (His words?)

As indicated by the question mark, the meaning of this phrase is anything but clear. The meaning of the first two words is relatively straightforward,[78] and in the context of the passage we will read it as a present-tense participle, as *yotzer* and *borei*. The more difficult phrase is *seḥo*, which is translated here as "his words" or "His words." First of all, does the pronominal suffix refer to God or man: does God tell humanity about their thoughts (as per the midrash mentioned in the footnotes) or does God reveal His thoughts/ intentions/ plans to humanity (perhaps via prophecy)?

Moreover, the meaning of *seḥo* is unclear. Does it mean speech, reflections,[79] wanderings,[80] or something else? Traditional and modern scholars have suggested a wide range of meanings, largely based on the phrase *"Vayetze Yitzchak lasuaḥ basadeh"* (Gen. 24:63).[81] This ambiguity raises a further question. If the prophet intends to communicate a clear message, why does he use such an ambiguous word? Perhaps the word *seḥo* expresses multiple meanings.

77. As read by Ibn Ezra and R. Eliezer of Beaugency, for example.
78. In spite of the famous, frightening midrash that "even innocuous talk that constitutes no sin is brought before man when he dies (Semahot 1:5), or the more specific version, "even unnecessary talk between a man and his wife they tell him at the moment of death" (Hagiga 5b).
79. Shadal, Genesis 24:63.
80. Ibn Ezra and Radak, Genesis ad loc.
81. Gary Rendsburg, "'Lasûah' in Genesis XXIV 63," *Vetus Testamentum* 45, no. 4 (1995): 558–560.

Who makes the morning darkness

Most commentators read this as a parallel to the evening blessing of the Shema "*Golel or mipenei ḥoshekh*," "Who rolls away the light from the darkness": Who turns light (*shaḥar*) into darkness (*eifa*), but this interpretation is problematic. Again, why are such unusual terms used – *shaḥar* instead of *yom* or *or*? *Shaḥar* refers to the earliest part of the morning, while it is still "black" outside and light is barely on the horizon; turning that into darkness is not the frightening and impactful feat that turning midday into black might be, if that were the intent.

Hakham suggests: "He makes the light *as well as* the darkness," but this is inconsistent with the rhythm of the hymn until this point.

Ibn Janah reads these words in their opposite sense:[82] *eifa* is light (based on the anagrammed root *a-y-p* in Job 10:22), while *shaḥar* is darkness (*shaḥor* = black): God causes the darkness to turn to light. To claim that the phrase suggests hope and redemption in this context, however, is problematic.

And treads on the high places of the earth

Unlike the rest of the passage, this description is firmly anchored in earlier text: "Happy are you, Israel, who is like you ... and you will trample on their high places (*ve'ata al bamoteimo tidrokh*)" (Deut. 33:29) – although that refers to the Jewish nation's defeat of its enemies. Amos's contemporary, Micah, uses the same phrase to describe God;[83] it also appears in wisdom literature.[84]

The Lord, the God of Hosts, is His name

This phrase functions as an extended "signature" and the object of the epilogue's praise. As previously stated, these descriptions all impart a powerful, frightening, and destructive image – but, again, what is their purpose here, at the end of this chapter of bitter reproach?

---

82. Ibn Janah, *Sefer Hashorashim* (Berlin: 1896), 360.
83. Micah 1:3.
84. Job 9:8.

To resolve this larger conundrum, let's begin with the introductory phrase "*Ki hinei.*" In prophetic or wisdom literature, these two words serve to introduce a declaration;[85] in Psalms, it usually signifies an observation,[86] but in prophetic rhetoric, it generally introduces a divine commitment: a threat of punishment or, rarely, a reward.[87] Thus *Ki hinei* might be read as "Just as" – as a variation of *kehinei*: *ki* as a poetically expanded prefix *khaf*, indicating similarity.[88] This hymn can thus be read as directly related to the aforementioned rebukes and the punishment that awaits the obstinate nation.

How is this hymn in dialogue with each of the chapter's disasters?

Famine: In ancient Israel, planting was done in valleys, surrounded by mountains; the plots of cropland were bounded by mountains. This is the case in the fruitful Jezreel Valley of the Samarian kingdom. Thus, God is referred to as *Yotzer harim – He who fashions mountains.*

Drought: The wind is associated with rainfall. God "makes the wind blow and brings down the rain" – the two are inextricably bound together. Elisha warns: "You shall not see wind, nor shall you see rain";[89] in wisdom literature: "The north wind brings forth rain."[90] Drought is a reminder that God is *Borei ruaḥ* – He who creates the wind.

Blight: Most readings of the obscure word *seḥo*, as noted, are related to the verse in Genesis 24, when Isaac goes out *lasuaḥ* in the field just before meeting Rebecca. Rashbam and others[91] link this to the literal meaning of *siaḥ*, a bush; Isaac was out in the field planting. This, perhaps, links the word to the agricultural blight Israel has suffered. "*Maggid le'adam ma seḥo,*" does not mean, of course, that God tells man which trees he (or He) has planted; it does refer to "plans" or "thoughts." Yet the connotation of this unusual word perhaps alludes to the creedal position that God is able to interfere with humanity's relationship with the earth, for *maggid le'adam ma seḥo* – He informs man of His words.

---

85. Joel 4:1; Isaiah 3:1; Jeremiah 25:29; Malachi 3:19; Psalms 92:10 (twice).
86. For example, Psalms 48:5.
87. Jeremiah 30:3.
88. In the same manner as *min*, which is contracted to the prefix *mi-*.
89. II Kings 3:7.
90. Proverbs 25:23.
91. See Ibn Ezra and Radak ad loc.

Pestilence: The fourth disaster concerns Egypt, perhaps hinting to the *dever* plague of the Exodus narrative or the attack on the young men going to (or leaving) Egypt. There, too, God demonstrated His ultimate power over light and dark, plunging Egypt into utter blackness for three days, while keeping His people in the light. He is *oseh eifa shaḥar* – the one who makes the morning darkness.

Destruction: Finally, the people experience (some form of) utter destruction, God's full power unleashed on them as on Sodom and Gomorra. The image of God trampling on the high places (this hints, no doubt, to both mountains and idolatrous *bamot*) evokes Moses's promise of Israel's victorious conquest of the Land. When we picture God turning against His own people with such fury, we see *doreikh al bamotei aretz* – He who treads on the high places of the earth.

Thus this final verse is not out of place; phrase by phrase, it praises the aspects of God's power that have brought the disasters of this chapter upon Israel.

Chapter 6

The Fall of Israel (5:1–17)

The seventeen verses describing the "Fall of Israel" form a chiasm of seven components. We will explore the structure and its individual components to uncover the message of this complex, moving rhetoric. Although all seven sections are part of one Masoretic paragraph (with the exception of a *setuma* after verse 15), their division is self-evident, as we will see below.

(א) שִׁמְעוּ אֶת הַדָּבָר הַזֶּה אֲשֶׁר אָנֹכִי נֹשֵׂא עֲלֵיכֶם קִינָה בֵּית יִשְׂרָאֵל:
(ב) נָפְלָה לֹא תוֹסִיף קוּם בְּתוּלַת יִשְׂרָאֵל נִטְּשָׁה עַל אַדְמָתָהּ אֵין מְקִימָהּ:
(ג) כִּי כֹה אָמַר אֲדֹנָי ה׳ הָעִיר הַיֹּצֵאת אֶלֶף תַּשְׁאִיר מֵאָה וְהַיּוֹצֵאת מֵאָה
תַּשְׁאִיר עֲשָׂרָה לְבֵית יִשְׂרָאֵל:

(ד) כִּי כֹה אָמַר ה׳ לְבֵית יִשְׂרָאֵל דִּרְשׁוּנִי וִחְיוּ: (ה) וְאַל תִּדְרְשׁוּ בֵּית אֵל וְהַגִּלְגָּל
לֹא תָבֹאוּ וּבְאֵר שֶׁבַע לֹא תַעֲבֹרוּ כִּי הַגִּלְגָּל גָּלֹה יִגְלֶה וּבֵית אֵל יִהְיֶה לְאָוֶן:
(ו) דִּרְשׁוּ אֶת ה׳ וִחְיוּ פֶּן יִצְלַח כָּאֵשׁ בֵּית יוֹסֵף וְאָכְלָה וְאֵין מְכַבֶּה לְבֵית אֵל:

(ז) הַהֹפְכִים לְלַעֲנָה מִשְׁפָּט וּצְדָקָה לָאָרֶץ הִנִּיחוּ:

(ח) עֹשֵׂה כִימָה וּכְסִיל וְהֹפֵךְ לַבֹּקֶר צַלְמָוֶת וְיוֹם לַיְלָה הֶחְשִׁיךְ הַקּוֹרֵא לְמֵי הַיָּם
וַיִּשְׁפְּכֵם עַל פְּנֵי הָאָרֶץ ה׳ שְׁמוֹ: (ט) הַמַּבְלִיג שֹׁד עַל עָז וְשֹׁד עַל מִבְצָר יָבוֹא:

(י) שָׂנְאוּ בַשַּׁעַר מוֹכִיחַ וְדֹבֵר תָּמִים יְתָעֵבוּ: (יא) לָכֵן יַעַן בּוֹשַׁסְכֶם עַל דָּל
וּמַשְׂאַת בַּר תִּקְחוּ מִמֶּנּוּ בָּתֵּי גָזִית בְּנִיתֶם וְלֹא תֵשְׁבוּ בָם כַּרְמֵי חֶמֶד נְטַעְתֶּם
וְלֹא תִשְׁתּוּ אֶת יֵינָם: (יב) כִּי יָדַעְתִּי רַבִּים פִּשְׁעֵיכֶם וַעֲצֻמִים חַטֹּאתֵיכֶם צֹרְרֵי
צַדִּיק לֹקְחֵי כֹפֶר וְאֶבְיוֹנִים בַּשַּׁעַר הִטּוּ: (יג) לָכֵן הַמַּשְׂכִּיל בָּעֵת הַהִיא יִדֹּם
כִּי עֵת רָעָה הִיא:

(יד) דִּרְשׁוּ טוֹב וְאַל רָע לְמַעַן תִּחְיוּ וִיהִי כֵן ה׳ אֱלֹהֵי צְבָאוֹת אִתְּכֶם כַּאֲשֶׁר
אֲמַרְתֶּם:

(טו) שִׂנְאוּ רָע וְאֶהֱבוּ טוֹב וְהַצִּיגוּ בַשַּׁעַר מִשְׁפָּט אוּלַי יֶחֱנַן ה׳ אֱלֹהֵי צְבָאוֹת
שְׁאֵרִית יוֹסֵף: ס

(טז) לָכֵן כֹּה אָמַר ה׳ אֱלֹהֵי צְבָאוֹת אֲדֹנָי בְּכָל רְחֹבוֹת מִסְפֵּד וּבְכָל חוּצוֹת
יֹאמְרוּ הוֹ הוֹ וְקָרְאוּ אִכָּר אֶל אֵבֶל וּמִסְפֵּד אֶל יוֹדְעֵי נֶהִי: (יז) וּבְכָל כְּרָמִים
מִסְפֵּד כִּי אֶעֱבֹר בְּקִרְבְּךָ אָמַר ה׳:

A: *KINA* ("DIRGE")
1 Hear this word which I take up for a lamentation over you, O house of Israel: 2 She has fallen and will never again rise, the maiden of Israel; she is cast down upon her land, there is none to raise her up. 3 For thus says the Lord *Hashem*: The city that went forth a thousand shall have a hundred left, and that which went forth a hundred shall have ten left, of the house of Israel.

B: SEEKING GOD
4 For so says *Hashem* unto the house of Israel: Seek Me, and live; 5 but do not seek Beit El, nor enter into Gilgal, and pass not to Be'er Sheva; for Gilgal shall surely go into captivity, and Beit El shall come to nothing. 6 Seek *Hashem*, and live – lest He break out like fire in the house of Joseph, and it devour, and there be none to quench it in Beit El.

C: REBUKE
7 You who turn judgment to wormwood, and cast righteousness to the ground;

D: HYMN
8 He that makes the Pleiades and Orion and brings on the shadow of darkness in the morning and blackens the day into night; that calls for the waters of the sea and pours them out upon the face of the earth; *Hashem* is His name; 9 that causes destruction to flash upon the strong, so that destruction comes upon the fortress.

C': REBUKE
10 They hate him that reproves at the gate, and they abhor the one that speaks uprightly. 11 Therefore, because you trample upon the poor, and take from him exactions of wheat; you have built houses of hewn stone, but you will not dwell in them, you have planted pleasant vineyards, but you will not drink of their wine. 12 For I know how many are your transgressions, and how mighty are your sins; you that afflict the just, that take a ransom, and that turn aside the needy at the gate. 13 Therefore the wise keeps silence in such a time; for it is an evil time.

B': SEEKING GOD
14 Seek good, and not evil, that you may live; and so that *Hashem*, the God of Hosts, should be with you, as you say. 15 Hate evil, and love good, and establish justice at the gate; perhaps *Hashem*, the God of Hosts, will be gracious unto the remnant of Joseph.

A': *KINA* ("DIRGE")
16 Therefore thus says *Hashem*, the God of Hosts, the Lord: Lamentation shall be in all the public places, and they will say in all the streets: "Alas! Alas!" and they shall call the farmer to mourning and proclaim

lamentation to such as are skillful of wailing. 17 And in all vineyards shall be lamentation; for I will pass through your midst, says *Hashem*.

INITIAL OBSERVATIONS

The seven paragraphs form a clear chiasmus. God's name, the Tetragrammaton, is used seven times, with an additional, eighth mention serving as the unit's signature (at the end of verse 17). God's name appears three times in the first half, once in the axis verse and three more times in the second half – but not in the two rebuke sections (C-C').

The opening and closing sections employ lamentation language (*kina, misped*). In addition, the opening dirge has three verses, whereas the final one has two, just as the opening "seek" section has three verses and the closing "seek" section has two. This sense of "tapering" is further bolstered by the use of *darash*, "seek," in the two "seeking God" sections: it appears three times in the first, but only once in the closing "seek" passage, as if grimly reflecting that God is no longer being sought out.

Furthermore, though the closing "dirge" section is shorter than the first, its grief and lament is far deeper: there is only one word for lamentation (*kina*) in the opening section, but seven such words in the closing section (*misped, ho-ho, evel, misped, nehi, misped*). The opening section's most explicit lamentation word, *kina*, is omitted in the final one, as if expressing that the final sense of torment and loss is of an entirely different nature.

At its heart is a surprising hymn, as seen before in Amos's oracles, and once again we will explore the cosmic praise's relationship with the rebuke in which it is embedded.

The rebuke section (including the hymn) comprises seven verses; various "sevens" continue to reflect Amos's penchant for the heptad.

First Impressions

The structure seems to follow a reasonable suasive order. First, the prophet proclaims lamentation – which is prognosticative, not descriptive. He then outlines the people's faults that, if left uncorrected, will lead to his predictions' tragic fulfillment. He continues with direct rebuke of their behavior in the hope it will move them to repent, and follows with a clearer vision of the society they ought to be building. All of this concludes with intense lamentation, which will come to pass unless they take Amos's reproach to heart.

There is another rhetorical progression at play here. The opening section mentions "house" seven times: the "house of Israel" three times, "the house of God" three times, and the "house of Joseph" once. In contrast, the word "house" appears twice in the second half, referring not to figurative houses that represent people (or God), but rather to concrete houses, to the mansions of the wealthy: "houses of hewn stone."

In apposition to the metaphoric houses of the first half, the second half refers to public locations seven times: the gate (three times), the vineyard (twice), the public square (once), and the outskirts (once). Note that the "house of Joseph" becomes "the remnant of Joseph" in the second half. Perhaps this serves to shame the Israelite elite: they cannot remain hidden inside the house, nor keep the poison fruit of their immorality hidden from view.

This also signals the destruction of the "house"; moreover, as expressed in the final lament, those who suffer the most will be the farmer and vintner as their crops fail.

Through this structure, Amos hopes against all odds that the people will recognize the poison that threatens their society and take measures before its fall. Although he fears that the northern kingdom's fall is inevitable, he still attempts to speak to their hearts and frighten them into repentance.

FIRST *KINA*

This is the third time Amos uses the ominous *shimu* opening. The previous rebuke sequence ends with a sense of foreboding: "Prepare to meet your God, Israel." The prophet continues by imploring his audience to listen to God's word (perhaps this is the true meaning of "Prepare to meet your God, Israel"). What they do not expect is for him to speak of the tragic future as if it were already realized.

1: Which I take up for a lamentation over you

The verb *nosei*, lift up, is commonly paired with the object "voice," usually in the context of wailing and crying[1] – as here, as voices raised in lament. Amos is the first prophet to utter a lament and, with the exception of David's laments,[2] this is the first appearance of the word *kina*.[3] Jeremiah, who often echoes Amos's rhetorical style, also raises his voice in lamentation.[4]

The preposition *aleikhem* ("over you") is jarring. Instead of lamenting *with you* or *on your behalf*, the prophet is lamenting *over you*, as if over a dead body. Amos is not inviting the audience to join him in the rites of mourning; rather, he is lamenting over them – in the hopes of rousing the Samarian aristocracy from their complacence.

The word *kina* itself is relatively rare, appearing eighteen times in the entire canon (including ten instances in Ezekiel). A *kina* is not only recognizable by its content – mourning a great and deep loss – but also by its form. Biblical poetry is generally balanced in meter and has a symmetrical relationship in stressed syllables between its constituent halves.[5] *Kina*-meter, however, is deliberately imbalanced, as if to reflect the mourner's destabilizing grief. The biblical audience intuitively seeks balance in poetry; the poetic imbalance is a sign that something is not right.

The book of Lamentations (which surprisingly lacks the word *kina*) is one long *kina* in five chapters. The first, second, and fourth chapters all demonstrate this "*kina*-meter." For instance, the famous opening verse has eight stressed syllables in the first half and only six in its second half; this generates a sense of catastrophe from the outset. The *mekonen*, the dirge-leader, seeks to awaken feelings of loss and disorientation among those present. In biblical times, professional mourners known as *mekonenot* would elicit feelings of loss and grief among those gathered.[6]

1. Genesis 21:16, 27:38, 29:11.
2. For Saul and Jonathan: II Samuel 1:17–27; for Abner: ibid. 3:33.
3. Curiously, David does not *raise his voice* in lamentation upon hearing of the death of his best friend and the king; Amos is the first to do so.
4. Jeremiah 9:9.
5. See the addendum to chapter 2.
6. Jeremiah 9:16 and *Mo'ed Katan* 3:8.

Amos does not adhere to this *kina*-meter, and his lament is composed of two balanced verses, with symmetrical content and syllables. Perhaps, given that the subject of his lament is alive before him, he cannot "grieve" to the full extent.

Amos uses the "house" motif throughout the first half of the rebuke sequence, lamenting the house of Israel, the house of God (Beit El), and the house of Joseph. By the end of the sequence, there will be no more protective walls or roofs; the lamenting will be held in open fields.

2: She has fallen and will never again rise[7]

The verb *nafal* implies more than just a "fall" – it carries with it the sense of an irrevocable plunge.[8] The added punch of *lo tosif kum* underscores the finality of the "fall" – which Amos describes as if it is after the fact.

The maiden of Israel

A young girl is a common metaphor for a nation. The nation feels youthful power, at the cusp of maturity, with its whole life ahead. Amos refers to them as *betula* to dash these expectations: she will be struck down just as her life is beginning, her potential unfulfilled (*betula* also means "virgin"). While Ezekiel and others use *betula* imagery as an expression of her infidelity or her status as a bride whose marriage has never been consummated,[9] Amos's use discusses her youthful vitality, power, and military strength.

She is cast down upon her land

The root *n-t-sh* bears a sense of abandonment;[10] more than just being "cast down" (*hushlekha*), which refers to the action, *nitesha* indicates an

7. Note the clever midrashic parsing that the community in the Land of Israel would use to read this verse favorably: *nafela lo tosif* (she will never fall again) – *kum betulat Yisrael* (arise, maiden of Israel)!
8. See, for instance, Esther 6:13.
9. Ezekiel 16; Joel 1:8.
10. I Samuel 12:22; Proverbs 1:8.

attitude of disengagement and an abrupt disavowal of responsibility or even relationship. Hence…

There is no one to raise her up

This final nail in the coffin may be understood in several ways: no one is willing to help her rise to power again, meaning that her allies have turned their backs on her; or that God has ended their relationship, preventing any future rise to power. Another reading is that there is no relief to her sense of abandonment, as long as He who has cast her away refuses to relent.

Amos now provides the reason for his lament. Since God has declared that there will be such devastating loss of life, it is a *fait accompli*; he mourns as if this reality has already been realized.

3: The city that went forth a thousand shall have a hundred left, and that which went forth a hundred shall have ten left

There are two ways to read this prophecy: as a devastating plague, or as a crushing military defeat.

The word *yotzeit* (going out) has military connotations.[11] If this is indeed a prophecy about a military defeat, echoing the threat at the first oracle's end, then the thousands, hundreds, and tens all refer to various military units. On the other hand, the maiden's corpse of v. 2 makes military imagery a less compelling read.

If we read the verse as a deadly plague, then the use of *yotzei* and the round numbers require explanation. The numbers can be read as mortality rates: that ninety percent of the population dies. The word *yotzei* may hint to the corpses cast out of the city when plague strikes. The definition of a plague in Mishna Ta'anit (3:1) is a city that "evacuates" (*motzia*) a certain ratio of the population. In all, it seems more likely that this lament refers to a deadly plague.

11. For example, Numbers 27:17.

Of the house of Israel

The prophet begins and ends his lament by calling to the "house of Israel," which creates an "envelope" structure. Moreover, the "house of Israel" itself is the corpse that will fall and never rise again.[12]

FIRST CALL TO SEEK GOD

4: For so says *Hashem* unto the house of Israel

Amos has already used the "messenger formula" to preface God's message to His servants. The more detailed *ki kho amar* formula used here was used in the previous verse, at the lament's end, announcing the looming deadly plague. Perhaps Amos uses the same formula here as a transition between the lament and his call for the people to seek God. It may also serve as a signal for the antidote: to prevent these catastrophes, this is what you must do…

The phrase *leVeit Yisrael* further cements the relationship between this call to return to God and the first lament, which begins and ends with *Beit Yisrael.*

Seek Me, and live

The root *d-r-sh* means "seek": to seek truth in judgment;[13] to seek out God;[14] not to "seek after the dead" (necromancy);[15] to seek the welfare of our city.[16]

To seek something usually means to achieve a certain goal: to determine whether a crime was indeed committed; to bring peace to the city. Seeking God, however, carries no secondary goal: it is an end in and of itself. This distinction is highlighted in our verse: *"Dirshuni – viḥyu!"* "Seek Me – and live!" The key to life is the very act of seeking God.

12. We will see how this "falling" is redeemed in Amos's eschaton with the raising of *Sukkat David* at 9:11. See our discussion there in chapter 12.
13. Deuteronomy 13:15, 17:4, 9.
14. Ibid. 12:5.
15. Ibid. 18:11.
16. Jeremiah 29:7.

5: But do not seek Beit El

Beit El, where Jeroboam built his southern sanctuary, was a common pilgrimage site.[17] Although there may be several places called "Beit El,"[18] the Beit El constantly mentioned in eighth-century BCE prophecy as a worship site is the one associated with Jacob's vision and altar, near the modern-day village of Beitin.

Nor enter into Gilgal

Note that in parallel to *lidrosh,* to seek, the operative verb here is *lavo,* to come or enter. The prophet does not focus on the worship there, but rather on the very act of visiting Gilgal (or Beit El or Be'er Sheva). Rather than a diatribe against idolatry, this reproach seems to focus on something more subtle and, if possible, more insidious.

And pass not to Be'er Sheva

Be'er Sheva is mentioned eleven times in Genesis, fourteen in the prophetic history,[19]and never in wisdom literature or Psalms; its only appearance in prophetic literature is twice in Amos. The place clearly has little significance in the context of prophetic rhetoric; if so, why is it suddenly mentioned here?

For Gilgal shall surely go into captivity

The phrase *haGilgal galo yigleh* has pleasing alliteration, but what does it mean? Idolatrous sites are usually threatened with destruction and desolation; why the emphasis on exile in this verse?

---

17. See I Samuel 10:3, and possibly Judges 19:18.
18. Judges 4:5.
19. And in the Second Temple histories, a total of seven times.

And Beit El shall come to nothing

This is another astute play on words (*Beit El yihyeh l'Aven*).[20] The book of Joshua records a town in Benjamin named "Beit Aven," to the west of Beit El. The name, read uncharitably, means "house of iniquity."[21]

DISCUSSION: BEIT EL, GILGAL, AND BE'ER SHEVA

Whereas I proposed that the earlier instance of Gilgal (4:4) refers to Elijah's Gilgal, this may not be the case here.[22] Most commentators assume that Amos always refers to Joshua's Gilgal because it was an ancient worship site – the Tabernacle was set up there until it moved to Shiloh. Samuel's Gilgal presumably refers to that same site. There are, however, no geographic markers in relation to Gilgal until the narratives of Elijah and Elisha,[23] which point to a different location in the Samarian hills. This, as we suggested earlier, is why Amos's first reference to Gilgal presumably refers to Elijah's Gilgal – ritual sites for other gods need not be associated with ancient Israelite worship, and it makes more sense that the Israelites are worshipping locally.

The mention of Be'er Sheva here, however, calls the identity of *this* Gilgal into question. Beit El's location is known; Be'er Sheva's location is known – do these two sites illuminate which Gilgal Amos is referring to?

There are two anomalies about the mention of Be'er Sheva here. First of all, Be'er Sheva is squarely in Judean territory, hardly a convenient worship site for Amos's Samarian audience. Moreover, there is no

---

20. I often point to this verse as an example of why Tanakh ought to be studied and taught in the original (Hebrew). So much of the glory and exquisite play of the text – not to mention the double- and triple-entendres that give birth to midrashic expansions – are lost in translation.
21. Keep in mind that we have already encountered *Aven* in the opening series of oracles (1:5), but that is in Syria. See our discussion in chapter 2.
22. See Radak, Amos 4:14, Hosea 9:15; see also Hakham, 28, fn. 1b, and Paul, 76. It should be noted that nearly all commentators assume that the Gilgal in all three citations is Joshua's; Andersen and Freedman have an extended discussion about the administration of the location and whether it was under Judean or Israelite control during the eighth century BCE (*Amos*, Anchor Bible, 430–433).
23. II Kings 2:1, 4:38.

biblical record of Be'er Sheva as a pagan site – as noted above, Be'er Sheva is never mentioned in prophetic rhetoric outside Amos.

Note the neat chiasm formed in these verses:

Beit El (do not seek)
  Gilgal (do not enter)
    Be'er Sheva (do not pass)
  Gilgal (will surely be exiled)
Beit El (will become "*Aven*")

This highlights Be'er Sheva as the chiastic central axis, at the center of Amos's reproach, even though it is not known as a site of idolatry. This spotlighting requires explanation.

Modes of Foreign Worship

Joshua's final address to the people points out two kinds of forbidden worship:

> And if it is bad in your eyes to serve the Lord, choose this day whom you will serve; whether the gods that your fathers served that were beyond the river, or the gods of the Amorites, in whose land you dwell.[24]

Prophets repeatedly warn against serving local gods. In ancient thought, it was terrifying to refuse to pay homage to the local deities and took absolute faith to deny their powers and worship God alone – hence the constant prophetic warning against serving the Canaanite gods. Joshua, however, also notes a less obvious temptation: worship of family deities who are familiar from stories about the past. Throughout Tanakh, we find people yearning for the "olden days."[25] After all, the patriarchs themselves worshipped God in ways that were prohibited after the Temple was built in Jerusalem – by building altars and monuments to God all over the

24. Joshua 24:15.
25. Numbers 11:5 ff; Judges 6:13; Ecclesiastes 7:10.

land. This passage, therefore, seems to denounce not idol-worship, but rather the kind of worship once practiced by their ancestors.

A key word in Amos's rebuke is *darash*. This is also a key word in Deuteronomy 12, when Moses warns the people that once they reach the Land, they must *seek* only the singular place God has chosen. Amos's use of *darash* in our passages, coupled with the unusual mention of Be'er Sheva, suggests that his focus here is not idolatry, but rather "ancestor-worship." His eschaton[26] envisions a full restoration of Judean monarchy – including the reunion of the kingdoms under one king and the recognition of Jerusalem and the Temple as the place that God has chosen.

Perhaps the Samarian community, drawn to the "old days and the old ways," were making pilgrimages to Beit El, already a "Royal Sanctuary"; to Gilgal, where Israel first camped upon their entrance into the Land; and to Be'er Sheva, where all three of the patriarchs worshipped.[27]

Note that Amos is not condemning actual worship, but rather "seeking," "coming," and "passing," which all may refer to pilgrimage. This explains why Be'er Sheva is the focal point of his rebuke – it is the most ancient and most direct link to the patriarchs, whose worship is certainly a beacon but should not become a lodestone, drawing the people away from the "new" place that God has chosen.

Excursus: A Brief Note on the Unique Status of Be'er Sheva

The town of Be'er Sheva, which does not appear in any of the books of the literary prophets save for ours, is one of the earliest cities to play a central role in Israelite history. Abraham, Isaac, and Jacob all settled there, each of them alternating their homes between Be'er Sheva and Hebron. It is a town with what seems like an obvious name – either meaning "the well of the seven" or "the seventh well," yet a closer inspection of the relevant texts shows a different and more confusing picture. The town is first named, seemingly, when Abraham and Abimelekh make a treaty there. Part of the treaty involved Abraham's giving Abimelekh seven lambs:

26. Beginning at 8:11 until the end of the book.
27. Genesis 21:33, 26:25, 47:1.

> Abraham set apart seven ewe lambs from the flock. Abimelekh asked him, "What is the meaning of these seven ewe lambs you have set apart?" He replied, "Accept these seven lambs from me as testimony that I dug this well." That is why that place is called Be'er Sheva, because there the two men swore an oath. (Gen. 21:28–31)

Subsequent to pointing to the "seven lambs," the text associates the naming of the place with the oath (*shevua* in Hebrew) – such that the location is best rendered, in translation, "the well of the oath."

The place is named, yet again, in the next generation:

> Abimelekh came to him [Isaac] from Gerar, with Aḥuzat his advisor and Pikhol the commander of his troops. Isaac said to them, "Why have you come to me? You hate me; you sent me away from you." They said, "We have seen clearly that the Lord is with you, so we say: Let there be a pact between you and us. Let us make a covenant with you that you will do us no harm, just as we did not touch you, just as we have done you nothing but good and we sent you on your way in peace. And now – the Lord bless you." Isaac made them a feast, and they ate and drank. Early in the morning they rose and exchanged oaths, and Isaac sent them on their way. They parted from him in peace. That day, Isaac's servants came and told him about the well that they had dug; they said, "We have found water." He named it *Shiva*, which is why the town is called Be'er Sheva to this day. (Gen. 26:26–33)

It is again unclear whether the *shiva* is the cardinal number – since the narrative reckoned six previous wells, making this well the seventh – or a reference to the oaths.

What is far more curious is the way that LXX translates the toponym. The general convention in all translations of the Bible, starting with the earliest one into Greek, is to render place names as transliteration. Hence Beit Leḥem ("house of food/bread/meat") is translated as Βαιθλεεμ (Beithle'em), and Canaan is Χανααν (Khanaan). Be'er Sheva, however, is usually translated as τῷ φρέατι τοῦ ὅρκου ("the well of the oath"). This is fairly consistent throughout the LXX and is only presented as Βηρσαβεε ("Beersabe'e" = Be'er Sheva) in those places where it is purely a geographic marker (as in "from Dan to Be'er Sheva"), but not when anything, important or trivial, happens there. Besides seeming to settle the question as to whether the *sheva* means "seven" or "oath" (clearly the latter), it may point us to a deeper understanding of the significance of that place, within the Israelite religious and historic consciousness.

It seems far-fetched to think that an oath between Abraham and/or Isaac and a local Philistine leader would be so momentous an event that it would forever shape the name and associations with this place, above other place names. I'd like to suggest that the event that crowned the place and caused it to be eternally associated with an oath included, vicariously, those two patriarchs – but directly involved the third:

> So Israel (Jacob) set out with all he had. When he reached Be'er Sheva, he offered up sacrifices to the God of his father Isaac. And God spoke to Israel in a night vision: "Jacob, Jacob."
>
> He replied, "Here I am."
>
> "I am God, the God of your father," He said. "Do not be afraid to go down to Egypt, for there I will make of you a great nation. I Myself will go down to Egypt with you, and I Myself will also bring you back; and Joseph's hand will close your eyes." (Gen. 46:1–4)

It was this commitment that God made to Jacob, on the eve of his departure from Canaan, that established the historic background for the foundational story of the Jewish people – the servitude and subsequent Exodus from Egypt. Hence, this place became forever associated with that mysterious night vision and would e'er be known as "the well of *the* oath."[28]

This may go a long way to explaining why, along with the northern worship sites of Gilgal and Beit El, Amos had to contend with people

28. See also Ziony Zevit, *The Religions of Ancient Israel: A Synthesis of Parallactic Approaches* (Bloomsbury Academic, 2002), 171–176, for a survey of the archaeological evidence for the existence of a cult site at Be'er Sheva.

desiring to go to Be'er Sheva (rendered "the well of the oath" in the LXX's translation of Amos) – this illuminates the association with "ancestor-worship" proposed above.

6: Seek *Hashem* and live

Amos voices God's threat in the third person – no longer *dirshuni,* but rather *dirshu et Hashem*; the sense is that even the mention of the Beit El/ Gilgal/ Be'er Sheva pilgrimages has distanced God from the people.

Lest He break out like fire in the house of Joseph

Beit Yosef often refers to the northern kingdom.[29] The motif of *bayit* functions effectively here, contrasting *Beit Yosef* with *Beit El.* If Joseph's house is burned, that will also mean the devouring and destruction of God's house (Beit El).[30]

And it devour, and there will be none to quench it in Beit El

This final line can be read in three ways:

1. There will be none *left* to quench the flames: the destruction of the north will leave no survivors.
2. There will be none *capable* of quenching the flames: people will stand by helplessly as destruction rages.
3. There will be none *interested* in quenching the flames: all those witnessing Israel's downfall will turn their backs and withdraw their assistance.

All three meanings stand: none who wish to help will remain; those who do will be unable or disinterested in helping.

29. For example, Jeremiah 31:19.
30. See how Obadiah turs this message inside-out and redeems *Beit Yosef* in Ob. 18.

FIRST AND SECOND REBUKE

This brings us to the rebuke section, which is interrupted by the hymn, the center of the chiasmus. This results in two rebuke sections – verse 7, then verses 10–13 – which we will analyze individually.

7: You who turn judgment to wormwood

La'ana, translated here as "wormwood," is a bitter, poisonous plant – most identify it as a species of the genus *Artemisia*. In five of its eight biblical instances, it is matched with *rosh* (or the "juice" of that root, known as *mei rosh*).[31] A metaphor for bitterness and punishment, its first appearance is at the covenant of the plains of Moab, where it symbolizes the bitter and poisonous growth of rebellion and apostasy (Deut. 29:17).

Amos later uses it again (6:12), together with *rosh*, to describe the warping of justice. The same bitter pill that offenders are forced to swallow is now the symbol of corrupted justice, when the innocent is subjected to the fate rightfully meant for his oppressors.

And cast righteousness to the ground

Though the verb used here (*hiniḥu*) is gentler than the translation, the intent seems to be closer to the word *hishlikhu*,[32] meaning "to cast down," usually in anger, resignation, or disposal.[33] The verb *hiniaḥ* appears elsewhere in this sense.[34]

This opening verse of the accusation is presented as a chiasmus:

Hahofekhim lela'ana
  Mishpat
  Utzedaka
La'aretz hiniḥu

31. Jeremiah 9:14, 23:15; once again, we see Jeremiah utilizing Amos's imagery.
32. Compare Daniel 8:7–12 and the three instances of *hashlekh* there.
33. Exodus 1:22 (!).
34. Isaiah 28:2.

This highlights the theme of justice, which will be the focus of this accusation.

The next two verses comprise the "praise-hymn" that interrupts the accusation; I will come back to this after discussing both rebukes.

10: They hate him that reproves at the gate

In the biblical period, the city gate was where the court and marketplace stood.[35] Accusations of corruption were made by the city gates and were thus heard not only by the accused judges, but also by a significant audience.

As Amos hints here, these rebukes have already been sounded. Rather than condemn the judges for their corruption, the people's reaction has been to "shoot the messenger."

This response is twice addressed in *Mishlei*:

He who despises rebuke is a fool (12:1)
He who despises rebuke will die (15:10)

Who is Mishlei's "hated *mokhiaḥ*"? Is it Amos himself,[36] or some other despised, ignored prophet? While Jeremiah's travails and the resistance he meets are recorded in full, there is no record of the *people's* response to him,[37] so we cannot answer this question.

And they abhor the one that speaks uprightly

Sanei and *ta'eiv* is a rare pair, which perhaps ought to be read as complementary rather than synonymous. *Sinah* is generally understood as personal and subjective; when a man has two wives and prefers one, the other is called *senua.*[38] *To'eiva,* on the other hand, suggests a more

---

35. Ruth 4:1; Deuteronomy 16:18.
36. Hakham (p. 40) raises this suggestion.
37. We do have numerous reports of how different leaders, including the king, reacted to Jeremiah's prophecies.
38. Deuteronomy 21:15–17.

categorical rejection (typically of idolatrous practices or forbidden sexuality) of things that are to be abhorred. We are never told "to hate," but we are told "to abhor."[39]

Perhaps Amos's rebuke should be understood as the people's two-stage response to prophetic reproach. First, they internalize a hatred toward their accuser at the gate. Next, they formally ostracize the source of the words, so that they may continue their perfidious behavior.

Although *tamim* is a relatively common adjective, the phrase *dover tamim* and the association of speech with this root is unique. Thus we have no frame of reference for interpretation. It may mean "a wholehearted speaker" (Radak's first proposal, Paul and Hakham), which is synonymous with "rebuker." Targum Yonatan explains: "one who speaks perfect things."

Once again, Amos's rebuke forms a chiasm:

Sanu vasha'ar (They hate at the gate)
  Mokhiaḥ (the rebuker)
  Vedover tamim (and the one who speaks uprightly)
Yeta'eivu (they abhor)

The focus is on the rebuke; after the hymn-praise, the prophet redirects the audience's attention to his rebuke of their "justice."

11: Therefore, because you trample upon the poor

The conjunctive adverb *lakhen* is just as likely to announce consolation as to reveal divine wrath.

The predicate in this clause *boshaskhem* is a *hapax legomenon* and must be interpreted from context. Rashi relates the word to the root *b-s-s*, as in "*bosesu et ḥelkati*" (Jer. 12:10), meaning "trample" (hence the translation here). Based on the Akkadian, Klein suggests "to draw farmrent," which seems consistent with R. Eliezer of Beaugency's commentary: "taking their house and inheritance in court." Further support may

39. Ibid. 7:26.

be found in the parallel stich, which accuses the people of withholding grain from the poor.

In any case, the implication is clear. The wealthy are exploiting the poor and depriving them of their basic needs.

And take from him exactions of wheat

Klein's interpretation of the above *hapax legomenon* is consistent with this accusation. A *maset* is a gift: Joseph gives his brothers gifts, *maset,* when they feast together (Gen. 43:34). It may also mean "tribute" and is associated with *mas,* a tax. If seized from the poor, it is certainly no gift; if it is in the form of grain (*bar*), then "farm-rent" indeed seems like a reasonable rendering.

One more detail about this clause: a tribute or farm-tax is usually *offered* by the debtor; the fact that the creditor "takes" it is another indication of exploitation.[40]

You have built houses of hewn stone

Hewn stone was considered a high-quality building material: in Isaiah, *gazit* (hewn stone) replaces *levenim* (bricks), much as cedars replace sycamore trees (9:9). Amos accuses Samaria's wealthy of using these immoral profits for luxury homes; but, he warns, they will never enjoy them.

But you will not dwell in them

The corrupt wealthy will not enjoy the fruits of their abuse. This warning is a departure from Amos's earlier threats: in his first oracle against Israel, the upper class successfully exacted payment from the poor and used it for their own selfish entertainment – the punishment was to come later, on the battlefield. Here, they will not benefit from their corruption. They will build their houses, but they will not live in them.

40. Compare with the description of the behavior of Eli's sons at I Samuel 2:13–16.

You have planted pleasant vineyards

Karmei ḥemed, pleasant vineyards, is a unique phrase; the closest biblical parallel is *sedei ḥemed,* desirable fields (Is. 32:12). Another phrase from Isaiah may further illuminate its meaning:

> On that day, they will respond: "This is a vineyard of wine" (*kerem ḥemer,* i.e., the vineyard has produced a good bounty of wine).(27:2)

Some even suggest that Isaiah's *kerem ḥemer* should be emended to *kerem ḥemed* (this is substantiated by several manuscripts). We will propose the reverse: *karmei ḥemed* should read *karmei ḥemer.* There are various examples of the *reish-daled* permutation.[41] Perhaps this is a bold suggestion, given the lack of any manuscripts supporting *ḥemer,* but the context does support it: "You will plant *wine-producing vineyards* but will not drink of their wine." *Ḥemer* makes more sense than *ḥemed,* desire; moreover, reading *ḥemed* as *ḥemer* produces a perfect parallel between *ḥemer* and *yeinam.*

But you will not drink of their wine

This verse warns about two of the three curses from the covenantal curse in Arvot Moab (Deut. 28:10):

> You will betroth a woman, and another man will lie with her; you will build a house, and you will not live in it; you will plant a vineyard, but will not use the fruit thereof.[42]

Amos beautifully reverses this curse in the book's conclusion.[43]

---

41. *Dodanim→Rodanim* (Gen. 10:4/I Chronicles 1:7), *Deuel→Reuel* (Num. 1:14/2:14); see Radak's comments at I Chronicles 1:7, Ibn Ezra, Eccl. 5:1; and Rashi, Job 15:24.
42. This curse famously reverses the order of the military exemptions in Deuteronomy 20:5–7; see Tosefta Sota 7:20; for an interesting follow-up, see *Hilkhot De'ot* 5:11 and *Kesef Mishneh* ad loc.
43. 9:13–15, esp. v. 14.

12: For I know

Amos has already mentioned God's *knowledge*: "You alone have I *known* of all the families of the earth" (3:2) to explain why Israel are held to such a high moral standard. This "knowledge" implies intimacy and revelation. This is what is expected of Israel, who have been exposed to God's knowledge; here, however, it is God's knowledge of His people's behavior that fuels this prophecy.

How many are your transgressions

Translation is difficult here: does the phrase mean "I know *how many* are your sins" (that God keeps count of their sins), or "I know *that* your sins *are many*"? These readings are equally compelling.

And how mighty are your sins

This is a straightforward parallelism. *Rabim* is matched with *atzumim* elsewhere.[44] Similarly, *pisheikhem* and *ḥatoteikhem,* while not synonymous, are used frequently in parallelism (see the discussion of *pesha* in chapter 2).

You, that afflict the just

Note the alliteration here. Rashi, quoting Targum Yonatan, reads *tzorer* as a transitive verb. Some read *tzorer*[45] as an intransitive verb, but this is not an appropriate parallel to *lokeḥei* and *hitu,* which are active predicates. R. Joseph Kara explains that the act of enmity expressed by *tzorer* here is taking bribes.

---

44. Exodus 1:7, 9.
45. Esther 8:1.

That take a ransom

Kofer means "ransom" and has both positive and negative connotations: depending on the context, it can be recommended[46] or disallowed.[47] In this context, it implies that those in power are accepting bribes to skew judgment against the poor.

And that turn away the needy at the gate

Are the poor literally "turned away," refused support, or is their path perverted ("turned away") at the gate (i.e., the court)? In context, the latter seems more likely.

Note that the "gate," true to its nature, opens and closes the core of Amos's rebuke:

Sanu vasha'ar mokhiaḥ…	*Ve'evyonim* ***basha'ar*** *hitu*
They hate him that reproves at the **gate**	And that turn away the needy at the **gate**

13: Therefore the wise keeps silence in such a time

The prophet concludes his rebuke with a mini-epilogue, evoking the central verse with *lakhen* (above, v. 11).

A *maskil* has deep understanding. The root *s-k-l* also means "to gaze" – to look carefully, in deep contemplation, before reaching a conclusion. Amos seems to be pre-empting the "haters" at the gate by stating that anyone who truly understands the situation will have nothing to say. This silence recalls Aaron's stillness at the tragic death of his sons (Lev. 10:2); at such times, there is nothing to say. As the prophet concludes:

For it is an evil time

The audience does not yet realize that a tragic time is at hand; a time of evil, in which rebuke ought to be heard without response.

46. Exodus 21:30, 30:12.
47. Numbers 35:31–32.

HYMN

At the heart of the chiastic structure, this hymn interrupts the prophet's rebuke.

8: He that makes the Pleiades and Orion

The constellation pair Pleiades (*Kima*) and Orion (*Kesil*) is mentioned twice in Job;[48] outside of Job, constellations are rarely mentioned in the Bible, even in paeans which praise God for Creation.[49] Although constellations were recognized in the ancient world,[50] they held little significance in our prophetic tradition. Surrounding cultures believed that the stars affected human fate, but Israelite prophets challenged this notion.[51]

And brings on the shadow of darkness in the morning

This phrase is an inversion of *Oseh shaḥar eifa* (4:13): God turns the morning (*shaḥar*) into darkness (*eifa*).[52] This phrase clearly means the opposite: He turns *tzalmavet* into morning.

Thanks to the well-known Psalm 23, *tzalmavet* is commonly rendered as "the shadow of death," based on reading the word *tzalmavet* as if it were a compound of *tzel* (shadow) and *mavet* (death). BDB does suggest this meaning, although it favors its interpretation as "deep shadows," arguing that the *mavet* component is not etymologically related to death.[53] Read thus, the word is pronounced *tzalamut*, an intense form of *tzel/tzelem*.[54]

---

48. Job 9:9, 38:31.
49. Psalms 104, 148, the numerous "creation hymns" in Deutero-Isaiah.
50. According to German archaeoastronomer Michael Rappenglück (cited, *inter alia,* in Graham Hancock's "Magicians of the Gods"), paintings found in the Hall of Bulls in Lascaux Cave in France dating back more than 17,000 years indicate an awareness of the night sky, and have a clear depiction of Taurus.
51. See Jeremiah 10:2; see also the medieval dispute in *Mishneh Torah, Hilkhot Avoda Zara* 11:16, and Nahmanides's commentary on the Torah at Deuteronomy 18:9–12.
52. As I noted above, Ibn Janah reverses the meaning at 4:13 and, as such, reads our clause as a variation of the same idea.
53. Although in Job 10:21–22, death is described as a place of *tzalmavet.*
54. See Amos Hakham, *Da'at Mikra* on Psalms, vol. 1, 125; the word *tzalmavet* is related

Two notes about *boker*. First of all, the word is etymologically associated with investigation – *bikoret*[55] – when things "come to light." The deep shadows of *tzalamut/ tzalmavet* turn to the bright, clear sunshine of *boker*. The choice of *boker* instead of *shaḥar* or even *yom* underscores the contrast between the obscurity of shadow and the clarity of daylight.

Second, the undefined *tzalmavet* turns to *haboker* (*laboker* is a contracted form of *lehaboker*), using the definite article. "He turns dark shadows into *the* morning," again emphasizes the difference between dim, frightening shadows and the clear, defined relief of daylight. Not only does God change night into morning; He also radically changes the atmosphere that accompanies this transition.

And blackens the day into night

Unlike its parallel in the previous hymn, the meaning of this phrase is clear. Biblical poetry often uses flexible syntax; here, the object (*yom*) precedes the subject (*laila*), and both are followed by the predicate (*heḥshikh*): the night comes and "blackens" (darkens) the day. This reflects nature: the day is clear and bright, and then night comes and darkens the sky as the light fades. One argument in favor of this reading is the absence of God's direct involvement in this change. Unlike the other four verbs in the verse, which express God's direct impact on the environment (*oseh, hofeikh, korei, yishpokh*), here the night itself darkens the day.

On the other hand, the hymn expresses how God effects this change; does this reflect God's intervention in the natural order, such as an eclipse (or *ḥoshekh Mitzrayim*)? Hakham suggests reading *veyom leleil heḥshikh*: that the *hei* at the end of *laila* is locative, meaning "to night," in which case God, not night, is the subject.

Broadly, these passages either praise God for establishing and maintaining natural order, or for His capacity to intervene and change natural order. Our reading may depend on how we understand this ode's

---

to similar words in Ugaritic, Akkadian, and Arabic, all meaning "deep darkness."

55. Leviticus 19:20; Ibn Ezra on Genesis 1:5.

"interjection" in the middle of Amos's rebuke; I will address this after analyzing this passage.

That calls for the waters of the sea and pours them out upon the face of the earth

This next description of God's power seems to express destructive intervention in nature, perhaps a tidal wave or tsunami; alternatively, this might reflect another facet of God's control of the natural world. Describing the regular movement of the waves that are "summoned" to the earth and spill their waters on its shores underscores God's constant hand in creation, however the theologians wish to define it.

***Hashem* is His name**

This signature is typical of a conclusion and thus generates surprise when this hymn continues for another verse; it does, however, indicate a shift in tone.

This first verse of the hymn praises God for His role as Master over Creation: for the hidden divine hand in its constant ebb and flow: the movement of the stars, day to night, night to day, and waves that cover the land and then recede. Another reading is that these verses praise God for His power to intervene in natural order. The approach we take affects the extent of surprise upon reading the subsequent verse.

9: That causes destruction to flash upon the strong

The root *b-l-g* appears just four times in the canon; the other three instances seem to mean "shine" or "gleam" according to the BDB (based on a similar Arabic cognate for "smile"); or "strengthen" according to Rashi, R. Joseph Kara, and R. Eliezer of Beaugency: God strengthens the pillagers in their destruction of the fortressed city. Paul points out that the context seems to render it parallel with *bo* (as in *mevi,* the causative form of *bo*). Therefore, he suggests that we read it as "brings." In any case, this clause expresses how God wreaks destruction on the "strong." This undefined object is explicated in the second bicolon as *mivtzar*, a fortress or walled city. God brings destruction – seemingly through human agents (hence *shod*) – on the strong, fortressed city.

So that destruction comes upon the fortress

Note the chiasmus: *mavlig* and *yavo* operate as an *inclusio*, with the pillaged city at the focal point.

Why the Hymn, Why Here?

R. Joseph Kara suggests that the hymn, which starts out with a description of God as "overturning" (*hofeikh*), is a response to the sins mentioned in verse 7: "Those who pervert justice into wormwood." In response to those who change justice into wormwood, Amos expresses that God changes day into night. If so, the descriptions of God's actions in v. 8 are destructive (although God's creation of the constellations and turning dark shadows into morning is not consistent with this theme).

This hymn can be read differently. It begins with praise for God and His constant hand in the natural order. Whether these rhythms are associated with astral bodies (as believed in the ancient world) or whether the astral movements themselves are part of that grand design is, for Amos's purposes, irrelevant.[56] In contrast to natural order, Amos's audience subverts God's justice and misuses God's blessing for oppression and exploitation. Thus, the hymn begins with its own *hefekh*: God's constant care for His universe is the *hefekh* of those who are *hofekhim lela'ana mishpat*.

At this point, the hymn seems to conclude with the signature form *Hashem shemo.*[57] But this is a false ending; in a surprising denouement, God's characterization changes from reliable Master of Creation to destroying pillager, enabling the otherwise impotent attacker to lay waste to the fortressed city.

The rhetorical effect is startling. Verse 8 could have left the audience with a sense of complacency: no matter what they do, God will

56. The question is highly significant from a cosmological-theological perspective.
57. Some manuscripts also have a *parasha setumah* here, indicating a break of sorts.

always keep His world turning. This hardly inspires fear. But then, with a surprising twist, the prophet reminds the people that God does not merely keep the engine running: as He creates, He also destroys. As His might drives the reliable rhythms of the world, His power can also turn those rhythms inside out, ravaging the mightiest of fortresses.

SECOND CALL TO SEEK GOD

14: Seek good, and not evil

This call can be understood in several ways. First, we need to determine if "good" here is an elusive adjective (an adjective with the attendant noun missing but assumed), an elusive noun (with a missing verb), or a simple, all-inclusive noun, as we have rendered it in the title above. Do we read it as "seek the good [thing]," "seek to do good," or "seek the good"? Ibn Ezra favors either the first or third, leaving it as an open question. Targum Yonatan reads it as "to do the good": as an elusive noun.[58]

Malbim suggests that *tov* is synonymous with God: that "seek good" is another way of saying "seek God"; *ra* thus refers to Beit El, Gilgal, and Be'er Sheva, those places the audience must *not* seek. Malbim then softens this idea by suggesting that *by* seeking good, they will effectively be seeking God.

Regardless of the meaning of *tov, ra* is its opposite; hence it might be read: "Seek the good things, and not the evil things"; or "Seek to do good, and not to do evil"; or "seek [the] good, and not [the] evil." Resolving this seemingly trivial question will have a surprising impact on the overall message.

Another question is how to interpret to "seek" here; this may depend on the meaning of *tov*. Does *dirshu* mean "look for," "yearn for," or "try to accomplish"? This will come to light below.

Moses bids the nation to "seek out" the place where God places His name (Deut. 12:5). Ramban reads this as an obligation to ask "where is the house of God?"; R. David Tzvi Hoffmann, in contrast,[59] states

58. As do Metzudot, Hakham, and Paul.
59. Hoffmann, along with Shadal and Malbim, were locked in a battle against the school

that *lidrosh,* when used with the prepositions *el* or *le* means "to look for." This doesn't mean that information is missing; we know where the place is, but may not know how to get there. Alternatively, it means "to yearn for," which concerns the state of mind that turns one from a neutral visitor to a *doresh.*

How do we understand "seek" here? Is Amos telling his audience that they ought to inquire what "the good" is or how to get to "the good place" (per Malbim); or is he adjuring them to yearn for good (or to do good) rather than evil (or to do evil)? We are not out of the literary woods with this hymn and will address this question below.

That you may live

This phrase, *lema'an tiḥyu,* directly echoes Deuteronomy.[60]

Note that all three cited instances of *lema'an tiḥyu(n)* do not merely refer to survival, but also to successful conquest and long life. To the Samarian audience, this phrase likely evokes the promises in Moses's farewell speech.

Amos is encouraging them to turn back to God's laws of justice and morality in order to ensure their continued presence in the Land. This is an uphill battle in a time of geopolitical quiet (the calm before the storm) and economic success, when it is difficult to rouse people from their complacency.

And so that *Hashem,* the God of Hosts, should be with you

This raises a glaring theological problem – is God not *with the people* when they sin? "*If* you seek good and eschew evil, *then* God will be with you." According to this reading, there seems to be no way around the frightening conclusion: God is *not* with the people when they embrace evil. This is not only a linear question (at what point does God

of Higher Criticism regarding the authorship, dating, and "agenda" of Deuteronomy (along with numerous other battles). As such, we ought to keep in mind that there may be a polemic at work in this discussion (see Shadal's comments at Deut. 12:5).

60. Deuteronomy 4:1, 5:29, 8:1.

abandon the sinners?); it also leads to a theological stalemate. If we posit that God's continued presence among the people is what keeps them alive and sustains them, then how can anyone claim that God is absent?

Traditional scholars read the verse thus, and suggest that the people are challenging this claim by pointing to their current prosperity. The prophet therefore attempts to correct them: though He is "with them" in a broader sense, God is *not* with them *in these endeavors*. Paul and Hakham share a similar approach, which they build on the next phrase, *ka'asher amartem*.

As you say

What have the people have declared? The aforementioned commentators explain that the people claim that God is still with them in their practice of "justice" and their pilgrimages to Beit El, Gilgal, and Be'er Sheva. These commentators would render the passage as follows:

> If you want God to be with you in all of your endeavors so that you may live, then you must abandon the worship at Beit El... and then He will be with you as you declare.

There is an alternate possible reading of the entire phrase and the intent behind it.

Rather than *viyhi khen* meaning a *consequence* of their actions, it can be read as an extension and clarification of the prophet's challenge to them:

> If you seek good and eschew evil so that you may (truly) live, and have the Lord, God of the Hosts with you as you claim...

This defines to "seek the good" as to strive for God's presence among them by adhering to the covenant of Deuteronomy. The next verse continues Amos's clarification of the prophetic demand, with the hopeful consequence coming at the end of that verse, as we will see. This defines the two verses as a complex condition and a single consequence, which appears at the end of the second verse.

15: Hate evil, and love good

The prophet now clarifies what the demand to "seek good" means: to develop and foster an affinity for that which is good and a revulsion for its antithesis. This is not a "quick fix," but rather a deep, exacting paradigm shift. The judges and aristocracy of Samaria must develop love for good and an innate hatred of evil, seeing it as anathema; they must also ensure that this is implemented on a practical and consequential level by fixing the corruption of the long-broken justice system.

FRACTURED CHIASMUS

This clause serves as the back half of a "fractured chiasmus," working in poetic antiphony with the previous verse:

> *Seek good*
> *and not evil...*
> *Hate evil*
> *And love good*

I refer to this as a "fractured chiasmus" because the composite parts of the structure are not proximate to each other. A standard chiastic structure presents either A-B-B'-A' or, with a central axis, A-B-C-B'-A'. There is nothing (besides incidental words, such as prepositions, names of members of the direct audience, etc.) between any of the segments of the structure.

Here, however, the second half of v. 14 "interrupts" the chiastic structure; and in an elegant flourish, the second half of v. 15 echoes the second half of v. 14.

There are instances of "fractured chiasmus" structures elsewhere in prophetic rhetoric, such as Isaiah's opening prophecy:

> How the *faithful city* has become a harlot, she that was full of justice! *Righteousness* lodged in her....[61] And I will restore your judges as at the first, and your counselors as at the beginning.

---

61. Isaiah 1:21.

> Afterward you shall be called the city of *righteousness*, the *faithful city*.[62]

With a full four verses intervening, the prophet creates a beautiful (and painful) picture of the Jerusalem that was against the Jerusalem that is – and then, the Jerusalem that could be. Jerusalem was once a "faithful city" and "righteousness" lodged there; [63] one day, "righteousness" will be its name and it will again be called "faithful city."

Here, too, this chiasmus underscores the essence of Amos's message: the Samarian audience must love the good and desire the ethical and upright – and abhorrence of that which is immoral and unjust should be a natural consequence of that great desire.

15: And establish justice at the gate

The demand to establish justice is not some distant goal, the end result of developing a love for that which is upright, but rather an immediate demand for change: the gates must become a place of justice, where poor and rich are treated equally, without prejudice or corruption.

The relatively rare word *hatzigu* ("establish," "set," "exhibit," or "station") appears only three times in prophetic literature.[64] The sense here is that Amos is compelling his audience to permanently "establish justice" as an unwavering, inherent part of the court, rather than as a fleeting trend.

Perhaps *Hashem*, the God of Hosts, will be gracious unto the remnant of Joseph

Again, Amos uses this longer form of God's name; this serves as a type of epistrophe.

---

62. Ibid. 1:26.
63. The first king of the city that we meet has the titular name *Malki-Tzedek* (Gen. 14:18); the first king of the city that the Israelites meet as a nation is *Adoni-Tzedek* (Josh. 10:1).
64. Hosea 2:5; Jeremiah 51:34; and Amos 5:15.

This phrasing is tragic: even if the people make drastic changes in their attitudes toward justice, they are still left with a mere hope that *perhaps*… The Talmud includes this among the verses that moved the Sages to tears:[65]

> When Rabbi Asi would get to this verse, he would cry: "Hate evil and love good and establish justice at the gates; *perhaps Hashem* the Lord of Hosts will be gracious…" – all this and (only) "perhaps"?

Many read the "remnant of Joseph" as the northern kingdom. Much of the northern kingdom was already exiled before Jeroboam II's time.[66] Rashi, however, believes this prophecy addresses the entire nation, given that Joseph sustained them in Egypt.[67] Hakham cites an anonymous commentator who suggests that *she'erit* means "family" rather than "remnant."[68] Yet others, he continues, read *she'erit* as remnant, but not as the result of any earlier exile or devastation. Rather, it refers to the divine decree already in place – and the hope that at least a remnant might remain.

SECOND *KINA*

16: Therefore

That *lakhen* ("therefore") portends a threat is confirmed by the ensuing call to lament. Both Ibn Ezra and Radak read *lakhen* as responding to the assumed condition of the rebuke:

> *Lakhen*: if you fail to listen (and heed), therefore (*lakhen*) evil will befall you: "in all the squares there will be wailing" (Ibn Ezra)

---

65. Hagiga 4b.
66. As pointed out by Radak, Ibn Ezra, and R. Eliezer of Beaugency.
67. He evidently infers this from Joseph's words to his brothers at Genesis 45:7.
68. Per *she'er* – Leviticus 18:6.

> *Lakhen*: if you do not return to Me, evil will befall you to the point that there will be wailing in all the squares (Radak)[69]

Lakhen usually appears at the beginning of a verse and is usually followed by some form of God's name; thus it usually creates a "drum-roll" effect, part of the rhetorical "pomp and circumstance" of the prophetic declaration of divine anger and punishment.

Thus says *Hashem*, the God of Hosts, the Lord

The name A-D-N-Y, which is uncommon in the Torah (a mere fifteen occurrences) and the historiographic books of the *Nevi'im* (only seventeen instances), is far more frequent in prophetic literature (Ezekiel uses it 222 times!). As Elitzur points out, it is used in direct address to God in the early biblical period and becomes a "name" for God only at a later point.[70] Since Amos is possibly the earliest of the literary prophets, he may be one of the first who introduces this address as a Name. Could it be that the combination of *lakhen* and *A-D-N-Y* here is no coincidence?

The role of the literary prophets is to address the people, exhort them, inspire them – and, to some extent, frighten them into introspection, all for the sake of social and religious reform. The "ominous" *lakhen* is part of that rhetorical scheme. The introduction of God's name of "My Master," with the royal honorific in plural form (*A-D-N-Y* instead of *Adoni*), once used to address God directly,[71] is now used for speaking *about* God.

69. It is unclear if they disagree about the syntax and its pursuant meaning: whether the threat is the lament, or that the lament will be the human and natural response to unspoken evils.
70. Yoel Elitzur, "The Divine Name ADNY in the Hebrew Bible: Surprising Findings," *Liber Annuus* 65 (2015): 87–106.
71. Genesis 15:2, 8, 20:4; Exodus 4:10, 13, 5:22; Numbers 14:17; Deuteronomy 3:24; Joshua 7:7–8; Judges 6:15, 22; II Samuel 7:18–20, 28–29.

Lamentation shall be in all the public places

In biblical Hebrew, *reḥov* means square (in modern Hebrew, *reḥov* means "street"). The word is rare in the Torah and prophetic historiography, but it takes on new significance in prophetic literature as a place of public mourning[72] or the place of desolation during a plague[73] or devastation.[74] It is here that desperate mothers bring their starving children to beg for food.[75]

Hesped/ Mispeid

Mispeid, meaning "eulogy" since rabbinic times, means "mourning" in biblical Hebrew, as is clear from its first instance in Genesis 23. Eulogy, in contrast, is not an expression of grief as much as a speech intended to elicit grief in its audience.[76] In its only other appearance in the Torah, in the context of Jacob's death (Gen. 50:10), *hesped* is a formal part of a mourning rite.[77]

Thus the above translation, "In all the squares there shall be wailing," is at least misleading, if not incorrect; it is perhaps more accurately rendered as "in all the squares there will be [the sounds of] mourning." This is consistent with the rest of the verse: "*Ho Ho,*" "Alas! Alas!" is hardly a eulogy; it is a cry of grief and desperation, the sound of mourning.

16: And they will say in all the streets, "Alas! Alas!"

Ḥutzot, parallel to *reḥov*; is the biblical term for "city squares," although the urban "streets" of biblical times differed greatly from modern streets. The *ḥutzot* (lit. "outer areas") seem to be marketplaces, as opposed to

72. Isaiah 15:3.
73. Jeremiah 9:20.
74. Lamentations 4:18.
75. Ibid. 2:11–12; note the beautiful way that Zechariah turns Jeremiah's "squares" into places of renewed life, in Zechariah 8:4–5.
76. Thus, in Berakhot 6b, Rav Sheshet states: *Agra dehespeida daloyei,* "The weeping it elicits is the reward for a eulogy."
77. See also Ecclesiastes 3:4 and Psalms 30:12; indeed, this very verse speaks to this definition: "You turned my *mourning* into a dance."

reḥovot, where mass gatherings were held (see Mishna Ta'anit 2:1). It may also mean "outskirts" – the areas bounding the city limits.

Weeping and mourning in the *ḥutzot* of the city, often in parallel with *reḥovot,* is a common motif.[78] They also feature prominently in Jeremiah's famous consolation: those same *ḥutzot Yerushalayim* of desolation and injustice will become a setting of rebirth and rejoicing (Jer. 33:10–11).

The onomatopoetic "*Ho Ho*" is one of various biblical phrases used to express sorrow: *hoi,*[79] *aha,*[80] *oi,*[81] *avoi,*[82] *ha,*[83] and *oya.*[84] Unsurprisingly, most of these sounds appear in prophetic literature (and, of course, Lamentations).

And they shall call the farmer to mourning

This phrase can be read in three equally compelling ways. Firstly, note Amos's alliteration: *vekare'u* – *ikkar*. Does this mean (1) the farmers are the object of *vekare'u,* being summoned to lament; or (2) are the farmers to summon *each other* to lament; or (3) are the farmers being called to summon others to lament?

This last reading seems less likely because it assumes a plural verb (*kare'u*) as modifying a singular noun (*ikkar*); keep in mind, however, that the "farmer" here is an example of the collective singular, a common biblical idiom for depicting a group.[85] In biblical text, a collective singular noun can be modified by a plural verb.

Before addressing these three possibilities, we ought to note that this is one of just six biblical instances of *ikkar.*[86] In two other instances

78. Isaiah 15:3.
79. Occurs fifty-one times in the canon, including twice in Amos.
80. Fifteen times, half of which are in Jeremiah and Ezekiel.
81. Twenty-three occurrences, including twice in the Torah.
82. Once matched with *oi* in Proverbs 23:29.
83. Ezekiel 30:2.
84. Psalms 120:5.
85. For example, Exodus 1:5; Deuteronomy 10:22.
86. The word has Akkadian roots, from the Sumerian (*ikkaru*).

they are matched, as here, with *kormim* (*vintners*).[87] Here and in Joel, farmers and vintners are summoned to mourn; Jeremiah 14:4 also appropriates this image of lamenting farmers (albeit without vintners).

Rashi has a curious take on our verse: "The groups of farmers who are plowing in the fields will encounter the voice of lament of the mourners crying out in the streets." This interprets the verb *vekare'u* with the preposition *el* as meaning "to have sounds meeting each other." Rashi resolves the verse's ambiguity and understands that the farmers are actively involved in this lament. This approach may seem awkward, but is consistent with the structure of this passage.

Ibn Ezra reads differently: "When they observed God's commandments, they would harvest, and the farmers would call out to rejoice and feast; now, they(?) will call them(?) to mourning." Note how he does not attempt to define *who* is calling *whom*.

Radak presents a clearer picture: "The farmer is the one who toils in the fields and they will call him to come to the mourning, since his work and labor will be for naught, since the seeds and plants have been plagued; they planted but did not reap." This clarifies the scene: others, who are mourning the destruction of the crops, will direct the farmers to go join the mourners.

Hakham reads: "the farmers will announce a lamentation"[88] – the verb *kara* means calling for weeping and lamentation. Alternatively, he suggests, the farmers may be the ones who are summoned to call others to join the lamentation.

Much of this nuanced debate depends on how we read the next phrase and its relation to this one.

And proclaim lamentation to such as are skillful of wailing

Amos uses *mispeid* as if people had died, though the sadness and lamentation is apparently over an agricultural plague. This is because crop failure results in famine, widespread suffering, and probable death. The farmers are the first ones to recognize when their toil bears no fruit.

87. Isaiah 61:5; Joel 1:11.
88. Building upon the phrasing in Isaiah 22:12.

In ancient times, professional "wailers" were hired to participate in funerals or other public displays of sadness in order to move the crowd with their lamentation.[89] The book of Lamentations may well have been composed with this intent: to provide a script for mourning that would inspire weeping and grief.

Perhaps a structural look at our verse may help solve the question of who is being summoned for whom:

	1	2
A:	*Bekhol reḥovot mispeid*	*uvkhol ḥutzot yomeru Ho Ho*
B:	*Vekare'u ikkar el evel*	*Umispeid el yode'ei nehi*

The passage is structured chiastically. The key word *mispeid* appears at the end of A1 and at the beginning of B2. The two verbs – saying (*yomeru*) and summoning/calling (*vekare'u*) – appear in A2 and B1. The farmer and those who are in the *ḥutzot* feature at the center, consistent with Rashi's interpretation. This implies that the farmers are called to act at the center of the lamentation – not to summon others, but rather to be the chief wailers.

Such as are skillful of wailing

Nehi is rendered here as "lamentation"; this seems to be its meaning in its six other biblical instances, which all appear in prophetic literature. Five of these are in Jeremiah, including four instances in one passage (9:9–19), where it is juxtaposed with *bekhi* (weeping), and paralleled with *dima* (tears) and *kina*. BDB reads all instances of *nun-hei-hei* as "mourning, lamentation." Koehler-Baumgartner,[90] however, assumes two distinct meanings: "to moan, lament," and "to follow eagerly," the second being the meaning in I Samuel 7. Klein reads this latter instance as a *hapax legomenon*, meaning "was attracted by, longed for."[91]

---

89. Jeremiah 9:16; see Mishna Moed Katan 3:8–9.
90. Vol. 1, 675.
91. Ernest Klein, *A Comprehensive Etymological Dictionary of the Hebrew Language for Readers of English* (MacMillan, 1987)..

We can read Amos's use of *nehi* as a deft combination of these two meanings. Unlike Jeremiah, who speaks to a nation on the cusp of destruction, Amos's mission is to inspire reflection and repentance. Perhaps those who are *yode'ei nehi* understand what it means to *long for* a better life, and grasp that if they fail to change their attitude, they will soon be *lamenting* their fate.[92]

Note that the brief two-verse segment at the end of our section is set off as a separate *parasha setuma* and concludes with Amos's signature formula *Amar Hashem*. The next verse begins a *parasha petuḥa*. These literary (and graphic) markers indicate that our section is independent of what follows and, as such, forms the conclusion of the lament-seek-rebuke-hymn-rebuke-seek-lament chiasmus.

The word *mispeid* appears just fourteen times (as a noun, with various suffixes and prefixes) in the entire canon, yet Amos uses it three times within these two verses. This spotlights the severity of the bitter mourning and dire weeping he attempts to warn his audience of, as we will revisit after our analysis of the next verse.

17: And in all vineyards there shall be lamentation

Noting that there will be mourning *in* the vineyards supports the reading that "*Vekare'u ikkar el evel*" means "Summon the farmers to lament" – for they will be the first to notice the failed crop.

Vineyards were a locus of celebration in ancient times;[93] the sectarian calendar found in Cave 4[94] suggests that the "grape-harvest feast" was celebrated on the fifteenth of Av.[95]

Thus mourning in the vineyards represents the apotheosis of tragedy, as expressed elsewhere in prophetic literature.[96] Mourning in the vineyards means that the essence of rejoicing, the source of wine

92. This may also be true of the aforementioned passage in Micah.
93. As suggested in Judges 21:19.
94. 4QMMT.
95. This supports the theory that the festival of Judges 21 is the festival mentioned in the Mishna, Ta'anit 4:8. See also Judges 9:27.
96. Isaiah 16:10; Jeremiah 48:33.

"which gladdens God and man,"[97] has turned sour; the heart of celebration has fermented to devastation.

For I will pass through your midst

This is an unanticipated ending; we would expect devastation and subsequent mourning to be an expression of God "hiding His face."[98] Surprisingly, the prophet suggests that God's presence results in mourning.

Tanakh presents two competing models about the impact of God's Presence. One suggests that defeat, exile, and oppression indicate God's absence:

> Then My anger shall be ignited against them in that day, and I will forsake them, and I will hide My face from them, and they shall be devoured, and many evils and troubles shall come upon them; so that they will say in that day: "Are not these evils come upon us because our God is not among us?" (Deut. 31:17)

The second is that God's presence is dangerous to mortals:

> And He smote of the men of Beit Shemesh, because they had gazed upon the ark of the Lord, even He smote of the people seventy men, and fifty thousand men; and the people mourned, because the Lord had smitten the people with a great slaughter. (I Sam. 6:19)

When God appears before Moses to express forgiveness for the sin of the Golden Calf, He says: "You cannot see My face, for man shall not see Me and live" (Ex. 33:20). Even Moses, who is able to "gaze at the visage of God" (Num. 12:18) will die if he sees God too intensely (Ex. 33:23).

---

97. Judges 9:13.
98. Deuteronomy 31:18.

Nevertheless, Isaiah promises that at the right time: "Yet shall not your Teacher hide Himself anymore, but your eyes shall see your Teacher" (30:20).

Is God's presence a source of life and blessing, or of destruction and death? There are several approaches to this apparent contradiction. We might posit that the nature of "God's Presence" depends on the *cause* of His immanence. If God is appearing in response to sinful behavior, His Presence is frightening and potentially lethal, while if He appears in response to oppression, exile, or a threat to His people, then we would assume the manifestation of His *Shekhina* to be protective and comforting. Metaphysically, we would then distinguish between what might conveniently be called *middat hadin,* the attribute of justice, and *middat haraḥamim,* the attribute of mercy or compassion. What this means is that God's essence depends on the cause of His "appearance."

Alternatively, we might posit that God's Presence is a static, intense reality, and that the difference in impact depends on the recipient. Bright sunshine is intense: it can be dangerous in certain circumstances, and warming and healing in others. Similarly, God's Presence affects those who long for Him differently than those entrenched in sin. As Resh Lakish observes about the "bright sun" of Malakhi 3:20:

> There is no Gehinnom in the world to come, rather, the Blessed Holy One will take the sun out from its cover, the righteous will be healed by it and the wicked will be judged by it… (Nedarim 8b)

Amos's mention of God's passing among the people as a frightening thing elegantly foreshadows his next prophecy about *Yom Hashem*. We will discuss this in the next chapter and continue our discussion about God's presence in this context.

Says *Hashem*.

Amos uses his familiar signature to indicate this prophecy's end, and to reaffirm that He speaks in this Master's name.

RECAP OF THE ORACLE

In this seventeen-verse oracle, Amos builds a masterful chiasmus with a beautiful praise-hymn at its heart. The entire piece is couched in lamentation, but note how the lamentation evolves.

The first section (vv. 1–3) describes a disaster: the nation "has fallen and will never rise again," while the closing lament bewails an agricultural crisis that subtly echoes the plagues against Egypt. The first "*dirshu*" section calls for yearning and seeking God rather than yearning and seeking cultic or ancestral worship. The closing "*dirshu*" section, however, refers to specific behaviors and attitudes to embrace: doing justice and seeking good. The rebuke condemns those selfsame interpersonal and social crimes and the corruption of the governing bodies.

Amos foresees devastating military loss as well as agricultural devastation. He ascribes this all to "looking in the wrong places" and the people's failure to long for God and seek His Presence. It is no surprise that the people's confused obsession with wanting to see "the day of the Lord" is Amos's next target.

Chapter 7

"Day of the Lord" (5:18–27)

(יח) הוֹי הַמִּתְאַוִּים אֶת יוֹם ה׳ לָמָּה זֶּה לָכֶם יוֹם ה׳ הוּא חֹשֶׁךְ וְלֹא אוֹר:
(יט) כַּאֲשֶׁר יָנוּס אִישׁ מִפְּנֵי הָאֲרִי וּפְגָעוֹ הַדֹּב וּבָא הַבַּיִת וְסָמַךְ יָדוֹ עַל הַקִּיר
וּנְשָׁכוֹ הַנָּחָשׁ: (כ) הֲלֹא חֹשֶׁךְ יוֹם ה׳ וְלֹא אוֹר וְאָפֵל וְלֹא נֹגַהּ לוֹ: (כא) שָׂנֵאתִי
מָאַסְתִּי חַגֵּיכֶם וְלֹא אָרִיחַ בְּעַצְּרֹתֵיכֶם: (כב) כִּי אִם תַּעֲלוּ לִי עֹלוֹת וּמִנְחֹתֵיכֶם
לֹא אֶרְצֶה וְשֶׁלֶם מְרִיאֵיכֶם לֹא אַבִּיט: (כג) הָסֵר מֵעָלַי הֲמוֹן שִׁרֶיךָ וְזִמְרַת
נְבָלֶיךָ לֹא אֶשְׁמָע: (כד) וְיִגַּל כַּמַּיִם מִשְׁפָּט וּצְדָקָה כְּנַחַל אֵיתָן: (כה) הַזְּבָחִים
וּמִנְחָה הִגַּשְׁתֶּם לִי בַמִּדְבָּר אַרְבָּעִים שָׁנָה בֵּית יִשְׂרָאֵל: (כו) וּנְשָׂאתֶם אֵת סִכּוּת
מַלְכְּכֶם וְאֵת כִּיּוּן צַלְמֵיכֶם כּוֹכַב אֱלֹהֵיכֶם אֲשֶׁר עֲשִׂיתֶם לָכֶם: (כז) וְהִגְלֵיתִי
אֶתְכֶם מֵהָלְאָה לְדַמָּשֶׂק אָמַר ה׳ אֱלֹהֵי צְבָאוֹת שְׁמוֹ:

18 Woe to you who desire the day of the Lord! Why would you
have the day of the Lord? It is darkness, and not light; **19** as if a
man fled from a lion, and a bear met him; or went into the house
and leaned with his hand against the wall, and a serpent bit him. **20**
Is not the day of the Lord darkness, and not light, and gloom with
no brightness in it? **21** I hate, I despise your feasts, and I take no
delight in your solemn assemblies. **22** Even though you offer Me
your burnt offerings and cereal offerings, I will not accept them,
and the peace offerings of your fatted beasts I will not look upon.

> **23** Take away from Me the noise of your songs; to the melody of your harps I will not listen. **24** But let justice roll down like waters, and righteousness like an ever-flowing stream. **25** Did you bring to Me sacrifices and offerings the forty years in the wilderness, O house of Israel? **26** You shall take up Sikkut your king, and Kiyun your star-gods, your images, which you made for yourselves; **27** therefore I will take you into exile beyond Damascus, says the Lord, whose name is the God of Hosts.

Amos is the first prophet to present "the day of the Lord," a theme that is then picked up by his contemporaries and becomes a *leitmotif* in numerous prophetic pericopes.

18: Woe to you

The lament *Hoi* first appears as an expression of mourning over the death of the "man of God" from the south who comes to Beit El, that mysterious forerunner to our own prophet.[1] This nameless prophet is killed by a lion after a local false prophet convinces him to defy God's word; at his burial, the guilty prophet mourns over him *"Hoi aḥi"* – "Woe my brother."

The word is used extensively during the first wave of literary prophecy:[2] "Woe to those who are smug in Zion" (Amos 6:1); "Woe to those who devise iniquity and work evil upon their beds" (Mic. 2:1). Most instances in Isaiah address sinful groups, lamenting their behavior and their impending punishment.[3] This differs from its original sense as a lament over one who has already died. The use of a lament-word is a powerful warning: a lament for those who are still alive and healthy but unaware of the deadly danger of their path might – hopefully – spur them to change their ways. Curiously, Zechariah inverts the meaning of this word, from a lament to a call for the exiles to return.[4]

---

1. I Kings 13:30.
2. Isaiah uses it eighteen times (!), Amos twice, and Micah once.
3. See, especially, the repeated use of *hoi* in Isaiah 5.
4. Zechariah 2:10–11; see Rashi, R. Joseph Kara, Ibn Ezra, and Radak ad loc.

Who desire the day of the Lord

While Amos is the first to mention *yom Hashem,* "the day of the Lord," we can assume that this concept was a well-known and anticipated event in the people's collective conscious – this is evident from the fact that there is need to "correct" people who await this day.

Where does this concept come from? Is the "day of the Lord" implied in earlier texts?

Hakham suggests that the premise of *yom Hashem* is found in Moses's song of *Ha'azinu*. Indeed, the final verses do speak of a time when the nations will be judged with God's sword: "Rejoice, you nations, with His people, for He will avenge the blood of His servants. He will render vengeance to His adversaries, and will make expiation for His Land, for His people" (Deut. 32:43). We might argue, however, that this can be read as part of the constant ebb-and-flow of human history and is not necessarily eschatological.

Another possibility is that the notion of *yom Hashem* – of a final Judgment Day – is built into any theistic system which posits two essential foundations: Revelation and Providence. So long as the faith-system assumes a direct interaction between God and the people (either directly or through a prophet) *and* it assumes God's constant awareness and involvement with the welfare of His people, perhaps this was perceived as an inevitable event in which God appears to punish all those who have defied Him and hurt His people.[5] If so, then the *yom Hashem* that Amos's audience anticipates is a built-in factor of their belief system and understanding of meta-history.

Finally, we may posit that the assumption of *yom Hashem* – a day of great and public divine revelation – may be anchored not in a divine promise (per Hakham), nor in a "built-in" factor of theistic belief; rather, it is the natural consequence of the Jewish people's own history. The people's nascence at the Exodus culminates at Mount Sinai, when

5. This may be part of the undercurrent of the Song of Songs, in which the intense relationship between the lover (in the parable, God) and the beloved (the Jewish people) is never fully realized. It concludes, oddly enough, with the beloved telling the shepherd-king, "Flee, my beloved..." It may be that Song of Songs can only describe the relationship as it has already been experienced, and waiting for the denouement of complete revelation is beyond the range of the parable.

the entire nation "meets" God. This foundational historic moment, it might be argued, is not only a pillar of the past, but also a hope for the future – that God's presence will be made known to all of humanity.[6]

In any case, Amos's prophecy assumes that the people are familiar with a notion of *yom Hashem*; Amos does not disabuse them of this notion, rather, he sharply corrects their assumptions about what that day will bring.

Why would you have the day of the Lord?

Thus the prophet quashes the people's naive fascination with the advent of *yom Hashem* and their belief that this day will bring the utter defeat of their enemies and universally demonstrate their status as God's chosen nation. This belief may have been substantiated by Jeroboam II's recent military successes and recapture of territory on the eastern border,[7] which inspired anticipation of *yom Hashem*.

It is darkness, and not light

The people expect this to be a day of light, but nothing could be farther from the truth. As R. Eliezer of Beaugency proposes, "it will not come to be light, for then numerous troubles will come one after the other."

19: As if a man fled from a lion

Something seems to be missing here, either at the phrase's beginning or end. We would expect the day's darkness either as a preface to the analogy of the lion, bear, and snake; or as its conclusion: "so will this day be" (*kein hayom hahu*).

This phrasing forces us to read this verse as the explication of the "darkness" – that it is not a literal darkness (as the Egyptian plague), but

---

6. Cf. the research done by Dr. Nili Samet on the parallels between the prophetic *Yom Hashem* and Akkadian lamentation literature – see, *inter alii*, *The Lamentation over the Destruction of Ur: A Revised Edition* (Winona Lake, IN: Eisenbrauns, 2014).
7. II Kings 14:25–26.

rather a constant shadow of doom hanging over the people. Even if they manage to avoid one threat, another awaits them immediately, without a moment of respite.

Why are these troubles described as "darkness" and not "war" or "plagues"? One answer is that the trope of *yom Hashem* in biblical and ancient Near Eastern sources is always associated with darkness. Here there may be a further consideration. Amos's hymn in the previous passage declares: "He...brings on the shadow of darkness into morning and blackens the day into night." This is how Amos uses the dark.

And a bear met him

This image expresses escape from predators rather than confrontation.[8] Lions and bears are common biblical predators:[9] terrifying, dangerous beasts. Anyone who escapes from an encounter with either is considered blessed to survive. Imagine, then, escaping the lion only to encounter the bear!

Or went into the house and leaned with his hand against the wall

After finally having reached their home – which is presumably safe from wild animals – the victim leans with "his hand against the wall." This is an act of resting, of weariness after tribulation, only to experience further terror:

And a serpent bit him

Having narrowly escaped death twice in a row, the victim is finally attacked from within his own domain.[10]

---

8. Contrast this to David's story about his saving the flock in I Samuel 17:34–35.
9. II Kings 17, 2:24.
10. This seems to be an expansion of the image in Moses's song – Deuteronomy 32:25; compare with Isaiah 24:17–18.

20: Is not the day of the Lord darkness, and not light?

This final verse of the section perfectly echoes the first:

> *Hu **ḥoshekh** velo or... Halo **ḥoshekh** yom Hashem **velo or**?*
>
> It is darkness, and not light... Is not the day of the Lord darkness, and not light?

This *inclusio* clearly defines the unit and underscores its topic: *yom Hashem* is not a glorious day of victory, as anticipated, but rather one of devastating punishment.

And gloom, with no brightness in it

The translation here corresponds to the verse's opening word *halo* – whose "rhetorical *hei*" turns the statement into a question.

Afel here is parallel to *ḥoshekh,* although *afel,* a *hapax legomenon,* is apparently an adjective; a more accurate translation, perhaps, would be "gloomy" (per BDB). There are ten biblical instances of *afela,* most famously in the plague of *ḥoshekh* (Ex. 10:22).

"*YOM HASHEM*" – *SHTAYIM SHEHEIN ARBA* (TWO WHICH ARE FOUR[11])

A biblical survey of the "day of the Lord" concept shows that this refers either to immediate events familiar to the audience, or to an eschatological vision of divine judgment. This "day of the Lord" seems to refer to the latter.

The first type falls into two categories: past events and imminent events. The prophet uses the former as fuel for his own laments and warnings about the latter.

The eschatological "days of the Lord" also fall into different categories. Some describe how God's revelation will put idol-worshippers

11. Cf. Mishna Shevuot 1:1.

to shame.[12] Another type, which characterizes this oracle, refers to a day of universal judgment, when all people will be called to account for their deeds – toward each other and toward Israel. This paradigm is essentially pagan, based on the pagan assumption that one god will prove to be the most powerful of all gods and bring victory and vindication for their worshippers. As with all polytheistic axioms, the biblical text seeks to undermine it.

Amos's audience apparently anticipates this kind of Judgment Day, but its underlying pagan assumption leads them to believe that they will emerge unscathed and victorious. The prophet seeks to shatter this smug assumption. God's chosen people are not granted a get-out-of-jail-free card; in fact, the opposite holds true. As Amos has already emphasized (3:2), being God's people means that they are held to a higher moral standard than the rest of the world, and thus, to more exacting judgment. Amos's audience expects that they will be safe from God's judgment, and that their own moral failings will be overlooked; but instead, these very flaws will condemn them to suffering and horror on the day of the Lord.

The next unit, seven verses long, expresses God's rejection of Israel's meaningless religious worship.

21: I hate, I despise your feasts

The opening pair of words seem repetitive; what is the difference between *sanei* and *maos* in this context? As discussed above,[13] *sanei*, "hated," can be read as relative.[14] All peoples can worship God, but He (usually) favors Israel; here, perhaps, God is stating that due to their corruption, Israel are no longer favored. *Maos* then expresses that not only have they fallen from grace, but also He absolutely rejects their empty offerings: "I have disfavored (in a relative sense), yea even rejected (in an absolute sense) your festive offerings."

---

12. Notably Isaiah 2–4, Zephaniah 1, and Zechariah 14.
13. See page 204.
14. For example, Genesis 25:28; note how Malachi builds on this in 1:2–3; see also Deuteronomy 21:15, which builds on Genesis 29:31.

ḤAG

The root *ḥ-v-g* means "circle"[15] and refers to a festive meal eaten in a circle – the participants gather in a circle, facing each other. God no longer favors "your festive gatherings," when the people come together to celebrate with an offering.

21: And I *no longer* take delight in your solemn assemblies

I have added the phrase "no longer" because this is the diatribe's tone: until now, as expressed throughout Leviticus, God has "savored" the "sweet smell" (*rei'aḥ niḥoaḥ*) of the offerings. The verb here, *ariaḥ*, meaning to smell, conveys divine "enjoyment" and "acceptance" of offerings.[16]

The *vav* at the beginning of our stich is not *vav* conjunctive (*vav haḥibbur*), but rather *vav habiur*: the *vav* of clarification. God now disfavors and even despises the people's festive offerings *because* He no longer takes delight in the people's solemn assemblies. Thus the *atzeroteikhem* of this second clause should not be read as parallel to *ḥageikhem*, but rather, *because* the people's solemn gatherings no longer please God, He rejects and despises the people's festive gatherings.

An *atzeret* or *atzara* is a gathering, usually of worship.[17] Jeremiah, however, employs this word to express a very different type of gathering; he ironically refers to the wayward people as *atzeret bogedim* – a gathering of rebels.[18]

Amos calls the gatherings *ḥageikhem* and *atzeroteikhem* – "*your* feasts" and "*your* gatherings," as if to point out that God is no longer interested in them and does not see them as motivated or defined by His worship.

---

15. See, *inter alii*, Rashi on Job 22:14.
16. See also I Samuel 26:19.
17. Numbers 29:35; Deuteronomy 16:8; and, as a generic, Isaiah 1:13. For a treatment of the meaning of *atzeret* in rabbinic Hebrew, see Henshke, *Simḥat haRegel beToratam shel haTanaim* (Jerusalem: Magnes, 2007), 205–219.
18. Jeremiah 9:1.

22: Even though you offer Me your burnt offerings and cereal offerings, I will not accept them

In legal literature, the word *ki* is often used to introduce the casuistic clause.[19]

In poetry, it is often declarative, "indeed," such as "Give thanks to God, *for* (*ki*) He is good, *for* (*ki*) His kindness is everlasting";[20] but it can also mean "rather":

> (Return us O Hashem…restore our days as of old): *Rather* (*ki*), you have completely rejected us… (Lam. 5:21–22)

The sense in our verse is that of "indeed," of intensification: Not only do I reject and hate your festive gatherings, when the participants share the festive meat – but I am also not even interested in your burnt offerings that are completely consumed on the altar.

An *olah* is an animal offering (cows, goats, sheep, or birds) that is fully burned on the altar; it is considered the prototypical "sacrifice."

The first offering commanded in Leviticus is an *olah* (1:3). A *minḥa*, which means "tribute" in both the sacrificial and general sense, is often paired with an *olah*.[21] This may be because like the *olah*, the donor does not eat any of the *korban minḥa*, the grain offering; rather, the *minḥa* is eaten by the officiating priests – but when a *minḥa* is donated by a priest, it is completely burned up like an *olah*.

Here, *olah* is presented without the genitive suffix, whereas *minḥa* is presented in this form: "*minḥoteikhem*." Paul suggests that the suffix in fact applies to both offerings.[22] This, however, may be understood thus: *olot*, the regular communal offering, will be rejected; and even if you offer up an individual, seemingly selfless *minḥa*, I will not accept it.

---

19. Deuteronomy 24:1, Exodus 22:6, among many examples.
20. Psalms 106:1, 107:1, 118:1, 29, 136:1; Ezra 3:11; I Chronicles 16:34; II Chronicles 5:13, 7:3.
21. Numbers 29:27; Joshua 22:23.
22. He argues that this is an inverted case of the syntactical rule of *Moshekh atzmo ve'aḥer imo*, "*It* pulls itself and another with it," which explains how a second item on a list is defined by the parameters of the first: here the second is defined as "your grain offerings," such that *olah* is understood as *oloteikhem*, your *olot*.

The root *r-tz-h*, "desire," means "accept" or "favor" in a sacrificial context, implying God's gracious acceptance of a person's offering. Two verbs associated with God's acceptance of offerings now express God's rejection: He will no longer smell them (*ariaḥ*) or accept them (*ertzeh*).

And the peace offerings of your fatted beasts I will not look upon

This singular form of *shelamim* – *shelem* – occurs just once in the canon. Its placement in the sequence here is odd: if the order indeed implies that He hates and rejects not only their festive gatherings, but *even* their burnt offerings, why then return to *shelamim*, which *are* eaten by the people in festive gatherings?

It seems that the key word here is *meri*, which is related to the Akkadian *maru* (to fatten up). The word appears eight times in Tanakh and always takes this same meaning of "fattened calf." Amos is tackling his audience's pagan conceptions of sacrifices. As we will develop below, in pagan thought the gods devour offerings; the fatter and richer the offering, the greater their pleasure. This perception is anathema to the Israelite religion and its staunch belief that for God offerings are not His "food," rather a measure of communal or individual devotion.[23]

Nonetheless, the people of Samaria (and Judah as well) are influenced by this thought throughout the First Commonwealth, as Jeremiah's prophecies testify; they believe that an expensive fatted ox will be more pleasing to God. Hence, Amos concludes with the message of divine rejection of this misguided perspective.

23: Take away from Me the noise of your songs

Music is an essential component of Temple worship. This begins in Numbers 10, when Moses is commanded to fashion two trumpets whose blast is to accompany "*al oloteikhem ve'al zivḥei shalmeikhem* – your burnt offerings and your slaughtered peace offerings."

---

23. Nonetheless, there are numerous phrases in Torah that could be understood in the more primitive mode, for instance *Et korbani laḥmi le'ishai*, "My offering, My food for My offerings by fire" (Num. 28:2).

Sacred music in worship is developed further in the prophetic histories,[24] and numerous musical instruments played in the Temple are listed in the Psalter.

Here, however, God insists that they remove this music "from before Me." The sweet sounds of worship are no longer music to God but rather noise, thus the use of the odd *hamon*. This word's original meaning, which later becomes "abundant," seems to be "noise" or "sound."[25]

To the melody of your harps I will *no longer* listen

This is the second phrase expressing God's rejection of music worship. Until now, the people's melodies have pleased God, but He no longer desires to hear them; we will soon discover why.

24: But let justice roll down like waters[26]

This *vav* is not a regular conjunctive or a *vav hahippukh*. Rather, it is a *vav* disjunctive – a *vav haniggud*: "*But* justice should roll down like water." This serves as a pivot in the oracle, turning from what *is* to what *ought to be*. This reading of the *vav* is almost unanimous,[27] although I will mention two surprising alternative readings among the traditional commentators.

The verb *veyigal* is generally translated as "roll," although not all *Rishonim* read it this way. Beginning with KJV, most standard English translations have some form of "roll." Relatively rare in verb form, the verb *galol* is often, but not always, associated with rocks.

The verb appears here in the passive *nifal* form, "justice shall roll." Why does Amos use this unusual word, which rarely appears in verbal form and even less frequently in a metaphorical sense? Why does he use the passive voice, as opposed to something like: and you shall roll justice

24. I Samuel 10; II Kings 3.
25. See Genesis 17:4 and II Samuel 18:19.
26. This verse is famous in Christian sermonics; perhaps the most well-known modern use of it is in Rev. Martin Luther King Jr.'s "Letter from Birmingham Jail" in 1963. It was a staple in the oratory of the civil rights movement in 1960s' America.
27. NLT goes so far as to translate: "Instead, I want to see a mighty flood of justice."

down like water? Moreover, what does the metaphor *mean*? How does justice "roll down like water"?

Before addressing the verb's meaning, it is worth noting two *Rishonim* who read the opening *vav* as *vav* conjunctive.

R. Joseph Kara comments as follows:

> *Veyigal kamayim mishpat*: like water which passes through temporarily; similarly, their judgments are rushed through.

Ibn Ezra's second commentary reads thus:

> *Veyigal kamayim mishpat*: the meaning of *veyigal* is similar to "Roll a rock toward me,"[28] and this is what the prophet states: you did not stand judgment upright and look at it carefully to extract its truth; rather, you rushed through it.

Both perceive this verse as a continuation of the indictment. We will consider below whether this approach works with the rest of the passage.

As mentioned, most read the *vav* as disjunctive and therefore understand this verse as a shift from the present state to the ideal.

Rashi, following Targum Yonatan, interprets *veyigal* as an abbreviated form of *yigaleh*, "it shall be revealed":

> This is what you ought to do and I will favor you; the justice that you buried and hid should become revealed and flood among you like e'er-sprouting water.

This also seems to be R. Eliezer of Beaugency's understanding, as well as the Vulgate's:

> *Et revelabitur quasi aqua judicium*
> Let justice be *disclosed* (*revelabitur*) like water

28. I Samuel 14:33.

Beginning with Ibn Ezra's first commentary, however, *veyigal* is traditionally read as a form of *galol.* In his first commentary,[29] he associates *veyigal* with the *gulot* (wells) that Caleb granted his daughter Akhsa, when she complained that her land lacked water.[30] This is an unusual interpretation, as it reads the noun, "well," in the sense of a verb. Radak also associates the verb with *gulot mayim*: justice should flow like water and not be stopped up.

Paul and Hakham both understand the imagery as more than prescriptive: in a land without water, nothing can grow; in the same way, a society without justice and righteousness cannot survive.

And righteousness like an ever-flowing stream

The pairing of *mishpat utzdaka* first appear in God's explanation for His selection of Abraham (Gen. 18:19):

> For I know, regarding [Abraham] that he will command his sons and his household after him, that they will guard the path of Hashem, doing acts of righteousness and justice.

Tzedaka umishpat is defined here as *derekh Hashem,* the path of God. Surprisingly, this pair appears just four more times in the first nine books of Tanakh (Genesis through Kings),[31] but is more frequent in prophetic literature (twenty-five instances). *Mishpat* is usually presented in parallel with *tzedaka,* but not synonymously. For example in Isaiah's prophecy against Jerusalem (1:27): "Zion will be redeemed through *mishpat* / and her returnees with *tzedaka.*" *Mishpat* is not *equated* to *tzedaka*; rather, both are necessary for true redemption. The same is true of all three occurrences in Amos.[32]

---

29. Ibn Ezra has two extant commentaries on Amos; his second commentary to this verse was referenced above.
30. Joshua 15:19; Judges 1:15.
31. Deuteronomy 33:21; I Samuel 12:7; II Samuel 8:15; I Kings 10:9.
32. The only one of the twelve "small prophets" to invoke the pairing at all.

A biblical survey of *tzedaka* (and its related *tzedek*) reveals that it is a mindset, an approach, a priority system that informs behavior: going lengths to help the poor debtor,[33] or trusting deeply in another.[34] In the apt words of R. David Tzvi Hoffmann:[35]

> *Tzedaka*: that is to say, the intent and action that are upstanding before Him is considered for [Abraham] to be a merit.

Mishpat, which has several related meanings (including "custom" and "ordinance"), in our context means "judicial process." *Tzedaka / tzedek* and *mishpat* are not synonymous; they are not even in the same semantic field. One refers to a certain attitude; the other to a particular process.

The combination of *tzedaka* and *mishpat,* therefore, is to internalize and practice proper attitudes toward others, and to enable and promote proper judicial procedure. When these two essentially unrelated terms are joined together, as in the description of David's rule,[36] it ought to be read as a "hendiadys," "two that are one." A hendiadys is two nouns that could each modify the other: for example, "Not for us … for *Your kindness,* for *Your truth*" (Ps. 115:1). Are we praying for God's truth or kindness? Rather, the phrase could be read thus: "Your kind truth" or "Your true kindness."

Similarly, *mishpat utzdaka* essentially means just righteousness, or righteous justice. Note that this hendiadys only appears in the context of a king or the King of kings (or in describing an ideal – but theoretical – person, as in Proverbs). The king, who is essentially responsible for the justice system, must ensure that the process (*mishpat*) is based on the proper underlying value system and attitude (*tzedaka*). This is why Jeremiah can make such a demand of Jehoiakim and invoke Josiah's proper leadership;[37] or why the psalmist prays that God grants His *mishpatim* to the king and His *tzedaka* to the crown prince (Ps. 72:1).

---

33. Deuteronomy 24:13.
34. Genesis 15:6; see Rashi and Ibn Ezra ad loc.
35. At Genesis 15:6.
36. II Samuel 8; I Chronicles 18.
37. Jeremiah 22:3.

Thus Amos is expressing that righteous justice – the proper attitude toward the poor, and a legal system that functions accordingly – must flow freely for all so that life and society may flourish and bloom. *This* is God's desire – not empty offerings and hymns.

25: Did you bring me sacrifices and offerings the forty years in the wilderness, O house of Israel?

The verse begins with rhetorical *hei*, turning the entire statement into a question that recalls God's response to David's request to build a Temple (II Sam. 7:5–7):

> Shall you build Me a house for Me to dwell in? For I have not dwelt in a house since the day that I brought up the Israelites out of Egypt, even to this day, but have walked in a tent and in a tabernacle. In all places wherein I have walked among all the Israelites, spoke I a word with any of the tribes of Israel, whom I commanded to feed My people Israel, saying: "Why have you not built Me a house of cedar?"

God does not desire this house or these offerings; or, at least, they are not crucial for His Presence among the people. Amos is stating: your ancestors did not offer *zevaḥim* or *menaḥot* to Me in the desert, yet My presence was constant; clearly, therefore, these physical expressions of worship are not central to the relationship. It is not that God does not desire these offerings (well over one hundred of the 613 commandments in the Torah concern the Temple environs and its worship), but rather they do not have intrinsic value and are worthless if they are offered up by a society whose values do not reflect the sanctity He commands.

Samuel expresses these sentiments three hundred years before Amos's time, as does Jeremiah two hundred years later.[38] These prophets all express that it is obeisance to God and the establishment of a just society that fulfills God's will, not the technical offering of sacrifices.

---

38. I Samuel 15:22; Jeremiah 7:21–23.

It is crucial to note that this is not a *rejection* of the sacrificial order, but rather a *contextualization* of worship that defines acceptable offerings as those accompanied by a broken spirit, purchased with honest gains, and offered by members of a moral society whose values are righteous and just.

26: You shall take up Sikkut your king

Verses 26–27, which conclude our heptad, turn back to the punishment awaiting Samaria. Verse 26 is, perhaps, the most inscrutable verse in the entire book.

This is Amos's only explicit reference to idolatry (as opposed to the forbidden cult sites of the northern kingdom, which were largely used for divine worship, albeit wrongly). The gods mentioned here, Sikkut and Kiyun, are not mentioned elsewhere in the canon.[39]

Most scholars believe that Sikkut is a Hebrew adaptation of *Sag-kud*, an Assyrian deity known from several cuneiform tablets; Ibn Ezra comments that Sikkut is the god of Saturn. Although some claim that the text is either a later interpolation or references something else, as Amos's career ends before the Assyrian conquest, Paul defends the text's integrity, arguing that Jeroboam II, who reigned in Amos's time, "expanded the borders of his rule to Damascus and Hama in northern Syria[40] and, thus, the Israelites came into contact with the Mesopotamian culture…here, there is an echo of Mesopotamian worship which infiltrated Israel via Aram."[41]

The most striking thing about this verse is its juxtaposition with an entirely different offense: improper sacrifices to God. Is Amos addressing different groups in the northern aristocracy – one that brings improper offerings to God, and another that shows forbidden devotion to foreign gods? Or is this all the same group, which, in true syncretistic fashion, attempts to "cover all bases" by bringing offerings to

39. Although the list of foreign gods worshipped by Sennacherib's exiles (II Kings 17) does mention Sukkot Benot, which may refer to the same god.
40. II Kings 14:28.
41. See also the entry in *Encyclopedia Mikra'it*, vol. 5, 1037.

its ancestral God as well as the regional gods of whom it has learned?[42] The latter reading is more likely, which further condemns their empty offerings: not only are they *acting* unethically, but their *devotion* to God is equally tainted.

Sikkut here is vocalized oddly; the deity's original name was likely something like Sakkat. Traditional and modern commentators point out that biblical narrative often mocks foreign gods by altering their name in a derogatory way, sometimes by changing the letters – Ba'al Zevul (lord of the high place) becomes Ba'al Zevuv (lord of the flies), and elsewhere by changing the vocalization. Here, the name is vocalized to echo *shik-kutz* ("disgusting thing," a biblical euphemism for idols). Thus *sak-kat* becomes Sikkut and *kavanim*[43] becomes Kiyun (see below).

Sikkut is called "your king." R. Joseph Kara reads this as a variation of Molekh – "your Molekh";[44] alternatively, it may mean "king," and the accusation is that the people have made this god into their ruler (so Radak and Ibn Ezra).

The image of the people carrying their idols with them into exile is poignantly portrayed in Isaiah 46:1–2, 7: these gods are incapable of carrying the people, so the people must carry them.

And Kiyun your star-gods

As is the case with Sikkut, Kiyun may be a deliberate mis-vocalization of *kavanim*, but this is less likely as *kavanim* might be a certain tribute brought before an idol, not the name of a god. Traditional commentators explain this *hapax legomenon* in various ways.

Rashi reads Sikkut as the same as Kiyun, two names for the same god; Ibn Ezra believes that they are both deities associated with Saturn. Radak also favors this view, although he also cites the theory that *kavanim* are cakes offered to the idols.

42. See I Kings 18:21.
43. Perhaps, see Jeremiah 44:19; but there and in 7:18 it means a type of offering given to the "queen of the heavens."
44. As do others, including R. Eliezer of Beaugency. Similarly, LXX and the Vulgate understand *mal'k'khem* as being pointed differently, rendering something like *molekh'khem*.

R. Joseph Kara and R. Eliezer of Beaugency read Kiyun as synonymous with *tikkun*, repair – i.e., "the proper form of your images" – this reading implies that the phrase is facetious.

Your images

Whether this phrase means that Sikkut and Kiyun are astral deities, or whether the construct form means that this image is "the star of your gods," the intent is the same. These are foreign deities associated with heavenly bodies; the only difference is whether the emphasis is placed on the image or on the star it represents.

The phrase's opacity is evident through the variety of its modern translations:

- Yet you bore Sikkut, your king, and Kiyun, your idol, the star of your god which you made for yourselves. (New Koren)
- But you have borne the tabernacle of your Molokh and Chiun your images, the star of your god, which you made to yourselves. (KJV)
- No, you served your pagan gods – Sikkut your king god and Kiyun your star god – the images you made for yourselves. (NLT)
- You have lifted up the shrine of your king, the pedestal of your idols, the star of your god – which you made for yourselves. (NIV)
- You shall take up Sikkut your king, and Kiyun your star-god, your images, which you made for yourselves; (RSV)

These translations show a wide range of interpretations for Sikkut, *Malkekhem,* Kiyun, and *Kokhav eloheikhem,* and these five are just a sample of the readings of this obscure phrase.

Which you made for yourselves

Throughout the canon, a vital component of the polemic against idolatry is the fact that the devotee fashions his own gods, which are literally "*ma'asei yedei adam* – the work of human hands."[45]

27: Therefore I will take you into exile beyond Damascus

In Amos's first oracle, he warns Aram that they will be exiled *from* Damascus (1:5); here, he warns the people that they will be exiled past that city. If the Samarian aristocracy and monarchy desire such close ties with Aramean culture and even show devotion to the Assyrian gods, then let them find their future in that land – an experiment doomed to fail. Hence, the sentence is exile beyond Damascus.

Another form of poetic justice may also be at work here. At this point, the northern kingdom has conquered territory all the way to Damascus and has entered the area as victors – and they have brought back images of the Assyrian gods of that region. Now, they are destined to return by the same route – but as exiles, shamefully carrying those selfsame gods as a sign of defeat and shame.

Says the Lord, whose name is the God of Hosts

Amos concludes a number of his oracles with *Amar Hashem*. He refers to God as *Tzeva'ot* nine times, but only twice does he add *shemo* – that *Tzeva'ot* is a *name* of God. The other instance is in 4:13, as part of the hymn which references the movements of the stars. Here, *Tzeva'ot* seems to respond to these foreign deities as *kokhav eloheikhem*, "the star-gods" or "the star of your gods." All these gods and their stars are so much

45. For example, Psalms 115:4.

vanity and nothingness; so says the Lord, whose name is "God of the [heavenly] Hosts."

THE STRUCTURE OF THE PERICOPE

Here is the full text of the seven verses we have just studied (Amos 5:21–27).

> I hate (*saneiti*), I despise (*ma'asti*) your feasts (*ḥagei**khem***),
> And I take no delight (*ariaḥ*) in your solemn assemblies (*atzrotei**khem***)
>
> > Even though you offer Me (***li***) your burnt offerings and cereal offerings (*minḥotei**khem***)
> > I will not accept (*ertzeh*) them
> > And the peace offerings of your fatted beasts (*shelem meri'ei**khem***) I will not look upon (*abit*)
> >
> > > Take away from Me (*me'**alai***) the noise of your songs (*shire**kha***)
> > > To the melody of your harps (*nevale**kha***) I will not listen (*eshma*)
> > >
> > > > But let justice roll down like the waters
> > > > And righteousness like an ever-flowing stream
> > >
> > > Did you bring Me (***li***) sacrifices and offerings the forty years in the wilderness
> > > O house of Israel?
> >
> > You shall take up Sikkut your king (*malke**khem***)
> > And Kiyun your star-gods (*elohei**khem***), your images (*tzalmei**khem***)
> > Which you made for yourselves (***lakhem***)
>
> I will take you (***etkhem***) into exile (*vehiglei**ti***) beyond Damascus
> Says the Lord, whose name is the God of Hosts

As can be seen from the graphic presentation, these seven verses are arranged as a chiasmus, with the pivot verse ("But let justice roll down like the waters / And righteousness like an ever-flowing stream") at its center. The structure's components are not perfectly balanced: for example, the concluding verse seems to be unmatched in the first half.

The first half is devoted to God's rejection of Israel's sacrifices, whereas the second half seems to impart three distinct messages. First, a familiar rebuke regarding God's attitude toward offerings; second, an obscure mention of the people's apparent engagement with Assyrian deities; finally their punishment, which recalls Amos's opening oracle against the nations.

In the above translation I have transliterated twenty words, eleven of which have the second person pronominal suffix *-khem* (plural) or *-kha* (singular). The other nine all have first person prefixes or suffixes, either as conjugated verbs (for example, *ma'asti*) or, as nouns, in the accusative case (*me'alai, li*). This interplay between "Me" and "you" (or "you all") may hold the key to understanding the oracle's structural wisdom and underlying message, as well as the obscure inclusion of Sikkut and Kiyun.

God's rejection of the people's offerings means that they *have* been worshipping Him; He cannot reject an offering that was not offered up to Him. Even so, these offerings are considered *your* offerings; God wants nothing to do with them because they are meaningless.

With this in mind, let's consider this structure from a new angle. As I noted earlier, Israelite worship of Assyrian gods at this point in time is highly unlikely, given the lack of interaction with Assyria. Hence *it is unlikely that the Samarian audience was ever involved in Sikkut-worship,* and that the mention of these Assyrian gods must have surprised them.

God is rejecting Samaria's *legitimate* worship because their society is corrupted with moral depravity that poisons the core of true "devotion."[46] In order for God to accept their offerings, society must reflect God's path of righteousness and justice, "*la'asot tzedaka umishpat.*"

Micah expresses this observation beautifully:

> Will the Lord be pleased with thousands of rams, with ten thousands of rivers of oil? Shall I give my first-born for my transgres-

46. See Isaiah 1:11–15 for an explicit expression of this model of divine rejection; see ibid. vv. 16–17 for the necessary repair that will allow their offerings to be once more accepted.

> sion, the fruit of my body for the sin of my soul? It has been told to you, O man, what is good, and what the Lord does require of you: only to do justly (*asot mishpat*), and to love mercy (*ahavat ḥesed*), and to walk humbly with your God. (Mic. 6:7–8)

AND BACK TO SIKKUT AND KIYUN

Though a central biblical agenda is to condemn and ultimately obliterate idolatry, the prophets sometimes use pagan practices or deities as a reference point for evil: they will refer to moral corruption as "idolatry" as a derogative term, even though the people are not in fact serving other gods.

When the elders pressure Samuel to appoint a king, God considers this an expression of rebellion against Him, of idolatry.[47] God is effectively stating: if you reject My principles and demand a human king, you might as well be worshipping other gods.

That may be the case here: Amos is accusing the people of serving Sikkut and Kiyun in order to convey God's rejection of their corrupt judiciary and society. Though they are not actually worshipping them, the prophet is expressing: "Your treatment of the poor is as grave as worshipping the foreign gods of a distant empire, an empire which will one day destroy you!"

Let's explore how this theory illuminates the oracle's structure.

The repetition of "you" and "Me" emphasizes that worship of God is necessarily about a relationship between "you" and "Me." Amos is conveying God's message to his audience: You are bringing offerings for yourselves, not for Me; if they are not brought in righteous justice, "I reject them," "I hate them," and "your songs sound like noise to Me." There is no relationship here; your offerings are meaningless, and "I utterly reject them."

The following retains the same structure, but redefines each section:

47. I Samuel 8:7–8.

A: [UTTER REJECTION OF THE "HOLY" GATHERINGS] I hate (*saneiti*), I despise (*ma'asti*) your feasts (*ḥageikhem*), and I take no delight (*ariaḥ*) in your solemn assemblies (*atzeroteikhem*)

B: [SPECIFIC REJECTION OF THE OFFERINGS] Even though you offer me (***li***) your burnt offerings and cereal offerings, (*minḥoteikhem*), I will not accept (*ertzeh*) them, and the peace offerings of your fatted beasts (*shelem meri'eikhem*), I will not look upon (*abit*)

C: [POINTED REJECTION OF THE VERY ACTIONS THAT SHOULD ENGENDER HARMONY] Take away from Me (*me'alai*) the noise of your songs (*shirekha*); to the melody of your harps (*nevalekha*) I will not listen (*eshma*)

D: [THE PIVOT – THIS IS WHAT **SHOULD** BE TAKING PLACE] But let justice roll down like the waters and righteousness like an ever-flowing stream

C': [EVOCATION OF THE PERIOD OF TRUE HARMONY[48]] Did you bring me (***li***) sacrifices and offerings the forty years in the wilderness, O house of Israel?

B': [EQUATING THEIR OFFERINGS WITH ODIOUS IDOLATROUS PRACTICES] You shall take up Sikkut your king (*malkekhem*) and Kiyun your star-gods (*eloheikhem*), your images (*tzalmeikhem*), which you made for yourselves (*lakhem*)

A': [UTTER REJECTION OF THE PEOPLE – EXILE AND DISPERSION] I will exile (*vehigleiti*) you (*etkhem*) beyond Damascus

Says the Lord, whose name is the God of Hosts.

48. See Jeremiah 2:1–3.

1: Amos begins by expressing God's broad rejection of the people's festive gatherings, gatherings that ideally constitute "meeting" (akin to *Ohel Mo'ed,* the Tent of Meeting in the desert) between the people and God. The final line expresses the exact opposite with poetic justice: You gather in false holiness; thus you will be dispersed (the opposite of "gathered") and exiled from your place.

2: God explicitly rejects the people's worship because they are only doing it for themselves: "for *you*" and not "for *Me*."

3: Singing to God should be a wondrous experience of connection to the Divine, yet God wants nothing of it. These are "*your* songs," not "*My* songs." The prophet reminds the people of their years in the wilderness, when true harmony between God and His people existed.

4: The pivot verse explains the core issue: Why are these offerings considered "for *you*" and not "for *Me*"? Why are these songs a cacophony to God? Because of society's grave corruption. But the people's relationship with God can be mended, and *minḥoteikhem* (*your* grain offerings) will once again be considered *minḥotai* (*My* grain offerings), if only justice would flow like water and righteousness would surge like an everflowing stream.

Chapter 8

The End of Power (6:1–14)

(א) הוֹי הַשַּׁאֲנַנִּים בְּצִיּוֹן וְהַבֹּטְחִים בְּהַר שֹׁמְרוֹן נְקֻבֵי רֵאשִׁית הַגּוֹיִם וּבָאוּ לָהֶם בֵּית יִשְׂרָאֵל: (ב) עִבְרוּ כַלְנֵה וּרְאוּ וּלְכוּ מִשָּׁם חֲמַת רַבָּה וּרְדוּ גַת פְּלִשְׁתִּים הֲטוֹבִים מִן הַמַּמְלָכוֹת הָאֵלֶּה אִם רַב גְּבוּלָם מִגְּבֻלְכֶם: (ג) הַמְנַדִּים לְיוֹם רָע וַתַּגִּישׁוּן שֶׁבֶת חָמָס: (ד) הַשֹּׁכְבִים עַל מִטּוֹת שֵׁן וּסְרֻחִים עַל עַרְשׂוֹתָם וְאֹכְלִים כָּרִים מִצֹּאן וַעֲגָלִים מִתּוֹךְ מַרְבֵּק: (ה) הַפֹּרְטִים עַל פִּי הַנָּבֶל כְּדָוִיד חָשְׁבוּ לָהֶם כְּלֵי שִׁיר: (ו) הַשֹּׁתִים בְּמִזְרְקֵי יַיִן וְרֵאשִׁית שְׁמָנִים יִמְשָׁחוּ וְלֹא נֶחְלוּ עַל שֵׁבֶר יוֹסֵף: (ז) לָכֵן עַתָּה יִגְלוּ בְּרֹאשׁ גֹּלִים וְסָר מִרְזַח סְרוּחִים:

(ח) נִשְׁבַּע אֲדֹנָי ה׳ בְּנַפְשׁוֹ נְאֻם ה׳ אֱלֹהֵי צְבָאוֹת מְתָאֵב אָנֹכִי אֶת גְּאוֹן יַעֲקֹב וְאַרְמְנֹתָיו שָׂנֵאתִי וְהִסְגַּרְתִּי עִיר וּמְלֹאָהּ: (ט) וְהָיָה אִם יִוָּתְרוּ עֲשָׂרָה אֲנָשִׁים בְּבַיִת אֶחָד וָמֵתוּ: (י) וּנְשָׂאוֹ דּוֹדוֹ וּמְסָרְפוֹ לְהוֹצִיא עֲצָמִים מִן הַבַּיִת וְאָמַר לַאֲשֶׁר בְּיַרְכְּתֵי הַבַּיִת הַעוֹד עִמָּךְ וְאָמַר אָפֶס וְאָמַר הָס כִּי לֹא לְהַזְכִּיר בְּשֵׁם ה׳: (יא) כִּי הִנֵּה ה׳ מְצַוֶּה וְהִכָּה הַבַּיִת הַגָּדוֹל רְסִיסִים וְהַבַּיִת הַקָּטֹן בְּקִעִים: (יב) הַיְרֻצוּן בַּסֶּלַע סוּסִים אִם יַחֲרוֹשׁ בַּבְּקָרִים כִּי הֲפַכְתֶּם לְרֹאשׁ מִשְׁפָּט וּפְרִי צְדָקָה לְלַעֲנָה: (יג) הַשְּׂמֵחִים לְלֹא דָבָר הָאֹמְרִים הֲלוֹא בְחָזְקֵנוּ לָקַחְנוּ לָנוּ קַרְנָיִם: (יד) כִּי הִנְנִי מֵקִים עֲלֵיכֶם בֵּית יִשְׂרָאֵל נְאֻם ה׳ אֱלֹהֵי הַצְּבָאוֹת גּוֹי וְלָחֲצוּ אֶתְכֶם מִלְּבוֹא חֲמָת עַד נַחַל הָעֲרָבָה:

1 Woe to those who are at ease in Zion, and to those who feel secure on the mountain of Samaria, the notable men of the first of the nations, to whom the house of Israel come! 2 Pass over to

Kalneh, and see; and from there go to Ḥamat the great; then go
down to Gath of the Philistines. Are they better than these kingdoms? Or is their territory greater than your territory, **3** O you
who put the evil day far away, and bring the seat of violence near?

4 Woe to those who lie upon beds of ivory, and stretch themselves
upon their couches, and eat lambs from the flock, and calves from
the midst of the stall; **5** who sing idle songs to the sound of the
harp, and like David invent for themselves instruments of music;
6 who drink wine in bowls, and anoint themselves with the finest
oils, but are not grieved over the ruin of Joseph! **7** Therefore, they
shall now be the first of those to go into exile, and the revelry of
those who stretch themselves shall pass away.

8 The Lord A-D-N-Y has sworn by Himself says the Lord, the
God of Hosts; I abhor the pride of Jacob and hate his strongholds;
and I will deliver up the city and all that is in it. **9** And if ten men
remain in one house, they shall die. **10** And when a man's kinsman, he who burns him, shall take him up to bring the bones out
of the house, and shall say to him who is in the innermost parts
of the house, "Is there still anyone with you?" he shall say, "No";
and he shall say, "Hush! We must not mention the name of the
Lord." **11** For behold, the Lord commands, and the great house
shall be smitten into fragments, and the little house into bits.
12 Do horses run upon rocks? Does one plow them with oxen?
But you have turned justice into poison and the fruit of righteousness into wormwood – **13** you who rejoice in Lo-devar, who say:
Have we not by our own strength taken Karnaim for ourselves?
14 For behold, I will raise up against you a nation, O house of
Israel," says the Lord, the God of Hosts; "and they shall oppress
you from the entrance of Ḥamat to the Brook of the Araba."

THE FIRST PART OF THE ORACLE – ILLUSIONS OF GRANDEUR (6:1–7)

1: Woe to those who are at ease in Zion
And to those who feel secure on the mountain of Samaria

We have already discussed the opening word *Hoi* at the beginning of the previous chapter. This is Amos's only other use of *hoi;* here it recalls Isaiah's repeated use of *hoi* as he also condemns the complacent revelers of a corrupt society (Is. 5).

Sha'anan is a rare word (fifteen biblical instances) that sometimes means "tranquil" in the pejorative sense of "complacent," and sometimes simply "at ease."[1]

Oddly, Amos's audience is "complacent" *in Zion*. Is he addressing a southern audience, which would counter his opening anthem of bringing the roaring voice of God *from* Zion to the north? Traditional and modern commentators read the verse thus, and associate it with Judah's inclusion is Amos's opening oracle (2:4–5).[2] In chapter 2, we entertained a strategy to understand the rebuke against Judah in that sequence, but that strategy would not explain *Zion* here.

Rather, I would like to suggest two alternative interpretations here:

First, this phrase, *sha'ananim beTziyon ubotḥim beHar Shomron,* may have been a common phrase at that time; prophets often employed contemporary idioms – sometimes with surprising modifications – as part of their rhetorical strategy.

Alternatively, Amos may be ironically expressing how the Samarian aristocracy *consider themselves as central as Zion;* perhaps as a result of the northern kingdom's establishment of their own center of worship.

---

1. Two exceptions (which are, in fact, parallel narratives: II Kings 19:28 and Isaiah 37:29) are considered from the root *sha'on* – i.e., a chaotic noisy tumult.
2. See, *inter alia,* Paul's comments in *Mikra LeYisrael,* 101.

The notable men of the first of the nations,
To whom the house of Israel come!

This is a challenging clause, explained in various ways. The opening word *nekuvei* seems to be an abbreviated form of *nekuv beshem*, i.e., designated by name;[3] those of important repute. Amos addresses those who consider themselves of importance, leaders of the nation, whose egos are inflated because the people come to them.

2: Pass over to Kalneh, and see
And from there go to Ḥamat the great;
Then go down to Gath of the Philistines.
Are they better than these kingdoms?
Or is their territory greater than your territory?

This passage poses additional exegetical challenges. Are these city-states currently in ruins? Or are they enjoying short-lived success? Why are these three places mentioned?

Some modern scholars suggest that this refers to Tiglath-Pileser III's campaign in the eighth century BCE. This is unconvincing, given that this took place after Amos's time. Moreover, by that time, the Samarian aristocracy was no longer sovereign, but rather Assyria's vassal state, with Hosea ben Ela its "puppet king" answering to the Assyrians. By then, this rebuke would have been given far too late.

Most reasonably, then, this chastisement takes place at a time when these kingdoms were at rest and secure. Kalnei was a neo-Hittite capital in northern Syria,[4] and Greater Ḥamat is likely al-Ḥama, on the banks of the Orontes River in central Syria. Gath-Pelishtim (as opposed to other cities known as Gath, such as Gath HaḤefer) is likely located near Tel as-Safi, a few miles northwest of Beit Guvrin (in the Lakhish area). As he did in his first series of oracles, Amos is creating a geographical sandwich, identifying powers to the northeast and one to the southwest – both of which presently stand secure.

3. Numbers 1:17; I Chronicles 12:32, 16:41; II Chronicles 28:15, 31:19.
4. See also Isaiah 10:9.

This is not the only instance of a prophet bidding the people to visit other nations to see how they honor their ancestral gods (and to contrast that with Israel's penchant to seek "new" deities to worship).[5]

Here, however, it is not clear what the purpose of this imaginary visit might be. Some *Rishonim* suggest that Israel is drawn to these particular city-states and their gods.[6]

Another possibility is to read the penultimate line as directed to Zion and Samaria. "Are your kingdoms better than these kingdoms?" implies that the amount of land you hold will not determine your future wealth and security.

The meaning of "these kingdoms" affects the meaning of the next line – does it refer to the aforementioned kingdoms, or to the audience?

3: O you who put the evil day far away

Hamenadim is a rare biblical verb; it appears in verb form only here and in Isaiah 66:5. The root is *n-d-h* (same as the nominal form *niddah*), the same as the post-biblical word *nidui* (excommunication).

The above translation (You who put the evil day far away…) suggests that it refers to the audience, but the most straightforward reading implies that the verb *hamenadim* refers to "these kingdoms." This is further supported by the opening word – *hoi* – and the verbal form that typically follows that vocative call, as we will discuss below. In the meantime, we will explore both possibilities.

If the referent is the other nations (as Ibn Ezra and R. Eliezer of Beaugency read it), then they have presumably managed to avert their day of reckoning, evidently by correcting their ethical behavior (Malbim); or they *imagine* that they have pushed it off (R. Eliezer). The difference between these two will be the referent of the next clause – who is bringing "the seat of violence" near? If this refers to the other nations, they are operating under the illusion that some other behavior or merit of theirs is keeping punishment at the door. If it is Israel (Malbim), then the

5. See Jeremiah 2:10–11.
6. Such as R. Eliezer of Beaugency.

contrast is stark: by correcting their behavior, these smaller, weaker kingdoms will outlast Zion and Samaria, who encourage violence and theft.

If, however, those who "push off the evil day" refers to the audience, then the text has left these neighboring nations and returned to the opening framework: direct rebuke of the Samarian aristocracy. If so, the verb *menadim* is necessarily illusory: the Samarian audience *imagines* that their day of reckoning is long in coming, but their behavior actually brings it ever closer.

This may depend on how we read the *vav* of *vatagishun*, below:

And bring the seat of violence near

If the *vav* opening this clause is *vav* explicative, then this clause explicates the previous one: both refer to the same group. If so, it is far more likely that this refers to the Samarian audience than to the other nations, as the audience has no way to know when the nations' day of reckoning is nigh.

If, on the other hand, we read the *vav* of *vatagishun* as *vav hanigud* (disjunctive *vav*), then the two clauses are, by definition, contrasting two different groups. Logically, only one reading follows: that the surrounding nations have successfully warded off the day of evil by behaving well (as Malbim maintains), *whereas* Samaria is institutionalizing and enabling the seat of violence, which will bring a swift and terrible "day of evil" in their near future.

4: Woe to those who lie upon beds of ivory

From this point on, the prophetic diatribe is unequivocally focused on the Samarian audience, which may have implications for our interpretation of the previous verse.

The word *shein* can mean "tooth"[7] or "ivory,"[8] as it does here. Why would beds be made of ivory?

---

7. Exodus 21:24.
8. I Kings 10:18 (= II Chronicles 9:17); I Kings 22:39; Psalms 45:9.

Sennacherib's boastful comments after his conquest of Judah illuminate this description. The famous Prism,[9] as reproduced by Pritchard,[10] describes how the Assyrian emperor claimed the following from Judah:[11]

> Hezekiah ... did send me, later, to Nineveh, my lordly city, together with 30 talents of gold, 800 talents of silver, precious stones, antinomy, large cuts of red stone, *couches (inlaid) with ivory,*[12] *nimedu-chairs (inlaid) with ivory*, elephant-hides, ebony-wood, boxwood, (and) all kinds of valuable treasures, his (own) daughters, concubines, male and female musicians.

Like the "ivory boats" of Ezekiel's tirade against Tyre (27:6), this clearly refers to extravagant beds inlaid with ivory – a valuable item owned by royalty and the wealthy.

As a side note, the "ivory houses" (Amos 3:15) and "ivory beds" suggest economic ties between Samaria and Africa.[13]

And stretch themselves upon their couches

The root *s-r-ḥ* (*samekh, resh, ḥet*) in almost all biblical instances means "stretch out" or "overhang."[14] This root may be related to *sin, resh, ayin*; the letters *sin* and *samekh* are often interchangeable as are *ayin* and *ḥet*. This root took on a different meaning in the rabbinic period: "stench," which is its common usage today. As is their wont,[15] the Sages eisegetically read their meaning of *saruaḥ* into the verse (Kiddushin 71b):

---

9. Both Oriental Institute as well as Taylor.
10. James Pritchard, ed. *Ancient Near Eastern Texts as Relating to the Old Testament* ("ANET"), 3rd ed. (Princeton, 1969), 288.
11. Although the references to ivory are but a small part of the list, the emperor's boasts are illuminative as to how the ancients recorded history – and more than a little entertaining; cf. II Kings 19 and Yeshayahu 37.
12. *Ershu-shinni* in the original Akkadian.
13. I Kings 5:14, 9:26, and 10:1–23.
14. Exodus 26:12.
15. The rabbis were aware that biblical Hebrew was of a different idiom than rabbinic Hebrew. For example, R. Yochanan states: "The terminology of the Bible is not the same as the terminology employed by the Sages" (Avoda Zara 58b). Yet for

> R. Yosi ben Ḥanina says that this refers to people who would urinate naked before their couches. R. Abbahu cursed this interpretation: Is that why it states [that their punishment would be] "Therefore, they shall be exiled at the head of all exiles"?! Rather, R. Abbahu explained that it refers to men who eat and drink with each other and attach their beds together and exchange their wives with each other and pollute their beds with semen that is not theirs.

Odious as this image may be, it is far from the straightforward meaning of the verse (see Rashi) – again, this is not the biblical meaning of *saruaḥ*.[16]

The parallel of *mita* and *eres* is well attested in the canon[17] and is used here in classic parallelism, implying that *seruḥim* is parallel to *shokhevim* – to lie or stretch out.

And eat the lambs from the flock and calves from the midst of the stall

Karim[18] and the singular *kar*[19] refer to the choicest he-lamb, to beasts so strong that they are used as "battering rams."[20] Sprawled on their fancy ivory-inlaid beds, the wealthy gorged themselves on the fattest lambs.

They would also take the calves from the middle of the stall, known as the *marbek*.[21] The words appear four times in *Tanakh*, always as a modifier for a calf, an *egel marbek*,[22] the choicest meat.

---

homiletic purposes, they were ready to see them as one and the same. A startling example is R. Yochanan's homily about God "enwrapping Himself as a *shaliaḥ tzibbur*" (Rosh HaShana 17b).

16. Although Klein suggests that Jeremiah 49:7 is a *hapax legomenon* and carries the meaning of "stench," this is not generally accepted.
17. As we had earlier in 3:12; Psalms 6:7, 41:4; and Job 7:13 (the latter two with *mishkav* in place of *mita*).
18. Deuteronomy 32:14.
19. Isaiah 16:1.
20. That is the provenance of that odd phrase; the earliest battering rams used to breach fortifications were shaped like a ram's head.
21. The source of the name Rivka – Mishna Eiruvin 2:1.
22. I Samuel 28:24; Jeremiah 46:21; Malachi 3:20 – and our verse.

There is no accusation here of any offense against the poor; this just seems to be a general critique of their hedonistic lifestyle.

5: Who sing idle songs to the sound of the harp
And like David invent for themselves instruments of music

The verb *poretim* is a *hapax legomenon* and can be interpreted from either the root (*p-r-t*) or the context. Rashi, citing Menachem's *maḥberet,* connects it to the only other instance of that root in *Tanakh,* as a noun: *peret karmekha,*[23] meaning individual grapes: "One who sings with an accompanying musical instrument sounds out the words in singular tones, per the beauty of the sound, going higher or lower."

Rashi apparently reads that *haporetim* refers to those who sing along with the Psalter.

R. Joseph Kara reads the word similarly (citing Dunash instead), but adds that they modify their voices to adjust to the sounds of the Psalter.

Ibn Ezra understands *poretim* as a form of improvisational composition, referring not to their musical ability but rather to their poetic range and talent.

However we read the phrase, the prophet is accusing these aspiring musicians of overrating their musical talents. They consider themselves to be "the next David" – whether this refers to David's compositional abilities (Ibn Ezra), his musical virtuosity (Radak), or his ability to fashion instruments.[24]

The spelling of David (*dvyd*) here is unusual; typically, until the Second Temple period,[25] the name is spelled without a *yod* (*dvd*). This may mean that we have to rethink our assumptions about the introduction of *matres lectiones* (Hebrew letters used as vowels); alternatively,

23. Leviticus 19:10.
24. See I Chronicles 23:5 and, more explicitly, the apocryphal Psalm CLI from Qumran, lines 4–5 (J. A. Sanders, *The Dead Sea Psalms Scroll* [Ithaca, 1967], 96–97). See also Rashi ad loc. for an interesting variation on this approach.
25. I Chronicles 29:10 and another 260 times.

perhaps the *yod* was added to distinguish it from the word *dod* (beloved), also spelled *dvd.*[26]

6: Who drink wine in bowls and anoint themselves with the finest oils

The use of *mizrakim* here is not incidental; neither is the wording of the second clause. A *mazrek* is a vessel used for "throwing" blood on the altar after it has been collected from the animal. The usual word used for a drinking cup is *gavia* or *kos* (both of which are used in the Joseph narrative); as Radak points out, both of those are smaller and used for the customary amount of wine, whereas a *mazrek* has a greater capacity. In addition to his criticism of their hedonistic lifestyle, Amos is *also* condemning the use of cultic vessels and materials for the people's own pleasure. Not only are they living self-indulgent lives, but they are also devoting more energy to indulging their material pleasures than to worship.

Wine and oil are the two liquids brought to the altar that may also be ingested by people (unlike blood). They are also the only two offerings brought to the altar that are edible in their raw state. Instead of bringing bowls of wine for libations on the altar, and finest oils for anointing the priests and vessels, the people are using them for their own pleasure.

But are not grieved over the ruin of Joseph!

Neḥelu, from the root *ḥ-l-h* (sick), implies making oneself sick, to hurt from someone else's pain.[27] *Shever Yosef* seems to allude to the disaster about to befall the northern kingdom. Yet the use of *shever* hints to its occurrence in Genesis, where *shever* is the corn (grain) that Joseph's brothers purchased in Egypt to bring back to Canaan.[28] While the other mention in Amos (8:5) as well as the one in Nehemiah (10:22) both relate to people selling grain, *shever* in Genesis is always in the context

26. Compare Song of Songs 7:12 with I Samuel 20:11.
27. See, for instance, I Samuel 22:8.
28. Genesis 41:56–57; 42:1–3, 5–7, 10, 19, 26; 43:2, 4, 20, 22; 44:2, 25; 47:14.

of the Joseph story. Thus, Amos's use of *shever* both means "tragedy" and evokes Joseph's grain.

This takes us back to the schism between Judah and Israel in Shechem (I Kings 12). The Midrash links this schism to the sale of Joseph, which also took place there.[29] The hedonistic people pay no heed to the terrible tragedy at the root of their very existence – their focus on their own pleasure thus dooms them to destruction.

7: Therefore, they shall now be the first to go into exile

In an ironic twist, those who perceive themselves as "the highest of the nations" will soon be the first in exile, their illusions of grandeur nothing but that – illusions.

And the revelry of those who stretch themselves shall pass away

The unusual word *mirzaḥ* appears only here and in Jeremiah, where it seems to refer to a meal taken by mourners (16:5). Various extra-biblical sources (Phoenician, Punic, Nabatean, and other texts) imply that it is some form of feast; it appears on the Medeba map (fourth c. CE) as the name of the Pe'or mountain where the Israelites sinned with the daughters of Moab. Thus the final line before God's terrifying oath is that all this feasting will come to an end when the people are led into captivity and exile.

Hoi

This introductory word to chapter 6 consistently follows a recognizable pattern.[30] All the verbs that follow this word are plural participles with the definite article – in this passage, *hasha'ananim* (v. 1), *habotehim* (v. 1), *hamenadim* (v. 3), *hashokhevim* (v. 4), *hashotim* (v. 6).

This rhetorical strategy may be calculated to address an audience without directly speaking *to* them; as if Amos is musing to himself about the fate of these revelers while the audience is "eavesdropping" on his

29. Sanhedrin 102a.

30. See above in chapter 7. See, for example, the *hoi* sequence in Isaiah 5.

words. This is a familiar strategy: when the "wicked son" of the Passover Seder challenges: "What is this worship to *you*," the father should *declare*:[31] "It is a Passover offering that God passed over our houses in Egypt when He afflicted Egypt and saved our houses" (Ex. 12:26). We respond as if to no one in particular, but make sure he hears it clearly. Similarly, the prophet is lamenting – as if to himself – about these sinners' fate, yet making sure they hear every word.

THE STRUCTURE

Once again, Amos favors the heptad.

Hoi
A: (1) ... to those who are at ease in Zion,
And to those who feel secure in the mountain of Samaria,
The notable men of the first of the nations,
To whom the house of Israel come!
B: (2) Pass over to Kalneh, and see,
And from thence go to Ḥamat the great;
Then go down to Gath of the Philistines;
Are they better than these kingdoms?
Or is their territory greater than your territory?
C: (3) O you who put the evil day far away,
And bring the seat of violence near;
D: (4) Who lie upon beds of ivory,
And stretch themselves upon their couches,
And eat lambs from the flock,
And calves from the midst of the stall;
C': (5) Who sing idle songs to the sound of the harp,
And like David invent for themselves instruments of music;
B': (6) Who drink wine in bowls,
And anoint themselves with the finest oils;
But are not grieved over the ruin of Joseph!

31. The missing preposition *elav* indicates that the father speaks aloud, but doesn't respond directly to the child.

A': (7) Therefore they shall now be
the first of those to go into exile,
And the revelry of those who stretch themselves
shall pass away.

Discussion

The relationship between the "A" sections is clear. The people of Samaria believe that they are the first and greatest among nations, whereas they will soon become the first among exiles. Their complacent leisure will soon turn to displacement and unrest.

The "B" sections seem to present a parallel rather than a contrast. They believe themselves superior to neighboring kingdoms; and they indulge in rich wines and oils. These particular neighbors may have been chosen deliberately. While wine is often biblically lauded, it can also serve as a metaphor for punishment, as in "the cup of My hot rage (*ḥamati*)."[32] Perhaps the surprising mention of Ḥamat hints to this "cup of hot rage." A "Gath," which literally means "winepress," may also be in dialogue with the Samarian aristocracy's indulgence in wine; moreover, winepresses are also used for pressing oil, which thus also alludes to the people's extravagant use of oil.

The "C" passages: we determined above that the subjects of v. 3 are the Samarians themselves. How would they "put off" the day of evil? By feigning unawareness of the signs and prophecies indicating the coming days of reckoning. Rather, they lie around and play music, imagining themselves as David, whose period of musical composition presumably took place after the kingdom was secured and his enemies were "put to rest" around him.[33] Unlike David's time, however, here the "seat of violence" creeps ever nearer, its ugly roar drowned out by the people's false and self-serving psalmody.

At the heart of this rebuke, Amos lays out four descriptions of the wealthy's hedonism in two couplets.

In the first, he caustically describes the fancy couches that they lie upon – alluding to the foreign trade (ivory) that has brought them

32. Isaiah 51:22.
33. II Samuel 7:1.

this wealth (connecting again to "B" and the neighboring countries) and to the smug arrogance of the aristocracy "stretched out" on their beds. The second couplet describes how they gorge on the fattest of the flock and the choicest of the herd. These descriptions of the aristocracy's indulgence serve as the central axis of this oracle: it is this smug self-aggrandizement that will ultimately be Samaria's undoing.

The Interconnected Web

Although we initially read these seven verses as a chiasmus, other more intricate and less obvious structural considerations may reflect Amos's deeper message here.

Amos, God's agent, is from Judah, from which the Samarian kingdom seceded when it established its own sovereignty nearly two centuries earlier. The northern kingdom was supposed to be a "temporary" corrective for the sins of the Davidic line.[34] But when Jeroboam established sanctuaries at Beit El and Dan, a more permanent sense of independence set in. By the time Ahab institutionalized Ba'al-worship, the die was cast and Samaria was, from Judah's perspective, a closely related but foreign state. Amos, however, still perceives the north as a renegade Jewish monarchy that veered sharply off course not only through its engagement in idolatry, but also in its very divorce from the true center of worship, Jerusalem. Beyond his criticism of the Samarian aristocracy's abuse of the poor, Amos also seeks to condemn their false sense of independence and disassociation from the Temple in Jerusalem.

As such, Amos's language evokes the Temple. First of all, he refers to *sha'ananim beTziyon,* a sardonic allusion to their sense of "feeling at home." He also mentions how the Israelites "come to them" in a mockery of pilgrimage. When criticizing their tolerance for violence, he uses the unexpected verb *vatagishun,* a word associated with offerings: rather than offerings, they bring violence near.[35] The fourth verse mentions *karim* and *eglei marbek,* both choice animals ideally used for offerings.[36]

34. See I Kings 11:1–13; 30–39 ff.
35. For example, Leviticus 2:8, 8:14, 21:21, 23.
36. Deuteronomy 32:14; I Samuel 15:9.

Perhaps the most overt slap comes in verse 5, where they are accused of having the temerity to compare themselves to David, playing on their instruments – a stinging allusion to their alienation from the Temple and the Davidic line.

Finally, in verse 6, *mizrekei yayin,* and *reishit shemanim* clearly evokes the Temple service.

The kingdom that has voluntarily exiled itself from its true home, and that indulges in empty imitations of life there, will now be forcefully exiled from their false center – first only among exiles.

THE SECOND PART OF THE ORACLE – ILLUSIONS OF VICTORY (6:8–14)

8: The Lord A-D-N-Y has sworn by Himself

Biblical oaths usually invoke God's name, as if associating the veracity of the claim with the truth of God's existence; another reason for including God's name is to declare that the oath-taker is prepared to accept God's punishment if their words are less than true.

There are various oath formulations. One common form in the prophetic histories is *ko ya'aseh Hashem vekho yosif.*[37]

Another is *ḥai Hashem,* "as the Lord lives," which again equates the truth of the oath's statement with the truth of God's eternity. This short oath-formula appears 41 times in the canon. *Ḥai Hashem* is used as an actual oath *and* in literary prophecy: Jeremiah uses it nine times,[38] and Hosea uses it once in an oracle reminiscent of Amos's rebuke in 5:5: "and no longer come to Gilgal, nor make a pilgrimage to Beit Aven, and do not swear 'as *Hashem* lives'" (Hos. 4:15).

Perhaps the most explicit discussion of using God's name in an oath is found in Leviticus: "Do not swear falsely by My name, as you will profane the name of your God" (19:12).

---

37. Nine times in Samuel and Kings and once in Ruth.
38. Of these, one describes how people swear false oaths (Jer. 5:2); another is when Zedekiah swears that he will spare Jeremiah (38:16); and the rest refer to other people taking oaths.

These examples all refer to humans taking oaths in God's name. But God *also* takes oaths, beginning with His commitment to Abraham, which is upgraded from a promise[39] to a covenant[40] to an oath.[41] This oath is repeated to Isaac,[42] and while it is not explicitly made to Jacob, he is included as its beneficiary throughout the rest of the Torah. The oath to the Patriarchs is introduced with the formula *bi nishbati*. Most translations render this "By Myself have I sworn."[43]

A different form appears in Numbers after the people react badly to the scouts' report. After acceding to Moses's plea to spare the people, God adds: "But truly, as I live, and as all the earth shall be filled with the glory of *Hashem*" (Num. 14:21). Rashi, R. Joseph Kara, R. Joseph Bekhor Shor, Radak, and Seforno (among others) all read this formula as an oath.[44] This same formula appears four verses later and, with a slight variation, in the coda of the Song of Moses.[45]

In sum, both people and God Himself take oaths using God's name as affirmation of that pledge. There are, however, only two places where God swears "*benafsho*."[46] Although some medieval commentators (Ibn Ezra, R. Eliezer of Beuagency, and Radak) read *Nishba Hashem Elokim benafsho* as essentially synonymous with *bi nishbati*, the question looms: Then why not just use *bi nishbati* here as well? To that end, Rashi interprets here: "With awareness and intent" – implying that this oath expresses more intent than others. While this raises certain theological issues, it does, perhaps, capture this variation's rhetorical intent. This oath is directly aimed at its audience and has taken into account all their sins and offenses, as detailed above. The next clause in this verse reinforces the sense that God's name intensifies its intent.

---

39. Genesis 12:1–3.
40. Ibid. chs. 15 and 17.
41. Ibid. 22:16–18.
42. Ibid. 26:3.
43. New English Translation (NET) has "I solemnly swear by My own Name" – not a literal translation, but perhaps catching the intent more clearly.
44. See, however, Ramban's dissent ad loc.
45. Deuteronomy 32:40. Subsequently it appears once in Isaiah, twice in Jeremiah, once in Zephaniah, and sixteen (!) times in Ezekiel.
46. Here and Jeremiah 51:14.

Says the Lord, the God of Hosts

The use of *ne'um* here comes as no surprise: Amos uses it 21 times, significantly more than his peers. The word means "utterance" and emphasizes the speaker's identity.

Amos frequently refers to God as "*Elokei Tzeva'ot*."[47] This Divine Name has clear military connotations, characterizing God as an aggressor who is prepared to do battle against His enemies – even when they are His own people. Stars and "the heavenly hosts" are referred to thus because the Bible views the stars as being aligned in battle, God's "front line" of attack.[48] This is consistent with Amos's "cosmic hymns," wherein the constellations are mentioned as part of God's great power.[49]

This mounting sense of adversarial power, conscripting the heavenly bodies to war against the Israelites, is underscored by the next word, an unusually harsh expression of rejection:

I abhor the pride of Jacob

The Rishonim understand the verb *ta'ev* in two different ways. Most, beginning with Rashi, read it as a variation of *ta'ev* with an *ayin* (instead of an *alef*). Similarly, BDB includes it as a secondary meaning, as a variation of *ta'ev* (with an *ayin*).[50] Both BDB and Koehler-Baumgartner acknowledge this to be the only instance of *ta'ev* (with an *alef*) with this meaning.[51]

However, Ibn Ezra, R. Eliezer of Beaugency, and Radak all read it in the opposite sense: Ibn Ezra reads *meta'ev* in the usual sense of the root *t-a-b: ta'ava*, "desire." He generally defines this root as "to be finished," in the sense that true desire completely consumes the one who desires. In that same sense, God is "finished" with these people. R. Eliezer and Radak read it as one of the various Hebrew verbs that function as contronyms: verbs that have two opposite meanings, such as *ikar* ("root," but the verb means "to *up*root") or *sharesh* (same as *ikar*). If so, *ta'ev*

47. He uses it nine times.
48. Judges 5:20.
49. 4:13, 5:8.
50. BDB, 1080; Koehler-Baumgartner, 1672–1673.
51. Some modern scholars, predictably, propose that there was an errant or deliberate textual emendation, and that the original was written with an *ayin*.

can mean both "desire" and "to no longer desire." In this context, the use of *meta'ev* is ironic.

The pride of Jacob

The phrase *ge'on Yaakov* appears in the Bible four times.[52] In Psalm 47, the referent seems to be the Land of Israel: "He chooses our inheritance for us, the pride of Jacob which He loves," while the instance in Nahum[53] is related to sovereignty in the Land, which God promises to restore. Amos's second mention seems to be an epithet for God (paralleling our verse, where God swears by His own name). Ibn Ezra explains that this refers to the Ark.[54] Radak allows for both possible translations, modifying the latter to the Temple.

Which of these four meanings applies here? What has God sworn to reject/abhor?

This can hardly refer to the Land; on the contrary, it is the Land that has been defiled by the nation's corruption.[55] Nor can it mean the Ark or Temple; neither are present in Samaria. And of course, God is not rejecting or abhorring His own name.

This leaves us with two options: either Nahum's meaning applies here, or it is an enigmatic phrase with some other meaning, unattested elsewhere.

Given that methodologically, consistent meaning within the same biblical period and genre is more likely, it is preferable to read this in the same sense as Nahum (who prophesies not long after Amos), rather than propose a new meaning.

Nahum's meaning is logical in this context: God is rejecting Samaria's *sovereignty* and is prepared to send these hedonistic aristocrats into exile. The parallel clause, immediately below, supports this interpretation.

52. Amos 6:8, 8:7; Nachum 2:3; Psalms 47.
53. "For the Lord restores the pride of Jacob, as the pride of Israel."
54. He quotes the Karaite Yefet b. Eli, this time with approval, per Ezekiel 24:21, following Psalms 78:61.
55. See Ramban, Leviticus 18:25.

And hate his strongholds

The use of the verb *sanei* here reinforces the reading of *ta'ev* above: He hates Jacob's palaces. This is also consistent with our reading of *ge'on Yaakov*.

And I will deliver up the city and all that is in it

The verb *hasger* (the causative form of *sagor*, to close up or close in) is generally understood as "hand over," as in handing refugees over to their masters:[56] "You shall not deliver (*lo tasgir*) to his master a servant who is escaped from his master to you."[57]

The referent of the causative form of this verb is usually a person or people.[58] Here, however, what is "handed over" seems to be the city's material wealth, rather than its people. First of all, the people will have already been exiled;[59] second, "*ir umelo'ah*" ("the city and all that is therein") suggests wealth and goods. This sense is found in Lamentations: "He has given up (*hisgir*) into the hand of the enemy the walls of her palaces" (2:7). This passage is in close dialogue with ours, as it is preceded by God's rejection of His altar (= *ge'on Yaakov*?).

The mention of "the city" may mean that this punishment will only affect Samaria's citizens; another option is that it refers to every city in the northern kingdom.

9: And if ten men remain in one house, they shall die

The "ten men" in one house may have survived the attack of the previous verse. Even if so many (ten being the definition of a group[60]) remain together, they will still have no hope; all of them will die. Most commentators understand that these are survivors of the sword who are then killed by the plague, but Rashi reads that these ten escaped both

56. Above, 1:9; see Leviticus 13 and, following that, Numbers 12.
57. Deuteronomy 23:16.
58. I Samuel 23:11, 30:15.
59. Verse 7.
60. Genesis 18:32.

sword and plague and then will be burned up in the house, as the following verse may suggest.

Some commentators link this to Amos's earlier warning that only ten percent of those who "go out" will survive.[61]

As we will also see in the next two verses, the "house" is central in this oath.

10: And when a man's kinsman, he who burns him, shall take him up ...

This clause has at least two linguistic difficulties.

Firstly, the word *unesa'o* is in singular form, "he will lift him." If the phrase "*dodo umesarfo*" refers to two different people, it should be in plural form, as rendered in LXX. If, however, the *vav* is a *vav explicative,* and "*dodo umesarfo*" refers to the same person, why would one person be described with two nouns?

Before we move on to the second problem, note that the word *dod* has two distinct yet related biblical meanings: "uncle" (specifically the father's brother) and "beloved." These meanings are interrelated: besides for the common practice of uncles marrying their brother's (orphaned) daughters, the father's brother had the responsibility of redeeming the family's land[62] or family members who were sold as slaves.[63] Thus a compound translation of *dod* would be "beloved relative who takes responsibility for the family's welfare."[64]

The second, more challenging word is *mesarfo*.[65] The most likely root might be *s-r-f*, to burn, but that poses three difficulties: (1) *s-r-f* is consistently written with *sin*, never *samekh*; (2) *sarof* only appears in *kal* form, but this word is in intensive *piel* form; (3) what could this possibly mean in this context? If the genitive suffix refers to the house being

61. See Rashbam at 5:3.
62. Leviticus 25:25.
63. Ibid. 25:49.
64. This is part of the subtext of Megillat Ruth and the role of Boaz.
65. The word is so challenging that R. Yosef ibn Kaspi (Provence, thirteenth–fourteenth century) comments (ad loc.): "As for me, what can I do if the Holy Tongue is not fully accessible to us."

"burned," then how does a house have a *dod* (uncle)? If, on the other hand, the referent is a person (the last survivor in the house?), then what does "his burner" mean?

Rashi cites the Targum Yonatan: *Veyatilinei karivei mi-yakida*, "His relative will pull him out of the fire." Thus he interprets *dodo* as "his relative," and *mesarfo* as "from the fire." This is consistent with Rashi's reading of the above verse: "those who were not killed by the sword or plague will be killed by fire," but this treatment of *umesarfo* is difficult and unattested.

Rashbam's approach is similar: he reads that the "uncle" saves one (of the ten) people from the fire, which is also consistent with his approach that only ten percent will survive, as in Amos 5:3.

R. Joseph Kara also reads *dodo umesarfo* as referring to one person, but he understands *mesarfo* as "the one who embalms him." He anchors this in several mentions of *misrefot melakhim*[66] which, he maintains, cannot mean a funeral pyre, but rather has a secondary meaning of preserving the body. This significantly impacts our understanding of the previous verse. Was the house destroyed by fire or otherwise?

Ibn Ezra points out that *mesarfo* is a *hapax legomenon*. He then quotes Ibn Karish,[67] who proposes that *dodo umesarfo* are a pair of relatives: *Dod* is the father's brother, while *mesarfo* refers to the mother's brother. Ibn Ezra rejects this as baseless, mentions and rejects the above commentators' readings, and then proposes his own interpretation: that *mesarfo* is some kind of undertaker[68] or funerary officiant.[69]

Radak cites Ibn Karish's explanation as well as the "mainstream" interpretation of "burning," and, citing his father, he explains: "That

66. Jeremiah 34:5.
67. Judah ibn Karish was a ninth-century Algerian Hebrew philologist and grammarian, and something of a pioneer in the study of Hebrew grammar, a discipline that Ibn Ezra considered vital for successful understanding of the biblical text.
68. In this vein, see Noble's article in the "for further study" section. I believe that his numerous emendations go too far, and his reconstruction of the verse, while insightful and clever, relies on too many scribal errors or "modifications."
69. Similarly, see Hakham, 52, although he suggests that the person in charge of this funeral practice was a relative, somewhat combining the "alternate relative" meaning first proposed by Ibn Karish.

friend ("beloved one") that came to burn up the flesh of his dead relative due to the stench and to remove the bones from the house." Radak's father apparently reads the *vav* of *umesarfo* as a *vav habiur*, meaning "his relative, that is the one who will burn him."

Ibn Kaspi writes:

> *Dodo* – Not necessarily his father's brother or [even] his mother's brother; rather [it could mean simply] his relative, as in, "My beloved is to me" (Song. 2:3).
>
> *Umesarfo* – Or *mesarfo*. As for me, what can I do if not all of the holy tongue is not fully accessible to us. But, in any case, this (*mesarfo*) is one of the close relatives.

He clearly favors Ibn Karish's general direction that *mesarfo* and *dod* are two separate people, albeit both relatives, but does not accept Ibn Karish's specific reading of *mesarfo*.

A "Hybrid" Solution

Perhaps the most likely meaning combines several of these proposals. Given the singular verb, let us read the *vav* as *vav habiur*, which explains that *dodo (she'hu) mesarfo* – his close relative (per Ibn Kaspi) *is* the one who performs the funerary rites (following Paul's reading of *mesarfo* as "embalmer").

If so, why would the text use this *hapax legomenon* instead of a well-known word like *sakh* (rub oil), *mashaḥ* (anoint), or the actual word for "embalm," *ḥanat*?[70] Perhaps the text seeks to create a sense of fiery death and destruction by using this rare word, which connotes fire and burning.

To bring the bones out of the house

Why would the bones be brought out of the house? There are two possible ways to read this, depending on our understanding of the cause of

70. Genesis 50:2–3.

death. If we read that the men in the house sought refuge (together – ten men in one house) after a military defeat, but were then killed by the plague, then the *dod/mesaref* presumably comes to the house a significant time later, when the corpses have decomposed and all that remains of these plague victims is their bones. If, however, they sought refuge from attack *and* plague, only to be burned to death in the house, then even if their relative comes right away, only their bones will remain because their bodies were burned in the fire – the latter reading makes Rashi's interpretation more compelling.

And shall say to him who is in the innermost parts of the house

Only one person is speaking here, which reinforces the MT's singular form: the scene portrayed here is one person who goes inside the house to find human remains for burial, then another – the relative/perfumer of one of the dead – enters and calls out to him.

The phrase *yarketei habayit* (innermost area of the house) appears just twice elsewhere. Solomon builds "twenty cubits of the innermost area of the house with cedar planks" (I Kings 6:15), but it is unlikely that Amos is attempting to allude to the Temple here. A more likely dialogue is between this scene and Psalm 128: a God-fearing man's wife is likened to "a fruitful vine inside your home" (*beyarketei veitekha*). Amos draws a subtle contrast between a thriving family safe in their home and the fruitless search for survivors in the innermost recesses of the destroyed house.[71] Moreover, this psalm expresses the joy and continuity of a God-fearing family for whom Jerusalem is their spiritual center: "May the Lord bless you from *Zion* and may you see the goodness of *Jerusalem* all the days of your life. And may you see children of your children, with peace over Israel." As discussed above, the subtext of this *hoi* rebuke reproaches the Northern Kingdom for their rejection of Jerusalem as their spiritual center.[72]

71. See Ibn Kaspi here, who uses the verse in Psalms to explain our verse.
72. This interpretation is not absolutely dependent on dating Psalm 128 to the early First Commonwealth; the motif and imagery were likely known from early in the monarchic period.

"Is there still anyone with you?"

The man waiting outside is carefully vague; he dares not ask *ha'od atzamot imakh*, for the scene is too horrific to describe explicitly.

This reading follows Ibn Ezra and others; Rashi describes a single rescuer who calls out to the lone survivor he finds in the house: "Are there any more (survivors) with you?"

He shall say, "No."

The other rescuer (or, per Rashi, the lone survivor) replies with a single word: *efes*. This word, which means "zero" in Modern Hebrew, appears forty-four times in the canon, usually indicating some form of negation, although its semantic use is broad (the edges of the earth are called *afsei aretz*). In any case, here, the respondent is clearly answering in the negative.

And he shall say, "Hush…"

The rare onomatopoetic word *has* – the biblical "hush!"[73] – appears only eight times in *Tanakh*; only Amos uses it more than once.[74]

"…We must not mention the name of the Lord."

What exactly is the problem here? Why does the rescuer silence him, and what does that have to do with God's name? Ibn Kaspi parses this verse creatively: "*has beshem Hashem, ki lo lehazkir*" – "it is appropriate to be silent in God's name."[75]

73. Indeed, some of the more creative etymologists claim that "hush" developed from *has*.
74. See Numbers 13:30.
75. Leviticus 10:3; Ezekiel 24:17.

11: For, behold, the Lord commands

The use of *metzaveh* here indicates that God will command an earthquake to bring down houses great and small. Is this the earthquake that looms over the entire book and brings devastation two years after Amos begins to prophesy?

Another reading is that God is commanding the enemy to attack Samaria and bring destruction to the entire city.

And the great house shall be smitten into fragments, and the little house into bits

The parallelism here is clear and would argue, as does Rashi, that *beki'im* are smaller (parts of the "small house") than *resisim* (parts of the "big house").

12: Do horses run upon rocks?

These rhetorical questions recall Amos's series of causal relationships in his "inevitability of prophecy" section,[76] which concludes with God's message inevitably being broadcast by His prophets. This couplet is taken from a world familiar to both speaker and audience.

In the mid-eighth century BCE, the northern kingdom enjoyed several decades of military success. While horses were not used for war in Joshua's or even David's time, by the ninth century BCE, cavalry and chariots were part of the military, and represented military prowess and success. The first explicit mention of their use in war is when Ahab employs horse-driven chariots in his second war against Aram.[77]

As for his first war against Aram, a brief digression will provide valuable background information about Amos's time. At the end of the miraculous campaign against the more powerful Aramean army, Ahab surprisingly extends an "olive branch" to Ben-Hadad, sparing him after miraculously defeating him. For this apparently treacherous action, he

---

76. See chapter 3.

77. See I Kings 22:4 – "my horses are as your horses."

is cursed by a prophet – but, religious sentiments aside, what could have been Ahab's motivation?

The answer lies in the looming threat from the east, which both Aram and Israel (and the entire region) was soon to face. The Assyrian empire was preparing to invade and conquer the western Levant and, to that end, former (and future) enemies Israel and Aram (and others) formed an alliance against Assyria. In the great battle of Qarqar (today's northwest Syria) in 853 BCE, this alliance prevented Assyria from conquering the territory (although they would prove victorious 130 years later). Ahab's "olive branch" extended to the defeated Ben-Hadad was part of this treaty-building which was, from a geopolitical perspective, a sage move (although this was denounced from a theological perspective, and God's prophet cursed Ahab).

What is critical for our purposes is what the alliance encountered in the battle of Qarqar. The Assyrians were the first Mesopotamian army with horse-driven chariots and riders. Though the Samarian kingdom knew of cavalry from their battles with Aram, they were presumably inspired by the extent of Assyria's technology and succeeded in imitating it by the time they faced Shalmaneser III. The famous Kurkh stela describes this battle and lists an army of 10,000 infantrymen as well as 2,000 chariots in Ahab's army. This seems to be the first time that any Israelite army had employed horses for any military use. As such, horses were not only a relatively recent upgrade for the Samarian army, but also a source of pride and, perhaps, national arrogance.

Does one plow them with oxen?

The translation of this passage is challenging. The *Rishonim* generally view it as a parallel to the first stich: just as a horse cannot run on rocks, oxen cannot plow [on rocks].

However, bothered by the incomplete parallelism, Michaelis[78] suggests reading the word *babekarim* as two words – *babakar* and *yam* – meaning, "is it possible to plow *the sea* with oxen?" This emendation was discussed and largely accepted by nineteenth–twentieth century

78. Johann David Michaelis, *Deutsche Übersetzung des Alten Testaments*, vol. 1, Göttingen.

scholars. Besides the missing parallel to *sela*, Michaelis was also bothered by the plural *bekarim*; elsewhere in Tanakh the plural form of oxen is *shor* or *bakar* (both collective singular) or *benei bakar* (in sacrificial law).[79]

Generally, textual emendations should be considered a last resort: such a change should only be suggested when the Masoretic text (MT) is indecipherable without exegetical/homiletical solutions or minor modifications. Here, however, the MT version of the phrase is easily explained, as above. As for the unusual form *bekarim*, Hakham suggests that the entire couplet was a known folk saying that used this rare form, which might even have been in common usage at that time.

But you have turned justice into poison, and the fruit of righteousness into wormwood

The opening word, *Ki*, explains this epigram's usage: Why are the people acting as foolishly as one trying to run his horses on rocks or plow his oxen on rocks? We have already noted that *la'ana*, translated here as "wormwood," is a poisonous grass.

Amos has already mentioned *la'ana* as a symbol of perverted justice (5:3); now, once again, Amos expresses that these violators are being punished for "turning righteousness to wormwood," this time with a subtle chiasmus:

Kihafakhtem (But you have turned)
    lerosh (into poison)
        mishpat (justice)
        uferi tzedaka (and the fruit of righteousness)
    lela'ana (into wormwood)

These metaphorical poisons frame the ideal virtue of righteous justice. I would like to explore the significance of this chiastic structure and the complex metaphor presented within this verse.

Chiasms generally highlight the center of the structure. The focal point here is not the poisonous weeds, but rather the justice and

79. Numbers 28–29.

righteousness the courts *ought* to manifest. The court's ideal "fruit" *ought* to be righteousness, not bitter wormwood.

A second issue concerns the correlation between the prophet's rhetorical questions and this second metaphor. Amos's questions highlight the futility of using animals in an inhospitable or unworkable environment. A horse cannot run on a round boulder, nor can an ox plow there. If we delve deeper into the imagery, we see an imperfect parallel: a horse *can* run on rocks, but it will be reluctant, slow, and possibly endanger itself; in contrast, an ox *cannot* plow rock. Amos is creating a subtle progression: he begins with something inefficient and continues with something inherently impossible.

Using the word *ki*, Amos conveys that this second verse follows from the first. Yet the second metaphor pair seems misaligned with the first: moral corruption is not about inefficiency, but rather about being unethical and immoral. Amos is not criticizing, say, a procedural roadblock in the court which keeps the system from moving, but rather the essential dysfunction of the court system, wherein justice that ought to bear sweet and nutritious fruit for society is, instead, producing bitter, toxic results.

We will need to plow deeper to understand the prophet's message. He is not merely addressing the perversion of justice, as he already has; rather, he is warning about the essential unworkability of the system and its inevitable implosion, which will take society with it. Horses or oxen cannot be used productively in an unsuitable environment. Similarly, trying to keep a society functioning and productive – or even "afloat" – when its base is rotted by corruption is doomed to failure. Here, Amos is addressing the practical, rather than the ethical, consequences of judicial corruption.

13–14: Background

The northern kingdom's military and political influence was restored and expanded by Jeroboam II: "He restored the border of Israel from the entrance of Ḥamat until the sea of the Arava" (II Kings 14:25).

This success generated a sense of arrogance and invincibility among the leadership. As is often the case throughout history – biblical and universal – national hubris often plants seeds of catastrophe.

Victory often leads to overconfidence; moreover, caution and prophetic warnings are thrown to the wind.[80] In this rebuke, and specifically these two verses, Amos tackles this hubris directly in the hope of shaking the leadership out of its complacency.

13: You who rejoice in Lo-devar

This is a clever play on words. The town of Lo-devar (documented as the town where Meriv-Ba'al[81] lived when David brought him to Jerusalem[82]) is in northwestern Jordan. (It may be the *lidevir* of Joshua 13:26; some read the vocalization there as *lodvar.*) Some identify it at Um A-Dabr. The phrase *lo davar* literally means "nothing," "no matter." The prophet refers to the people's rejoicing over their re-conquest of Lo-devar, but, in reality, their celebration is much ado about nothing.

Rashi, Radak, and Ibn Ezra understand *lo davar* as "illusory": the people are rejoicing over their powerful status, but it will not endure.

R. Eliezer of Beaugency, in contrast, reads their "illusion" as their confidence in their own power, whereas it in fact comes from God.

R. Joseph Kara reads *lo davar* as *lelo devar Hashem*: instead of rejoicing over their victory or newfound power, they rejoice over not having to listen to God's word. This completely changes the tone of the rebuke; instead of criticizing their *hubris,* the prophet is condemning the people's willful *rejection* of *devar Hashem.*[83] They are happy to do without "the Word." Accordingly, R. Joseph Kara interprets the previous verse thus: "just as a horse cannot run on rocks and an ox cannot plow on rocks, similarly, you (the audience) are incapable of following God's path." Both R. Joseph Kara and R. Eliezer point to the people's rejection of God as the source of their hubris.

---

80. See, *inter alii,* Jeremiah 34.
81. Meriv-Ba'al was Yonatan's son, who was lamed at an early age. He is called Mefiboshet in Samuel, but that is almost assuredly a "censored" version of his name, which Chronicles (I 8:34, 9:40) faithfully records as Meriv-Ba'al.
82. II Samuel 9:4–5, 17:27.
83. As an aside, it is always curious to hear prophets rail against those who turn a deaf ear to the word of God – as delivered by the prophets. Who, exactly, is their audience?

One note about syntax: the predicate *samo'aḥ,* when followed with the prepositional prefix *le-,* often is understood as "mock" or "laugh *at.*" This applies when the object is an individual[84] or a group,[85] but when the object is an event (conquest), the verb retains its usual meaning of "rejoice" and the prefix points to the source of this joy.[86]

Who say: "Have we not by our own strength taken Karnaim for ourselves?"

Here, as above, Amos refers to the audience in the third person, expressing the danger of the people taking credit for their military success instead of acknowledging that all power comes from God.[87] This general warning applies to all kinds of success and wealth.

The military's arrogance and overconfidence in its own power carries with it the potential to unravel the entire spiritual fabric of society.

Lakaḥnu lanu, translated above as "we took for ourselves,"[88] emphasizes *lanu* – us, our power, our might – we ourselves took it, without outside (or divine) help.

The *karnayim* mentioned here, as with *lo-davar,* may also be a clever word play on the name of a town Jeroboam II restored to Israelite rule. Archeological evidence shows that two adjacent cities approximately 4 kilometers apart – one called Ashterot[89] and the other Karnayim – were in the Bashan, adjacent to the Yarmukh's headwaters. These two towns are mentioned together in the battle of the "four kings" in Genesis 14.

84. Psalms 38:17.
85. Obadiah v. 12.
86. See Proverbs 17:5; Job 3:22. Note that both of these speak of *inappropriate* causes for rejoicing.
87. This is one theme of Moses's farewell address (Deut. 8:11–18; see also ibid. 20:3–4). It is not completely tangential to note that this speech, which makes up most of Deuteronomy, is at its core a charge to the army on the eve of their great battle for the Land.
88. Most of the translations generally render it in that spirit – that *lanu* means "for ourselves."
89. Ashterot is best known as the capital or seat of power of Og, King of Bashan.

Keren also means "horn," and is a famous biblical symbol of power.[90]

Thus this phrase is an adroit triple-entendre:

1. We conquered the town of Karnayim.
2. We have appropriated for ourselves immense power.
3. (Through our own might) we have captured the great power of the enemy.

We might even suggest a fourth, more insidious intent: "We have taken divine might for ourselves."

14: For, behold, I will raise up against you [a nation], O house of Israel

Here, unlike verse 12, the introductory *Ki* does not provide an explanation for the previous clause;[91] rather, it mocks Israel's arrogant elation. Though they are convinced of their own invincibility, heady with their recent victories, they should cease their rejoicing – for they are about to be utterly defeated – by divine order, no less.

As readers, safe from the immediate implications of the warning, we have the luxury to take note of the powerful poetic justice here. The nation that *should* acknowledge God's hand in their victory is blind with self-congratulation, but soon the very God they shunned will become explicitly and immanently manifest in their defeat.

Says the Lord, the God of Hosts

Amos frequently uses God's Name to "sign" his oratorical pronouncements. As mentioned, he sometimes does this to mark the end of prophetic units. Here, however, even though this verse concludes this oracle, it serves a further purpose: it underscores the role of God, who has been utterly

90. See, for instance, Psalms 75:5–11.
91. More accurately, in verse 12 it introduces the solution to a riddle – "in what way is our behavior/attitude akin to trying to run horses on rocks," etc.

overlooked in the national consciousness. This same God, the "Lord of Hosts" – which alludes to military power and His role as leader of the Israelite army,[92] is about to employ that very military might *against* His nation.

And they shall oppress you from the entrance of Ḥamat

Levo Ḥamat is in the northern half of the Beka'a Valley, the northern point of Moses's scouts' tour of Canaan,[93] and the Land's northernmost border.[94]

To the Brook of the Araba

This unmatched phrase likely refers to a *wadi* to the Dead Sea's north. In the parallel phrase in Kings, the conquest that the people are evidently celebrating includes *Yam haArava*: "He restored the border of Israel from the *entrance of Ḥamat* until the sea of the *Araba*" (II Kings 14:25).

Amos foretells of Israelite enslavement and oppression in those very areas recently restored to Israelite dominion. Because the Samarian military completely misunderstood the meaning and source of their victory, those same places would become the focal points of their bitter downfall.

92. Exodus 12:41, 51; I Samuel 17:45; among others.
93. Numbers 13:21.
94. Ibid. 34:8.

Chapter 9

The Visions (7:1–8:3)

INTRODUCTION

Until now, Amos has employed various rhetorical tools in efforts to persuade Samaria's aristocracy and leadership to mend their ways. His tactics have included imaginary audiences, cosmic metaphors, and earthly similes, as well as various allusions to earlier books in Tanakh. The one prophetic tool we have not yet encountered is perhaps the most obvious: prophetic vision.

When God attacks Miriam and Aaron for considering themselves Moses's prophetic equals, He defines how prophecy works for all seers besides Moses: "Hear now my words. If there is a prophet among you, I the Lord will make myself known to him in a vision. I will speak with him in a dream" (Num. 12:6).

Prophetic "vision" is called *mar'eh*, which implies that the prophet envisions some image or form – either static or active – which conveys a message to his audience. Until now, Amos's oracles have been auditory – emanating from the roar of God's voice from Zion; for the rest of the book, they are based on visions. Amos has four or five visions, depending on how we understand the relationship of the beginning of chapter 9 to the earlier sections.

The first three visions take place within nine verses; each is three verses long. These are followed by the only narrative scene in the book: Amos's interaction with the High Priest at the Royal Sanctuary at Beit

El. This is followed by another vision – like the first three, it is three verses long. These visions, although interrupted by a narrative scene, form a deliberate sequence that is part of Amos's underlying message. We will explore this below, after a brief introduction to the idea of prophetic vision.

VISIONS: A PROPOSED TAXONOMY

A survey of prophetic visions – when a prophet describes seeing an image that conveys a divine message – presents us with various types of images. Although we could theoretically categorize and sub-categorize visions to the point of defining each as its own category, that would not help us understand vision *types* and the reason that a particular vision is one type rather than another.

Some biblical prophets never report "visions" at all. Perhaps all prophecies are received through a "vision," but unless the prophet specifically reports an image, the reader has no way of knowing whether the prophet had a vision. With the exception of Amos and Zechariah, none of the *Trei Asar* reports a specific *mar'eh,* whereas the books of Isaiah, Jeremiah, and Ezekiel are replete with images.

Visions: Static or Dynamic?

First, we must distinguish between static visions and animated or dynamic visions. Jeremiah sees "an almond staff" (1:11), a single, unchanging image, which conveys a prophetic message (*makel shaked* → *shoked ani al devari*). He then sees a "a boiling pot facing the north." Whether he actually watches the pot coming to boil (a dynamic image) or just sees a boiling pot (a static image) is irrelevant, as this image conveys the message nonetheless: "The troubles will begin from the north."

In contrast, Isaiah's inauguration vision is dynamic, an active scene with shifting imagery, beginning with *va'ereh* ("and I saw," 6:1). This particular vision also has two elements that are important categories of prophetic taxonomy.

Dynamic Visions: Is God Part of the Vision?

In Isaiah's inauguration vision, God Himself is present in the scene. Such visions do not describe God, but rather focus on His surroundings and actions. Does this mean that the prophet only perceives God's Presence and cannot be more specific, or that he deliberately withholds these secrets from his audience? This information is unavailable to the eternal audience (i.e., the readership).

Other dynamic visions do not involve God. Zechariah's seven visions are all dynamic, but God is not overtly present in any of them.

Dynamic Visions: Is The Prophet Active or Passive?

Sometimes the prophet plays an active role in his vision, but in others, he merely watches from the side, a passive onlooker. Zechariah interacts with the angel in his visions; in Ezekiel's visions of the Divine Chariot, the prophet is a passive spectator.

The Role of the Prophet – Dialogue with God or Mere Reporter?

A further useful distinction, which will play a critical role in understanding Amos's visions, is the prophet's role in the vision itself. In some visions, the prophet and God actively discuss its meaning and implications.

For example, once Zechariah understands the message of each vision, he appeals to God, beseeching Him to show His people favor. When Isaiah experiences his inauguration prophecy, he initially refuses to act as God's agent, as he is "impure, living among an impure people." God's response is to send a *seraph* to burn his lips with a hot coal, purifying him for God's agency. This even occurs in static prophecies: God engages with Jeremiah when He shows him two baskets of figs.[1]

Thus dialogue about the vision may occur whether it is static or dynamic, whether God is present or absent, and whether or not the

1. Jeremiah 24.

prophet is an active player. This dialogue may concern the vision's meaning or the prophet's response.

In sum, we have several considerations to take into account when encountering a prophetic vision. Is the vision static or dynamic? Is God present in the vision? Is the prophet present? If so, is he an onlooker or actively involved? Is there interaction between the prophet and God in the vision?

AMOS'S VISIONS

Amos's first two visions follow a consistent pattern and are clearly interrelated. They are both introduced with the phrase *Ko hirani A-D-N-Y Elokim* (Thus the Lord God showed me), followed by *vehinei*, "and behold." After the vision itself, Amos turns to God and begs him to forgive the people and cancel the punishment shown in the vision. He argues, *Mi yakum Yaakov, ki katan hu* – "Can Jacob withstand this? He is so small!"

Both times, God responds with favor: *niḥam Hashem al zot*, "God has repented from this"; regarding the second vision, He adds: *gam hi*, "this also," which links the two visions. Neither "will come to pass." Both visions conclude with the promise of forgiveness and a divine signature.

These first two visions recall the plagues of Egypt.

The third vision deviates from this pattern, as God is involved in the vision itself, and asks Amos "What do you see?" (echoed in the opening scene of Jeremiah). Amos answers, but from that point on, only God's voice is heard, roaring with Israel's looming punishment. Amos remains silent, with no opportunity to beg for divine mercy.

The fourth vision combines elements of the first three prophecies. God shows Amos the vision but is not part of it, as the first two; on the other hand, He asks Amos what he sees, like the third, but after his reply God pronounces Israel's punishment, and Amos is given no chance to plead for forgiveness. Thus the first two and the second two visions can be considered as two distinct pairs.

THE FIRST VISION (7:1–3)

(א) כֹּה הִרְאַנִי אֲדֹנָי ה׳ וְהִנֵּה יוֹצֵר גֹּבַי בִּתְחִלַּת עֲלוֹת הַלָּקֶשׁ וְהִנֵּה לֶקֶשׁ אַחַר
גִּזֵּי הַמֶּלֶךְ: (ב) וְהָיָה אִם כִּלָּה לֶאֱכוֹל אֶת עֵשֶׂב הָאָרֶץ וָאֹמַר אֲדֹנָי ה׳ סְלַח נָא
מִי יָקוּם יַעֲקֹב כִּי קָטֹן הוּא: (ג) נִחַם ה׳ עַל זֹאת לֹא תִהְיֶה אָמַר ה׳:

1 Thus the Lord God showed me; and, behold, He formed locusts at the beginning of the shooting up of the late crop; indeed, it was the late crop after the king's mowings. 2 And as they made an end of eating the grass of the land, so I said: Lord God, forgive, now; how will Jacob stand? For he is small. 3 The Lord relented concerning this; "It shall not be," said the Lord.

1: Thus the Lord God showed me

This opening refrain introduces three of the four visions: all but the third, where God Himself is *in* the vision, which thus begins *Ko hirani vehinei.*

Amos frequently introduces his oracles with the word *ko,* including his opening oracle (*Ko amar Hashem, Al shelosha pishei* – 1:2). Assuming he prophesies to the same audience throughout the book, they should already be able to anticipate a reproach following a warning of punishment.

The repetition of the pronominal suffix *hirani* emphasizes that the speaker is conveying a vision that he alone was shown for the purpose of sharing this vision and its message with his audience.

God's name has an unusual form in the second and fourth visions. This combination, using the letters *A-D-N-Y,* which literally means "my Lord(s)," is the customary oral representation of the Ineffable Name. Since the first Name is written this way, the second, which is the Tetragrammaton, is pronounced *Elokim.* The effect is as if it were written *Y-H-V-H Elokim.*

Why does Amos use this "unconventional" form of God's name so frequently – over twenty times in his short book, whereas none of the other "minor" prophets use it more than once? Of the literary prophets, only Ezekiel uses it more. Moreover, in the context of these visions, it appears eight times within twelve verses.

A-D-N-Y Elokim – An Introduction and Overview

The combination A-D-N-Y Y-H-V-H, with the Tetragrammaton vocalized as "*Elokim*," appears 293 times in Tanakh, with an unusual distribution: only four times in the Torah[2] and twelve times in Joshua-Kings. All but one appear in the context of prayer.[3]

All seven instances in Samuel appear within the twelve verses of David's prayer to God after he learns that he will not build God's House; perhaps this frequency can illuminate its use in Amos. The first mention in Kings deviates from this pattern, and it may help explain Amos's frequent use in general and concentrated use in his visions.

As for its appearance in prophetic literature, this name appears once in Micah, Obadiah, and Zephaniah; eleven times in Jeremiah; twenty-two times in both Isaiah and Amos – and an astounding 217 times in Ezekiel's visions and prayers.

Amos's Use of *A-D-N-Y Elokim*: Four Proposals

We will propose four approaches to understanding Amos's use of this Divine-Name combination in his prophecy in general, and specifically in these visions. These proposals are not mutually exclusive, and all contribute to understanding of Amos's rhetorical choices.

Proposal #1: The Prayerful Mode

Amos is apparently the first prophet to formally use *A-D-N-Y Elokim*, and given its consistent appearance in the context of prayer, it stands to reason that Amos is similarly invoking these two names to establish a prayer-oriented context. Indeed, Amos's response to these visions is to pray that they will not come to pass. Moreover, all the prayers with this Divine-Name combination were either of dire national concern (such as Moses's plea after the sin of the Golden Calf) or of personal survival

2. Twice in Genesis and twice in Deuteronomy.
3. I Kings 2:26.

(such as Gideon after "seeing" God). In the same vein, Amos is shown visions of the people's devastating destruction, and he prays that they will be spared.

Proposal #2: Establishing the Source of His Visions

If Amos is indeed the first to share a "vision" with his audience (in fact, he may be the first prophet to receive a "vision," as we are defining it, at all), he must persuade his audience that this vision is truly from God and not his own dream or imagination. He prefaces God's word with *ko amar Hashem* and its variants, but here *ko amar* is not relevant, since God has shared an image, not a message.

By first invoking A-D-N-Y, literally "My Lord," he states that this image is not of his own making, but rather what his "Lord" has shown him; he then emphasizes that this Lord is none other than Y-H-V-H, God of Israel.

Proposal #3: To Emphasize His Qualifications, Despite His Background

The visions are interrupted by an eight-verse narrative about Amos's confrontation with Amazia, the priest at Beit El. Amaziah tells Amos to leave, telling him to "go flee away to the land of Judea ... and prophesy there ..." to which Amos famously answers: "I am neither a *navi* nor a *ben navi*."

Since Amos is neither a "professional prophet" nor a member of the "prophetic guild," he needs to establish his credentials as one who has visions. (This may be why he uses *ko amar* and its variants so regularly – something that is not true of Isaiah, who appears to be a "professional prophet.") Amos does so by stating that the vision was given by "my Lord," perhaps adding Y-H-V-H for emphasis. Both this and the previous approach point to his need to establish his position as "seer."

Proposal #4: Contextual Significance – The "Beit El" Standoff

As we already noted, Amos's four visions are interrupted with its one narrative scene – a confrontation between the prophet and the temple priest. Amos's use of this specific name may help him establish his political stance, given the differences between Judah and the northern kingdom.

Here, a brief tangent will help clarify this approach. Although it is generally assumed that David and Solomon's "united kingdom" was of a single religious orientation and common theological base, and the schism was no more than a political move to avoid paying Rehoboam's heavy taxes, even a cursory read through the post-conquest period of settlement and early monarchy reflect a different picture. In Saul's first war, which is the first cross-tribal army since Joshua's time, the army is described as comprising 30,000 soldiers from Judah and 300,000 from the rest of Israel.[4] When David becomes king, he is first "crowned" in Hebron by his own tribe of Judah,[5] and is only accepted later by the northern tribes,[6] whereupon he establishes the capital in Jerusalem. When David returns after Absalom's rebellion, the tribal leaders of Judah and Israel fight over who has "bragging rights" over the king.[7] Throughout this period of "unity," there is a consistent and recognizable divide between north and south.[8]

Perhaps most telling is a narrative from the period a few decades after Amos's career. II Kings 17 describes the population transfer engineered by the Assyrians, moving the indigenous Israelite population of Samaria throughout the captured lands of the empire, while bringing in other foreigners from Kuta, Sefarvayim, and other parts of Asia minor. When the new population is attacked by lions as a punishment by God for their idolatrous practices, they send a message to the empire asking for help. The government finds *kohanim* among the captive population and sends them back to Shomron to teach the new emigres the "law of the God of the Land" (*mishpat Elokei ha'aretz*). Why didn't the Assyrians bring *kohanim* from Judah instead? One suggestion is that by this point, after two centuries of separation from Jerusalem, the Samarian religion differed significantly from Judean religion, and the locals wanted to learn the "local" customs and practices.[9]

---

4. I Samuel 11:8.
5. II Samuel 2:4.
6. Ibid. 5:1–3.
7. Ibid. 19:41–44.
8. It is tempting, and not completely inaccurate, to compare the situation with the confederation of the United States from the early nineteen century until the latter half of the twentieth century – a division evident in dialect, culture, religion, and more (some would argue that this is still the case).
9. I am indebted to my teacher and friend Zev (Jabo) Erlich for this insight.

Confronting a northern priest, with the northern calendar and northern practices,[10] Amos wanted to establish that these visions are from *his* Lord – that is, Y-H-V-H, the One who roars from Jerusalem – and that these represent *His* response to the north's wayward behavior. Moreover, he uses the Divine-Name combination used by David seven times (!) in the context of his prayer regarding the building of the Temple, which further emphasizes Jerusalem's centrality and what constitutes the proper worship of God – especially here, at the pseudo-sacred "Royal Sanctuary."

We will now explore the visions themselves.

1: And, behold, He formed locusts

God is depicted as *yotzer govai,* forming locusts. The image is terrifying. A locust plague is a frightening phenomenon; a swarm can devour a crop at a devastating rate, as described in the Egyptian plague. Joel uses a plague of locusts as a metaphor for a devastating foreign army.[11] This image is all the more terrifying given that God Himself is forming the weapons that will destroy His own people.

The word *govai* is an unusual term for locusts, as opposed to the more common *arbeh*[12] and *gazam, yelek,* and *ḥasil* (found in Joel). *Govai* appears in one other prophecy: "Your guards are like locusts, your officials like swarms of locusts that settle in the walls on a cold day (*kegov govai* – Nahum 3:17). This may suggest another association between the lexicon of these two prophets, as we already saw in parsing *ge'on Yaakov.*[13]

At the beginning of the shooting up of the late crop

Alot – the "shooting up" of a stalk – expresses the beginning of growth.[14]

---

10. I Kings 12:32.
11. According to the approach that the depiction in Joel chapter 1 is a metaphor. There is a significant school of thought that this plague was a real locust infestation.
12. In Exodus 10.
13. Above, chapter 8.
14. See Isaiah 5:6.

The *lekesh* (a *hapax legomenon* related to *malkosh,* late-season rains) refers to late-season growth.[15] When locusts attack at the beginning of that growth, then both early crops ripe for harvesting and late crops just beginning to sprout are lost, resulting in complete famine for the year.

Indeed, it was the late crop after the king's mowings

This last clause is difficult. Rashi writes: "The *lekesh* would grow after *gizei hamelekh* – after they harvested the king's produce. Before it would grow on the stalk, they would cut it as straw to feed the animals." They would first prune the king's produce before it was ripe to help it grow better (and they would feed these early cuttings to the animals), and the locusts came at this point. R. Joseph Kara reads this line the same way.

Ibn Ezra, in his second commentary, explains that this was when the king's flocks would be sheared. Malbim picks up on this explanation and clarifies that the sheep-shearing festival (*ḥag hageiz*) takes place in the middle of the summer, at which point only the later crops (*lekesh*) are still growing.

R. Eliezer of Beaugency believes that the locusts attack right after the harvest of the king's produce – the first to grow, like *bikkurim* – before the people's crops are harvested.

R. Yosef ibn Kaspi's intriguing interpretation is that this refers to cuttings for the king's horses (similar to Rashi's view), but that the locusts here are a metaphor for the king of Assyria, who will come and devour everything. The "king" here doubles back as part of the parable as well as the object lesson.

2: And as they made an end of eating the grass of the land

The language here evokes the locust plague in Egypt. Unlike the locust plague (real or metaphoric) in Joel, where the disaster has already taken

15. On the Gezer calendar, which is dated to the tenth century BCE and lists the various agricultural seasons by name, the two months of the end of winter are called in Canaanite *yarchu lakesh,* the months of late planting.

place, Amos's vision is just a warning, and he prays that the decree be revoked.

The locust swarm that "*kila le'ekhol*" ("made an end of eating") recalls the devastation in Egypt: "There remained nothing green, neither tree nor herb of the field, throughout all the land of Egypt" (Ex. 10:15). As in Amos's "call to return" (4:6–13), evoking the plagues of Egypt within a warning of the punishment about to befall Israel, expresses a terrifying threat of God's fury.

First of all, it means that God is turning His anger against His people as He would toward an enemy. The plagues of Exodus are portrayed as a war that culminates at the sea.[16]

Specifically, the plague of locusts was a deathblow, the final nail in the coffin of Egyptian agriculture: "They shall eat the residue of that which has escaped, which remains to you from the hail, and shall eat every tree which grows for you out of the field" (Ex. 10:15).

To be threatened with such complete ruin should move the people to reflect and repent; the prophet presumably chose to evoke the locusts of Egypt in the hope that it would stir them; but this, alas, was not to be.

I said: Lord (A-D-N-Y) God *Elokim* (Y-H-V-H)

Amos tells his audience how he prayed to God so they will understand the severity of this existential threat. This recalls how Moses tells the people of his desperate prayer to God to let him see the Land.[17]

Perhaps Amos, drawing from Moses, shares the words of his prayer with his audience in order to move them with the sense of the deep *personal* anguish he feels upon learning of this threat.

16. Exodus 14:14, 25, 15:3.
17. Deuteronomy 3:23–25; see also ibid. 9:25–26. Note that Moses shared not only the contents of his petition (and of God's refusal) with the people, but also his phrasing, including the salutatory *A-D-N-Y Elokim*.

Forgive, now…

The word *na* is often read as "please" or some other form of entreaty, as in Modern Hebrew. Ibn Ezra repeatedly asserts that it means "now,"[18] and it is indeed often used when there is a sense of urgency; this is certainly appropriate here.

Amos's plea that God "forgive" (*selaḥ*) should not be misunderstood. He is not asking God to postpone or even cancel the punishment; rather, he begs God to forgive the people for their grievous sin. The biblical word *selaḥ* acknowledges wrongdoing and asks for the *consequence* to be waived; as opposed to other similar words such as *m-ḥ-h* (or *m-ḥ-l* in later literature), which asks that God "look away" rather than punish, even though they are guilty.

As we will soon see, God's answer is encouraging… for now. First, Amos must support his request with an argument. One tactic he could employ is justice – that the people are not guilty as accused; alternatively, he could appeal to divine compassion.

How will Jacob stand?

Amos argues that the northern kingdom cannot withstand such an attack, for they are "small." He refers to Samaria as "Jacob" as he did in 3:13.

The use of *mi* here is unusual. To translate it as "who" is strained, although R. Joseph Kara does so: "If I [Amos] do not pray on their behalf, who (*mi*) among them will stand up to help?"

Ibn Ezra also reads *mi* as "who," but interprets it differently: "Who among them would be able to stand up in the face of this catastrophe?"

Mi is used elsewhere to express a rhetorical question;[19] see also Radak here: "For he is small, and how could he possibly stand with all of these decrees as he is small [= few] and only a few are left of the many."

18. For example, Genesis 12:11, 27:2; Numbers 10:31, 12:11–12; Isaiah 5:1; Psalms 80:15.
19. Isaiah 51:19.

For he is small

This is the crux of Amos's argument: Jacob is "small" (or "few") and cannot withstand such harsh decrees. This is a weak argument for *seliḥa* because it does not justify why God should cleanse "Jacob's" record. Perhaps Amos uses this argument and shares it with his audience nonetheless because he knows that, surprisingly, they have been forgiven.

There seems to be another rhetorical-suasive ploy here. Amos's argument is that Samaria is *katon*, small and weak, and this is what moves God to spare them. What does this convey to Samaria's haughty aristocracy? Besides demonstrating God's deep capacity for forgiveness, it also underscores their insignificance. Amos's appeal is thus a masterful rhetorical stroke, for it stirs God's compassion for the defendant while simultaneously forcing the defendant to face their own inadequacies – a truth his audience was assiduously avoiding in the throes of their arrogance.

3: The Lord relented concerning this

The root *n-ḥ-m* always conveys a change in sentiment, whether from the negative to the positive, as in "comfort" and "consolation,"[20] or from the positive to the negative, as in "regret."[21] Whether God indeed changes His mind is explored in the context of Saul's failure to destroy Amalek. God informs Samuel, "I *regret* (*niḥamti*) that I set Saul up as king" (I Sam. 15:11); yet later on in the chapter, Samuel tells Saul: "Israel's Eternal will not betray or *waver* (*yinaḥem*), for He is not a mere *wavering* human" (15:29).

Does God "change His mind" or not?[22] In our case, God's change of mind is good for Israel – although this is not quite what Amos asked for: forgiveness. God has annulled this decree, but the guilt is still there.

This discrepancy creates the sense that Amos has bought temporary respite for the people, but at some point, the guilt will build up and punishment will not be forestalled anymore. This evokes the book's opening refrain, *Al shelosha pishei* – For three sins... God only forgives so much.

---

20. Beginning with Noah's name – Genesis 5:29.
21. Beginning with God's disappointment in humanity, which leads Him to bring the Flood – Genesis 6:5.
22. The commentators grapple with that problem there.

"It shall not be"

Again, it is the punishment that will "not be" – or are we reading too optimistically? Perhaps God's reply conceals a greater threat. What if *niḥam* refers not to their punishment, but rather to the people themselves – evoking the antediluvian divine regret? And what if *lo tihyeh* should be read in the second person – "Jacob, you will no longer be"? Amos's words are hopeful, but the alternate reading lingers – and tragically, comes to pass a few decades later.

Said the Lord

Amos's familiar signature serves as a divine imprimatur to his audience, and as a literary marker to us, the distant audience.

THE SECOND VISION (7:4–6)

(ד) כֹּה הִרְאַנִי אֲדֹנָי ה׳ וְהִנֵּה קֹרֵא לָרִב בָּאֵשׁ אֲדֹנָי ה׳ וַתֹּאכַל אֶת תְּהוֹם רַבָּה
וְאָכְלָה אֶת הַחֵלֶק: (ה) וָאֹמַר אֲדֹנָי ה׳ חֲדַל נָא מִי יָקוּם יַעֲקֹב כִּי קָטֹן הוּא:
(ו) נִחַם ה׳ עַל זֹאת גַּם הִיא לֹא תִהְיֶה אָמַר אֲדֹנָי ה׳:

4 Thus the Lord God showed me: And, behold, the Lord God called to contend by fire; and it consumed the great deep, and devoured the land. 5 Then I said: O Lord God, cease, I beg. How will Jacob stand? for he is small. 6 The Lord relented concerning this; "This also shall not be," said the Lord God.

4: Thus the Lord God (*A-D-N-Y Elokim*) showed me:

This opening follows the pattern established in the first vision (and which will be repeated in the next two visions, with a minor but significant variation).

And, behold, the Lord God (*A-D-N-Y Elokim*) called to contend by fire

As mentioned, the word *hinei* regularly introduces a dream or vision setting. This clause has unusual syntax. We would expect:

Vehinei A-D-N-Y Elokim korei lariv ba'eish

with the subject (God) presented before the predicate (*korei lariv?*) and the object (*ba'eish*). Yet another difficulty in this clause concerns the word *lariv*. We will see how these two issues may help resolve each other.

The verb *lariv* – "to contend" or "to dispute" – is usually followed by a preposition introducing the accused party, for example, *Vayiḥar Yaakov vayarev beLavan,* "Yaakov was angry and he *disputed* Lavan" (Gen. 31:36). Here in verse 4, *lariv* is followed by the *vehicle* of His judgment (the fire). God is not contending *against* the fire but punishing the people *with* fire.

The *Rishonim* do not address the syntactic problem; they presumably read it as an unusual but not unprecedented variation, in which God is doing the summoning. They present three distinct approaches to interpreting the meaning of "fire": as a supernatural fire of punishment (Rashi); as a searing heat accompanied by drought that will destroy all the crops (Ibn Ezra, Radak); or as a metaphor for an attacking nation (R. Joseph Kara, R. Yosef ibn Kaspi).

Accordingly, there are also three readings regarding the object of *korei* – whom or what is being summoned? Either God is summoning His heavenly hosts to attack with this fire (Rashi); or He is summoning Jacob to judgment by fire; or He is calling the "fire-nation" to come and punish His people.

Textual Criticism

Even traditionalists who accept the MT as authoritative recognize that some alternate readings can be considered legitimate, especially when they are supported by early translations, by citations in rabbinic literature, or when reliable texts differ in their orthography. Given that the biblical text has no vowels, and that certain scribal errors such as letter transposition are more common among copyists, there can be room to consider certain errors in transmission when the MT seems inscrutable.[23]

Traditional scholars will not entertain a textual emendation without testimony of its existence; in contrast, modern textual critics (beginning with the nascence of Biblical Criticism in the late eighteenth century) are willing to suggest alternative readings of the text without any attestation, based on various principles and some "educated guesswork."

The challenging words and phrases in our clause have been cause for consternation among textual critics for over a hundred years. Most begin with the premise that the MT is "corrupt" and must be emended. The challenges seem so insurmountable that Morgenstern records eleven different proposals for text-emendation, and then proposes his own twelfth "repair."[24] Ehrlich suggests that the *bet* of *ba'eish* was errantly repeated from the previous word, and the original words were *lerov eish.*[25] Krenkel proposes that the letters *lrb bes* are all correct, but that at some point the two words were incorrectly divided – taking just the consonants of these two words results in "*lrbbes.*" Since ancient texts were often written without clear division between words, it is possible that the original words were *lrbb es* – or, with vowels, *lereviv eish,* meaning "a rain of fire." Hillers references Krenkel's 1866 observation in an article in 1964.[26]

Simone accepts this "mis-division" theory, suggests that the original consonantal text read *lrvv es,* and then, based on the fact that *reviv* is always in plural form, suggests that there was a letter transposition to *bet*

23. The literature here is vast. An intriguing starting point is the lengthy comment of R. Akiva Eiger in his *Gilyon haShas* at Shabbat 55b; also see the nineteenth-century work, *Mishpakhat Soferim.*
24. J. Morgenstern, *Amos Studies* (Cincinnati, OH: Hebrew Union College Press, 1941), 59, 64.
25. Arnold B. Ehrlich, *Mikra KeFeshuto,* vol. 3 (Berlin, 1901), 413–414.
26. Delbert R. Hillers, "Amos 7:4 and Ancient Parallels," *The Catholic Biblical Quarterly* 26, no. 2 (1964): 221–225.

from *kaf*, so that the "original" oracle in fact read: *hinei korei lerekhev eish* (consonantal: *lrkv es*): "God is summoning a *chariot of fire*."[27]

A New Proposal

As noted above, the verse's awkward syntax is not addressed by *Rishonim*; modern scholars either ignore the problem or suggest that the inclusion of the two Divine Names was a "later interpolation" (or "gloss") intended to maintain the use of this Divine-Name combination within the vision series.

Perhaps the syntax is deliberately awkward, part of the original text, and holds the key to understanding of the whole phrase.

Instead of reading the verse as

vehinei korei lariv ba'eish, *A-D-N-Y Elokim,*

read it as,

vehinei korei lariv, *ba'eish-A-D-N-Y Elokim.*

God's names are not only the subject, but also serve as an adjectival noun, defining the fire: instead of "behold, the Lord God was summoning a trial by fire," it should be read: "behold, He was summoning a quarrel, using the fire of the Lord God." This fire may either be the medium of the ordeal or the punishment awaiting the guilty people and their land at the trial's end.

No changes need be made to the orthography, although the vocalization of the *bet* of *ba'eish* is best changed to *schwa, be'eish,* to agree with the construct state. The deliberate delay of God's names here thus makes double use of those names – God is the One summoning the trial and the source of the fire as well. It is a Godly fire.

27. Michael R. Simone. "A 'Chariot of Fire' in Amos 7:4: A Text Critical Solution for *qōrēʾ lārīb bāʾēš*," *Vetus Testamentum* 66, no. 3 (2016): 456–471.

4: And it consumed the great deep

As noted, this "fire" has been variously interpreted as a supernatural fire, as an intense heat wave / drought, and as a metaphor for an enemy nation (i.e., Assyria). Although all three readings are possible, a literal fire seems to fit best with the vision's next line. How would a heat wave or an invading army "devour the great deep"? Indeed, anything but a cosmic, supernatural attack would be hard to posit here, although this naturally depends on how we understand the "devouring of the great deep."

Various ancient mythologies – including some alluded to in Tanakh – reference either a pre-Creation or apocalyptic war between the Divine and "the deep chasm" or the beasts that inhabit that space. The second verse in the Torah speaks of the chaos that ruled in the "chasm" before God brought order and light. Isaiah praises God for His acts against the sea at the Exodus, along with His "war" against the deep and its monsters at the time of creation:

> Are you not the One that hewed Rahab in pieces, that pierced the dragon? ... Are you not the One that dried up the sea, the waters of the great deep; that made the depths of the sea a way for the redeemed to pass over?[28]

Amos describes how God wishes to summon supernatural fire to lay waste the earth, a fire that will rage so powerfully that even the deepest watery chasms will be scorched dry of all life.

What seems problematic is that why should all of existence be annihilated because of the northern kingdom's sins? How can this be an act of divine "justice"?

The word *tehom* is usually associated with water. The Creation story and the Flood narrative imply that this is a single immense watery abyss below the earth's surface, but a careful biblical survey indicates otherwise.

28. Isaiah 51:9–10; see also ibid. 27:1. See Hakham's comments in *Da'at Mikra, Yeshayahu* ad loc.

> *Deep* calls to *deep* (*tehom el-tehom kore*) in the roar of your waterfalls; all your waves and breakers have swept over me. (Ps. 42:8)

By definition, "deep calls to deep" implies a *tehom* that is separate from another *tehom*. Therefore, the word sometimes refers to a specific and geographically limited underground space where water is found.

I believe that in this context, *tehom* does not refer to the single primordial abyss, but rather to a specific area that Amos chooses to characterize in cosmic terms. Where is this *tehom*, and what is Amos's rhetorical strategy here?

In order to address this, one more exegetical conundrum remains. In our verse, the "fire" is described as *vatokhal* the abyss; then, it is *ve'akhla* the field. Are these two verbs using different tenses? If so, what are those tenses, and what difference does this reflect? If not, why use two different conjugations to communicate the same tense?

The *Rishonim* do not address this variation; contemporary translations, however, reflect different approaches. Some read the verbs as varying forms of the past tense: that Amos's vision describes an already devoured deep and fields. Others have the first verb in the past perfect ("had already devoured"), whereas the second is the ongoing present ("and was now devouring"). Either way, the sequence is odd. We would expect that the fire would first devour the above-ground fields, and only then reach the great deep. Why this order? Perhaps a broader look at the visions and their context will help.

Who Is Jacob?

In the first two visions, the "target" is called "Jacob," and Amos petitions God to withhold punishment because "Jacob is too small" to withstand the locusts and the fire. We interpreted the first vision as if Jacob was another name for the northern kingdom (which is the prevalent reading), although we questioned why Samaria was called "Jacob" (instead of, say, "Ephraim"). Besides this epithet, there are other indications that we may not have gotten the full story. In the first vision, the locusts follow "the king's shearings," which is generally explained as referring to the first harvest or some other aspect of harvest time associated with the royal house. It is, in any case, an odd way to mark a time within the harvest season.

Even stranger is the framework of the narrative sandwiched between the third and fourth visions, the narrative that comprises the chapter's second half. There the Beit El priest sends a message to the king:

> ... Amos has conspired against you in the midst of the house of Israel; the land is not able to bear all his words. For this is what Amos said: "Jeroboam will die by the sword, and Israel will surely be led away captive from his land." (7:10–11)

Where do Amos's words specifically target Jeroboam? Why are these prophecies more threatening to the royal house than the first two-thirds of the book?

These first two visions are aimed directly at the royal house, not at the entire kingdom or even the aristocracy. Until now, Amos's rhetorical charges have focused on the north's general leadership: the judiciary, the wealthy, and the court. Now, for the first time, Amos accuses the royal house itself – the house of Jeroboam II, who enjoyed political and military triumph during the mid-eighth century BCE. Despite his military success,[29] he was found sorely lacking in his loyalty to God and his moral leadership.[30]

As seen in this chapter, Jeroboam II's centers of worship were the sanctuaries in Beit El (where this confrontation takes place) and Dan. The sanctuary at Beit El is even called a "royal sanctuary."

The first vision's *gizei hamelekh* should not be read as chronological markers, but rather as the locusts' target: they will devour everything, not *after* (Heb: "*aḥar*") the king's produce has been harvested; rather, they will *follow* ("*aḥar*") the king's harvesters and devour the produce they have just reaped.

The second vision threatens the king himself. This king, who has maintained the political-religious policies of his eponymous forebear and who resides at the core of the rot that corrupted the northern "high society," is the "Jacob" of Amos's prophecies. After the first vision, Amos

29. II Kings 14:25.
30. Ibid. v. 24.

pleads with God on *Jeroboam's* behalf, claiming that he is not strong enough to withstand such a threat – and God accedes to his request.

In this vision, *tehom* refers to a specific aquifer (rather than to the universal watery abyss); we can read this "fire-ordeal" as an attack on a specific *tehom* – the king's aquifer that rests under and nourishes his fields.

This is a vision of trial-by-fire against the king – a fire that, in Amos's vision, first dries up the underground aquifer, *tehom rabba*. The word *rabba* here may just mean "great,"[31] implying that the singular *tehom rabba* is not necessarily *the* global deep.

If so, we can explain the rest of the verse thus: Amos adds *rabba* here as a deliberate rhetorical flourish. The king presumes himself to be far greater than he actually is – he is, after all, the leader of a relatively small kingdom, not a major player on the world stage. He is a loser as often as a winner in regional skirmishes. Yet he appropriates for himself the embodiment of the people Israel – hence "Jacob" – and he believes his royal house has ultimate significance[32] – hence *tehom rabba*.

4: And devoured the land

While, as mentioned, translations present the two verbs in various tenses, the most accurate reading seems to present both in the ongoing present. Amos is, after all, presenting a vision; he sees the fire devouring the king's underground aquifer and then moving on to consume the[33] *ḥelek*, a word that elsewhere refers to a *specific* field.[34] This is the king's field – which is why Amaziah now, and only now, sends an urgent message to Jeroboam, claiming that Amos is calling for his demise.

As noted, there are several ways to understand this "fire" and how it affects the deep (aquifer) and then the field. A supernatural fire might first dry up the aquifer and then the field itself as an expression

31. See Psalms 78:15.
32. See, in an Egyptian context (where such presumptions had, at least, some hold in reality), Ezekiel 29:3.
33. See Radak ad loc., who interprets the use of the definite article as referencing the king's field.
34. See, *inter alia*, Ruth 2:3, 4:3.

of God's power. Alternately, if this describes a searing heat and resultant drought, then the field would dry up only after its underground water source is depleted.

5: Then I said: O Lord God (*A-D-N-Y Elokim*), cease, I beg

This verse has one crucial difference from its parallel in the previous vision. Instead of *selaḥ na* ("forgive immediately"), which is *not* granted, Amos begs *ḥadal na* – "cease now," realizing that God will not *forgive* the sins of Jeroboam's house. Instead, taking a cue from God's previous response, he beseeches God to stay the punishment.

How will Jacob stand? for he is small

Amos's argument remains the same: "Jacob" is feeble, too weak to withstand such a blistering attack. Imagine how these words sounded in Jeroboam's ears, and we get a fuller picture of what drove Amaziah to send his message to the royal house.

6: The Lord relented concerning this; "This also shall not be"

Once again, God "repents" and promises that this disaster will not come to pass. It is clear from God's words, *gam hi*, that this vision followed the first, and that Amos's prayer and God's response followed the same pattern as the locust plague.

Said the Lord God (*A-D-N-Y Elokim*)

Amos concludes with the same Divine Name signature.

THE THIRD VISION (7:7–9)

(ז) כֹּה הִרְאַנִי וְהִנֵּה אֲדֹנָי נִצָּב עַל חוֹמַת אֲנָךְ וּבְיָדוֹ אֲנָךְ: (ח) וַיֹּאמֶר ה' אֵלַי מָה
אַתָּה רֹאֶה עָמוֹס וָאֹמַר אֲנָךְ וַיֹּאמֶר אֲדֹנָי הִנְנִי שָׂם אֲנָךְ בְּקֶרֶב עַמִּי יִשְׂרָאֵל

לֹא אוֹסִיף עוֹד עֲבוֹר לוֹ: (ט) וְנָשַׁמּוּ בָּמוֹת יִשְׂחָק וּמִקְדְּשֵׁי יִשְׂרָאֵל יֶחֱרָבוּ
וְקַמְתִּי עַל בֵּית יָרָבְעָם בֶּחָרֶב:

7 Thus He showed me; and, behold the Lord stood upon a wall made by a plumbline (*ḥomat anakh*), with a plumbline (*anakh*) in His hand. 8 And the Lord said to me: "Amos, what do you see?" And I said: "A plumbline (*anakh*)." Then the Lord said: Behold, I will set a plumbline (*anakh*) in the midst of My people Israel; I will not pardon them anymore. 9 And the high places of Isaac will be desolate, and the sanctuaries of Israel will be laid waste. And I will rise against the house of Jeroboam with the sword.

7: Thus He showed me

Note that the pattern *ko hirani A-D-N-Y Elokim* is broken here. God presented the first two visions and was active in them (forming the locusts, summoning the fire). In this third vision, however, God is not only present in the vision, but He also discusses its meaning with Amos, which implies that unlike the locusts and the fire, Amos cannot understand this vision without God's explanation. Perhaps for this reason the phrase cuts to *ko hirani.*

God's name may be omitted from the introduction because He will be actively involved in the scene; alternatively, it may be that Amos does not wish to claim that *A-D-N-Y Elokim* "showed him" the vision until he was certain of its meaning.

And, behold the Lord stood upon a wall made by an *anakh*

Back to form, the vision is introduced with *hinei.* Amos describes God as standing on an *anakh* wall (see below) – but unlike the rest of this series, in this vision he only uses the Name A-D-N-Y, without the Tetragrammaton. We will discuss this anomaly below.

The key word in this vision is undoubtedly *anakh.* A *hapax legomenon,* it only appears in this scene – four times within two verses; there is no other reference to shed light on its meaning. Moreover, its meaning is even obscure in context, although it seems to be associated with building (a tool? material?). We will discuss its meaning after analyzing the rest of the vision.

The image of God "standing" (or "sitting") is not unheard of in prophetic visions. It dates back to what may be the earliest vision in our tradition, when God "stands" over Jacob.[35]

Jacob's "ladder" is not just the *vehicle* for divine information – it is also part of the message: that this place is the nexus between heaven and earth, *axis mundi*,[36] as demonstrated by the angels ascending and descending.[37] Similarly, God's "standing on the *anakh* wall," as well as God's "standing (*nitzav*) on the altar"[38] possibly indicates some metaphysical centrality. This is self-evident in the latter instance as the altar is a clear site of Divine Presence, especially given Amos's anti-separatist agenda against the northern sanctuaries. The significance of the *ḥomat anakh* and its relation to God's presence is less obvious.

The preposition *al* usually means "atop," but most translations of this verse have "beside" presumably based on Amos 9:1, where God is seen as standing *al* the altar. That vision, in turn, was likely translated based on the story in I Kings 13, where Jeroboam was standing *al* the altar – in that context, "beside."

The difference between these two possibilities has tremendous implications for the vision's impact. "Beside" has God standing next to a wall and pointing at it, while "on" conjures up the terrifying vision of God *looming over* the scene, with the people unable to escape their fate. Hakham persuasively claims that here, *al* means "upon," for the vision is far more impactful if God is described as standing atop the *anakh* wall.

35. Genesis 28:12–13; see also Numbers 22;23, 31; and Isiah 3:13.
36. Cf. Mircea Eliade, *The Myth of the Eternal Return* (New York: Pantheon Books, Bollingen Series XLVI, 1954).
37. Otherwise, they seem to serve no purpose in the vision.
38. Amos 9:1.

With an *anakh* in His hand

What is the meaning of this key word? Is God holding a piece of metal or a building tool? Both are unlikely. It seems that the wall is made of some material – *anakh* – but if He were holding some of that material, the text would use a phrase that would indicate a "piece," such as *betza anakh*. This gives rise to a third possibility, that *anakh* has two meanings: God stands on a wall made of *anakh,* holding something *else* that is also called *anakh.*

If so, then the words may be semantically related but with distinct meanings: one such example would be *kesef,* which means "silver" as well as "money"; another is *adama,* which means "earth" in the sense of "ground"[39] *and* "world."[40] Perhaps the most striking example of this linguistic phenomenon is the word *ḥerem,* which is used in four distinct (yet related) ways in Joshua 6.

Another possibility is that this word is a strategically employed homophone, seen in the verse *kol demei aḥikha tzo'akim elai min ha'adama* (the voice of *demei* – meaning both "blood" as well as "silence" – of your brother cries out to Me from the ground).[41] Given that *anakh* is a *hapax legomenon,* it would be difficult to find – and prove – that there are two separate meanings for this obscure word.

As such, we will attempt to find a single concept that is flexible enough to suit all four instances of the word.

8: And the Lord said to me

Each of the visions in this sequence includes a dialogue between God and Amos, who reports it to his audience. This is the first vision in which God initiates the conversation.

---

39. For example, Deuteronomy 26:10.
40. Numbers 12:3.
41. Genesis 4:10, God's words to Cain after the murder of Abel.

"Amos, what do you see?"

The question *ma atah ro'eh* appears seven times in Tanakh – all in literary prophecy, always asked by God.[42] This question is calculated to rhetorically manipulate the prophet into explicating aloud what he is seeing. This serves to make the vision "real" for the audience: not a mere vision soon to be dispelled by petition and prayer, as the locusts and fire were. By forcing Amos to say the word, it becomes an irrevocable reality, as will be realized by the end of the vision dialogue.[43]

And I said: "An *anakh*"

This third instance of the key word *anakh* may have the same meaning as either of the instances above; or possibly yet a third meaning. Note that Amos does not say *anakh ani ro'eh,* but merely *anakh*. Rather than emphasize his ability as a seer,[44] he wishes to focus on the *anakh,* which evidently spells doom for his audience.

Then the Lord said

The Divine-Name combination *A-D-N-Y Hashem* appears throughout the first two visions, but here they are split: first "*Hashem*" (Y-H-V-H) asks Amos "what do you see," to which Amos answers "*anakh*." Then A-D-N-Y explains the meaning of the vision. It is as if the combination of awe-inspiring Lordship (A-D-N-Y) was tempered by the compassion implicit in the Tetragrammaton – until now. With the *anakh* vision, that tempering is over, and although the familiar, compassionate Y-H-V-H asks Amos what he sees, it is the Lord, *sans compassion,* who declares the meaning.

42. Three times in Jeremiah and twice each in Amos and Zechariah.
43. This suggestion came from a delightful conversation I had with my daughter, Ariella. The same might be applied to God's question of Jeremiah in Jeremiah 24.
44. Unlike Jeremiah with the *makel shaked* in Jeremiah 1:10.

Behold, I will set an *anakh* in the midst of My people Israel

Is this the *anakh* of the wall, or what God holds in His hand? We can be fairly confident that Amos's one-word answer refers to one of the two – what of God's reply?

I will not pardon them anymore

Unlike His response to Amos's first two petitions, God declares that He will no longer pardon the people. He forgives once and twice – but not a third time. This is unlike the divine justice of the opening chapters, where God forgives *three* times, but the fourth "crosses the line." Indeed, the phrase *lo osif avor lo* is hauntingly evocative of *lo ashivenu*. Has divine judgment grown harsher as the north's corruption has gone from bad to worse? Or are we to understand the "three-four" rhetoric of the opening chapters as a poetic device unrelated to the number of actual offenses?[45] We will leave these questions open for now and address them at the end of our analysis of this vision.

Anakh

Besides early *Targumim*, the first rabbinic interpretation of *anakh* is found in the Talmud (Bava Metzia 59a):

> R. Ḥisda says: All the gates of Heaven are apt to be locked, except for the gates of [prayer for victims of] verbal mistreatment (*ona'ah*), as it says: "And behold, the Lord stood upon a wall built with an *anakh*, and an *anakh* in His hand." R. Elazar says: In response to all transgressions, God punishes the perpetrator by means of an agent, except for mistreatment [*ona'ah*], as it says: "And an *anakh* in His hand."

Note that in Israel (R. Elazar) as well as Babylonia (R. Ḥisda), the two centers of Torah scholarship during the talmudic period, *anakh* is read similarly: as related to the word *ona'ah*. The two words share similar but

45. See the discussion about the three-four pattern in chapter 2, pp. 16–18.

distinct roots; we will explore below whether this aggadic connection seems lexically legitimate.

One salient point regarding the *aggada* itself: Rashi points out that the image of God holding the *anakh* in His hand indicates that He does not appoint an agent to punish, but rather uses the *anakh* Himself.[46] This implies that rather than being related to *ona'ah*, *anakh* is a tool for punishing the violation of that crime. We will return to this approach below.

Anakh: The *Rishonim*

Rashi begins by citing the Targum – *shura dedina* (lit. "a wall of justice"). He then explains (following Dunash)[47] that in Arabic, an *anakh* is a plumbline (or a "level"), a device that uses lead as a ballast to ensure that walls and frames are perfectly even.

Rashi does not comment on the separate *anakh* in God's hand, or on Amos's one-word answer, but he does explain that God's pronouncement means "Behold, I will judge them according to the strict line of justice."

Thus according to Rashi, all four instances of *anakh* have the same meaning, which functions metaphorically in God's pronouncement.

R. Joseph Kara first cites Menachem's[48] suggestion that *anakh* relates to *nekhim,*[49] meaning "shattered," and that God is holding the tool He used to shatter the wall. This is a difficult reading, and Dunash convincingly dismisses this suggestion. R. Kara then follows Rashi in citing Dunash's interpretation, explaining that just as an *anakh* sets the wall to be straight, with no stone protruding on either side, similarly God will not "incline" to forgive Israel's sins without first executing judgment. As he does not comment on the other instances, we can assume that like Rashi, R. Kara reads all four as plumbline.

---

46. Rashi ad loc. s.v. *uv'yado.*
47. Dunash b. Labrat, North African philologist who later lived in Cordoba; died 990.
48. Menachem ibn Saruq, Spanish philologist; died c. 970.
49. Psalms 35:15.

Among the early grammarians (we already cited Dunash and Menachem), Ibn Janah argues that *anakh* is tin, rather than lead; these two translations are still the two most common readings today.[50]

Ibn Ezra believes that all four instances mean "lead": the vision is of a lead wall, sturdy and impenetrable, and God declares He will set up a lead wall between Himself and the people so that He will no longer hear their petitions – that is how Ibn Ezra reads *lo osif avor lo*. He reads *avor* as "forgive" (as in *over al pesha*[51]), and makes no mention of "plumbline."

Radak prefers tin to lead here, based on the Arabic, but he then argues for plumbline,[52] as these are typically made using tin (or lead). The wall is straight, "built with the line of judgment and the weights of justice." God will judge the people based on their deeds just as He holds the plumbline in His hand – but just as He holds it "in His hand," He also holds compassion, and He will not utterly destroy them as they deserve. Radak then cites the above talmudic passage, explaining it as if the creditor is standing over the debtor holding his loan document.

One surprising element of Radak's explanation is that he reads this third vision as less harsh than the first two, and thus he explains Amos's silence:

> The prophet did not cry out in response to this vision because he did not see that God was causing total destruction [as he did in the locust and fire visions], but rather that He was going to judge them with affliction and exile. Therefore, He said to him, "What do you see – that you didn't cry out as you did in the first two visions?" and Amos responded: "I saw an *anakh* – that you would judge them with proper, aligned judgment."

50. See Tzvi Novick, "Duping the Prophet," *Journal for the Study of the Old Testament* 33:1 (2008): 115–128.
51. Micah 7:18.
52. In this, he follows his father, R. Joseph Kimhi, in the *Sefer HaGalui*, who also cites Menachem and Dunash and favors Dunash's interpretation.

In this, Radak deviates significantly from most other exegetes, who view this third vision as far more severe than the first two. His logic is convincing, especially his explanation of Amos's silence.

R. Yosef ibn Kaspi shares Rashi's line of thinking, but adds that the metaphor carries an additional message. First of all, an *anakh* (plumbline) is generally used to build, but here, the image of God holding it atop the wall signifies destruction – God will destroy Israel's firm, secure walls. This is the first message, from the vision itself; God's pronouncement *hineni sam anakh bekerev ami Yisrael* then conveys that all of His judgements are carefully and precisely measured out. Ibn Kaspi then cites: "And I will make justice the line, and righteousness the plummet" (Is. 28:17).

Modern Commentaries

Some modern scholars adopt various aspects of the traditionalists' readings to form their own conclusions. Hakham fuses Rashi's plumbline with Ibn Kaspi's interpretation that the *ḥomat anakh* represents the northern kingdom's fortifications, which they believe are impenetrable, and that God declares that He will destroy them. He reads Amos's silence as his being confused by the vision and not understanding its message – hence he cannot pray for its annulment.

Mays, based on Assyrian etymology, reads *anakh* as a lead plumbline.[53] He then explains that the apparent innocuity of the vision – as opposed to destructive locusts and fire – keeps Amos from interceding, and that Israel was once straight but now needs straightening (hence the *anakh* in His hand).

Andersen and Freedman survey various emendations, including Horst's reading of *anaḥah* (with a *ḥet* in place of the final *kaf*), meaning "groan," as well as Riedel's suggestion of *anakeh* (I will clean out).[54] Both of these only refer to the final mention of *anakh*, while the first three instances are all read as "plumbline."

53. James L. Mays, *Amos*, Old Testament Library (Westminster Press, 1969) (henceforth "OTL"), 132.
54. Anchor Bible, 758.

Novick suggests that the fourth vision holds the key to the third.[55] There, too, God asks Amos what he sees, and Amos's answer is then the basis for wordplay – the word *kayitz* is modified to *ketz,* which leads to God's pronouncement. Similarly, Novick maintains that the word *anakh* is a homonym Amos does not know: when asked what he sees, Amos says *anakh* – not knowing that the word has another unrelated meaning and that by uttering it himself, he has sealed his audience's fate, with no hope of praying for the decree's annulment. One of Novick's suggestions for the second instance of *anakh* is that it is related lexically to *anaḥah,* as per Horst.[56]

Novick's claim that Amos, a southern prophet, is unfamiliar with the northern dialect, and is thus "trapped" into passing sentence on Israel, is highly problematic, but the connection with *anaḥah,* suggested by Horst, may nonetheless hold the key to understanding this vision.

The Two-Radical Root

Hebrew roots famously contain three letters, but some linguists argue that in some word-families, the essential root contains two radicals, and the third narrows a broader meaning down to a specific one.

For instance, the many roots that begin with *peh resh* (פר) all have a common meaning. To list just four of many examples: P-R-Z – to be unwalled; P-R-M – to slice vegetables; P-R-S – to slice bread; P-R-K – to break something down. All these and ten more share a single broad meaning: to break down one entity into smaller parts. This theory may be applied to various word families.

Back to the Aggada

We began with the passage in Bava Metzia, which connects *anakh* to *ona'ah.* Both roots begin with *alef-nun,* as does the root of *anaḥa* – "sighing." If we apply the above theory about two radical roots sharing certain elements of meaning, there may be a thematic connection between the three concepts. I would like to propose that *anakh* has two meanings,

55. See footnote 50, above.
56. Friedrich Horst, "Die Visionsschilderungen der alttestamentlichen Propheten," *EvT* 20 (1961): 193–205 (201).

both known to Amos. The prophet sees a plumblined wall, the plummet itself made of tin or lead and held by God, who stands atop that wall. Amos correctly identifies the object as *anakh*, a word related to *anaḥa*, *anaka*, and *ona'ah*. All of these speak of grievous pain – a pain not of crying out, but rather one of resignation. The victims of *ona'ah* are silent in their shame; the person who sighs (*anaḥa*) expresses his sense of impotence in the face of troubles; and the people who are *ne'enakim* (from *anaka*) are typically imprisoned[57] or desperately impoverished.[58] Perhaps Ezekiel expresses this best when God commands him to mark the foreheads of those "*Hane'enaḥim vehane'enakim*," who "sigh and cry."[59]

This deft use of an otherwise unattested but convincing homonym, where *anakh* describes the vision of the wall as well as the people's future sighs, teaches Amos that God's judgment has moved from an active, terrifying threat that can be forestalled with prayer to a more subtle threat that will leave the people hopeless. Amos, understanding this, responds with the only appropriate response – silence.

9: And the high places of Isaac will be desolate, and the sanctuaries of Israel will be laid waste

This passage builds on one of the curses in the rebuke at the end of Leviticus (26:30–31). When God punishes His people, sanctuaries of God's worship will be destroyed together with cultic sites of idolatry.

Until this point, the warning given at Sinai was never actualized; for the people, it was a distant storm cloud with no direct consequences. Amos turns this around with a single phrase: reviving the age-old rebuke, he is able to point to the specific "high places" and "sanctuaries" that would be laid waste.

Until Solomon's Temple, God's chosen place, was built, *bamot* were an acceptable locus of worship. A *bama* – rendered here as "high

57. Psalms 79:11, 102:21.
58. Ibid. 12:6.
59. Ezekiel 9:4.

place" – was a local worship site established at the highest place in the town.[60]

The first instance of problematic *bamot* are Solomon's *bamot* for his foreign wives (I Kings 11). From that point on, *bamot* appear in Kings in one of two contexts: as alternate worship sites to God, which are perceived as a "mild" violation of the law; or as idolatrous worship sites – particularly in the northern kingdom.

One of Jeroboam ben Nebat's first political moves was to build *beit habamot,* literally "the house of high places" (I Kings 13:2). Both Radak and Ralbag explain that he built a single temple with multiple "high places" (i.e., altars) – the opposite of the *Mikdash* in Jerusalem, which had only one altar (for offerings). The "impostor" priests that Jeroboam appointed (from the Ephraimite tribe) are referred to as *Kohanei HaBamot.* Although this worship was ostensibly for God, it was seen as a significant violation of God's will.

In this sense, Amos's use of the curse in Leviticus is doubly intense: not only is he announcing the imminence of a previously theoretical punishment, but he is also redefining once legitimate *bamot* as idolatrous, offensive sites due to the people's sins.

Moreover, the use of the plural *mikdashim* (*mikdeshei*) no longer refers to the legitimate existence of multiple sanctuaries (before Jerusalem was chosen). Now it is the problem itself; the existence of any *mikdash* outside of Jerusalem and the implied rejection of the centrality of that city and the Davidic dynasty is an essential part of the problem.

"Bamot Yisḥak"

The patriarch's name takes an unusual form, with a *sin* in place of a *tzadi.* But before addressing that unusual orthography, why does Amos refer to these sinful worship sites as *bamot Yisḥak,* given that Israel is consistently associated with Jacob/Israel? There would be no question if the prophet were to call these high places *bamot Yosef* or *bamot Efrayim;* the northern kingdom is often called by those names, since the reigning tribe in the area was Ephraim, son of Joseph. Why "Yisḥak" – and why is it spelled with a *sin*?

60. I Samuel 9:12–14, 19, 25; 10:5–7.

Few *Rishonim* address these problems. Ibn Ezra enigmatically comments: "*Venashamu bamot Yisḥak – Bamot Yisrael veEdom.*" He reads this prophecy as foretelling the destruction of both Israelite and Edomite (!) worship sites, evidently based on the use of the name Isaac, father of Israel (Jacob) and Edom (Esau). Why Ibn Ezra mentions Edom here is unclear; moreover, he does not address the odd spelling *Yisḥak*.

Radak notes the unusual spelling, but dismisses it by noting that *saḥok* and *tzaḥok* are interchangeable. He then addresses the mention of Isaac:

> The prophets never referred to the people by the name "Abraham" nor "Isaac," because Abraham and Isaac had other children … This prophet, however, called the tribes of Israel by the name "Yitzḥak" in two places in this book … Perhaps his intent in invoking *bamot Yisḥak* was because Yitzchak his father was bound atop the altar to fulfill God's will and His command. Yet here his children are angering God with their *bamot* and their idols. The [referenced] *mikdeshei Yisrael* are Beit El, Gilgal, and Dan, for that is where the major *bamot* were, and there they built big houses for the *bamot* …

As we can see, neither of these *Rishonim* – the only ones before Abravanel to address either question – provide a compelling explanation for the mention of Isaac (Radak's "perhaps" is telling). Radak is correct that *sin* and *tzadi* are interchangeable, but why does Isaac's name appear in such unusual form here? The roots *s-ḥ-q* and *tz-ḥ-q* may be virtually synonymous, but we never call Yitzḥak "Yisḥak" because his name is "Yitzḥak." Clearly, more is at play in this vision.

Don Isaac Abravanel tackles these issues directly and proposes that the deliberate misspelling of "*Yisḥak*" indicates that this is not a reference to the patriarch Isaac, who is always called Yitzḥak. Rather, the name alludes to Israel's foolish ways and empty vanities: their *bamot* are *bamot Yischak* – meaning "folly" and "ridicule," and their worship is mocked and ridiculed by God.[61]

61. See Psalms 2.

While Abravanel's comments answer both questions and his explanation of the variant spelling is compelling, I believe that there is still one piece of the puzzle missing.

The variant spelling *Yisḥak* appears only four times in Tanakh: once later in our chapter (7:16) and once in Jeremiah 33:26:

> Then will I also cast away the seed of Jacob and of David My servant, so that I will not take of his seed to be rulers over the seed of Abraham, *Yisḥak*, and Jacob; for I will cause their captivity to return and will have compassion on them.

The fourth time is in a historiographic Psalm (105:9):

> [The covenant] which He made with Abraham, and His oath unto *Yisḥak*.

This spelling is all the more unusual because in the psalm's parallel version in Chronicles, the name is spelled in its usual form, Yitzḥak (I Chr. 16:8–36). While these deviations can be explained as local to their specific books, since no biblical books contain both spellings of Isaac's name, variant spelling of proper names is nonetheless unusual enough to require further explanation.

Back to Abravanel

Abravanel's theory that *Yisḥak* expresses the ridicule of Israel's worship can be developed further. Although "the house of Yitzḥak" initially sounds like a noble cognomen, the name can actually be read as "the house of ridicule," similar to Amos's earlier gibe at the worship sites at Gilgal and Beit El (5:5).

There is no reason to believe that *Yisḥak* became the standard spelling and pronunciation of the patriarch's name in the eighth century BCE. Jeremiah draws heavily on Amos's rhetorical strategies, so in his only mention of the patriarchs, he employs this variant of the name with its negative connotations. The verse in question, quoted above, expresses strong rejection; evoking Amos's use of the name thus reminds the people of the pain of God's rejection.

As mentioned, the fourth and final instance of *Yisḥak* is in Psalm 105, but its parallel in Chronicles has the usual form *Yitzhak*.

Psalms 105–107 comprise one long sequence that describes God's selection of the Patriarchs, the descent to Egypt, the servitude, the plagues, and the Exodus, the travels in the wilderness (105); followed by a more detailed and less flattering portrayal of the Israelites in the wilderness (106); and concluding with a psalm of praise that anticipates God's redemption of the exiles (107). I would like to suggest that this series was composed during the Babylonian exile to inspire hope and anticipation within the exiled community,[62] employing the "history of the past" to help imagine the "history of the future." In order to covertly interject a note of realism, however, the author uses the name *Yisḥak* to express that this "reality" is not yet a reality.

Once the community were able to return from exile, the Chronicler edited this psalm for use in the new Temple, and replaced the sardonic form *Yisḥak* with the joyous, historic name of *Yitzḥak*.[63]

9: And I will rise against the house of Jeroboam with the sword

This third vision ends with a focused and explicit threat against the king. This is the first time that Amos calls him out by name, which leads to an unpleasant interaction with Amaziah. Indeed, as the *Rishonim* point out, Jeroboam's son is killed by the sword.[64]

62. See Psalms 51:20–21 and R. Moshe HaKohen Giqatilla, "one of the sages of Spain," cited in Ibn Ezra's commentary on 51:20. See also Psalms 126, 137 among others.
63. This also explains a well-known conundrum about *Pesukei DeZimra*, which is largely based on Psalms, yet the opening passages of *Hodu* are taken from the version in Chronicles. This explains why: that passage in Psalms was not the one recited in the Temple, and *Pesukei DeZimra* is an attempt to envision praising God in His House. Hence, the *Yisḥak* of exile (Psalms) becomes the *Yitzḥak* of Jerusalem (Chronicles).
64. Zechariah, his son, was killed by Shalum ben Yabesh (II Kings 15:10). That death put an end to the fourth northern dynasty, the house of Yehu.

AMOS'S CONFRONTATION AT BEIT EL (7:10–17)

The interaction at Beit El, the only narrative scene in Amos, shares significant parallels with a much earlier confrontation in Beit El. In the book of Kings, just after Jeroboam ben Nebat establishes the worship sites at Dan and Beit El as local alternatives to the Temple in Jerusalem, a mysterious visitor arrives there:

> And, behold, there came a man of God out of Judah by the word of the Lord to Beit El; and Jeroboam was standing by the altar to offer. And he cried against the altar by the word of the Lord, and said: "O altar, altar, thus says the Lord: Behold, a son shall be born to the house of David, Josiah by name; and upon you he will slaughter the priests of the high places that offer upon you, and men's bones shall they burn upon you. (I Kings 13:1–2)

Note the parallels – a "man of God" from Judea comes to the altar at Beit El and predicts the site's future destruction. The prophecy is delivered to Jeroboam, and the priests of the high places ("*kohanei bamot*") will be the victims of God's anger.

Does Amos deliberately choose Beit El in order to reenact that earlier scene? Is it significant that Amos's target is the only king who shares a name with the founder of these worship sites? Our analysis of this confrontation will reveal even more parallels between the two scenes.

The Text

(י) וַיִּשְׁלַח אֲמַצְיָה כֹּהֵן בֵּית אֵל אֶל יָרָבְעָם מֶלֶךְ יִשְׂרָאֵל לֵאמֹר קָשַׁר
עָלֶיךָ עָמוֹס בְּקֶרֶב בֵּית יִשְׂרָאֵל לֹא תוּכַל הָאָרֶץ לְהָכִיל אֶת כָּל דְּבָרָיו:
(יא) כִּי כֹה אָמַר עָמוֹס בַּחֶרֶב יָמוּת יָרָבְעָם וְיִשְׂרָאֵל גָּלֹה יִגְלֶה מֵעַל
אַדְמָתוֹ: (יב) וַיֹּאמֶר אֲמַצְיָה אֶל עָמוֹס חֹזֶה לֵךְ בְּרַח לְךָ אֶל אֶרֶץ
יְהוּדָה וֶאֱכָל שָׁם לֶחֶם וְשָׁם תִּנָּבֵא: (יג) וּבֵית אֵל לֹא תוֹסִיף עוֹד לְהִנָּבֵא כִּי
מִקְדַּשׁ מֶלֶךְ הוּא וּבֵית מַמְלָכָה הוּא: (יד) וַיַּעַן עָמוֹס וַיֹּאמֶר אֶל
אֲמַצְיָה לֹא נָבִיא אָנֹכִי וְלֹא בֶן נָבִיא אָנֹכִי כִּי בוֹקֵר אָנֹכִי וּבוֹלֵס שִׁקְמִים:
(טו) וַיִּקָּחֵנִי ה׳ מֵאַחֲרֵי הַצֹּאן וַיֹּאמֶר אֵלַי ה׳ לֵךְ הִנָּבֵא אֶל עַמִּי יִשְׂרָאֵל:
(טז) וְעַתָּה שְׁמַע דְּבַר ה׳ אַתָּה אֹמֵר לֹא תִנָּבֵא עַל יִשְׂרָאֵל וְלֹא תַטִּיף עַל

בֵּית יִשְׂחָק: (יז) לָכֵן כֹּה אָמַר ה׳ אִשְׁתְּךָ בָּעִיר תִּזְנֶה וּבָנֶיךָ וּבְנֹתֶיךָ בַּחֶרֶב
יִפֹּלוּ וְאַדְמָתְךָ בַּחֶבֶל תְּחֻלָּק וְאַתָּה עַל אֲדָמָה טְמֵאָה תָּמוּת וְיִשְׂרָאֵל גָּלֹה
יִגְלֶה מֵעַל אַדְמָתוֹ:

10 Then Amaziah the priest of Beit El sent to Jeroboam king of
Israel, saying: Amos has conspired against you in the midst of the
house of Israel; the land is not able to bear all his words. **11** For
thus Amos has said: Jeroboam shall die by the sword, and Israel
shall surely be led away captive out of his land. **12** Then Amaziah said to Amos: Go, you seer, flee to the land of Judah, and
there eat bread, and prophesy there; **13** but never again prophesy at Beit El, for it is the king's sanctuary, and it is a royal house.
14 Then Amos answered, and said to Amaziah: I am not a prophet,
neither am I a prophet's son; but I was a herdsman, and a dresser
of sycamore trees; **15** and the Lord took me from following the
flock, and the Lord said to me: Go, prophesy to My people Israel.
16 Now therefore hear the word of the Lord: You say: Do not
prophesy against Israel, and do not preach against the house of
Isaac. **17** Therefore, *ko amar Hashem*: Your wife will be a harlot in
the city, and your sons and your daughters will fall by the sword,
and your land will be divided by the survey line. And you yourself will die in an unclean land, and Israel will surely be led away
captive out of his land.

10: Then Amaziah the priest of Beit El sent to Jeroboam king of Israel, saying

Jeroboam appointed non-Levites to act as his priests (I Kings 12:28–29, 31); we do not know whether this priesthood became dynastic. Although Jeroboam I established these sanctuaries for worship of the God of Israel, by Ahab's time a century later, they may have become devoted to Ba'al worship. That is why the *Rishonim* assume Amaziah was a pagan priest, without mentioning his tribal identity. It may also be that each change of royal dynasty (Jeroboam, Baasha, Omri, Yehu) brought a change in the officials overseeing the cult.

The end of the third vision (verse 9) and the first two verses of this narrative are the only places where Jeroboam is mentioned by name in the book of Amos.

Amos has conspired against you in the midst of the house of Israel

Amaziah sees Amos as more than a troublesome prophet from the south; he perceives him as a rabble-rouser, whose rebukes and visions of doom have the potential to generate popular rebellion against the crown.

This message is odd, considering his prophecies so far: nearly all of Amos's oratory is aimed at the aristocracy, the corrupt judiciary, and the royal house – hardly the exploited masses, the plebian "house of Israel." We must consider the possibility that Amaziah sees Amos as a personal threat. Remember that Amos has already warned the people not to worship at Beit El (or Gilgal or Be'er Sheva). If the leadership heeds him, the populace is likely to follow suit. This may pose a threat to the priests at Beit El: to both their authority and their livelihood. Perhaps Amaziah's message to the king is tinged with hysteria and exaggerated in order to spur the king to action against Amos.

Amos may have been pronouncing these prophecies – notably, the visions in this section – in Beit El, at the site of the royal sanctuary, as suggested by Amaziah's ensuing words. This is a central site, where crowds of people would have heard him and perhaps been inspired to rebel.

The word *kesher*, "conspiracy," which appears approximately twenty times in Samuel, Kings, and Chronicles, appears only twice in the literary prophets (here and Isaiah 8:12): it is a word often relevant in historical narrative, but rare in prophetic rhetoric.[65]

The land is not able to bear all his words

This is a curious image. Radak explains that "the land" refers to its people: the people loyal to the crown cannot bear to hear so many bad things about their own nation. Abravanel, in contrast, explains that Amos's

65. See, however, Saul's words in I Samuel 22.

words may incite rebellion against the king. Hakham, in this same vein, explains that Amos's words are like fermenting wine which, when poured into a barrel, will burst the barrel – that is, his provocative words are likely to generate rebellion among the people.[66]

The latter approach presumes that the people's loyalty to the king is weak if their initial reaction would not be to despise the "southern man of God" who threatens the king, but rather to side with him.

It is worth noting that there is historical precedence of prophets identifying and anointing northern kings – Ahija elects Jeroboam ben Nebat, and Elisha elects Hazael and Jehu. It may be that Amaziah perceives Amos as yet another prophet aiming to unseat Jeroboam and the house of Yehu and replace him with another king (perhaps a Judean vassal).

Paul points out the alliteration in this phrase – *tukhal lehakhil kol.* A subliminal message of this alliterative scheme would be *okhel hakol* – Amos's words will lead to *everything* in the north being devoured.[67]

11: For thus Amos has said

This short phrase is heavy with implication. The priest uses the same familiar introductory "messenger formula" Amos himself employed for his first series of oracles. As mentioned, this formula is used when delivering a liege's words to their vassal: "*Ko amar Balak,*" "*Ko amar Par'oh,*" and "*Ko amar Yosef.*" The understated power of "*Ko amar Amos*" preceding a message to the king is clear – Amos presumes himself the superior of Jeroboam, his servant. This is not Amos's position, of course; rather, this is how Amaziah wants to portray the Judean prophet to his king.

Moreover, the phrase *Ko amar Amos* is misleading in itself. Amos would not have said *Ko omar* ("Thus say I"), but rather *Ko amar Hashem.* The omission of this vital aspect is calculated to make Jeroboam believe that these are Amos's words – not God's! This reduces Amos to a mere troublemaking orator from the south, not the agent of God Himself.

66. Hakham, 59.

67. Paul, 122.

Jeroboam shall die by the sword

This intentionally misquotes Amos's last vision: "I will rise up against *the house of* Jeroboam by the sword." Amos warns that doom will befall Jeroboam's *descendants,* but Amaziah deliberately rephrases this as a more immediate, personal threat against the king himself in order to spur immediate and drastic action against the Tekoite interloper.

And Israel shall surely be led away captive out of his land

As noted, the commentators are divided about Amaziah's first warning – "the land will not be able to tolerate/contain all of his words." Some, such as Ibn Ezra and R. Eliezer of Beaugency, read that the people naturally sided with their king and would not tolerate Amos's threats. Others, however, notably Abravanel, define this phrase as part of the threat: Amos is riling "the whole land" against the king. The latter interpretation seems incompatible with the warning that "Israel will surely be exiled." For if the threat is against all the people of the northern kingdom, it is far more likely to result in the people's lynching of Amos than in rebellion!

Abravanel's approach can nonetheless be salvaged if we read the relationship between the two clauses differently: instead of reading the two clauses as sequential – first the king will be killed and *then* Israel will be exiled – it can be read as conditional. That is, Amaziah is claiming that Amos is rallying the people: "Jeroboam *must* die by the sword *or else* Israel will be exiled!"

These first two verses relate Amaziah's manipulative and near-hysterical message to the king. The next few verses present the exchange between "priest" and prophet.

12: Then Amaziah said to Amos

Was Amos privy to Amaziah's message to the king? Did Amaziah declare it publicly, or was it sent as a private message to the court? If we interpret *Vayomer* here as, "Also, Amaziah said," as in various translations (KJV, JPS), this implies that Amaziah's first statement was also public. He first addressed a royal messenger in the presence of those gathered *as well as*

Amos, and sent his urgent message to the court; he then turned to Amos to confront him directly.

On the other hand, if we interpret *Vayomer* as "Then Amaziah said," these may be the first words that Amos (or anyone else present) heard.

Go, you seer, flee to the land of Judah

Amaziah uses an archaic term for prophet – *hozeh*, literally "seer." We will revisit this in the context of Amos's response, which uses the term *navi*.

And there eat bread, and prophesy there

We will soon discuss why Amaziah tells Amos to go eat bread elsewhere. He perceives him as an unwelcome southerner, out of his element, with no right to orate in the north.

13: But never again prophesy at Beit El

This phrase gives us the impression that Amos has been prophesying in Beit El for some time. There are several reasons why this was an ideal location. First of all, it was a royal sanctuary, where the king himself may have come to participate in the cult practices. It was also a popular pilgrimage site.[68] Moreover, one reason Jeroboam I originally chose this site was for its proximity to Judah. It was, for a time, the southernmost city in the Israelite kingdom. This may have made it a "safer" place for Amos to preach, given its distance from the capitol in Samaria.

For it is the king's sanctuary

Whether Amaziah is defining Beit El as "the *king's* sanctuary" or "a *royal* sanctuary" is significant. The former implies that Amaziah is telling Amos to leave because this is Jeroboam's personal "property," and the king himself may arrive at any moment. It is more likely to be the latter,

68. See Judges 19:18 and I Samuel 10:3.

which frames Amos's oracle as an insult to the crown – coming into a royal sanctuary and preaching against the king.

The phrase *mikdash melekh* (which we know from a more positive context, in R. Shlomo Alkabetz's *Lekha Dodi*) appears only here in Tanakh. The notion of a *mikdash melekh* is familiar, albeit from foreign, pagan nations, where divinity and royalty are one and the same. In a sense, Amaziah's clumsy description of the altar at Beit El speaks volumes, although this is not a point that Amos ever directly attacks. Jeroboam established the temple at Beit El to prevent the people from making pilgrimage to Jerusalem, which he feared would lead to their renewed loyalty to the Davidic line and the resultant end of Jeroboam's power. Beit El and Dan were set up to provide "local and convenient" places to worship God, but their real purpose was to maintain Jeroboam's own power – they were, essentially, "a royal sanctuary" privileging the kingship over loyalty to God.

And it is a royal house

This conclusion emphasizes this purpose: the sanctuary's first priority is not communion with the divine, but rather a place that ensures the monarchy's power. Thus the real intruder is not someone impure or corrupt, but rather one who threatens the kingship.

14: Then Amos answered, and said to Amaziah

Again, we assume that this confrontation takes place publicly, and that Amos's response is aimed at the onlookers more than at Amaziah himself.

I am not a prophet, neither am I a prophet's son

This is Amos's famous claim that he is not part of a professional guild of prophets, nor is he a prophet by vocation.

But I was a herdsman

Amos is a rancher, who herds animals. In other words, he is not part of the scholastic or ascetic class, but rather a "regular person."

And a dresser of sycamore trees

The word *boles* is a *hapax legomenon*. The most prevalent interpretation is that it refers to the puncturing of sycamore-figs; still practiced in Egypt today, this evidently hastens ripening without exposing the fruit to worm infestation. This was only done during a specific part of the season, so Amos was both herder and "sycamore dresser."

15: And the Lord took me from following the flock

This description clearly evokes God's words to David (II Sam. 7:8). Like David, Amos did not seek power; he was content tending his flock and dressing his sycamores when God singled him out and sent him on this vital but difficult mission. Amos emphasizes that he was "plucked" from a hard-working but serene and pastoral life and thrown directly into the crucible of conflict with kings, priests, and judges.

And the Lord said to me

This underscores what Amaziah deliberately omitted: Amos's words are not his own – they are God's words, a divine message, ignored at one's own peril.

Go, prophesy to My people Israel

This completes the picture. Amos was *sent*; he did not go of his own volition. When Amaziah tells him to "go," this assumes that Amos chose to come and may now choose to go. This is not the case, as Amos spells out for him.

PROPHET OR SEER?

The priest speaks directly to Amos and calls him *ḥozeh* – literally "visionary" or "seer." He then tells him to go back to Judea and "prophesy there" – *sham tinavei* – using the same root as *navi*. Amos replies that he is not a *navi*. Are *ḥozeh* and *navi* synonymous? Why does Amos respond thus, instead of using the priest's own epithet: *lo ḥozeh anokhi velo ben ḥozeh*?

Only one biblical character is called *ḥozeh*: Gad the Ḥozeh, who is David's "court prophet" from the beginning of David's rise to power, while he is still fleeing from Saul;[69] he is most famous for his role in the tragic story of David's census.[70] When Gad is first mentioned in this scene, the text characterizes him with seemingly redundant terms: "...and the word of the Lord was given to Gad the prophet (*hanavi*), the seer (*ḥozeh*) of David."

The term *navi* remains independent, but the *ḥozeh* belongs to David – *ḥozeh David*. Gad is also noted as one of the three authors of David's chronicles:

> Now the acts of David the king, first and last, behold, they are written in the words of Samuel the *ro'eh* and in the words of Natan the *navi* and in the words of Gad the *ḥozeh*.[71]

Elsewhere, the term *ḥozeh* is used disparagingly. Ezekiel consistently refers to false prophets as *ḥozim*,[72] juxtaposing them with *kosmim* (wizards). The most famous *kosem* in Tanakh (Bilam) refers to himself as one who *maḥazeh Shaddai yehezeh* ("sees the visions of Shaddai") – but never calls himself a *navi*.

This underscores the essential difference between a *ḥozeh* and a *navi*. A *ḥozeh* is a court prophet, the king's employee who serves as his royal oracle.

Whereas a *ḥozeh* works for the king, the *navi* works for God; he brings God's word to the court, the leaders, and the people.[73]

This implies that Amaziah assumes Amos is working for the Judean king – that he has been sent to Beit El to set the local populace against their king in an attempt to restore Davidic sovereignty to the north.

---

69. I Samuel 22:5.
70. II Samuel 24 (= I Chronicles 21).
71. I Chronicles 29:29. *Ro'eh* is synonymous with *ḥozeh* but used almost exclusively to identify Shmuel – the one exception being Hanani in II Chronicles 16.
72. Chiefly in Ezekiel 12–13.
73. Some have suggested that the root of *navi* is *havei*, bringer, i.e., of the Word.

This explains Amaziah's odd phrase – "eat bread there." Amaziah believes that Amos works for the Judean court, and that he "eats bread at the king's table" like the false prophets under Jezebel's hire, who "dine at Jezebel's table" (I Kings 18:19).[74]

When Amos responds that he is not a *navi,* he is emphasizing that he has not chosen this vocation. Nor is he even a *ben navi,* a member of the guild of students who, at least in Elisha's time, adopted a life of penury in their quest to "study" prophecy.

Rather, he is a "regular" person, fully occupied with his chosen profession. Speaking to God's people on His behalf was never his choice. He is not a professional *ḥozeh* or *navi* who "belongs" to a court; he represents one thing and one thing only – God's word to His people. He cannot return to Judea and eat bread there, for although he comes *from* there, he is not *supported* there. He is not in the employ of the southern king. It may be that Amaziah was not even aware of any other kind of prophet, and Amos's words open his eyes to a new kind of revelation.

16: Now therefore hear the word of the Lord

The word *ve'ata* appears in the canon over 250 times, with fifty-five instances in prophetic literature, but this is its only appearance in Amos. The meaning "now therefore" always expresses causality and is usually found in the middle of a passage:[75] this has happened, *now therefore* comes the consequence.

Here, *ve'ata* is used in an unexpected context: rather than following the description of an offense, it follows Amos's autobiographic sketch of his call to divine agency.

Paul reads *ve'ata* as a transition: Amos has concluded justifying his agency and now shifts (*ve'ata*) to the pronouncement. Hakham, however, interprets *ve'ata* as causal: "Now that I have confirmed my

74. Nili Samet, "Between 'Eat Bread There' and 'Do Not Eat Bread': The Motif of Eating Bread in Two Stories in the Prophets and Its Relationship to the Perception of Prophecy in the Bible" [Heb.], in *Masekhet: Say To Wisdom: You Are My Sister,* vol. 2 (2004), 167–181.

75. Notable exceptions are Deuteronomy 4:1, 10:12.

agency from God, I have prophecy regarding you, Amaziah…" This fits its usual biblical usage.

The placement of the clause "hear the word of the Lord" seems curious: instead of following with God's word, he then describes Amaziah's words to Amos. This implies that God himself is condemning Amaziah's attempt to silence Amos.

> *Ve'ata* – and now, here is the prophecy that God has sent me to deliver: "You tell me (or Me) not to deliver prophecy against Israel and not to rebuke the house of Yisḥak. Therefore, this is what Hashem says…"

Amos's paraphrase of Amaziah's words are not his own personal response; rather, they are part of God's response to the attempt to silence God's word at Beit El.

You say: Do not prophesy against Israel, and do not preach against the house of Isaac

Amos uses *tinavei* in parallel with *tatif.* The root *natof* means "drip" in most of its rare appearances (eighteen in total).[76] This meaning is then used metaphorically to convey prophetic words of rebuke, which "drop down" from heaven.[77]

This helps underscore the dynamics of this interaction. Amos is standing at Beit El, beneath the altar, looking up at the priest officiating there. He is at the bottom, and the priest looks down at him. The word *natof* thus expresses a directional orientation that is a foil to this scene – specifically here, where Amos's role and agency is directly challenged as he stands *below,* he stresses that his words are coming "down" from *above,* like dew or hail.

---

76. For instance, in the opening lines of Devora's song, poetically describing the cosmological reaction to God's appearance at Sinai – Judges 5:4; see also Psalms 68:9. The root's other appearance in Amos is part of his consolation epilogue, where it retains its original meaning and conveys divine blessing.
77. Ezekiel 21:2, 9. This root is also used thus in Micah 2:6, 11, and Job 29:22. The expression is still used in Modern Hebrew.

The alignment of *hinavei* with "Israel" and *tatif* with "Beit Yisḥak" is deliberate and elegant. The classic, familiar word *navi* is associated with Israel, whereas the rebuff implied by *tatif* specifically targets "Beit Yisḥak" – the sardonic play on the name Yitzḥak that turns it from a name of divine favor and joy to one of ridicule and frivolity. Amos's prophecy rains down from on high on the northern kingdom's "high" places.

17: Therefore, *ko amar Hashem*

Amos is already delivering God's words. Why add this introductory phrase?

Amos's response can be understood as two separate divine responses to Amaziah. The first is a strong-arm rebuff of Amaziah's attempts to silence God's prophet. The second describes the punishment due to Amaziah (and presumably, his sovereign) in light of their attempts to silence Amos.[78]

Ironically, perhaps this harsh pronouncement was originally only intended for the king, but since the priest tried to prevent the prophet from announcing God's words to the king, they now apply to his minions at Beit El as well.

This curse has five prongs to it, a rhetorical pattern that Amos has used several times. Five disasters (4:6–11) each conclude with "and still you have not returned to Me"; five cosmic wonders are listed in 4:13.

Your wife will be a harlot in the city

R. Eliezer of Beaugency explains that the wife in question will *voluntarily* go out to commit harlotry/adultery; whereas an adulterer is usually discreet, to heighten the shame she will do so publicly. Paul suggests that this refers to Amaziah's wife: the wives of real priests acted with virtue (and priests could not marry harlots), but this false priest's wife will bring him shame.

78. Whether this curse is aimed at the king or his priest – or both – depends on how we read the pronominal suffixes in this curse.

Both of these commentators, one medieval and the other modern, assume that the act of *tizneh* is voluntary and brazen, but this does not fit the context: the rest of the curse describes an enemy conquering the land, killing their children, dividing up the land, and exiling the people.

A more likely reading is that the wife in question (again, whose wife? Perhaps everyone's?) will be so desperate for food that she will turn to whoring – in the city, publicly, as her situation will have become so dire that she will do anything to save herself and her family.[79]

This reading is consistent with the rest of the verse, which is not a random group of five tragedies, but rather a sequence ending in exile (a common biblical motif). First, there will be such desperate hunger that even the wives of nobles will offer sexual favors for food. This suggests a siege – not the first siege in Samarian history[80] – which will be followed by invasion, mass slaughter, conquest, and finally the exile of the leaders, who have seen their own wives, children, and land taken from them. Now they will be led away from Israel to die "in an unclean land."

And your sons and your daughters will fall by the sword

This suggests massacre – but if so, then why aren't the leaders killed as well? One might expect that the leaders would be killed first.

A more likely possibility is that even the young women joined the fighting in desperate times, as is evident in Joel: "Let the bridegroom go out from his room and the bride from her wedding canopy" (2:16). Though contextually that mention seems to be about communal prayer, the Sages read it as a call to conscription.[81]

And your land will be divided by the survey line

The conquering enemy dividing the spoil is a common biblical image.[82]

---

79. See Deuteronomy 28:54–55; see also, of interest, the comment of R. Eliezer of Beaugency on Joel 4:3.
80. II Kings 6:25 ff.
81. Mishna Sota 8:7.
82. Joel 4:3.

And you yourself will die in an unclean land

Does the phrase "unclean land" imply that all foreign lands are impure, or does it refer specifically to death upon enemy soil? From the perspective of Israelite sovereignty and recognition that conquest and exile reflect a breach of the covenant, we can posit that death in the captor's land – hence eternal exile – is what constitutes the impurity.

And Israel will surely be led away captive out of his land

The curses in Leviticus 26, Deuteronomy 28, and throughout prophetic literature – all biblical downward spirals end with displacement and exile.

THE FOURTH VISION (8:1–3)

(א) כֹּה הִרְאַנִי אֲדֹנָי ה׳ וְהִנֵּה כְּלוּב קָיִץ: (ב) וַיֹּאמֶר מָה אַתָּה רֹאֶה עָמוֹס
וָאֹמַר כְּלוּב קָיִץ וַיֹּאמֶר ה׳ אֵלַי בָּא הַקֵּץ אֶל עַמִּי יִשְׂרָאֵל לֹא אוֹסִיף עוֹד
עֲבוֹר לוֹ: (ג) וְהֵילִילוּ שִׁירוֹת הֵיכָל בַּיּוֹם הַהוּא נְאֻם אֲדֹנָי ה׳ רַב הַפֶּגֶר בְּכָל
מָקוֹם הִשְׁלִיךְ הָס:

1 Thus the Lord God showed me; and behold a basket of summer fruit. 2 And He said: "Amos, what do you see?" And I said:
"A basket of summer fruit." Then the Lord said to me: The end
is come upon My people Israel, I will not pardon them anymore.
3 And the songs of the palace shall be wailings in that day, says
the Lord God; the dead bodies will be many; in every place
silence will be cast.

1: Thus the Lord God showed me

This vision did not necessarily follow immediately after his confrontation with Amaziah at Beit El – it may have taken place earlier – but it is reported here. This order once again follows the 3 + 1 pattern, which evokes Amos's opening oracle against the nations, and lends further meaning to the phrase *ko amar*. *Ko amar Hashem*: three visions are followed by a fourth, the most terrifying of all, and "the fourth I will not forgive."

And behold a basket of summer fruit

The word *keluv* appears twice here and one more time in Jeremiah: "As a *keluv* is full of birds, so are their houses full of deceit" (5:27). Radak explains that a *keluv* is a container made of wooden boards for raising birds – a coop. Shadal points out that this is associated with Jeremiah's earlier bird-trapping metaphor.

Amos's *keluv* contains fruit. Generally translated as "basket," the sense of "trap" nonetheless lingers.

The *keluv* holds *kayitz*. "Summer" in modern Hebrew, the word is derived from the root *k-tz-h,* meaning "end"[83] (the agricultural year ends with the summer harvest). The fruit harvested at the season's end is called *kayitz.*

The specific meaning of this summer fruit is subject to dispute, which may reflect a more profound debate about this vision's message.

The Meaning of *"Kayitz"*

The basic debate here is whether "*kayitz*" refers to inferior fruits (as opposed to *bikkurim,* the first fruits, which are considered the finest),[84] or is simply a neutral word for "summer fruits." Rashi and R. Joseph Kara favor the former approach, while Ibn Ezra and Radak prefer the latter.

The word *kayitz* appears twenty times in Tanakh; nine instances refer to summer fruit (as opposed to the season). There seems to be little support for reading *kayitz* as inferior grade fruit: for example, when fleeing Absalom, David is brought a large gift that includes "a hundred of summer fruits – *kayitz*" (II Sam. 16:1) – which clearly does not refer to inferior fruit. Why, then, do Rashi and R. Kara take this approach?

83. See, however, Ibn Kaspi on our verse, who argues that the root of *kayitz* is *k-y-tz* and the root of *ketz* (end) is *k-tz-tz.* Even if these are not anchored in a single set of radicals, the roots are clearly of a single family and are related.
84. See Pesahim 6b; see also *Tosefta Ma'asrot* 3:5 and *Tosefta Beitza* 4:2 (according to some versions, the first word is *sokhei*).

One immediate response comes to mind. We have consistently argued that Jeremiah built his rhetorical strategy on the model established by Amos. Here, too, when God asks Amos *ma ata ro'eh*, God's famous question to Jeremiah comes to mind.

One of Jeremiah's famous visions is the "baskets of figs" (ch. 24), in which he sees a basket of finest figs and a basket of inedible figs – the latter a symbol of the sinful people. Perhaps this image moved Rashi to perceive Amos's summer fruits as inferior. Alternatively, he may have been influenced by Micah's lament: "Woe is me, for I am as the *last of the summer fruits – ke'ospei kayitz*" (7:1). Rashi interprets *kayitz* there as: "the summer harvest, the *sofei te'einim*, which are bad."

A different explanation can be derived from the vision itself. How closely does the message adhere to the vision? Since its meaning is derived from wordplay (as we will see in the next verse), it may or may not be significant what the basket actually contains. Ibn Ezra would say that the quality of the fruit is of little consequence, whereas Rashi seems to believe that the content of the basket is tied to the content of the message: even though the fruit only appear for the sake of wordplay, their quality ought to be symbolic of Israel's moral rot, and inferior fruit are a more fitting metaphor for the northern kingdom.

A further dispute concerns the nature of God's providence. If we follow Rashi's approach that the fruit themselves represent the people, then who will be punished here? Is it only the *sofei te'einim*, the worst among the target audience, or is it all of them?

2: And He said: "Amos, what do you see?"

Like the third vision, Amos does not have the opportunity to interpret the vision himself and then pray, because God immediately engages the prophet: *Ma ata ro'eh Amos*?

And I said: "A basket of summer fruit"

As he did in the *anakh* vision Amos faithfully responds, briefly: *keluv kayitz*.

Jeremiah's responses to the same question are wordier,[85] perhaps because the newly inaugurated prophet – unlike Amos – needs to emphasize that he is indeed seeing the visions God shows him: *makel shaked ani ro'eh.*

Then the Lord said to me

As he did in the third vision, Amos faithfully reports God's words of doom, which are the response to Amos's correct identification of the object in the vision.

The end is come upon My people Israel

In response to Amos's answer of *kayitz* (figs/summer fruit), God announces that the end is nigh: the people's *keitz* – end – has come. While the wordplay seems weaker than that employed in the *anakh* vision, since the words *kayitz* and *keitz* are vocalized differently,[86] Paul points out that in the Gezer calendar, the summer month is called *yerach keitz* (not *kayitz*), and notes:

> Amos ... while addressing his northern audience, affected their very own dialectical pronunciation in order to heighten the similarity of sounds. By pronouncing both substantives as *keitz*, he produced a very poignant and powerful paronomasia.[87]

---

85. 1:11, 1:13, 24:3.

86. Kutscher, in his brilliant monograph *Milim VeToldoteihem*, points out that archaeological evidence indicates that the northern dialect apparently elided the *ayi* diphthong and pronounced it as *ei*. Using Kutscher's example, wine, which is pronounced in the Judean (and our common) dialect as *yayin*, was pronounced *yein*. Note that we all pronounce it that way when in the construct state – for example, *ḥamat taninim yeinam* (Deut. 32:33). Based on several ostraca found in the Shomron, Kutscher concluded that even in the nominative state, the word was pronounced that way in the north.

87. Paul, *Amos: A Commentary on the Book of Amos* (Fortress Press, 1991), 254.

To modify Paul's claim: this wordplay is not Amos's own. Rather, God manipulates him into pronouncing sentence on the people, as in the third vision. At that point, he is unable to turn back to God and ask for this sentence to be revoked; thus the punishment is put into irrevocable motion.

I will not pardon them anymore

These visions, as mentioned, evoke Amos's opening series of oracles, with their *Ko amar* opening and the "three/four" number scheme. This phrase, *lo osif avor lo,* the proverbial nail in the northern kingdom's coffin, reminds us of the repeated phrase there: *ve'al arba'a lo ashivenu.*

3: And the songs of the palace shall be wailings in that day

Heikhal

The biblical word *heikhal,* "palace," is used in both secular and sacral sense.

Significantly, the secular sense is only used in reference to *foreign* palaces (most commonly *heikhal melekh Bavel,* the palace of the Babylonian king). The Judean or Israelite king's palace is called *armon* or *beit hamelekh*; only once does *heikhal* refer to an Israelite king's palace (I Kings 21:1), and this is presumably employed intentionally, to hint that Ahab is as corrupt and tyrannical as a foreign king who considers himself a deity. Amos is borrowing this deliberate sting from the Ahab story to insinuate that the palace in Samaria has become like a foreign, oppressive power, rather than the seat of a king who leads and protects his people, as is expected from an Israelite king.

In a sacral sense, the word exclusively applies to the house of God; foreign temples are *never* called *heikhal.* "*Heikhal*" comes from *ekallu* in Akkadian – borrowed, in turned, from the Sumerian *e-gal,* "great house," which is not inherently sacred *or* profane. This changes by the time it enters *Tanakh* in the pre-monarchic period,[88] where it initially

88. I Samuel 1:9.

refers to the Tabernacle. When Solomon builds the Temple, the meaning of *heikhal* evolves to refer to a vestibule through which *kohanim* may enter the *Mikdash*. One thing is clear – "off-site" shrines to God are *never* referred to as *heikhal*.[89]

Since the biblical word took on connotations of sanctity, it is inappropriate to use it for pagan temples. Its application to foreign kings' palaces, however, underscores the temerity and haughtiness of these self-appointed (or culturally assigned) demigods – describing a foreign palace as *heikhal* is thus essentially ironic. Judean kings never presume that their own abodes are of equal grandeur and holiness to the Temple, but this is not true of foreign kings – and as such, their palaces are sardonically called *heikhal*.

Shirot Heikhal

The subject in this clause is *shirot heikhal*. While the plural *shirim* appears four times in *Tanakh*, this plural form of *shir* or *shira* is unmatched. Why this unusual form, rather than the usual *shir* or the genitive *shirei*?

Conventionally, *shirot* is read as "songs," but a more likely possibility is that it means "singers," possibly written in a northern dialect. Some critics propose that the *yod* is a scribal corruption, and the word was originally *sharot*. Whether we arrive at *sharot* via alternative dialect or text emendation, this meaning fits the syntax more smoothly: it is not the *songs* but the *singers* that will soon wail rather than sing sweetly.

Sharot weep and lament over the death of Josiah: "And Jeremiah lamented for Josiah; and all the singing men and *singing women* (*vehasharot*) spoke of Josiah in their lamentations."[90]

Some suggest a more invasive emendation, reading *shurot* (from the Aramaic "walls"), substituting the *yod* with a *vav* (this is certainly a reasonable scribal error, considering these letters' shape; in any case, the text is written in *plene* spelling, *ketiv malei*): "the palace walls will

89. Mays renders *shirot heikhal* as "the hymns of the temple." He then expands on this: "The hymns of the temple were songs of exultant joy and hope in Y-H-W-H, but under the last of Y-H-W-H's wrath, the sounds of wailing, the howling chants of lamentation would replace them." I find this approach most surprising and hard to accept, based on the evidence presented here.

90. II Chronicles 35:25; see also II Samuel 19:36, and Ecclesiastes 2:8.

wail," an image found elsewhere in Tanakh.[91] Though this poetic image fits the context well, academic integrity – not to speak of religious sensitivity – dictates that such emendations are only recommended when the Masoretic text is incomprehensible as is.

If we read "female singers," why are the *female* singers highlighted? All three biblical instances of *sharot* appear together with *sharim*, male singers. Why are there only female singers here? If we read "songs," why the unique plural form? Perhaps the unusual opening word of this clause, "*Veheililu*," will help solve this conundrum.

Heililu

The root of this word is *y-l-l*, "wail." The word is typically associated with people who usually sing celebratory songs, or nations that would otherwise be celebrating.[92] Here, too, *shirot heikhal* will soon turn to sounds of mourning.

What is unique about *heililu* here is that all other instances of *heililu* in the causative *hifil* stem are understood as imperative, while ours alone is rendered in the future imperfect – the word would be consistent with other biblical appearances if it were *veyeililu*.[93]

How we read *shirot* effects the meaning of *heililu*. If we understand it as "songs," then the imperative doesn't fit; even the imperfect is awkward. If, on the other hand, we read *shirot* as either a form of *sharot* (or *shurot*), then the imperative is appropriate: commanding the singers to wail is equivalent to directing the farmers and drinkers to lament.

Perhaps most translators read *heililu* as future tense due to the prefix *vav*, which doesn't usually appear before an imperative. However, if we understand this *vav* as explanatory rather than conjunctive, the phrase fits nicely.

The previous verse concluded with God's statement that He will no longer forgive the nation. Amos is turning to his audience and *instructing them how to respond* to the threat: "[therefore] Wail! You singers in the palace" – all songs of joy should turn to wails of mourning. For this

91. Psalms 96:12, Habakuk 2:11, and, more to our point, Isaiah 14:31.
92. Joel 1:5, 11.
93. For example, Isaiah 15:3.

reason, he addresses the *sharot*, given that women were usually those trained as professional mourners:[94] this is how they ought to respond on the day of punishment, when He no longer forgives.

3: Says the Lord God

Amos frequently evokes God's "signature" mid-verse;[95] perhaps for the sake of rhetorical variation, as this signature usually appears at the end of a passage or at least at the end of a verse.

The dead bodies will be many

Is this a description of the punishment, or the anticipated/ commanded words of the lament? The word *peger* is a collective singular;[96] it is more degrading than *halal* (corpse) and is used for both human and animal carcasses.

In every place silence will be cast

This clause is inscrutable; this translation is only one of several possibilities, none more convincing than others. The *Rishonim* suggest various readings:

Rashi, citing Targum, reads that there will be so many carcasses everywhere that "in every place" people will say "cast [the corpses] away." He does not explain the word *has*.

Ibn Ezra only addresses *has*, and explains that the command to be silent (*Has!*) is intended to keep the listeners from collapsing.

94. Jeremiah 9:16.
95. 3:10, 6:14, 8:9, 11.
96. See, for instance, the use of the collective singular at Genesis 32:6. Also see p. 222.

Radak explains that those who dispose of the bodies will tell each other "Silence!" as an expression of confirming and accepting God's justice.

Abravanel believes that *hishlikh* refers to God, who has cast down all of these carcasses. He then understands *has* as Amos's words to Amaziah: Amos is telling Amaziah that he should be silent and stop challenging Amos's prophetic mission.

Paul suggests that these two clauses ought to be read as short, staccato wails, and that the active causative *hishlikh* ought to be read as the passive *hoshlakh*, i.e., "have been cast down."

> *Rav hapeger!*
> *Bekhol makom hishlikh (hoshlakh)*
> *Has!*

We would thus translate:

> So many carcasses!
> They have been cast down everywhere!
> Silence!

This is a convincing parsing of the phrase.

One question remains: Is this Amos's vision of the future punishment and the people's response, or is this the call the wailing singers ought to sound?

The latter approach is more convincing, and it reads as follows:

> Oh songstresses of the palace, wail on that day, saying: There are so many carcasses! They have been cast down everywhere! Silence!

We will now take a panoramic look at this last vision, followed by a broader look at all four visions, their sequence, and their overarching message.

The Fourth Vision: A Summary

While we have analyzed specific aspects of this vision – its association with Jeremiah's vision, the wordplay of *kayitz-ketz*, and the notion that God has Amos pronounce Samaria's sentence – there is also a larger picture at play.

The description *keluv kayitz* is vague and detached. Is it being held? Is it hovering in mid-air? This contrasts sharply with the third vision, which carefully describes how the *anakh* is held by God, who is atop a wall. The lack of context and detail in the fourth vision is even starker in comparison to the first two visions, which are created and dispatched by God.

This sequence is part of Amos's rhetorical strategy, which I will outline and analyze after one last discussion of the *keluv kayitz* image and its own internal logic.

Amos sees a *keluv kayitz*, a basket of summer fruit. While one purpose of this vision might be to "trap" Amos into pronouncing Israel's sentence – *kayitz* (= *keitz*) – this does not seem to encapsulate the vision's entire meaning – there are other ways to express the looming "end" (a cup = *saf* = *sof*?). Why figs, and why figs in a *keluv*?

Figs appear frequently in Tanakh, both fruit and tree, often together with the grape or vine,[97] symbolizing both sweetness[98] and discarded, inedible fruit.[99] Jeremiah and Hosea both use the fig as a metaphor for Israel.[100] Whether the fig plays such a central role as an example of God's blessing because of its sweetness, its ubiquitousness, or its unusual harvest cycle is unclear.[101] Intriguingly, the fig is the first specific fruit tree mentioned in Tanakh (Gen. 3:7); it provides humanity with their first garments, and thus becomes a symbol of emerging

97. For example, I Kings 15:5 and II Kings 18:31.
98. Judges 9:10–11.
99. Isaiah 34:4.
100. Hosea 9:10.
101. Rabbinic literature assumes multiple harvest cycles for the fig, but only for the fig. See Peah 1:4, where a single harvest time is presented as a necessary condition for the obligation of *peah*. The Talmud (Shabbat 68a and Pesahim 56b) understands that this phrase pointedly *excludes* the fig tree.

human consciousness. Amos sees a basket of figs – not a single fig, but a symbol of collective consciousness. Why is the basket called a *keluv*?

Note that this vision is presented (and perhaps first seen) only after Amaziah's confrontation with Amos, where the priest tells Amos to "go back to the south and prophesy there." Beyond our explanation that Amaziah assumes Amos has been sent by Judah to stir up rebellion in the northern kingdom, Amaziah is expressing an underlying "regionalist" worldview: that prophecy spoken by a Judean prophet belongs in Judah, and Samaria's fortunes are independent of its southern neighbor's.

Amos thus receives a vision of *a basket of* fruit: all Israel, north and south, Samaria and Jerusalem, are one; what befalls the north will ultimately affect the south. This basket of fruit is a response to Amaziah's attempt to distance the "southern messenger" from the northern audience.

Moreover, this explains why the basket is referred to as a *keluv*, rather than *eifa, dud, sal,* or *teneh*: a *keluv* also connotes "cage." These figs, representing all of Israel – Samaria and Jerusalem, Ephraim with Judah – are trapped together in one cage; their destiny is as intertwined as is their history.[102] The *keluv* is presented without context – not being held or situated anywhere specific – because it represents an ontological reality about the nation, and is thus presented without any context that might diminish this essential message.

Within this paradigm, the meaning of *heikhal* does in fact allude to the Temple in Jerusalem. Although its primary meaning is Jeroboam's palace in Samaria, Judah and Samaria's fates are inextricable – and Jeroboam's continued sinful behavior will ultimately lead to mourning in the Temple. Even a southern prophet is concerned about the north's fate.

102. Whether or not this is how history unfolded (it is decidedly not) is irrelevant to Amos's message here. He is defending his mission: beyond being sent by God, his message as a southern prophet is relevant to the north and he should not be seen as a Judean prophet would be seen if he were to go to, say, Damascus, and prophesy (II Kings 8:7).

The Four Visions: Sequence, Structure, and Message

As discussed in the introduction, prophetic rhetoric functions on different levels. Amos's original audience undoubtedly experienced his oratory in ways we can never fully appreciate – and certainly cannot replicate. Reading a record or transcription of the presentation will never come close to how Isaiah or Jeremiah's audience feels when Isaiah rails against injustice, or when Jeremiah offers poignant words of consolation.

That said, we readers have a distinct advantage over the original audience. According to the Sages, prophecy was only written down if it was valuable for future generations. If so, we can assume that their words were arranged in a way that would best convey its message to future readers.

Thus, again, we ought to read the text on two planes: as if we were *listeners*, the prophet's original audience in Jerusalem's square, or bound in chains past Ramah, or at the royal sanctuary at Beit El. This requires not only imagination but also careful research about that period's society, commerce, and government. Alliteration, wordplay, the prophecy's meter, and even syntax, punctuated by the Masoretic trope marks, all contribute to bringing the prophet's words to life.

We should also approach the text as *readers*, seeking out the text's structure and textual juxtapositions that may have been lost on the original audience. As readers, we have the advantage of being able to consider the impact of a longer prophetic sequence, as here.

Amos's first two visions are clearly a couplet. They both begin with *"Ko hirani A-D-N-Y Elokim"*; they both describe how Amos sees God summoning agents for Israel's destruction. In both cases, Amos understands the vision's import and cries to God that Jacob is too "small" to withstand such punishment, and God accedes to Amos's petition.

The third and fourth visions are likewise a couplet. In both, Amos sees not God's action but rather an unusual image that carries certain wordplay; Amos is asked to identify the object, but does not seem to understand its meaning until God explains this wordplay; Amos has no chance to appeal, and the threat of Samaria's utter destruction remains.

The scope of destruction grows wider and more intense from vision to vision: from a locust plague, destructive but temporary; to a devastating conflagration with a harsh impact on agriculture; to the obliteration of all of the royal places ending with the death of the royal family; to the grievous finality of *keitz* – ending – with wailing and mourning in place of celebration.

This sequence is interrupted by a narrative scene in a surprising place – instead of coming after Amos presents all four visions or between the couplets, the scene is placed after the third vision.

As listeners, standing at Beit El, the reason for this interjection is obvious. The third vision specifically, explicitly, targets the royal family: as a result, Amaziah intervenes after this vision. Why, however, is this sequence maintained in the text? Why not keep the visions together and then report the narrative, or place the narrative between the two pairs of visions?

One answer is that Amos wants his future readers to experience the same sequence of events as his contemporary audience. Whether or not this is his goal, this particular sequence results in an even more powerful subtext.

Amos's opening sequence of oracles against the seven surrounding nations all maintain a pattern of "*Al shelosha pishei X, ve'al arba'a lo ashivenu,*" "For the three sins of nation X [I will forgive] but for the fourth one I will not forgive." This common biblical pattern of 3 + 1 thus becomes Amos's trademark. He even plays with this pattern when he reaches the eighth nation: Israel, his rhetorical audience. Instead of listing a fourth sin, he lists seven: *three + a fourth* become *three and **another** four*.

This pattern, delivered against Israel at the end of his opening set of oracles, effectively hovers over the entire book. Amos has already decried the worship at Beit El;[103] now, once again at Beit El, he delivers a three-plus-one series that concludes with the ominous news of Israel's end: *Ba hakeitz el ami Yisrael,* "The end has come to My nation, Israel."

103. 4:4 and 5:5.

Chapter 10

Summation and Judgment (8:4–10)

This next passage echoes Amos's first rebuke of his northern audience.

(ד) שִׁמְעוּ זֹאת הַשֹּׁאֲפִים אֶבְיוֹן וְלַשְׁבִּית ענוי[1] עֲנִיֵּי אָרֶץ: (ה) לֵאמֹר מָתַי יַעֲבֹר
הַחֹדֶשׁ וְנַשְׁבִּירָה שֶּׁבֶר וְהַשַּׁבָּת וְנִפְתְּחָה בָּר לְהַקְטִין אֵיפָה וּלְהַגְדִּיל שֶׁקֶל
וּלְעַוֵּת מֹאזְנֵי מִרְמָה: (ו) לִקְנוֹת בַּכֶּסֶף דַּלִּים וְאֶבְיוֹן בַּעֲבוּר נַעֲלָיִם וּמַפַּל בַּר
נַשְׁבִּיר: (ז) נִשְׁבַּע ה׳ בִּגְאוֹן יַעֲקֹב אִם אֶשְׁכַּח לָנֶצַח כָּל מַעֲשֵׂיהֶם: (ח) הַעַל
זֹאת לֹא תִרְגַּז הָאָרֶץ וְאָבַל כָּל יוֹשֵׁב בָּהּ וְעָלְתָה כָאֹר כֻּלָּהּ וְנִגְרְשָׁה ונשקה
וְנִשְׁקְעָה כִּיאוֹר מִצְרָיִם: (ט) וְהָיָה בַּיּוֹם הַהוּא נְאֻם אֲדֹנָי ה׳ וְהֵבֵאתִי
הַשֶּׁמֶשׁ בַּצָּהֳרָיִם וְהַחֲשַׁכְתִּי לָאָרֶץ בְּיוֹם אוֹר: (י) וְהָפַכְתִּי חַגֵּיכֶם לְאֵבֶל וְכָל
שִׁירֵיכֶם לְקִינָה וְהַעֲלֵיתִי עַל כָּל מָתְנַיִם שָׂק וְעַל כָּל רֹאשׁ קָרְחָה וְשַׂמְתִּיהָ
כְּאֵבֶל יָחִיד וְאַחֲרִיתָהּ כְּיוֹם מָר:

1. I have included the *ketiv* (the written form) in shadow and the *keri* (the way in which the word is read) in regular font.

> **4** Hear this, you who swallow up the needy, and destroy the poor of the land, **5** saying: "When will the new moon be past, that we may sell grain? And the sabbath, that we may trade wheat? Making the ephah small, and the shekel great, and falsifying the balances of deceit; **6** that we may buy the poor for silver, and the needy for a pair of shoes, and sell the refuse of the wheat?" **7** The Lord has sworn by the pride of Jacob: surely I will never forget any of their works. **8** Will the land not tremble for this, and everyone mourn who dwells in it? It will rise up wholly like the River; and it will be troubled and sink again, like the River of Egypt. **9** And it will come to pass in that day, says the Lord God, that I will cause the sun to go down at noon, and I will darken the earth in the clear day. **10** And I will turn your feasts into mourning, and all of your songs into lamentation. And I will bring up sackcloth on every waist, and baldness upon every head. And I will make it like mourning for an only son, and the end like a bitter day.

A CLARION CALL

4: Hear this

"Shimu zot" seems to be a contracted version of the standard *"Shimu et hadavar hazeh."* The lengthier introduction allows for slight pause before the prophet's voice storms in direct rebuke;[2] here, however, he gets straight to the point.

Perhaps this is yet another example of Amos's "three plus one" rhetorical strategy, with "one" being the final nail in the coffin. Amos's pronouncement here closely recalls his first rebuke of Israel in tone, meaning, and even lexicon; the most striking connection is his condemnation of "selling the needy for a pair of shoes."[3]

---

2. Note the first phrases in each of 3:1, 4:1, and 5:1, the three prior instances of *shim'u*.
3. The main discussions regarding word choice, allusions, etc., are found in chapter 2.

You who swallow up the needy

We have rendered *sho'afim* as in chapter 2 – "trample" or "swallow." Here, too, this portrays an upper class who exploit the downtrodden for their own indulgence. This verse seems to be a general statement followed by examples of how the destitute are trampled.

Most translations have: "you who swallow the needy," but JPS changes the tense: "you that *would* swallow the needy,"[4] which implies that the avaricious audience is still plotting how to exploit the poor but hasn't yet done so. Perhaps this translation is based on the rest of the verse: "when will the new moon be over" – they are biding their time until the perfect opportunity arises. If we read *Hasho'afim evyon velahashbit aniyei aretz* as the "topic sentence" or general statement (*kelal*) followed by the details (*perat*), this reading makes sense.

And destroy the poor of the land

Traditional commentators read *lashbit* as the causative *lehashbit,* to get rid of.[5] The plain meaning is that the wealthy merchants intend to rid the land of its poor. Can this be, given that the wealthy exploit them and use them to enrich themselves? Nonetheless R. Eliezer of Beaugency argues that the rich wish "to rid from among them the poor of the land, and to live alone in the land"; while Radak explains: "meaning, they intend to make them disappear from the world, as they take what is theirs deceitfully and unjustly."

Hakham and Paul understand *l(eh)ashbit* as equivalent to *hamashbitim*:

"You who trample the poor" / "You who rid the land of the poor."

These two clauses are either (1) parallel: the merchants are doing two things – trampling the poor as well as ridding the land of its poor; or (2) causative: they are doing one thing: trampling the poor, which will *lead* to the poor being gone from the land.

---

4. Similarly, ASV (American Standard Version). HNV (Hebrew Names Version) presents a similar phrase: "you who desire to swallow up the needy."
5. Ibn Ezra points out that the *pataḥ* under the *lamed* is there to indicate the missing *hei.* Rashi cites two examples of this phenomenon: II Kings 9:15 and Isaiah 23:11.

The second reading is more persuasive, given that this portrays the merchants as corrupt, but not intentionally self-destructive. If so, then the *vav* of *velashbit* should be understood as a *vav* explicative.

The word *aniyei* is written "*anvei,*" "the humble [of]." There are, however, various biblical examples where *anavim* is synonymous with *aniyim*, the poor.[6]

Some biblical dictionaries conflate the two, reading the word as "poor, humble, meek" but the two roots, although related, are distinct. Some modern English translations render the word as "needy" or "destitute"; some even translate it as "oppressed," reading the root as *a-n-y* (*ayin-nun-yod*).

Samaria's wealthy merchants are accused of trampling the needy; as a result, the humble/ poor/ oppressed will disappear from the land.

5: Saying

The word *leimor* appears at the beginning of a verse just nine times throughout Tanakh, including here. In five of the other eight cases,[7] the word is in the middle of a longer passage that, due to syntax and length, is divided into a separate verse just before *leimor*, so it isn't properly considered to be the beginning of a verse. Two further occurrences are explicatory:[8] "And He established it unto Jacob for a statute, to Israel for an everlasting covenant, saying (*leimor*): "Unto you will I give the land of Canaan, the lot of your inheritance."

The one instance that seems to mirror our usage is in Jeremiah:[9] "for the Lord has rejected the ones whom you did trust, and you will not prosper in them, *saying*: If a man divorces his wife, and she goes away from him, and becomes another man's wife, may he return to her again?" The commentators' attention to this phrase underscores how unusual its usage is in this verse.

---

6. For example, in Isaiah 11:4, *anvei aretz* is clearly "the poor of the land," as it stands in parallel with *dalim*, the destitute.
7. Isaiah 49:9; Jeremiah 25:5, 42:14; Zechariah 7:3; Psalms 71:11.
8. Psalms 105:10–11 (= I Chronicles 16:17–18).
9. Jeremiah 2:37–3:1; what makes this *leimor* glaring is that, serendipitously, it begins verse 1.

While few commentators discuss *leimor* as an opening word here, Paul suggests that Amos is quoting the merchants back to themselves, allowing their own words to serve as testimony to their greed.

SHABBAT, COMMERCE, AND EXPLOITATION

The merchants' greedy anticipation highlights a common problem with religious practice. Tanakh and rabbinic literature have many examples of religious selectiveness, wherein people are stringent about certain religious practices but show absolute disdain for others. Saul provides one of the earliest examples of such hypocrisy.[10] Isaiah rebukes people who bring offerings to the Temple, while their hands are "filled with blood."[11] Here, Amos calls out the duplicity of merchants who will not work on Shabbat yet are obsessed with strategizing how to cheat and exploit the poor.

While commerce on Shabbat was not always avoided in biblical times,[12] Amos's audience does seem to observe this prohibition; another reading, however, is that these scofflaws are also inherently disrespectful of Shabbat, but their markets are closed to public barter, so they have no choice but to wait. We will explore another possibility below.

5: When will the new moon be past, that we may sell grain?
And the sabbath, that we may trade wheat?

In biblical times, the New Moon – Rosh Ḥodesh – was a proper holiday, one of the occasions marked by the blast of the sacred cornets (Num. 10:10). In the early days of the monarchy, sacred feasts were held on the New Moon, known as "Ḥodesh."[13]

The pair "*ḥodesh veshabbat*" appears once in the historiographic books[14] and seven times in the literary prophets,[15] its pairing an indication

10. Compare I Samuel 13:12 with ibid. 22:19.
11. See, pointedly, Isaiah 58:6–7.
12. Jeremiah 17:21–27 and Nehemiah 10:32, 13:15–17.
13. I Samuel 20:18 ff.
14. II Kings 4:23.
15. Isaiah 1:13, 66:23; Ezekiel 45:17, 46:1, 3; Hosea 2:13; and our verse.

that Rosh Ḥodesh had a similar status to Shabbat. This explains the merchants' impatience with these days' restrictions of commerce.[16]

The Targum, however, reads both *ḥodesh* and *shabbat* within the context of a larger calendar cycle. Targum Yonatan understands *ḥodesh* as "month" (rather than "the New Month")[17] and *shabbat* as a reference to the *shemitta* year. Rashi and R. Joseph Kara cite the Targum and interpret accordingly; Ibn Ezra and Radak, without referencing the Targum, take a similar approach.

Rashi writes:

> "When will the *ḥodesh* pass…" – This is the anticipation; they await a time when the price of grain will go up and they will sell it to the poor [on credit] with interest and then will take their fields [for defaulting on their payments].
>
> "Will the *ḥodesh* pass (*ya'avor*)" – Yonatan [Targum] translates: When will the year be expanded (*titabber*) by adding the extra month [of Adar]; this phrase refers to "pushing off," per "The appointed time is pushed off (*he'evir*)" (Jeremiah 46:17); since they push off the offering of the Omer [brought on 16 Nissan and permitting the new grain to be sold and eaten] and the year is extended, the old grain becomes more expensive.
>
> "And the *shabbat*, that we may open up our grain stores" – When will *shemitta* [also called "*shabbat*," for example, Lev. 25:2] arrive, and the price of grain will go up and we will open up our grain stores.

Ibn Ezra also reads *ḥodesh* as month, but not as the extra month of a leap year: "Perhaps a year of famine will come, when *this month passes* and no

16. As read by Ibn Kaspi and R. Eliezer of Beaugency; Paul brings epigraphic evidence to the cessation of work on Rosh Ḥodesh; Hakham concurs.
17. This is in spite of the fact that the phrase *rosh ḥodesh* does not appear anywhere in *Nevi'im* or *Ketuvim*; the first day of the month is referred to as *ḥodesh,* although this term may also mean an entire thirty-day period, depending on context.

rain falls; then we will sell the grain at an inflated price." Rather, these merchants wait until food is in low supply and they can raise their prices.

Radak suggests that the merchants are waiting for the "harvest month" to pass, when the gifts to the poor such as gleanings are finished, after which they will keep them hanging for yet another "*shabbat*": "When that month passes and the poor come to buy, we will defer them by a week, saying: Let this week pass, and next week we will open up our grain stores and we will sell. We will keep pushing them off until the price of grain goes up and then we will sell as we wish."

There are, we see, two broad views of what *ḥodesh* and *shabbat* mean. One reads these as specific days when commerce is forbidden. The second perceives them as periods of time that affect the market to the extent that greedy merchants can inflate their prices and exploit the poor.

Amos quotes these merchants as using two relatively uncommon words for grain, *shever* and *bar*, rather than the more common *tevuah* or *dagan*.

The root *sh-b-r* in this sense appears a total of twenty-one times in Tanakh, fourteen of them in Genesis, all in the story of Joseph, "who gives the grain (*hamashbir*) to the people of the land."[18] The other noun used here, *bar*, appears just fourteen times in Tanakh in this sense – five times in the Joseph story. (In contrast, *dagan* appears forty times and *tevuah* forty-one.)

I believe that the use of these uncommon words for grain is an intentional allusion to the Joseph story; Amos's audience, after all, are identified as "*Beit Yosef*"[19] and "Ephraim."[20]

The Joseph story presents the image of a single powerful person controlling the harvested wheat, holding the keys to the grain stores, doling out portions to supplicating would-be buyers. Amos subtly evokes the north's ancestor, as if asking them: "You who open your storehouses of grain, are you as wise, fair, and selfless as your ancestor Joseph?" Do you aristocrats and merchants bring honor to the eponymous ancestor

18. Genesis 42:6.
19. See Ezekiel 37:15–28.
20. *Efrayim* appears nearly sixty times in the canon of the literary prophets. See, most poignantly, Jeremiah 31:6, 9, 18, and 20.

who gives you your claim to power, your distinct regional and political identity?

Furthermore, this association with Joseph may justify Ibn Ezra's above interpretation of *ḥodesh* – that the merchants are waiting until the poor are desperate so as to bleed them; a painful and ironic inversion of Joseph's plan regarding the years of plenty and famine in Egypt.

Making the ephah small, and the shekel great, and falsifying the balances of deceit

Dishonest measures and weights are the focus of several prohibitions with severe implications.[21] "Making the ephah (*eifa*: the dry weight measure) small" is straightforward: the merchants are accused of using smaller measures, so buyers pay for what they believe is an *eifa* of wheat, but they receive less.

"To make the shekel great" is also related to unfair business practices: they would use a heavier counterweight to measure out the silver owed them. Thus, if the price of an *eifa* of wheat was, for example, one *ma'a* of silver, the merchants would cheat the buyer in two ways: the measuring basket marked "*eifa*" would hold less than an *eifa*, but the scale for silver weighed more, so the buyer would have to put more than a *ma'a* of silver there.

Mozenei mirma appears four other times in Tanakh;[22] this was evidently a widespread problem in Samaria during Jeroboam II's reign.

6: That we may buy the poor for silver, and the needy for a pair of shoes

This is a paraphrase of Amos 2:6:

---

21. Leviticus 19:35–36; Deuteronomy 25:13–16, juxtaposed to the obligation to remember Amalek; see also Rashi at Deuteronomy 25:17.
22. Twice vilified in Prov. 11:1, 20:23; the other mentions are in prophetic rhetoric from our period, all directed at Samaria – Micah 6:9–16; Hosea 12:8; and our verse.

> Because they sell the righteous for silver,
> And the needy for [the price of] a pair of shoes (2:6)

The parallel verses share five identical words (*hasho'afim, evyon, eretz, dalim, bakesef*); one pair *written* identically, although the *keri* in chapter 8 differs (*aniyei, anavim*); and one identical phrase (*ba'avur na'alayim*). The *mikhram* of the first oracle is neatly matched by *liknot*. The word *hasho'afim* appears exclusively in these two passages in Tanakh, as does the phrase *ba'avur na'alayim*. Although the virtually synonymous *dal, evyon,* and *ani/anav* appear many times throughout Tanakh, the specific combination of these three terms further connects the two passages.

The first passage is a direct indictment of Israel's offense; this second passage is in fact presented as the merchants' corrupt intentions. Here, it is not clear that they consciously plan this barter of humans, but their actions do set the destruction of the economy and society into motion.

I believe that Amos echoes this indictment here to generate the same *heptad of accusation* employed in his first sequences of oracles, those against the nations. There, Amos pronounces seven offenses, followed by seven of God's kindnesses, followed by seven punishments. The parallel accusation here evokes this seven-link chain.

And sell the refuse of the wheat

Amos continues to use unusual words – *mappal* appears in just one other place in Tanakh – in Job, where it describes the scales of the mighty Leviathan (Job 41:15):

> ***Mappelei*** *vesaro daveiku*
> *Yatzuk alav bal yimmot*
> The flakes of his flesh are joined together.
> They are firm upon him; they cannot be moved.

There, Rashbam explains *mappelei* as either "the falling off (*nefilat*) of pieces [of its flesh]," or, based on the talmudic phrase *pela'ei peluyei,* "dents" or "splits" – that is, "cracked." This connotes scales, flakes – in the case of grain, it presumably refers to parts of grain that have fallen off.

Rashi, following Targum, explains that the merchants plot to sell "the waste that fell from the wheat in the sifter… at an inflated price." Similarly, Ibn Ezra and Radak understand *mappal* as equivalent to the meaning in Job – the coarse flakes that have fallen away.

Radak, in a slightly milder reading, explains that when the price of wheat rises, the poor are willing to buy the coarse bran that is usually fed to animals. There is no actual deception, but the poor are exploited to the point where they can only afford food that is barely fit for human consumption.

R. Eliezer of Beaugency, in contrast, understands *mappal bar* as the empty larder in their houses: the merchants say, "we can charge a steep price because they are desperate – they have no wheat at home." This reading is consistent with the allusion to Joseph, and maintains the difference between their venal exploitation and Joseph's thoughtful and compassionate salvation of Egypt.

One final note on this phrase. As Paul points out, ending the indictment with a mention of *bar* and the verb *nashbir* creates an *inclusio*: it began with the merchants plotting "*venashbira shever… veniftecha bar*," and ends, in chiastic fashion, with the phrase "*mappal bar nashbir*."

7: The Lord has sworn by the pride of Jacob

Amos has already used this rhetorical device twice;[23] this seems to be a trademark of his, as he is the only prophet to use it more than once[24] until Jeremiah.[25]

Paul reads this phrase as connected to 6:8 – the people's arrogant pride in their palaces, in their own power – and perceives this phrase as a deliberately caustic preface to their punishment. God swears by the people's brazen arrogance:

23. 4:2, 6:8.
24. Isaiah 62:8 dates from the period of *Shivat Tziyon*.
25. Another example of Jeremiah's heavy reliance on Amos's rhetorical style.

Surely I will never forget any of their works

A biblical oath usually has three components: the "oath-form," such as "*Bi nishbati,*" "*Ḥai Hashem,*" or the like; the second, most central component is the conditional statement introduced with the particle *im* or *im lo*; the third and final element is the apodosis – the curse one must accept if their words prove false – that is, if the condition is not fulfilled.

This apodosis, however, is generally omitted – perhaps because the declarant does not want to explicitly voice such a curse. Another possibility is that the ellipsis accomplishes far more than an explicitly stated curse. By leaving the imprecation unstated, the terror of the unsaid may outweigh the potential horror of any actual image.

Park, in contrast, suggests that the *im/im lo* components should be read as rhetorical questions.[26] For example, when God pronounces that Israel must wander for forty years, He takes this oath:

> Yet indeed, *as I live* [oath-form]… for all of those men… and have not listened to My voice… *if they will see the Land which I swore to their fathers…* (Num. 14:21–23)

We generally understand the phrase "*im yiru et ha'aretz*" as the protasis: "If they do see the Land," and the apodosis: "such and such terrible thing will happen to Me" as elided. Park prefers to read the conditional clause as a rhetorical question, with nothing elided; here, she would translate:

> As I live (oath), regarding these men… will they see the Land which I swore to their fathers…?

This theory, if accepted, would impact our understanding of many key biblical passages, and is especially compelling when this formula is used by God. After all, does an oath taken by God indicate His commitment to suffering the consequences if His words do not come true? A broader question might be posed here: Why does God express Himself in oaths at all? A person typically swears to gain credibility – something which

26. Grace J. Park, "Polar *'im* in Oaths and the Question of Literacy in Lachish 3," *Zeitschrift für Die Alttestamentliche Wissenschaft* 125, no. 3: 463–478.

makes no sense in the context of God speaking with people, be they His loyalists,[27] His nation,[28] an enemy nation,[29] or the entire world.[30]

Here we can apply R. Yishmael's principle of hermeneutics: "The Torah speaks in human language." Not only does the Bible utilize anthropomorphism (for example, "God's outstretched arm") and anthropopathism ("God was jealous") to generate some level of accessibility to God, it also uses what we might coin *anthropologos*: God's words are presented as human speech. Even the notion of God's "speech" may be a borrowed term; after all, we don't know if prophets have any auditory experience when receiving prophecy, yet the prophet responds to God, "Your servant is listening" (I Sam. 3:9). In the same way, God utilizes various levels of intensity of speech to denote increasing severity or commitment. A divine decree is stronger than a divine promise; a divine oath is yet stronger; a divine covenant tops them all.

Just as God's "oath" expresses a strong commitment that cannot be revoked, the elided consequence simply follows oath conventions – not that we would ever imagine a real imprecation there.

Here, God "swears" that He will never forget the aristocracy and merchant class's corruption.

8: Will the land not tremble for this?

The opening *hei* here is the rhetorical *hei,* which turns the phrase into a question. Scholars unanimously understand *zot* as the merchants' greed and exploitation of the poor, as described in verses 4–6. Why, however, is the singular *zot* used, rather than the plural *eileh,* as is more common when referring to multiple offenses?[31] This is the only instance of *ha'al zot* in the canon.

One approach is somewhat consistent with the mainstream interpretive strategy. Rashi comments: "Is *this sin* (*avon zeh*) not enough

27. Genesis 26:3.
28. Deuteronomy 31:23.
29. Isaiah 14:24.
30. Isaiah 54:9.
31. Jeremiah 5:9, 29; 9:8; see also Isaiah 57:6, 64:11.

to cause the land to be destroyed?" Similarly, and perhaps with more accurate use of the feminine, Radak states: "Will the land not tremble/quake for *this evil* (*hara'a hazot*)?" Both are attuned to this issue, and thus condense the merchants' evil plans into one consummate evil. This is, however, inconsistent with the passages cited above, in which the prophet lists several manifestations of one crime[32] and yet refers to them with the plural *eileh*.

Perhaps *zot* here refers not to the offenses, but rather to the *oath* that introduces the punishment. God has sworn that He will not forget their deeds – is that terrifying and ominous oath not enough to shake the earth? This also explains the use of the feminine *zot* (in gender agreement with *shevuah*).

Tirgaz Ha'aretz

The root *r-g-z* appears over fifty times in Tanakh, meaning "quake"[33] or, less frequently, "anger."[34] The combination of *rogez* and *eretz* occasionally creates the impression of an earthquake, beginning with the confusion that shakes the Philistine camp when Saul's son Jonathan attacks (I Sam. 14:15). The image of the earth quaking expresses the pandemonium that rages in the military camp. From a physical and auditory perspective, the noise and tumult seem to have the same effect as an earthquake; moreover, the anger, confusion, and terror that tears through the camp is aptly conveyed through the word *rogez*.[35] Thus the phrase "*vatirgaz ha'aretz*" is a vivid merging of the external perception and the internal reality.

This sense is also conveyed in Isaiah 13:13, even though it doesn't directly use *rogez* with *eretz*:

> Therefore I will make the heavens to *tremble* (*argiz*) and the *earth* (*ha'aretz*) will be shaken out of its place at the wrath of the Lord of Hosts and for the day of His fierce anger.

---

32. In Jeremiah 9:8, regarding dishonesty.
33. For example, Exodus 15:14.
34. For example, I Samuel 28:15.
35. See, respectively, II Kings 19:28 (=Isaiah 37:29); Psalms 99:1; and Job 3:26.

The earth shakes from God's anger – hence both senses of *rogez*: *geo* and *theo.*

As noted, this phrase employs the rhetorical *hei.* This further takes us back to his opening oracle against Israel, his series of riddles we called "the inevitability of prophecy" (3:3–8), which culminates in this rhetorical question:

> *Aryei sha'ag,* ***mi lo*** *yira?*
> *A-D-N-Y Elokim dibber,* ***mi lo*** *yinavei*?
> The lion has roared, who can but fear?
> The Lord God has spoken, who can but prophesy?

And everyone mourn who dwells in it?

Amos uses personal mourning, both in feeling and in ritual, as the reference point for the national mood after the impending destruction; he relies on an immanent awareness of mourning among his listeners and uses it to convey the nation's fate.

Avelut in Prophetic Oratory

Evel (mourn, mourning) both as noun and verb, appears thirty-two times in prophetic rhetoric. Before comparing Amos's use with that of his fellows and literary disciples, it is of interest to note how this use plays out in Isaiah. Of the ten instances in Isaiah, the first five refer to a specific group (the fishermen in 19:8), to the doorways of homes whose owners have been killed (3:26), to the agricultural yield (the wine in 24:7), or to the land itself (24:4, 33:9). In other words (with the exception of the fishermen), *people* don't mourn, *things* do. This stands in stark contrast with the five instances in the last eleven chapters of Isaiah (which seem to be addressed to listeners in the beginning of the Second Temple era), where the mourners are people – not specific guilds but the people who mourn the loss of Jerusalem and, presumably, can now rejoice in her rebuilding.[36] In much the same way, Jerimiah's uses of *avelut* overwhelmingly uses the metaphoric mode – the land, the maiden,

36. Isaiah 57:18, 60:20, 61:2, 61:3 [twice], 66:10.

mourning – until his last use of the word. In his beautiful vision of *Shivat Tziyon*, he prophesies:

> Then shall the maiden rejoice in the dance and the young men and the old together. For I will turn their *mourning* into joy and will comfort them and make them rejoice from their sorrow. (Jer. 31:12)

We get the sense that until the destruction of Jerusalem in 586 BCE, *avelut* was seen as the province of the individual and provided an imagery that could be employed with land, crops, houses, and so forth to express the aftermath of devastation. With the anticipation of a return to Jerusalem on the part of a mourning nation, *avelut* became much more "real," and the models slipped away in favor of speaking to a bereaved people and comforting them in the midst of their national mourning.

In Hosea, again the land mourns (4:3) but the devotees of Ba'al are also depicted as mourning (10:5). In Yoel, in an echo of Hosea, the land mourns (1:10) but the *kohanim* of the *Mikdash* also mourn (1:9) – seemingly because of the paucity of gifts being brought as offerings, decreasing their food supplies.[37] Besides Amos, there is one more use of *evel* in the oratory of the prophets. In his opening prophecy, Micha (1:9) describes *himself* as walking around disheveled, "mourning like the ostriches" in response to the anticipated destruction of Shomeron at the hands of the Assyrians. We see that in the early era of prophecy, *avelut* was not by and large used (at least within oratory) in reference to mourning as we know it; rather, it was a poetic image used to evoke scenes of devastation and ruin and the accompanying solitude (for example, the imagery of Jerusalem in Lamentations 1).

Here is where Amos seems to stand out with his rhetorical bravery and brilliance. Alone among his contemporaries, he references *evel* as the personal and communal experience of mourning, without resorting to the imagery of his colleagues.

The first time that Amos invokes "mourning" is in his anthemic opening:

---

37. See Radak on Yoel 1:10.

> He would say: "The Lord roars from Zion, and from Jerusalem he sends forth His voice. The pastures of the shepherds will become parched (*avel*), and the top of the Carmel will wither. (1:2)

In an inversion of the usage of Isaiah, Hosea, and Yoel, Amos uses "mourning" as a metaphor for the withered land.

In 5:16, Amos invokes a call for public mourning, summoning the farmer (who, we would expect, would be rejoicing at his harvest) to come and mourn: *Vekar'u ikar el evel*, "They shall call the farmer to mourning."

In the verse that comes two verses after ours, Amos uses *evel* twice:

> And I will turn your feasts into *mourning* (*evel*), and all of your songs into lamentation. And I will bring up sackcloth on every waist, and baldness upon every head. And I will make it like *mourning* (*evel*) for an only son, and the end like a bitter day. (8:10)

Here, Amos uses personal mourning, both in feeling and in ritual, as the reference point for the national mood after the impending destruction. Again, he relies on a very real awareness of mourning among his listeners and uses it to convey the fate of the nation.

His final mention brings together the beginning of the book and our verse:

> For A-D-N-Y, the God of Hosts, is He that touches the land and it melts and all that dwell there *mourn* (*ve'avelu*); and it rises up wholly like the River, and sinks again, like the River of Egypt. (9:5)

BRINGING IT ALL TOGETHER

As mentioned, the earthquake motif and mourning in this line hark back to Amos's anthemic opening line. Together with the image of selling the needy for a pair of shoes and the pointed use of rhetorical questions, this prophecy forms an *inclusio* with Amos's opening prophecy, coming full circle in what proves to be a false ending.

Amos has more in store for us as he presents his vision of the end of days.

8: It will rise up wholly like the River

The previous clause indicates that the subject here is the Land. We can only presume that the image of the Nile overflowing its banks and then receding was known to the people even then.

The picture of the earth rising up in this manner is frightening – and certainly relatable for those who have lived through powerful earthquakes.

Most scholars assume that *kha'or* is some version (variant or scribal error) of *ki'or* ("like the River"). Rashi and R. Joseph Kara suggest that it means "light" and refers to a cloud – as the latter explains, a dark cloud that carries heavy amounts of rainwater.

And it will be troubled and sink again

Nigresha, based on the root *g-r-sh,* is used elsewhere to refer to the "washing away" of mud and detritus in a storm.[38]

Like the River of Egypt

This assumes, safely, that the people are familiar with the cycles of the Nile. Egypt had, after all, been a regional superpower for millennia.

9: And it will come to pass in that day, says the Lord God, that I will cause the sun to go down at noon, and I will darken the earth in the clear day

It is tempting to read this passage locally, as a poetic (or literal) depiction of what will happen on the day of the earthquake. Hakham indeed suggests that the darkening day is a poetic description of how an earthquake stirs up the earth's dust and dirt and darkens the sky. He also

38. Isaiah 57:20.

proposes a metaphorical meaning based on a midrash also mentioned by others, below.

Rashi and R. Kara, based on this midrash,[39] explain that "sun" refers to the Davidic dynasty.[40] The midday sunset represents the people's intense sense of loss at the passing of their generation's greatest luminary. In classic homiletic fashion, this is linked to the death of a popular, righteous king: Josiah on the battlefield at Megiddo.

This reading, however, is problematic. The audience here is Israelite, not Judean; we are witness to the north's enmity toward the south.[41] Why would Amos warn the audience at Beit El about the downfall of the Judean dynasty a century in the future? Furthermore, why would it be introduced with the momentous "*Vehaya bayom hahu*"? Rather, as Hakham suggests, this refers to the day of the great earthquake.

Radak understands *bayom hahu*, the day of the earthquake, as "the day of the land's destruction," explaining that a midday sunset is a metaphor for great suffering. He supports this with a passage from Micah: "It will be dark for you, that you will not divine; *and the sun will go down upon the prophets*, and the day will be black over them" (3:6).

Abravanel also interprets "that day" as the day of destruction foretold in the previous verse, but he interprets the midday sunset as a surprising and immediate destruction, without warning. He explains "clear day" (*yom or*) thus: the people will be incapable of explaining their downfall as anything but God's hand, just as one cannot explain how a day became dark with clouds when the sky had been cloudless.

Vehaya Bayom Hahu

This exact phrase appears thirty-two times in Tanakh, all in prophetic literature. The first thirteen are within the first twenty-seven chapters of Isaiah, which seems to date this phrase's origin to the seventh or eighth century BCE. In fact, the seven occurrences in Zechariah take place in

---

39. Moed Katan 25b.
40. Per Psalms 89:37–38.
41. See Amaziah's words to Amos in 7:12–13.

its last six chapters, which are commonly ascribed to an earlier prophet closer to Amos's time.[42]

The phrase is mostly used in an eschatological context (as in Isaiah,[43] Ezekiel,[44] Zechariah[45]); although it sometimes conveys non-eschatological destruction (as in the first instance in Jeremiah,[46] Hosea, and Zephaniah[47]). Although the phrase usually introduces destruction, it sometimes refers to visions of future redemption and an idyllic, perfect world (see Isaiah 10–11, the later occurrences in Hosea, and the surreal imagery in Joel[48]).

I propose that Amos, the brilliant rhetorician, introduced this powerful phrase, although its original meaning varied slightly from how it eventually came to be used. *Vehaya bayom hahu* portends a looming apocalypse that brings on the eschaton – the "end of days." Amos's eschatological scene begins properly in the next chapter with the equally ominous phrase *hinei yamim ba'im*. First there is "that day," the day of the earthquake, the day of the sun setting at midday, the day of great mourning...to be followed by "days that are coming," the eschaton, the end of days.

Here, the phrase *"vehaya bayom hahu"* seems to refer back to Amos's earlier prophecy against those who would "desire the day of the Lord" (5:18) – on this day, too, the sun sets at midday; indeed, as the verse concludes, the day is "darkness and not light."

This is a further illustration of Amos's powerful rhetorical influence. This is the first instance of the phrase *"vehaya bayom hahu"* and here it alludes to *Yom Hashem*. The phrase's association with the eschaton renders it into a synonym for *Yom Hashem*, which later prophets then use in that sense.

42. See Ze'ev Yabetz, *Toledot Yisrael*, vol. 2 (Jerusalem-Tel Aviv: 1927), 189 ff. and his support of Berthold's proposal.
43. 7:18, 21, 22; 10:20, 27; 11:10–11; 17:4; 22:2; 23:15; 24:21; 27:12–13.
44. All in chapters 38–39.
45. Zechariah 12:3, 9; 13:2, 4; 14:6, 7, 13 – note 14:9!
46. Jeremiah 4:9.
47. Zephaniah 1:10.
48. Joel 4:18–19.

10: And I will turn your feasts into mourning

The root *h-f-kh* expresses a complete turnaround, from one extreme to its opposite. It is used to describe utter destruction;[49] a sudden, surprising shift during a battle;[50] an extreme physical change, such as the complete whiteness of *tzara'at* (skin-blight);[51] or a change of heart, such as Pharaoh's sudden regret at letting the Israelites go:

> When the king of Egypt was told that the people had fled, the mind of Pharaoh and his servants *was turned* (*vayeihafeikh*) against the people, And they said, "What is this we have done, that we have let Israel go from serving us?"[52]

A variation of this change of attitude is a change of mood, a deep emotional shift from one state to its opposite. The penultimate verse of Psalm 30 is a well-known example:

> You have *turned* (*hafakhta*) my mourning into dancing for me.

As we see in Ecclesiastes,[53] the opposite of *mispeid* (mourning) is *rekod* or *maḥol* (dancing).

We can now appreciate the sense of cataclysmic upheaval Amos pronounces here: celebrations and festivities, all anticipated with great excitement, will be turned to ashes and sackcloth. Without warning, the people will be swept from one extreme to the other.

This verse implies that *ḥag* and *evel* are opposites. Although the most accurate translation of *evel* is "mourning," we usually read that word as a state of mind (or heart), not in its formal ritualistic sense. Here, however, as a foil to *ḥag*, *evel* may be read as a formal or public expression of mourning; this interpretation is supported by the Midrash.[54]

49. For example, Genesis 19:25; Jonah 3:4, Haggai 2:22; see also Judges 20:39–41.
50. Chiefly in Joshua, Kings, and Chronicles.
51. Famously, Jeremiah 13:23.
52. Exodus 14:5; see also Psalms 105:25.
53. "A time for mourning and a time for dance" (Eccl. 3:4); the pairs in this passage of twenty-eight are opposites.
54. Moed Katan 20a; Y. Moed Katan 3:5.

Jeremiah once again draws on Amos's rhetoric to describe an era of redemption (31:12):

> Then shall the maidens rejoice in the dance, and the young men and the old shall be merry. I will *turn* (*vehafakhti*) their mourning into joy, I will comfort them, and give them gladness for sorrow.

And all your songs into lamentation

Kina, its unique metrical form, and professional *mekonenot* are discussed above in the context of chapter 5 (v. 1).

Just as *ḥag* will turn into a period of mourning, festive songs will turn into dirges; just as festivity is elevated by *shira*, *evel* is intensified by *kina*.

And I will bring up sackcloth on every waist

The custom of donning sackcloth is well documented in Tanakh and appears in a number of popular narratives. For example, Jacob is the first to don *sak*, in mourning for Joseph,[55] and David directs his courtiers to wear *sak* to demonstrate their mourning for Avner.[56]

It is also worn as an expression of contrition and as part of the process of *teshuva*. The king of Nineveh commands his people to don sackcloth in response to Jonah's prophecy;[57] Ahab puts on sackcloth when Elijah confronts him about Nabot's murder[58] (and God accepts this repentance).

Here, sackcloth seems to be an expression of mourning.

---

55. Genesis 37:34. *Sak* is also occasionally used to describe a bag taken with food for travel, for instance in Joshua 9. Perhaps this is deliberately chosen to denote the grain-bags of Joseph's brothers in Genesis 42 (as opposed to the expected *amtaḥat*), to allude to the *sak* worn by their father at the time.
56. II Samuel 3:13
57. Jonah 3:5, 6, 8.
58. I Kings 21:27.

And baldness upon every head

This is also a well-attested expression of mourning.[59]

And I will make it like mourning for an only son

This is the widely accepted translation of *evel yaḥid*,[60] based on Zechariah 12:10:

> They will lament for him as one laments for a *yaḥid*, and there will be a bitter cry for him like the bitter cry for a firstborn.

The explicative phrase "for a firstborn" (*al habekhor*) clarifies that the *yaḥid* is an only son. The death of a child is certainly a deep tragedy; the death of a parent's only child infinitely more so.

And the end like a bitter day

The question is whether this last phrase is a further expression of helpless sadness or a parallel phrase to its antecedent.

Radak favors the latter and explains that the mourning for an only son is the bitterest of days.

R. Eliezer of Beaugency, however, reads this as a further state of desperation. This mourning – as bitter as a parent's grief for their only child – will not come to an end, but rather will continue with lingering sorrow.

Paul notes that the *kaf* (*keyom mar*) is not a *kaf* of analogy, but rather one of emphasis: a "truly bitter day."[61]

The end is coming to Samaria, and it will be a truly bitter day.

---

59. Isaiah 22:12; also Jeremiah 48:37; there may also be an allusion to this custom found in Deuteronomy 14:1.
60. See the parallel verse at Jeremiah 6:26.
61. Cf. Radak at Genesis 25:31.

Chapter 11

Eschaton – End of Days (8:11–9:12)

THE COMING FAMINE (8:11–14)

(יא) הִנֵּה יָמִים בָּאִים נְאֻם אֲדֹנָי ה׳ וְהִשְׁלַחְתִּי רָעָב בָּאָרֶץ לֹא רָעָב לַלֶּחֶם
וְלֹא צָמָא לַמַּיִם כִּי אִם לִשְׁמֹעַ אֵת דִּבְרֵי ה׳: (יב) וְנָעוּ מִיָּם עַד יָם וּמִצָּפוֹן וְעַד
מִזְרָח יְשׁוֹטְטוּ לְבַקֵּשׁ אֶת דְּבַר ה׳ וְלֹא יִמְצָאוּ: (יג) בַּיּוֹם הַהוּא תִּתְעַלַּפְנָה
הַבְּתוּלֹת הַיָּפוֹת וְהַבַּחוּרִים בַּצָּמָא: (יד) הַנִּשְׁבָּעִים בְּאַשְׁמַת שֹׁמְרוֹן וְאָמְרוּ
חֵי אֱלֹהֶיךָ דָּן וְחֵי דֶּרֶךְ בְּאֵר שָׁבַע וְנָפְלוּ וְלֹא יָקוּמוּ עוֹד:

11 Behold, the days are coming says the Lord God, that I will send
a famine in the land. Not a famine for bread, nor a thirst for water,
but of hearing the words of the Lord. 12 They will wander from
sea to sea, and from the north to the east; they will run to and
fro to seek the word of the Lord, and they will not find it. 13 On
that day, the fair maidens and the young men will faint for thirst.
14 Those that swear by the sin of Samaria, and say: "As your god,
O Dan, lives," and "As the way of Be'er Sheva lives," but they will
fall down and not get up again.

11: Behold, the days are coming

Although the ominous introduction *"Hinei yamim ba'im" sometimes* refers to a contextually anticipated time,[1] its connotations here are primarily eschatological: at one point in the future, this unique "famine" will come.

Jeremiah is the only other prophet who uses this phrase, and he does so fifteen times. Many of his visions introduced with this phrase are promising, while others are threatening; all are eschatological.

The Sages largely read this prophecy in that sense; they occasionally homiletically interpreted it as an allusion to their own time.[2] Curiously, the Midrash also perceives this prophecy as a literal famine for food, overriding the metaphor,[3] although the *Rishonim* largely overlook this interpretive tradition.

Rashi suggests that the reason for the thirst will be that *ruaḥ hakodesh,* prophecy, will have left the people – he thus seems to read this passage as a prophecy that had been realized before the talmudic era.

R. Joseph Kara more explicitly points to the famine as the lack of prophecy at the end of the First Commonwealth.

Ibn Ezra notes Amos's deliberate irony: Amaziah orders him *not* to prophesy, and Amos now speaks of a time when prophecy will cease.

In sum, most *Rishonim* hold that Amos's prophecy will be fulfilled soon after his own time, with the end of prophecy. The Midrash, in contrast, reads this as a vision of the distant future. Might we be so bold as to suggest that it may point to the existential crisis that grips modern humanity?

I believe that this text is intentionally ambiguous and thus allows for both readings. To Amos's immediate audience, it heralds the end of prophecy. To its eternal audience, the Jewish people over the generations, it speaks of one potential end-of-days scenario.

---

1. I Samuel 2:31; Amos 4:2.
2. Tosefta Eduyot 1:1; see the expansion of this passage in Shabbat 138b.
3. Theodor-Albeck, *Genesis Rabba,* par. 40 and par. 64; Lerner, *Ruth Rabbah,* par. 1.

Says the Lord God

We have already noted Amos's repeated use of *ne'um Hashem* and explained that this may reflect Amos's insecurity. Given his lack of prophetic training (*"Lo navi anokhi velo ven navi,"*) and, perhaps, the fact that he operates in a region where his dialect and accent are considered foreign and possibly inferior, he feels a need to emphasize that his words are the words of God – hence his repeated use of *ne'um Hashem*.

The Midrash hints to this:[4]

> R. Azaria, quoting R. Judah ben R. Simon, expounded the verse ["You love righteousness and hate wickedness. Therefore God, your God, has anointed you with the oil of gladness above your fellows"[5]] as referring to Isaiah.
>
> Isaiah said: I was strolling[6] in my study house and I heard the voice of the Holy One, who is blessed, saying: "Whom shall I send and who will go for us?"[7] I sent Micah and they were hitting him on the cheek, as it says: "With a rod they strike upon the cheek."[8] I sent Amos and they were calling him *pesilusa*.[9] They said: Doesn't God have anyone else to place his Divine Presence upon than this tongueless man, a *pesilusa*?
>
> R. Pinchas observed: Why was his name Amos? Because he was weighed down (*amus*) by his tongue.

This midrash, which discusses Isaiah's readiness to fulfill God's mission, also illuminates Amos's character. While there is no textual indication of any such speech defect, perhaps this characterization was extrapolated from the intense frequency of *ne'um Hashem*, along with the explicit awareness of Amos's "foreignness" to his northern audience.

---

4. Margoulies, *Vayikra Rabba*, vol. 1, 197; compare *Pesikta deRav Kahanah* 16:4.
5. Psalms 45:8.
6. See Margoulies, *Vayikra Rabba*, 197, footnote to line 6.
7. Isaiah 6:8.
8. Micah 4:14.
9. One unable to pronounce certain letters; stammerer (Jastrow).

That I will send a famine in the land

Famine is one of the most common motifs of sin and punishment in the ancient world, and it is usually presented as an expression of God's providence. Here, God's hand is made even more explicit than usual: this is one of only two instances where a prophet specifies that God will "send" a famine.[10]

Not a famine for bread

Here, Amos startles his audience with a surprising twist. A "bread-and-water" famine is a dreaded cataclysm that decimates kingdoms and alters the course of history. The next phrase, unprecedented in the prophetic canon, turns things on their head. Soon, the very thing the people *have been avoiding* will become the thing they crave as desperately as their daily bread.

Note that *leḥem* in Tanakh essentially means "food";[11] as the staple food of the ancient Near East in that period, bread, too, was called *leḥem,* and it is not always clear if *leḥem* means "food" in general, or the more specific "bread." Here, given that biblical famines are associated with failure of the grain crop, the image is more powerful if *leḥem* here is understood to refer to bread.

Nor a thirst for water

Although "thirst" is not part of the original threat – just *ra'av,* famine – famines are usually the result of a drought, which implies that there is also a lack of water.

But of hearing the words of the Lord

The biblical *ki* often means "rather."[12]

10. The other is Ezekiel 14:13.
11. See Numbers 28:2; Psalms 147:9; I Samuel 14:24, 43–44.
12. For example, Deuteronomy 21:17.

Note the gapping here – the full intent of the phrase is: *ki im ra'av vetzama lishmoa et divrei Hashem.* There may be another consideration at play here. By isolating what the people *will* desire, he subtly promotes the image of people listening to God's word without the painful association of famine and thirst, thus making this dream more appealing to his audience.

12: They will wander from sea to sea

Who will wander and who will run to and fro? Perhaps the undefined subject implies general movement: everyone will wander; all will run to and fro, seeking God's word. However, the next verse may help define the referent.

The root *n-v-a* (translated here as "wander") first appears in Cain's punishment of exile for killing his brother (Gen. 4:12); he is not banished anywhere specific – the emphasis is on his displacement. In some cases, the verb expresses wild movement.[13] This "wandering" is not aimless, but rather desperate, frantic, frenzied: they are desperate to find God's word.

And from the north to the east

In prophetic literature, "north" often refers to Mesopotamia.[14] If so, does "east" allude to Jordan? A more reasonable approach is that these refer to the Land's borders; seeking God's word therein is more logical. This, in turn, helps clarify the previous clause "from sea to sea." Ibn Ezra explains:

> They will travel from the Reed Sea, which is south of the Land of Israel, to the Great (Mediterranean) Sea at the setting of the sun (i.e., west).

---

13. Psalms 107:27; more pointedly at Isaiah 24:20.
14. Jeremiah 1:13–15.

Radak concurs and adds:

> [Amos] mentions the four directions; behold, in the Land of Israel they will not find words of prophecy, all the more so outside of the Land during days of exile.

There are, however, several problems with understanding one of the "seas" as the Reed Sea, *Yam Suf*. First, it is never referenced as one of Israel's borders;[15] second, the south is not typically mentioned as a direction of wandering (Egypt, to the south, is usually mentioned by name).[16] The Psalmist, when presenting a picture of the ingathered, *omits* the south and mentions the west twice.[17] Finally, and most significantly, the phrase *miyam ad yam* appears twice elsewhere, both times a metaphor for "everywhere" rather than referring to a specific body of water: "He will rule from sea to sea and from the river until the ends of the earth" (Ps. 72:8). Commentators debate whether this psalm refers to Solomon's rule or the Messianic age.

The other mention of *miyam ad yam* seems to refer to the latter:

> Rejoice greatly, O daughter of Zion! Shout aloud, O daughter of Jerusalem! Lo, your king comes to you; triumphant and victorious is he,
> ...His dominion shall be from sea to sea (*miyam ad yam*),
> And from the river to the ends of the earth. (Zech. 9:9–10)

Weiss cites Zeligman's suggestion that the phrase "*miyam ad yam uminahar ad afsei aretz*" may be Mesopotamian in origin, meaning "to the four corners of the earth."[18] This does seem to be the most reasonable reading of our text: that people will search for God's word *everywhere*.

---

15. The southern border (in the expanded version of Gen. 15) is the "River of Egypt," regarding which there are a number of well-respected opinions (the Nile Delta, Wadi El-Arish among others).
16. For example, Isaiah 27:13.
17. Psalms 107:2–3.
18. Meir Weiss, *The Bible and Modern Literary Theory* [Heb., *HaMikra Kidmuto*] (Jerusalem: 1987), 180–186.

They will run to and fro to seek the word of the Lord, and they will not find it

The verb *shotet* is parallel to *noa,* but the words are not synonymous. The root *sh-t-t,* which appears seventeen times in Tanakh, means "search high and low."[19] They will be desperate, and they will search high and low – they will *search* for God, but they will not *find* him. This verb pair first appears in this sense in the hopeful turn of Moses's warning of exile (Deut. 4:39). Reading our vision against the backdrop of Moses's words, do those who seek God fail to find Him because they are not seeking Him with all their might? Or, as Hosea hints (10:6), is the situation even worse than Moses envisioned – has God abandoned the people, never to be found no matter how desperately they seek Him?

13: In that day, the fair maidens and the young men will faint for thirst

The root *'a-l-p* appears six times in Tanakh. Its basic meaning is "to be completely covered," or, as BDB defines the root, "being so covered as to have one's senses obscured" – that is, "faint."

Although this verb refers to both young women and men, it takes on the feminine conjugation, *titalafna* (as opposed to *yitalefu*) – despite the general rule in Hebrew grammar that a mixed group assumes the masculine conjugation. The simple explanation is that here, *betulot* are mentioned first, and the verb is forward-gapped to apply to the young men as well; a deeper interpretation, as we will see below, is that the image of young women suffering is more painful.

The biblical pairing of *baḥur* (young man) and *betula* ("maiden") is common enough;[20] the tragedy of exile and defeat is sometimes underscored with the mention of how vital, beautiful young people with their whole lives ahead of them are lost.

It is perhaps significant that when this pair appears within a larger list of people,[21] the *baḥur* is mentioned first, but when only these two

19. Jeremiah 5:1; II Samuel 24:2 (see also v. 8).
20. Deuteronomy 32:25; Lamentations 1:18.
21. For example, Jeremiah 51:20; Psalms 78:63–64.

are mentioned, highlighting either the boundless joy of youth or the epic tragedy of young lives taken, the *betulot* appear first. Such is the case in Lamentations 2:21,[22] and such is the case here. The term *betulot* (as opposed to *ne'arot* or *almot*) highlights the loss of potential, a future unfulfilled and unconsummated.

As this is the case, since our "famine" is a dearth of God's word and the hunger is intellectual-spiritual – why highlight the young men and women?

Radak proposes that "even the young maidens and young men who are generally engaged in worldly pleasures will have such a thirst for the word of God." This is consistent with Radak's approach that this "famine" will be the cessation of prophecy during the Second Commonwealth.

If read as an eschatological vision, however, this cannot refer to a cessation of prophecy; rather, something else is meant by *devar Hashem*. Why the focus on young men and women in their prime? To apply Radak's approach, people in the prime of their youth would search wide and far for God's word and, unable to find it, would become faint from this thirst.

Yet Midrashic tradition understands this as a real famine – of a lack of food and water. Where does the Midrash get the notion that our vision ought to be included in the "meta-history" of famines?

THE "*LO VELO KI IM*" PATTERN

The answer may lie in the pattern of *Lo [X] velo [Y] ki im [Z]*, which presents a negation of two familiar elements in favor of an unexpected one.

This pattern presumably negates the expected meaning of the key word (here, *ra'av*) and replaces it with a different component (*lishmoa et divrei Hashem*). Indeed, in legal texts, this is invariably the intent:[23]

22. A careful reading of Lamentations 2:21 leads to the same result: the elders and youths starve *baḥutzot*, whereas *betulotai uvaḥurai* are slaughtered and die by the sword.
23. For example, Exodus 23:34; Joshua 23:7–8.

worshipping other gods or swearing by their names is absolutely banned; the *only* legitimate avenue of swearing is using God's name.[24]

In some texts, however, this pattern does not negate X and Y, but rather *includes* Z as well. For example, in Moses's recounting of the Revelation at Sinai, he declares:

> The Lord *did not* make this covenant with our fathers, *rather* with us, even us, who are all of us here alive this day. (Deut. 5:3)

Moses does not intend to *exclude* the previous generation, who all stood at Sinai, from the covenant; rather, his point is:

> The Lord *did not* make this covenant *only* with our fathers, *rather even* with us.[25]

Thus, not only does the pattern "*lo... velo... ki im...*" not always serve to negate X and Y, but it also sometimes adds a new (surprising) Z – or even privileges Z ahead of X and Y.

One apt example is found in Zechariah's night of seven visions, when the angel tells him:

> Then he answered and spoke unto me, saying: This is the word of the Lord unto Zerubbabel, saying: *Not* by might, *nor* by power, *rather* by My spirit,[26] says the Lord of Hosts. (Zech. 4:6)

Although many read this prophecy as a negation of using financial power (*ḥayil*) or military might (*ko'aḥ*) to rebuild the Temple and reestablish Jerusalem under Persian rule, there are several mitigating factors. Per Ezra 5:1–2, both Haggai and Zechariah provide the moral impetus and support for the rebuilding. Haggai's four visions revolve around

---

24. See also Joshua 22:26–27.
25. See also Jeremiah 16:14–15, paralleled at 23:7–8; see Tosefta Berakhot 1:10. According to the majority opinion, the text is to be read as we suggest "not only X but also Y..."; see also Jeremiah 7:21–23. I am indebted to my teacher, Prof. Yoel Elitzur, for pointing me to some of these passages.
26. *Lo veḥayil velo vekho'aḥ ki im beruḥi.*

military might and Zerubbabel's return to power. In addition, the *two* olive branches in front of the Menorah represent the two "sons of Yitzhar."[27] Rashi, Ibn Ezra, and others understand that this refers to two leaders who are to be anointed with olive oil: the king and the high priest. In other words, *both* political and military power as well as spiritual purity *will* be needed to rebuild.

As such, the verse should more likely be read as follows:

> Then he answered and spoke unto me, saying: This is the word of the Lord unto Zerubbabel, saying: **Not** (***only***) by might, **nor** (***only***) by power, **rather** (***also***) by My spirit, says the Lord of Hosts.

Not only will financial and military strength be necessary; the surprising element is that spirit, too, will play a role in the Temple's rebuilding.

This interpretation can resolve the various issues with Amos's vision:

> **Not** (***only***) a famine of bread nor (***only***) a thirst for water,
> **Rather** (***also***) of hearing the words of the Lord.

The famine that Amos envisions is first and foremost a real drought. As with any famine, the beautiful young people will swoon from thirst and faint from hunger. But there will be deep hunger for God's word as well.

This may mean that the people will realize that the lack of food stems from their distance from God; to resolve their physical hunger, they will attempt to come back to God's word. This is an optimistic reading – perhaps too optimistic for Amos.

Alternatively, we might read God's word as a metaphor for actual rain.[28] If so, the difference between other famines and this one is that the people realize that rain is a manifestation of God's blessing, and they will seek that out. This, however, frames the people's spiritual yearning as secondary to their actual hunger, while our above analysis argues that

27. Per Zechariah 4:14.
28. See Psalms 147:18; Isaiah 55:10–11.

the *ki im* clause is central. Moreover, reading *devar Hashem* as "rain" is uncommon and it may be difficult to build a case for this meaning.

I believe, rather, that Amos is warning the people that one day, they will finally realize that the famine is the result of their own wayward behavior (something Amos has been striving for throughout). They will then seek such a prophet but will not find one; thus, they will have no idea how to return to God, bring divine favor back to the Land, and bring an end to the famine. Amos is emphasizing that right now, there are prophets bearing God's word, but no one will heed them – but *the day will come*, long after the cessation of prophecy (it is, after all, an eschaton), when troubles come to the Land. Then, the people will long for prophets who can commune with God, but alas, such prophets will no longer be available.

14: Those that swear by the sin of Samaria (*ashmat Shomeron*)

Literally: "Who swear by the guilt of Samaria." One recurring issue with idolatry is swearing by the name of other gods. Indeed, the Sages rule against forming a partnership with a pagan,[29] concerned that this will lead to the Jew going to the local court to settle a dispute, where they will be forced to swear in the name of a foreign deity.

Oaths are sworn to establish credibility. When an oath is taken "by the life of the Lord," it implies "just as God lives, so these words are true." As Ibn Ezra explains:[30]

> Someone who invokes the Name over something and does not fulfill it, it is as if he has denied the Name; for the reason that he mentioned it is this: "Just as the Lord is true, so are my words."

This illuminates the Torah's strong reservations against swearing (or even invoking) the names of pagan gods. By doing so, the person is staking the truth of his own words on the truth of their existence, power, and rule.

29. Bekhorot 2b; *Mishneh Torah, Hilkhot Sheluḥin VeShutafin* 5:10.
30. R. Avraham ibn Ezra, long commentary to Exodus 20:6.

The meaning of *ashmat Shomeron* (a *hapax legomenon*) is not at all clear, although it is fairly evident that it some form of foreign deity.

Radak is the only medieval commentator who addresses its meaning, but his interpretation is incomplete and problematic:

> ...the [Golden] Calf, which is in Beit El; he associates it with Samaria because the capital of the kingdom of Ephraim (Israel) is Samaria. The kings are the ones who support the "worship of the calves," and the people follow them.

Not only does Radak fail to explain the meaning of *ashma,* but his explanation also seems forced. Why would the people swearing by the calf in Beit El refer to it as *ashmat* ***Shomeron,*** and not *ashmat* ***Beit El***? Moreover, if the southern worship site is associated with Samaria, why is the northern site called *elohekha* ***Dan*** (below)?

Finally – and this is a much larger issue – is the worship at Beit El truly foreign service, literal *avoda zara*? Jeroboam I established them as alternatives to the Temple, and the Golden Calf constructed at each place was inaugurated with the words, "Behold your god, Israel, who took you up out of Egypt" (I Kings 12:28). Although the north is later guilty of idolatry, the sites at Beit El and Dan were not established for this purpose.[31]

And say, "As your god, O Dan, lives"

Radak, who maintains that *ashmat Shomeron* refers to the Golden Calf at Beit El, explains that the second person suffix, *elohekha* instead of *elohai* ("my god"), expresses how the worshippers swore to each other there.

Hakham suggests that this may have been the common way of referring to the calf in Dan, based on the inaugural declaration, "*hinei elohekha Yisrael.*"

31. But see Hosea 10:5; see also the intriguing proposals of Hakham and Beinart in his article in the biblical encyclopedia: *Encyclopedia Mikra'it* [Heb.] (publisher 1950), vol. 1, 762.

Another possibility is that the prophet makes this subtle switch to avoid uttering these offensive oaths explicitly.

And "As the way of Be'er Sheva lives"

We have already discussed Be'er Sheva's possible significance as a worship site, even though it is in Judean territory.[32] The northern tribes would have revered it as part of their "ancestral worship," which helped to justify the sanctification of older sites like Beit El (Jacob), Dan (Abraham), and Gilgal (Joshua). To swear on this "road," however, is odd.

Rav Joseph Kara suggests that besides swearing by worship sites, people would also swear by the roads that took them there. This presents three difficulties: First, why would the road itself be considered sacred? Second, for Samarians, the road to Be'er Sheva leads away from Beit El and Dan. Finally, since this rebuke is aimed at the northern kingdom, why is the road to Be'er Sheva relevant?

Radak proposes that the people believed they would earn *sekhar halikha,* merit for traveling to reach a holy place – "from Dan to Be'er Sheva."[33] Given that Jeroboam established the sites at Beit El and Dan for the sake of convenient pilgrimage, and to prevent the people from traveling to Jerusalem, this is highly unlikely, besides the anachronistic reference. Nor is there any record of people traveling north from Judea to worship in Beit El (or Dan).

This stems from a different reason. We are aware of the north's reverence for Be'er Sheva (Amos 5:5). Given, however, that traveling to Be'er Sheva itself was arduous, the people may have worshipped the *road* to Be'er Sheva instead, as the "best they could do."

But they will fall down and not get up again

This phrase is familiar to us and recalls Amos's earlier prophecy: "She has fallen, the maiden of Israel, and will never arise again" (5:2). Here, too, the scene ends with the fall of the entire people – who are earlier

32. See pages 199–202.
33. I Samuel 3:20; II Samuel 24:15.

symbolically referred to as "the maiden of Israel"; this is in ingenious dialogue with the *maidens* of the previous verse, who faint and fall from thirst.

NO ESCAPE (9:1–6)

The Text

(א) רָאִיתִי אֶת אֲדֹנָי נִצָּב עַל הַמִּזְבֵּחַ וַיֹּאמֶר הַךְ הַכַּפְתּוֹר וְיִרְעֲשׁוּ הַסִּפִּים וּבְצַעַם
בְּרֹאשׁ כֻּלָּם וְאַחֲרִיתָם בַּחֶרֶב אֶהֱרֹג לֹא יָנוּס לָהֶם נָס וְלֹא יִמָּלֵט לָהֶם פָּלִיט:
(ב) אִם יַחְתְּרוּ בִשְׁאוֹל מִשָּׁם יָדִי תִקָּחֵם וְאִם יַעֲלוּ הַשָּׁמַיִם מִשָּׁם אוֹרִידֵם:
(ג) וְאִם יֵחָבְאוּ בְּרֹאשׁ הַכַּרְמֶל מִשָּׁם אֲחַפֵּשׂ וּלְקַחְתִּים וְאִם יִסָּתְרוּ מִנֶּגֶד עֵינַי
בְּקַרְקַע הַיָּם מִשָּׁם אֲצַוֶּה אֶת הַנָּחָשׁ וּנְשָׁכָם: (ד) וְאִם יֵלְכוּ בַשְּׁבִי לִפְנֵי אֹיְבֵיהֶם
מִשָּׁם אֲצַוֶּה אֶת הַחֶרֶב וַהֲרָגָתַם וְשַׂמְתִּי עֵינִי עֲלֵיהֶם לְרָעָה וְלֹא לְטוֹבָה:
(ה) וַאדֹנָי ה׳ הַצְּבָאוֹת הַנּוֹגֵעַ בָּאָרֶץ וַתָּמוֹג וְאָבְלוּ כָּל יוֹשְׁבֵי בָהּ וְעָלְתָה כַיְאֹר
כֻּלָּהּ וְשָׁקְעָה כִּיאֹר מִצְרָיִם: (ו) הַבּוֹנֶה בַשָּׁמַיִם מעלותו מַעֲלוֹתָיו וַאֲגֻדָּתוֹ עַל
אֶרֶץ יְסָדָהּ הַקֹּרֵא לְמֵי הַיָּם וַיִּשְׁפְּכֵם עַל פְּנֵי הָאָרֶץ ה׳ שְׁמוֹ:

1 I saw the Lord standing beside the altar; and He said: Smite the capitals, that the posts may shake; and break them in pieces on the head of all of them. And I will slay the remnant of them with the sword; not one of them will flee away, nor will one of them
escape. **2** Though they dig into the netherworld, My hand will take them from there; and even if they climb up to heaven, from
there will I bring them down. **3** And though they hide themselves atop the Carmel, I will search and take them out from there; and though they be hidden from My sight at the bottom of the sea, from there will I command the serpent, and he will bite them.
4 And though they go into captivity before their enemies, from there will I command the sword, and it will slay them; and I will
set My eyes on them for evil, and not for good. **5** For the Lord, the God of Hosts, is He that touches the earth and it melts, and all that dwell there mourn; and it rises up wholly like the River,
and sinks again, like the River of Egypt. **6** It is He who builds His

upper chambers in the heaven, and has founded His vault on the earth; He summons the waters of the sea and pours them out upon the face of the earth – the Lord is His name.

This vision is more reminiscent of Isaiah's inauguration (Is. 6:1–4) than of anything earlier in Amos: both scenes begin with the *navi* describing himself as "seeing." In Amos's earlier visions, he reports that God "showed me" – *ko hirani*. In Amos, God stands atop the altar; Isaiah sees God sitting atop a throne, which is beside the altar (6:6). In both visions, the *sipim* (posts) shake – Isaiah's shake with the tremor of revelation. What of Amos's?

Amos's earlier visions are images of the mundane (locusts, fire, the plumbline, and the summer fruit), but here God is seen in a place of royalty, of sanctity. Moreover, each of these earlier images was then used to convey a message to the people. Here, however, the setting and objects are not part of the message, which is stated, explicitly and with terrifying clarity, by God Himself.

Some hold that the vision's altar is the altar in Beit El,[34] others understand it to be *the* altar in Jerusalem[35] – perhaps based on the scene's close parallel to Isaiah's prophecy, which is presumed to be set in Jerusalem.

A vital difference between the two visions, of course, is that Isaiah's is his inauguration, and it conveys his reluctance to accept his mission. Amos's vision, in contrast, is an eschatological scene at the end of his book, a "doomsday" vision. Some *Rishonim* maintain that this frightening prophecy was realized at a particular point in history; another possibility is that it belongs to the distant future: the "end of history."

This vision is the longest single *mar'eh* in the book. Its structure is clear: the first four verses are the vision itself, which consists of two parts: the first is the first half of verse 1 – the vision of God atop/aside the altar, commanding terrible shaking; verses 1b–4 are the terrifying consequences of this "shake-up" for God's people. This entire section

34. This seems to be the opinion of Ibn Ezra in his second commentary and of R. Eliezer of Beaugency; see also Paul, 138, and Hakham, 68.
35. Rashi, following the Targum, as well as R. Joseph Kara and Radak.

is presented as a monologue; it should be imagined as enveloped in quotation marks.

God's name does not appear in this first section after the introductory *ra'iti et A-D-N-Y*. God's name here is A-D-N-Y, which Amos uses frequently. In his earlier visions, he uses A-D-N-Y with *Hashem* (vocalized "*Elokim*"); here, only A-D-N-Y is used.

Verse 5 shifts to the prophet's praise of God, where he again invokes A-D-N-Y, but this time adds "*Hashem*."

Verses 5 and 6 complete the vision with a paean similar to his earlier hymns.[36] This paean is also divided into two parts: v. 5 praises God for His immanence and destructive powers; v. 6 speaks more transcendentally about God and His power over the sea. He concludes the section and the entire passage with *Hashem shemo*, a common signature for Amos.

While the two sections are distinct, clear contextual and literary markers also bind them together.

Subtle chiasm in verses 2–3 describes God's presence in the depths and the heights:

A: dig into the netherworld...
  B: climb up to heaven (v. 2)
  B': hide themselves in the top of Carmel...
A': hidden from My sight in the bottom of the sea (v. 3)

In verse 5, God is praised as One who "touches the earth and it melts." The biblical image of melting earth is most often associated with mountains, especially Sinai.[37] There is no escaping God, even on the highest of mountains; He will merely touch the earth and melt it. Verse 6 praises God's power over the sea and its depths: people cannot even hide from God at "the bottom of the sea." The hymn (vv. 5–6) serves as an explication of the threats (vv. 1–4).

36. 4:13; 5:8–9.
37. See Judges 5:4–5; Psalms 68 and 114.

One final introductory note about the vision. God describes five avenues of flight that will prove futile;[38] God Himself will find those who flee under the earth, in the heavens, and in the caves of the Carmel. Those who attempt to hide at the bottom of the sea will be attacked by God's agent, the sea monster *naḥash.*[39] This also recalls the story of Jonah. Finally, those who are taken as captives will be pursued by the sword. Besides the oddity of imagining a sword as acting under divine agency, the nature of the attempt to flee in v. 4 is striking:

> And though they go into captivity before their enemies, from there I will command the sword, and it will slay them; and I will set My eyes on them for evil, and not for good.

It is as if even being taken into captivity is an (un)intentional attempt by the people to flee God's presence – and nonetheless, He will find them there and the sword that He commanded will slay them there.

1: I saw the Lord standing beside the altar

The abrupt opening *ra'iti* is nearly unmatched in prophetic introductory rhetoric.[40] Even Isaiah's inaugural prophetic experience opens with an introductory phrase that helps ease the listener (and reader) into the vision.

All of which raises the question: Why does Amos's oratory, usually so measured, suddenly take a shocking turn? Like a Mahler symphony, Amos's prophecy is harmonious and brooding for measures on end, then suddenly jarring and discordant.

I would like to propose two possible explanations for this abrupt opening. The first acknowledges Amos's rhetorical genius; the second is a literary observation.

---

38. Amos, as we have noticed several times, seems to have an affinity for the number five in his rhetoric.
39. See Isaiah 27:1.
40. See Zechariah 1:8; I Kings 22:19 (= II Chronicles 18:18).

One approach to this sudden *ra'iti* is that Amos wants to shock his audience into dread and panic about their imminent destruction. His first four visions did not convince them, so Amos changes his tune, as if splashing cold water on his audience. Not only is the opening word startling, but instead of describing God *showing him something*, Amos describes *seeing God Himself*; instead of symbolic messages, they are explicit – and brutal. In this sense, the vision can be considered part of the series,[41] the culmination of the vision sequence; at the same time, it is clearly distinct.

Another way to understand the sequence is to take a more panoramic view of this eschatological presentation. This *ra'iti* follows the people's hunger "for the words of God," which seems to signal the beginning of the eschaton. As the people wander from sea to sea, swooning and fainting from the famine, God will appear and declare their doom. Read thus, *ra'iti* is not an abrupt opening, but rather the next stage of the vision.[42]

Amos's omission of the name Hashem in the vision, which he subsequently incorporates into the hymn in verse 5, is a telling lacuna. This is the only one of 24 instances of A-D-N-Y in Amos that is not followed by *Hashem*, although in the *anakh* vision, the starker image of a "master" (*Adon*) is not tempered by the merciful Tetragrammaton (although the name does appear in the adjacent verse, 7:7–8).

It is as if the image of God "standing up" over the prophet is so terrifying that the only fitting name is "My Master."

The verb *nitzav* evokes the image of Jacob at none other than Beit El.[43] Whether the envisioned altar stands at Beit El or Jerusalem, Amos is likely delivering this *prophecy* at Beit El. His use of *nitzav* hints to Jacob's vision there and his subsequent commitment to building an altar at the site.[44]

Here, as in the *anakh* vision, *nitzav al* could mean that God stands *on top* of the altar or *beside* it. If we read this vision as pronouncing

41. Here we have yet another example of Amos's use of "fives."
42. Closer to Zechariah and Micaiah's sequence.
43. Genesis 28:12–13.
44. Ibid. 35:7.

Samaria's demise, then this phrase neatly and deliberately recalls the vision pronounced against Jeroboam I in I Kings 13.

The parallel is stark. The northern kingdom's sinful ways began with Jeroboam's two worship sites, and its demise is announced with a similar scene – not the wayward king at the altar, but rather God Himself standing there.

If, as Abravanel and others read, this prophecy refers to Judah and Israel alike, then the parallel to Jeroboam is irrelevant.

Either way, what is the nature of this altar? The use of the definite article – ***hamizbe'aḥ*** – implies that this is *the* altar in Jerusalem. Rashi (following Targum) and R. Joseph Kara cite a midrash that this vision is "one of the *Shekhina*'s ten exiles/journeys," which implies that this is the altar in Jerusalem. Radak states this explicitly: "He [Amos] said that he saw, in a prophetic vision, the glory of Hashem standing atop the altar in the Temple."

This does not necessarily imply that the vision refers to both Judah and Samaria, or to the Temple's destruction over a century later. Perhaps, rather, God seated on the altar in Jerusalem is a manifestation of Amos's anthemic "roaring from Zion."

Both Paul and Hakham, however, argue that this is the altar at Beit El. Paul's argument is literary: the previous prophecy refers to prohibited worship sites, so this must be the same.[45] Hakham presents a convincing thematic connection:

> …Those who worship there [in Beit El] believed that God, so to speak, stands next to the altar to accept their offerings with favor. And the prophet says to them: Indeed, I saw A-D-N-Y standing next to the altar, not with love and favor, but rather with anger and wrath. He is pleased neither with your service nor with you.

45. Paul, 138. Mays (OTL *Amos*, 152) assumes, without question, that the altar in question is the one at Beit El. Andersen and Freedman (AB, 835) address the possibility of it being the sanctuary in Jerusalem, but reject it in favor of the altar at Beit El on contextual grounds, as that is the only worship site where the text locates Amos (7:10–17).

One strong argument in favor of this reading is that God then shakes and destroys the building. Nonetheless, both possibilities stand.

And He said: Smite the capitals

God here is directing (someone) to strike the *kaftor*, a word that appears elsewhere only in context of the Menorah in Exodus.[46] A *kaftor* is a protruding architectural element; here, it refers to the column capitals – the oversized pieces that connect the column tops to the roof. A hard blow to the capitals will shake the entire building.

The *Rishonim* assume that God is addressing an angel;[47] in the words of R. Yosef ibn Kaspi, an "avenging angel." This is convincing, given the vision's subtle dialogue with Isaiah's inauguration vision.

That the posts may shake

The word *saf* has two distinct meanings – "basin" or "goblet,"[48] and "threshold"[49] – and the two are occasionally confused.[50] Here, it clearly means threshold; but why would the striking of the capitals cause the thresholds to shake?

R. Eliezer of Beaugency (and, following him, Radak) understands that the columns are below the floor; shaking the capitals will cause the threshold to come crashing down, bringing the building with it. Most other *Rishonim* read these as two separate actions, and not that the striking of the capitals will cause the threshold to shake. Some *Rishonim* read this metaphorically: the columns represent the heads of the people, and the threshold the "common folk."[51]

The verb used here is pointed and pregnant with meaning: *ra'ash* (earthquake) is a reference point for Amos's prophetic career. Amos's

46. Twelve times, all in the context of the Menorah.
47. Paul raises the possibility that God is addressing "a" prophet, that is, someone other than Amos.
48. Exodus 12:22; II Samuel 17:28.
49. Isaiah 6:4 (!); Zephaniah 2:14.
50. For example, Esther 2:21, and the commentaries ad loc.
51. See Ibn Ezra's second explanation and the comment of R. Eliezer of Beaugency.

use of the same word in verb form here might serve to connect this disturbing vision with the imminent earthquake.

In any case, the building where this altar is found is doomed and will come crashing down. This is a fitting fate for the sanctuary at Beit El, but what if this refers to the altar in Jerusalem? Can it be that the vision is set in Jerusalem, but the building marked for destruction is the sanctuary at Beit El?

And break them in pieces on the head of all of them

God then turns His anger from the building to the people inside – presumably the cult priests. This may be Amos's ultimate response to Amaziah who is himself *rosh kulam* – the head of the priestly cult at Beit El.

There is clear irony in using the sanctuary's capitals and threshold – the building's top and bottom – to destroy the cult priests. Beit El's destruction will not come from outside, but rather from the building itself, which will implode and take its officiants with it.

This phrase is not, however, without its exegetical challenges. Both the verb *betza* (with the pronominal third person plural suffix *mem*) and the object *berosh kulam* are not fully clear. Some read *rosh* as the poisonous weed;[52] others emend *rosh* to *ra'ash,* in line with *yirashu* in the previous phrase. Even if we read *berosh* as meaning "the head," does it mean to shatter the columns on *everyone's* head, or on *the person who stands at* the head? Hadjiev suggests reading "kill the ones at the front of all of them"[53] – those who stand at the front. This fits the next phrase neatly; *aḥaritam* means "those in back," and the image is complete.

And I will slay the remnant of them with the sword (*ve'aḥaritam baḥerev eherog*)

No matter how we interpret *berosh kulam* (if we agree that *rosh* means "head"), the word *aḥarit* works symmetrically. God will punish the

52. Already mentioned by Amos at 6:12.

53. Tchavdar Hadjiev, "Kill All Who Are in Front: Another Suggestion about Amos IX 1," *Vetus Testamentum* 57, no. 3 (July 2007): 386–389.

leaders, and their followers, too, will also be killed; perhaps this refers to their children (Ibn Ezra), or simply to those who are standing in the back.

Not one of them will flee away

This threat recalls Amos's first rebuke of Israel. No matter how they try to flee God's wrath, they will not escape, as is explicated in the following verses. Note Amos's clever use of *nus* here: as both verb and noun. He cannot do so in the parallel phrase, as there is no nominal form of the root *malet*.

Nor will one of them escape

This phrase, a parallel to the previous one, has its own wordplay: although, as noted, there is no nominal form of *malet*, Amos uses the noun *palet*. We have already discussed how similar roots may have similar meanings; perhaps the same sometimes applies when the variant letter is the first letter of the stem?

A Panoramic View

> *Verse 1*: I saw the Lord standing beside the altar; and He said: Smite the capitals, that the posts may shake; and break them in pieces on the head of all of them.
>
> And I will slay the remnant of them with the sword; not one of them will flee away, nor will one of them escape.
>
> *Verse 2*: **Though** they dig into the netherworld, **from there** shall My hand take them;
>
> **And though** they climb up to heaven, **from there** will I bring them down.
>
> *Verse 3*: **And though** they hide themselves atop the Carmel, I will search and take them out **from there**;

> **And though** they be hidden from My sight in the bottom of the sea, **from there** will I command the serpent, and he shall bite them.
>
> *Verse 4*: **And though** they go into captivity before their enemies, **from there** will I command the sword, and it shall slay them;
>
> And I will set My eyes upon them for evil, and not for good.

The rhythm of this passage is clear.

> *Im* (if) – location where they flee or are taken
> *Misham* (from there) – God's method of catching and punishing them

The people attempt to flee along five routes: the netherworld (below), the heavens (above), the top of the Carmel (above), the bottom of the sea (below), and, finally, captivity (neither above nor below). Note that the fate of the "followers" in the previous hemistich is death by the sword; the same fate awaits those taken into captivity. We will revisit this below.

Structurally, it is clear that verses 2 and 3 work as double-nested parallels. In other words, not only does each hemistich contain its own if-then parallel and each hemistich parallels the other half of its verse, each entire verse also parallels the other:

V2: *If* they hide in She'ol	→	*from there* I will take them
If they climb up to heaven	→	*from there* I will bring them down
V3: *if they* hide atop the Carmel	→	*from there* I will take them down
If they hide in the sea	→	*from there* I will command the snake…

This repetition of up and down movement implies that the people cannot flee to the highest heights, to the lowest depths, or anywhere else in between. What is unusual is Amos's fourfold focus on height and depth, rather than the more common "four directions." Instead of describing flight to the four ends of the earth, he describes the impossible (hiding in the netherworld, climbing up to heaven, hiding at the bottom of the sea). This divergence from the usual biblical convention begs explanation.

Moreover, these four balanced points are followed by a fifth: one possible "route of flight" to be taken is into captivity. This fifth point is a rhetorical slap in the face for Amos's audience.

The addition of a fifth element that upsets the balance of height and depth is itself surprising. In addition, these first four directions are unrealistic and seem symbolic,[54] whereas being taken into captivity is far more feasible and will soon befall the northern kingdom. In this manner, his audience is transported from the symbolic to grim realism.

A third rhetorical twist concerns the nature of captivity. People never willingly go into captivity, so unlike the first four descriptions, how can this be an attempt to *flee* God?

Finally, this description is ironic. The people presumably attempt to flee God to maintain their lives and their freedom. If they are taken into captivity, they have already lost this freedom; why should God pursue them anymore?

I would like to propose two solutions to this conundrum.

As mentioned above, the fate of death by the sword reserved for those taken into captivity is the same punishment meted out to the *aḥarit* in verse 1. Perhaps this is the *only* punishment awaiting "everybody else." The first four attempts to flee are merely hyperbole, whereas the final fate of captivity is, in fact, what will befall the people. To paraphrase Amos's words:

> I will smash those that are the leaders and will go after the rest with the sword. No matter where they try to flee – no matter how high or how low they go – they will ultimately be taken into captivity and slaughtered there.

54. The symbolism of hiding out atop Mount Carmel is addressed below.

This solves another issue in v. 1: God commands a member of His heavenly retinue to strike the capitals of the columns and shake the threshold, which will bring the house down. Those who are *berosh kulam* (either the leaders or the ones standing in front) will be killed by the impact of this destruction. Those who are not killed by this *ra'ash* will then be killed by the sword. Which sword? We can now suggest that this is the captors' sword mentioned in v. 4: The captors, God's agents, will kill them with the sword, thus fulfilling the opening threat – *ve'aḥaritam baḥerev eherog*.

If the first four attempts to flee are metaphoric, they can be explained as a poetic barrier between God's threat and the method of its fulfillment.

This vision is part of Amos's larger eschaton. One of the seminal verses in this end-of-days prophecy is the famine for God's word. In that famine, a deprivation of physical nutrition together with a thirst for God's word, the starving people wander "from sea to sea and from north to east" to find God's words – to no avail. These comprise *four points on the horizontal axis of the compass*: the starving people will search *everywhere*, seeking God. Here, the targeted population will attempt to escape God and try to disappear – to hide, to be *nowhere* by going to *four points on the vertical axis of the compass.* Whereas the starving people will go sea to sea, the targeted people will flee below ground and to the bottom of the sea. Whereas the starving young men and women will go to the north and east, those fleeing God's wrath will seek refuge on Mount Carmel (in the north) and in heaven. In ancient maps,[55] east was always on top – from Amos's audience's perspective, going east was going "up."

Though the people will not really attempt to flee God, Amos is contrasting their movement with that of those who desperately seek Him. When the people are starving for food and His word, they will search high and low to "hear God's word"; but when it comes to accountability, they will do anything and go anywhere to escape God's wrath.

Another possibility is that these four attempts to flee are not a metaphor, but rather hyperbole based on models that would have been familiar to Amos's audience.

55. For example, the Madaba map, dating from the sixth century CE.

Jonah, She'ol, and the Sea

The image of attempting to burrow to *She'ol* (the underworld or the grave) brings one character to mind from the same era and region. As Jonah was an older contemporary of Amos; the latter's audience would have been familiar with the story of Jonah[56] and his failed attempt to escape God and His word.

Jonah repeatedly "goes down" – down to Yafo, down to the boat, and down into the hold before going to sleep:

> ***Vayered*** *Yafo...* ***vayered*** *bah... veYona* ***yarad*** *el yarketei hasefina...* ***vayerad****am.*

The use of the relatively rare *vayeradam* (instead of the more common *vayishan*) manipulates this series into a "3 + 1" pattern. Jonah wishes to go down – down – down – to sleep and death. Even his prayer begins with a call to God *mibeten She'ol* – from the belly of the underworld/grave.[57]

This is in salient dialogue with fleeing "to the floor of the sea." God commands the fish to swallow Jonah, then directs the fish to vomit him out upon the shore. This comes daringly close to Amos's description:

> And though they hide from My sight at the bottom of the sea,
> There I will command the sea-serpent and it shall bite them.

Elijah, Carmel, and the Heavens

One generation earlier, a charismatic prophet and miracle-worker lived, preached, and taught would-be prophets in the northern kingdom. Perhaps the most legendary of prophets, Elijah of Gilead, also tries to flee from his responsibilities and, like Jonah,[58] asks God to take his life.[59]

Elijah's most powerful and impressive moment is *atop Mount Carmel,* where he challenges and defeats hundreds of prophets of Ba'al,

56. Regardless of how we understand its historicity (see chapter 1).
57. Jonah 2:3.
58. See *Mekhilta,* Exodus 12:1, which compares and contrasts Jonah and Elijah. See also *Pirkei deRabbi Eliezer,* ch. 32, where Jonah is identified as the son of the widow in Zarefat whom Elijah revives.
59. I Kings 19:4.

leading to a temporary religious revival among the people and the immediate demise of his pagan rivals.[60] Immediately after that success, however, he flees from Jezebel, who seeks to kill him *by the sword*. He arrives at a *cave* in Sinai/Horeb, where God asks him, "What are you doing here, Elijah?"

Amos's description of hiding in a cave on Mount Carmel combines the two extremes of Elijah's career – his astounding victory in God's name and his flight to a cave where he encounters God.

With his hyperbolic rhetoric, Amos is perhaps hinting to these two men of God, men worthy of prophecy, who nonetheless tried to flee God's word – to no avail. This underscores the futility of trying to run from God: for wherever they go, "the Omnipresent has many executioners."[61]

2: Though they dig into the netherworld (*She'ol*)

All biblical instances of *maḥteret-ḥatar* mean "to dig, unseen" in order to steal something. There are two exceptions, both in prophet texts: here and in Jonah. Consistent with the general sense of not wanting to be seen, both instances mean "to burrow," to hide away – not to steal something, but rather to evade a threat. Here, too, Amos's use of the unusual *ḥatar* may be calculated to evoke Jonah's failed flight from God: when the pious sailors in Jonah, intent on saving their boat without sacrificing the Hebrew prophet, try in vain to navigate the stormy waters back to shore, the text reports: "The men *rowed hard* (*vayaḥteru*) to bring it to the land but they could not, for the sea grew more and more tempestuous against them" (Jonah 1:13). Rashi sees the use of this word as an analogy: "They toiled and worked hard *like someone who was digging a tunnel.*"

60. Ibid. 18:38–40.

61. Ta'anit 18b; see Adiel Schremer, "'The Lord Has Forsaken the Land': Radical Explanations of the Military and Political Defeat of the Jews in Tannaitic Literature," *Journal of Jewish Studies* 59:2 (Autumn 2008): 183–200; and see there note 25 for further references.

R. Joseph Kara read it literally: "They were digging with their oars in order to bring the boat back to dry land due to the strong wind, but were unable" (similarly, Ibn Ezra).

R. Eliezer of Beaugency makes an intriguing observation:

> *Vayaḥteru* – this way and that to find some way to bring the boat back to dry land so that [Jonah] wouldn't go with them and wouldn't flee [with them] from God's presence, because they thought thus they would repair the sin of his flight and that God would favor them.

This unusual verb, he observes, alludes to that original *maḥteret* in Exodus 22, a breach where someone sneaks in to avoid being seen. Similarly, these sailors are trying to remove the man who "stole" into – and within – their ship (*vayered **bah*** – "he went down into [the ship]"; 1:3).

R. Eliezer of Beaugency presents the same approach here, in Amos:

> *Im yaḥteru*: A *maḥteret* is in the depths; similarly, it is the way of boatmen, since they operate in the depths of the waters like people tunneling into houses, he calls it *ḥatira*, as in "the men 'dug' to return to dry land" (Jonah 1:13).

The story of Jonah illustrates that *yaḥteru* does not only mean sneaking *in*, but also sneaking *away*. This also explains the unexpected preposition ***be**She'ol* (rather than the expected ***le**She'ol* – to She'ol). Someone who is trying to break in to steal something – the classic *maḥteret* – is attempting to get in there, where the desired item is. Someone who is trying to break in to find refuge is intent on staying hidden, to burrow ever deeper, and to remain out of sight: not ***le**She'ol* but ***be**She'ol.*

My hand will take them from there

The image of God's hand reaching down into She'ol is in ironic dialogue with Hosea 13:14, *mi-yad She'ol efdem* – "Shall I redeem them from the grave?" Some of the Rishonim explain this as a statement of past kindness: "I *did* redeem them from the grave."

It is not clear what God will do with them after He has taken them out; the same is true of the first three escape routes. Perhaps they will then meet the fate described in verse 4: "I will command the sword and it will slay them." The verb *lakaḥ* here may also hint to another prophetic figure.

And even if they climb up to heaven

Elijah's ascent to heaven follows the familiar literary pattern – which we discussed at some length in Chapter 2 – of 3 + 1.[62]

"When the Lord raised Elijah *up* to the heavens," the verb *lakaḥ* is used six times, in three pairs – twice by Elijah's students, twice by Elijah about his own impending ascent, and twice in reference to his disciple Elisha.[63]

The phrase *yadi tikaḥem* at the end of the previous clause, juxtaposed with this clause, connects the Jonah-image to the Elijah-image of going up to heaven. Although Elijah did not go up to heaven to escape from God, he earlier expressed a desire to evade his mission; like Jonah, he went so far as to express a wish to die.

Thus Amos references these two figures, one who ascends to the highest heavens and one who descends into the deepest depths, to describe the impossibility and futility of flight from God.

From there will I bring them down.

This final verb – *oridem* – says it all. God will literally and figuratively bring them down, no matter how high they have climbed.

One final point before moving on. The stories of Jonah and Elijah are subtly interwoven into this verse and the next. Just as the use of

---

62. He bids farewell to Elisha at Gilgal, then at Beit El, then in Jericho (3), and then the two of them go into the Jordan river where the master's departure is realized (+1).
63. II Kings 2.

yadi ***tikaḥem*** in the "She'ol unit" is a bridge to the Elijah allusion, the ominous *oridem* similarly brings us back to She'ol.

As mentioned, the beginning of Jonah presents another example of the 3 + 1 literary pattern when Jonah "goes down" three times: (1) down to the port, (2) down to the boat, (3) down to the hold, and then (4) down to sleep (wishing to die).

God's threat to "bring down" anyone who tries to escape to heaven ingeniously reintroduces the Jonah story into the second clause, just as Elijah is subtly brought into the first clause through "*yadi* ***tikaḥem***."

3: And though they hide themselves atop the Carmel

"Carmel" in *Tanakh*

Carmel has two distinct meanings in Tanakh: "fresh garden" or "pasture,"[64] and "fresh produce."[65] "Carmel" is also a toponym of two places in Israel. One is a settlement in the southeastern sector of the Hebron hills, most famously the place where Nabal's sheep-shearing feast takes place.[66]

The Carmel Mountain range in northern Israel is the site of the modern city of Haifa. Approximately twenty-four miles long, bisecting the coastal plain and the Jezreel valley, the entire range is referred to as "Carmel," while the mountain at its northwestern end is known as Mount Carmel. While not impressively high,[67] Mount Carmel is often mentioned in literary prophecy and poetry together with the Bashan,[68] Lebanon,[69] and Tabor.[70] This mountain is the setting of Elijah's confrontation with the prophets of Ba'al.

---

64. According to BDB (ad loc.) and Gesenius (*Gesenius's Hebrew Grammar*, 1910, Clarendon Press, 2nd English ed., rev. in accordance with the 28th German ed. [1909] / by A.E. Cowley. sec. 85, par. 52), it is a modified form of *kerem* with *lamed* afformative. See II Kings 19:23 (= Isaiah 37:24); Isaiah 10:18, 29:17.
65. Leviticus 23:14; 2:14; and II Kings 4:42.
66. I Samuel 25:1; see also 15:12.
67. The peak is 1791 feet above sea level.
68. Isaiah 33:9; Jeremiah 50:19; see also Nahum 1:4.
69. Isaiah 35:2; see also Nahum 1:4.
70. Jeremiah 46:18.

This mountain became famous[71] during the era of the charismatic prophets (Elijah and Elisha), to the extent that prophets referred to it as "HaCarmel"[72] – evidently replacing the southern village as *the* Carmel. Elijah is so deeply associated with this location that one of the Arabic names for the mountain is "Jabal Mar Elias."

Har HaCarmel, Elijah, and Elisha

Elijah's fiery triumph on Mount Carmel was miraculous, but it did not involve prophecy.[73] It is also likely that Elijah interacted with Ahaziah's three delegations (the first two of whom were doomed by Elijah's fire) on Mount Carmel.[74] Much of Elisha's story also takes place in this area – perhaps, as Abravanel suggests, to better channel the spirit of Elijah that rests upon him.

Carmel and Amos

Amos's anthem describes how God's voice withers the top of the Carmel and burns its lush greenery in an apt evocation of Elijah's fiery miracles there.

In our verse, Amos employs various Elijah-images to continue the theme of the futility of fleeing from God. He mentions "hiding" – *yeḥavu* – which, together with the location, recalls how Obadiah courageously hid a hundred of God's prophets in caves.[75]

Note that when Amos mentions Carmel, he does not refer to it as "***Har** HaCarmel*," but rather as "***Rosh** HaCarmel*"; we will address this below.

71. An additional reason for this shift is that the focus of the text, from the split kingdom, was on the northern kingdom, as can be seen by a cursory comparison of Samuel-Kings with Chronicles.
72. In all five mentions in Kings, as well as one mention each in Isaiah and Jeremiah, besides both mentions in Amos.
73. I Kings 18.
74. See II Kings 1.
75. I Kings 18:4.

3: I will search and take them out from there

The prepositional *mem* of *misham* is added to maintain the rhythm, as established in the previous verse, where *misham* makes contextual sense.

The only other occurrence of *aḥapes* is in Zephaniah:

> *Vehaya ba'eit hahi aḥapes et Yerushalayim banerot…*
>
> At that time I will search Jerusalem with lamps, and I will punish the men who have settled like sediment, saying in their hearts that the Lord can do neither good nor harm.[76]

In both cases, God is searching for sinners who are apparently trying to hide from Him.

And though they be hidden from My sight

This is clearly ironic as no one can hide from God;[77] rather, it should be read: "And though they *think to hide* from My sight."

At the bottom of the sea

This clear reference to Jonah completes the chiasm:

> Jonah (*she'ol*) → Elijah (*shamayim*); Elijah (Carmel) → Jonah (*yam*)

Of the eight biblical instances of *karka* (floor), the other seven refer to the floor of the Sanctuary. Why does Amos use this word – usually used in reference to the *Mikdash* – to refer to the seabed?[78]

This can be illuminated through context. Amos's vision begins with an image of God standing atop the altar; then to the Carmel; then to

76. Zephaniah 1:12; it is entirely possible that Zephaniah borrowed this phrasing from Amos's image of God "searching" for those hiding from him atop the Carmel.
77. See Genesis 3:8 ff and Psalms 139:7.
78. R. Joseph Kara, undoubtedly bothered by *karka* and following the Targum, reads it as "islands," which, of course, have *karka*, but this is not consistent with the vision's imagery or poetic symmetry.

the bottom of the sea – *karka*. This hints that the entire world, from the highest of mountaintops to the depths of the sea, is God's territory – His presence is everywhere, just as it rests in His *Mikdash*.

From there will I command the serpent, and he will bite them

Again, the prepositional prefix is used here for rhetorical rhythm, matching the *misham* of the doubled couplet.

Targum Yonatan and Rashi read this *naḥash* as a metaphor for "the nations, which are strong like a snake," while Ibn Ezra and Radak point to the sea serpents mentioned by Isaiah.[79]

4: And though they go into captivity before their enemies, From there will I command the sword, and it will slay them

The *vav* at the beginning of this verse implies that this scenario is merely another option in line with the earlier four: "If they hide in She'ol… if they climb up to heaven… if they hide atop the Carmel… if they hide on the sea floor… if they go into captivity," but this may be deliberately misleading.

This final "escape route" differs from the first four, which describe how people attempt to flee from God in various ways. This fifth "way" is neither a choice nor a certain destination: rather, the people are being led into captivity against their will.

This fifth "way" also differs in terms of orientation: the first four operate on a vertical plane, while this verse describes horizontal movement as the people are led away from their land by the invading army.

Finally, while the fate of the first four groups is not entirely clear (what happens after God reaches them?) in this final passage, there is no ambiguity regarding their fate: God's sword will kill them.

It seems that this verse presents the only real description in the vision, whereas the first four are merely rhetorical devices, and that this sword is the same as the sword in verse 1, which slays those who are

79. Isaiah 27:1.

aḥaritam.[80] The rhetorical interlude leads the audience into believing that these threats are hyperbolic and figurative, but this final verse – with a resounding slap – describes the grim fate that awaits these complacent sinners.

Shevi – Which Captivity?

Radak, who believes that the altar of this vision is the altar in Jerusalem, sees the captivity mentioned here as the Babylonian destruction of Jerusalem in the early sixth century BCE.

While this reading has certain merit – its eschatological tone is consistent with the fact that it is only fulfilled a century after its pronouncement – its problems nonetheless outweigh its advantages. Above all, this event has *nothing to do with Amos's audience.* Samaria is far too estranged from Judah to care about their fate a century later.

Rather, I would like to suggest that the "captivity" here is deliberately vague,[81] and the interpretation of this prophecy cannot be ascertained without the aid of a prophet.

Much as we might be tempted to point to a seminal event and recognize the realization of an ancient prophecy, we cannot make such a claim without the confirmation and divine imprimatur of a prophet. This leaves us looking at "remote prophecies" with the consistent anxiety of doubt; perhaps this is theologically calculated to ensure that we always keep these frightening images in the constellation of our possible futures.

There is, however, a more hopeful way of looking at these remote visions. Rabbinic tradition holds that all divine decrees of punishment are revocable.[82] Though we may always dread a "famine for the word of God" or the "sword of God," this may never come to pass – it is a metahistoric possibility, but not a divine inevitability.

We might, therefore, consider the horrific image of the enemy's sword as God's agent of destruction as one possible way that things

---

80. Paul sees the sword in our verse as forming an *inclusio* with the sword in the first verse.
81. For examples of this, compare I Kings 13 with II Kings 2:15–16; and I Kings 16:34 with Joshua 6:26.
82. Unlike His promises of recompense, consolation, and restoration.

might play out, but it is certainly not the only way for them to play out. There is no need to look at specific epochs in Jewish history, painful and bloody though they were, and assign them the realization of this frightening judgment.

4: And I will set My eyes upon them for evil, and not for good

This is ironic: God usually places "His eye" on someone for protection, not destruction.[83] This frightening vision thus ends with a double blow: the people learn that if there are any survivors, God will keep His eye on them, but His gaze is not one of compassion or protection. Rather, it will bring further punishment: *Vesamti eini aleihem – lera'ah* ***velo*** *letova.*

5: For the Lord, the God of Hosts

The sequence *A-D-N-Y Hashem Tzeva'ot* appears a few times in prophetic oratory,[84] but this particular form, with the definite article before the last name (***ha****Tzeva'ot*), is rare. Three of its four appearances are in Amos.[85] The two earlier instances in Amos both appear in the context of warnings of dire punishment of the imminent destruction of the palaces and power of Samaria's aristocracy.[86]

Here, the prophet uses this name in the meta-future context of his eschaton. This vision also begins with the shaking and destruction of a house or sanctuary as a symbol of the fall of the leaders. These once powerful people can no longer find refuge in their homes; they cannot find it at the farthest reaches of the world, nor even when being led away in captivity. God is the Lord of *all* hosts, *Elokei* ***ha****Tzeva'ot,* and no house is strong enough to provide shelter from His judgment.

83. Genesis 44:21; see Ramban and his dissent from Ibn Ezra's position ad loc.
84. And once in Psalms 69:7.
85. The only other place is in Hosea 12:6, in his description of Jacob's struggle with the angel. R. Eliezer of Beaugency explains that this is an expression of Jacob's prince-like mastery over God's hosts. I am discounting I Chronicles 27:3, as *tzeva'ot* there refers to David's honor guard rather than to any divine being or celestial body.
86. 3:13, 6:14.

One final note before moving on. The use of the definite article poses a challenge in translation; most translations avoid the problem altogether and omit the definite article: "Lord of Hosts" rather than "Lord of *the* Hosts."

I propose that we understand the phrase as if it were written as *vaAdonei* ***haTzeva'ot*** – i.e., "the Master of (all of) the (heavenly and earthly) hosts" – reading the opening Name in the construct form, with a *tzerei* under the nun. The element of the Tetragrammaton here changes the vocalization of the previous word, and thus the Name reverts to the more familiar *Ado-nai,* but we should understand it as *Adonei.*[87] This would work seamlessly in all three of Amos's uses of this rare form, as well as in Hosea.[88]

Is He that touches the earth and it melts

Given the biblical principle of minimizing divine anthropomorphisms, God is rarely depicted as "touching" anything. In Psalms, God touches the mountains, and they smoke,[89] which evokes God's power and might at Sinai. Here, God touches the earth, and it melts – this is not merely a description of God's power, but also of terror and fear. The verb root *mog* appears seventeen times in Tanakh, roughly half in reference to the nations, whose collective hearts melt in fear.[90] Only four instances of *mog* refer to the earth melting; two are in Amos: here and in the book's beautiful and uplifting coda.[91] Perhaps this latter instance is calculated to redeem this "melting" motif along with the hills, the Land, and God's people.

---

87. See also Hakham, 70, where he makes a somewhat similar suggestion, reading *Elokei haTzeva'ot.*
88. As noted above (note 2), the fifth use of *hatzeva'ot* has a completely different meaning and context, and even though the *masorah parva* note indicates "five times" at each of these occurrences, that is for orthographic considerations alone and does not impact on meaning.
89. Psalms 104:32, 144:5.
90. Exodus 15:15; see also Joshua 2:9, 24.
91. See chapter 12.

And all that dwell there mourn

When God "touches" the earth, it melts. The image of dry earth melting as if to liquid is an ironic foil to the drying up and withering of its inhabitants.

The word *avel* has already appeared in the verse before Amos's eschatological sequence: thus this double-entendre of "mourning" and "withering" forms a neat *inclusio*.

And it rises up wholly like the River, and sinks again, like the River of Egypt

This couplet echoes the end of Amos's "pre-eschatology" prophecy (8:8) and invites comparison between them:

(8:8) וְעָלְתָה כָאֹר כֻּלָּהּ וְנִגְרְשָׁה וְנִשְׁקְעָה כִּיאוֹר מִצְרָיִם:

(9:5) וְעָלְתָה כַיְאֹר כֻּלָּהּ וְשָׁקְעָה כִּיאֹר מִצְרָיִם:

The first difference is in the first line – *ka'or* has morphed into *kaye'or*. Most scholars assume *ka'or* to be a form (variant? scribal error?) of *keye'or* – Radak notes that *ye'or* here is the same as the one before, "which was missing the *yod*."

The earlier passage also contains *venigresha*. It is based on the root *garesh*, used elsewhere to refer to the "washing away" of mud and detritus in a storm (Is. 57:20). Radak points out that the passive is used in chapter 8 (*venishke'a*) and the active (*veshake'a*) in our verse, as if noting the variants of what are otherwise two parallel verses.

Another possibility is that the earlier verse describes a "cleansing": the waters bring up the silt and then wash it away, following normal tidal movements. Our verse, on the other hand, describes movement that is intentionally destructive: the river floods the land and then drains all the water away.

Finally, note the powerful parallelism in our verse (9:5), which suggests that Amos deliberately borrows his earlier wording to create this image of destruction:

Hanoge'a ba'aretz ***vatamog*** (wet) ***ve'avelu*** *kol yoshvei vah* (dry)
Ve'alta *khaye'or kulah* (wet) ***veshake'a*** *kiy'or Mitzrayim* (dry)

6: It is He who builds His upper chambers in the heaven

Ibn Ezra explains that since all the heavenly powers that have influence over the earth are built into God's "upper chambers," there is no place that is beyond His reach, beyond His "touch":

> ***Haboneh***: The reason for mentioning this is because He created the earth and all of its inhabitants, so where could they hide and flee from His presence? He is able to touch anywhere on the earth and it immediately melts, all the more so any one of the millions of people who dwell there. Then [Amos] states that the earth cannot stand without the support of the heavens.

Ibn Ezra is clarifying the relationship between this hymn and the judgment segment of the vision. In verses 2–3, Amos reminds his audience of the futility of attempting to flee God. The hymn turns this reality from rebuke to praise – from rebuke of those who would dare flee to praise for the One from whom fleeing is impossible.

R. Eliezer of Beaugency's interpretive direction is similar: he reads all the terms of praise for God in this verse as a response to the "escape" routes presented in verses 2–3:

> Therefore, if they burrow into She'ol, it will vomit them up from there and not absorb them in the presence of all who dwell there (!), even if they are at the very bottom of the earth.

And in our verse, he continues:

> And if they ascend and hide atop the Carmel, after all *He builds in the heavens*: Very high...

> *His upper chambers*: To climb up after them to the top of the Carmel and to find and seize them.

Whereas Ibn Ezra presents the heavens as far above human reach – so that human attempts to escape to the "highest heights" are laughable – R. Eliezer's approach minimizes heaven's exalted height to stairs that go "high enough" to reach the top of Carmel.

And has founded His vault (*aguda*) on the earth

Rashi, R. Joseph Kara, and Ibn Ezra interpret *aguda* as all of God's creatures.

Radak explains that the word *aguda* refers to the four elements of creation: "fire, wind, and water, each of which is layered one atop the other, and they are over the earth," and that the verse praises God as creator of all, above and below, which means that He can destroy the entire structure of creation if His people continue to sin. (He notes that Ibn Ezra's first approach is similar.)

Abravanel rejects "all of this philosophizing about nature," and maintains that it is wrong to think that if God takes His chosen nation and suddenly exiles them among the nations, this represents an essential change in His nature. This approach reflects an internal consistency. The hymn is about God's power over His creatures and, as such, is not a lesson in metaphysics, but rather an exploration of how God relates to His people.

Insightful and creative as his explanation may be, it has two difficulties. Whereas Abravanel rejects Ibn Ezra and Radak's notion that the prophet is "philosophizing about science," his reading similarly philosophizes about theology.

In addition, the word *ma'alot,* which can mean "advantages" in medieval Hebrew, does not have that meaning in Tanakh, where it always refers to a physical vehicle for ascent, such as steps or stairs.[92]

R. Eliezer of Beaugency takes an entirely different approach: just as he minimizes the height and depth of the heavens and the

92. As to the famous superscription in Psalms 120–134, see Hakham's introduction to that section in *Da'at Mikra* for a survey of meanings; however, none of those suggestions reflect Abravanel's proposal here.

netherworld in relation to the people's attempted flight from God, he explains this hymn in much humbler terms:

> *Agudato:* The binding of the city wall together, and the wall and its foundations is founded upon the earth.[93]

Should the people try to hide behind city walls, those walls are all founded on the earth that, at God's touch, melts, dissolving the foundations and rendering the walls useless.

These phrases, however, seem to be more poetic than technical (in either the scientific or theological sense) or tactical. The "upper chambers" of heaven (mentioned in Psalms 104:3, 13) seem to be either a general term for "heaven," or celestial "stairs" that link one layer of heaven to the next. Similarly, *aguda* may refer to the lowest level of heaven – the layer of sky visible from the earth.

If so, the hymn remains a paean that speaks of God's greatness and power but does not directly provide support for the punishment and judgment of the previous four verses.

Note the chiastic structure:[94]

Boneh
    bashamayim
        ma'alotav
        Va'agudato
    al eretz
yesada

93. He bases this explanation on a related verb in the context of wall building in Nehemiah 3:38.
94. Paul notes this.

He summons the waters of the sea and pours them out upon the face of the earth – the Lord is His name.

This clause is identical to the conclusion of Amos's earlier hymn (5:8). This raises two questions. First, why is it repeated here? Second, is its meaning the same in this context?

Most of Amos's eschatological vision draws on the ideas, phrases, and themes he presents in his first seven and a half chapters of oratory. As such, the meaning of this phrase should be understood against the backdrop of its earlier invocation.

Chapter 5's "spilling of the sea" is prefaced with a description of God's control over the stars and the cycle of night and day. We read this as examples of God's infinite tools for meting out punishment and destruction. If we take the same approach here, it is consistent with the *Rishonim*'s model that the entire hymn is a response to the futile flight described in the first four verses.

If, however, we read this hymn as independent of that judgment-sequence, then this phrase evokes God's power during the Flood, which expressed His absolute dominion over the universe. God's ability to obliterate the land by summoning the waters not only shows His capability to destroy, but, in the deepest and most elemental sense, also establishes His absolute sovereignty over both land and sea.

IS ISRAEL STILL CHOSEN? (9:7–12)

(ז) הֲלוֹא כִבְנֵי כֻשִׁיִּים אַתֶּם לִי בְּנֵי יִשְׂרָאֵל נְאֻם ה׳ הֲלוֹא אֶת יִשְׂרָאֵל הֶעֱלֵיתִי
מֵאֶרֶץ מִצְרַיִם וּפְלִשְׁתִּיִּים מִכַּפְתּוֹר וַאֲרָם מִקִּיר: (ח) הִנֵּה עֵינֵי אֲדֹנָי ה׳ בַּמַּמְלָכָה
הַחַטָּאָה וְהִשְׁמַדְתִּי אֹתָהּ מֵעַל פְּנֵי הָאֲדָמָה אֶפֶס כִּי לֹא הַשְׁמֵיד אַשְׁמִיד אֶת
בֵּית יַעֲקֹב נְאֻם ה׳: (ט) כִּי הִנֵּה אָנֹכִי מְצַוֶּה וַהֲנִעוֹתִי בְכָל הַגּוֹיִם אֶת בֵּית
יִשְׂרָאֵל כַּאֲשֶׁר יִנּוֹעַ בַּכְּבָרָה וְלֹא יִפּוֹל צְרוֹר אָרֶץ: (י) בַּחֶרֶב יָמוּתוּ כֹּל חַטָּאֵי
עַמִּי הָאֹמְרִים לֹא תַגִּישׁ וְתַקְדִּים בַּעֲדֵינוּ הָרָעָה: (יא) בַּיּוֹם הַהוּא אָקִים אֶת
סֻכַּת דָּוִיד הַנֹּפֶלֶת וְגָדַרְתִּי אֶת פִּרְצֵיהֶן וַהֲרִסֹתָיו אָקִים וּבְנִיתִיהָ כִּימֵי עוֹלָם:
(יב) לְמַעַן יִירְשׁוּ אֶת שְׁאֵרִית אֱדוֹם וְכָל הַגּוֹיִם אֲשֶׁר נִקְרָא שְׁמִי עֲלֵיהֶם נְאֻם
ה׳ עֹשֶׂה זֹּאת:

> 7 Are you not like the children of the Ethiopians unto Me, O
> children of Israel? says the Lord. Did I not bring up Israel out
> of the land of Egypt, and the Philistines from Kaftor, and Aram
> from Kir? **8** Behold, the eyes of the Lord God are on the sinful
> kingdom, and I will destroy it from off the face of the earth; yet
> I will not utterly destroy the house of Jacob, says the Lord. **9** For,
> surely I will command, and I will sift the house of Israel among
> all the nations, as one shakes with a sieve, but no pebble shall fall
> to the ground. **10** All the sinners of My people shall die by the
> sword, who say: "The evil will not overtake nor confront us." **11**
> On that day I will raise up David's fallen tabernacle, and close
> up its breaches. And I will raise up his ruins, and I will rebuild
> it as in the days of old; **12** that they may possess the remnant of
> Edom, and all the nations upon whom My name is called, says
> the Lord who does this.

7: Are you not (*Halo*) like the children of the Ethiopians unto Me, O children of Israel?

The opening *Halo,* employing rhetorical *hei,* expresses surprise and anticipates the audience's surprised reaction – Amos uses it twice in this verse as if to highlight how surprising this question should be to his audience. By extension, these questions should also surprise us, Amos's eternal audience.

Israel's chosen status as the culmination of a process that began with Abraham's selection is a foundational theme throughout Tanakh. Amos, too, embraces this theme. When Amos states: "I have known *only you* from all the families of the earth," it is clear that the election of Israel is central to his prophetic mission. God has chosen Israel, and this status comes with responsibility. When God's chosen people sin, they are held more accountable: "therefore I will visit upon you all of your iniquities."

Thus the *halo* question of this opening line is surprising because it implies that God does not consider Israel any different from any other nation – so surprising that it rates a *halo* introduction, and even a second *halo* before the idea is explicated.

But why Cush (Ethiopia)? Why compare Israel to the Cushites? Is it a random choice, as if to say "you are no different than any other nation"? Even so, the choice of a nation that features minimally in biblical historical drama is mystifying. Cush is first mentioned as one of the sons of Ham, Noah's son, in the Table of Nations.[95]

The land of Cush is typically presented as an example of a distant place, such as the southwestern border of the Persian empire,[96] although it is sometimes paired with Egypt.[97] Two Cushites are mentioned in biblical narrative, although neither is a notable character.[98]

The word *li* (*atem li*) is significant here – the prophet is not making an objective equation, but rather a relational one. He is stating that God relates to the Cushites the same way He relates to Israel. This underscores the inherent difficulties in this passage – how can it be that God's connection to the distant Cushites is no different than His relationship with Israel?

One final note about the Cushites here. Elsewhere, they are called simply Cushites;[99] here, they are called *Bnei Kushi'im*. This is calculated to further equate them to Bnei Yisrael and thus mock the Israelites that the special connection they assumed to have with God is no more.

Says the Lord

Amos has used this signature formula throughout his oracles, always to express divine threat or disapproval (although this will change in its

95. See Genesis 10:6–7. The land of Cush (south of Egypt, generally identified with Ethiopia) is first mentioned in Genesis 2:13, in identifying the rivers that leave from Eden. The "Gihon" is commonly understood to be another name for the White Nile. Genesis 2:11 identifies the "Pishon" river as going around the land of "Havila," just as the "Gihon" circumnavigates "Cush." Havila, as we will see forthwith, was a son of Cush; the entire area of the headwaters of both the Blue and White Nile are considered to be the "land of Cush" – i.e., Ethiopia.
96. For example, Esther 1:1 – see also Isaiah 18:1.
97. For example, Isaiah 20:3–5.
98. Tirhaka – see II Kings 19 (= Isaiah 37); perhaps, depending how we read *eved-melekh* – see Jeremiah 38.
99. For example, II Chronicles 14:11–12.

final appearance in 9:13, below). This intensifies the sense of desertion Amos wishes to convey to his audience.

Did I not (*Halo*) bring up Israel out of the land of Egypt

In the second half of this verse, Amos mentions three other nations and their corresponding locations.

Earlier, Amos mentions the Exodus as an expression of God's special relationship with His people (2:10, 3:1), but here he uses it in the opposite sense: to *equate* God's relationship with Israel to His relationship with other nations. If God redeemed the Philistines and Arameans just as He redeemed Israel, then there is nothing left of the special bond between God and His "treasured nation."

And the Philistines from Kaftor

It is broadly accepted that the Philistines of the settlement period originated in the Greek Islands;[100] early Egyptian texts refer to them as the "sea-peoples." Most associate Kaftor with Crete or another of the Greek Islands; some identify it with Cyprus. In any case, the mention of Kaftor connects this stage of Amos's eschaton with the beginning of the previous vision, where God commands, "*hakh hakaftor*" – strike the *kaftor*.

This phrase equates the migration of the "sea people" into Egypt and the Levant (generally dated to the thirteenth century BCE) with Israel's Exodus from Egypt. Both of these nations began as conquering armies and eventually settled the Land; there was perpetual tension between them until and through David's time. The parallels, drawn

100. There were two distinct groups of "Pelishtim" in Israel. During the Patriarchal era, both Abraham and Isaac had interactions with the "Pelishtim" who appeared to be a settled group, with a king (Abimelech) and an agricultural lifestyle. By the time Israel returned as a nation, a different group called "Pelishtim" lived there in various cities along the Mediterranean coast – organized as a military force, led by "captains" (*seranim*) instead of kings. The Pelishtim here – and in chapter 1 – are these latter arrivals. The name "sea-peoples" first appears in the inscriptions of Ramesses III (1182–1151 BCE).

together in this verse, should be too close for comfort – which is Amos's very purpose.

And Aram from Kir?

The Arameans originally came from Kir, which Elitzur identifies with Diacira in northeastern Mesopotamia.[101] Amos presents the relationship between the Arameans and Kir in his first oracle: Aram's punishment concludes with their exile (back) to Kir, their original place.[102]

Rashi reads Aram's relationship with Kir differently, as a prophecy: God *will* bring the Aramean nation *back* from Kir when their Assyrian captors fall from power. Rashi presumably thinks that the Arameans originated in Aram, west of the Euphrates, and, as such, could not have originally come from Kir.

In any case, this verse is clearly calculated to undermine Israel's status as the chosen nation.

The Larger Question

Does this verse signify a reversal of Israel's chosen status? Are they no longer considered God's "treasure"? Is Amos's intent to *threaten* the people with a demotion to "regular-nation" status, or is there a more profound message to unearth here?

I will begin by noting the *Rishonim*'s understanding of this passage.

Rashi believes that this equation points to the essential equivalence between Israel and other nations: that although God's relationship with Israel began with the Exodus, God also moved other nations around and dispossessed inhabitants to make way for them – so the Exodus *is not an automatic guarantee* that this special relationship will remain. Rashi also points out that since all humanity is descended from Noah, we are not fundamentally different from the children of the "cursed" son, Ham.

---

101. Yoel Elitzur, "Kir, the Birthplace of the Arameans: A New Look" [Heb.], in *Annual for Biblical and Ancient Near East Studies* 21 (2012): 141–152.
102. This exile is documented in II Kings 16:9.

R. Joseph Kara concurs, and emphasizes that since Israel has failed to keep the covenant that was the goal of that Exodus, their movement is just like the movement of any other nation.

R. Eliezer of Beaugency's approach is similar. He adds that the Arameans originated in Kir, and conquered and established a powerful monarchy in Syria – but will fall from power and be exiled back to Kir. In the same way, Amos's audience will lose their sovereignty and be exiled.

Radak believes that Amos mentions the Cushites as prototypical slaves – and that God's statement here is that Israel *ought* to have had the same fealty to God. He then reads the rest of the verse as a rhetorical question: "I brought Israel up out of Egypt, *did I bring Pelishtim from Kaftor or Aram from Kir?*" He then suggests that this question, although written in the past tense, should be understood as the future – that the Philistines will (again) be exiled to Kaftor and the Arameans to Kir – but He will *not* bring them out of their exile, unlike what God will do for Israel. Radak admits that this interpretation is not without its challenges and adds that the reader should consider other opinions and choose the most convincing one.

In an entirely different take, Abravanel reads the verse as a dialogue between God and the people. Unlike the earlier exegetes, he understands the opening statement as the beginning of Amos's "consolation coda" here – that this opening in fact *emphasizes* Israel's chosen status. He begins by borrowing from Radak: just as the Cushites are the quintessential slaves, Israel will always be God's slaves – ever since He brought them out of Egypt. Abravanel writes:

> And if you say that I also brought the Philistines from Kaftor and the Arameans from Kir, and other nations from under the rule of yet other nations who enslaved them for a long time yet they did not become My slaves ... this is just the way of the world, so it was and so will it be.... If so, the statement "Philistines from Kaftor and Aram from Kir" is what Bnei Yisrael will respond to God.

"Are You Not Like the Cushites unto Me?" Setting Up the Next Verse

I would like to recommend a different approach to this verse, one inspired by a panoramic view of the book. Amos's opening prophecy is a series of oracles against the nations, the first six of which are Israel's surrounding neighbors. The first of these nations is Aram – whose final punishment will be to be exiled (back) to Kir.

Amos's eschaton is entirely drawn from the material of his prophecies throughout the book: each is a necessary building block in the great edifice of his "end-of-days" vision.

The gist of his first series of oracles is that all nations are held accountable to God and will ultimately stand in judgment before Him. Like the rest of the nations, Israel will also be held accountable for their deeds – but given its special relationship with God, Israel is held to a higher standard, as Amos eloquently states after his first indictment of Israel (3:2).

Here, as the book of Amos nears its end, the prophet turns back to this opening message: that Israel is a nation like every nation and yet a nation apart.

We began our analysis of this section by asking "Why Cush?" Amos deliberately selects Cush; he begins this penultimate message by pointing to a distant, irrelevant nation. As noted, Cush is virtually insignificant in Israelite history; descended from a different Noahide family, they have had nothing to do with Israel's geopolitical history. Amos wishes to emphasize that every nation – no matter how near or far – has a relationship with God and is accountable to Him. God has redeemed other nations, shifted other populations, enslaved and liberated countless others. Israel is no different from any other nation.

But here, too, Amos is planning a surprise for his audience. His opening prophecy was designed to lull his Samarian audience into a sense of relief and complacency at the description of their enemies' punishment. Then he surprised them by turning and accusing them of the worst corruption of all. His first series of oracles boxed Israel in before he turned on them with a caustic attack.

Here, however, Amos aims for the opposite effect. He begins by puncturing the audience's sense that they are special. He mocks them: you are no different than any other nation. Other nations have a relationship with God. God has taken other nations out of slavery and made them conquerors in other lands as well. He cruelly breaks them down…

only, in the next verse, to build them up. Amos wields the same force of rhetorical surprise – but in the opposite direction. Here, at the end of the book, Amos uses his surprise to comfort and console, rather than to reproach. In the next verse we will see how the fraught tension, the possibility of "sameness" that is so threatening to Israel, is resolved in favor of "chosenness" and *segulah*. This verse lowers Israel's morale to restore their sense of equilibrium in the next; to surprise them with the reassurance that ultimately, when all the dross is burned away, the pure silver core of the covenant remains, and always will.

8: Behold (*Hinei*), the eyes of the Lord God

The phrase *hinei yamim ba'im* marks a sea change, a shift in tone, and we are ready for something unexpected. As a result, we anticipate something new with the brief *Hinei* introducing the next stage of this message.

Throughout his prophecies – from his first series of oracles – Amos emphasizes that what God demands of His people is more than what He expects from others. The neighboring nations are called to judgment for war crimes of a most more sensitive nature. Judah's crime is a lack of fealty to the Torah – an offense of a higher nature. And when the prophet zeroes in on his target audience – Samaria – he accuses them not merely of "3 → 4" offenses, but of "3 + 4," listing seven offenses. Grave though they may be, they fall significantly short of the war crimes for which the other nations are indicted and sentenced.

But here, Amos clarifies that these higher demands also come with a lifeline. God, who not only took Israel out of Egypt but also took the Philistines from Caphtor and the Arameans from Kir, judges all nations and will punish each one. This includes Israel – in fact, His judgment of Israel is far more exacting than His judgment of the other nations. But while the other nations sin, are sent into exile, and fade away forever, Israel will never suffer such final punishment. God will always preserve the house of Jacob. This significant theological statement will be developed over the next verses.

We might explain the "eyes" of God as *hashgaḥa,* but not in the modern sense of the word, which always expresses positive Divine Providence. The *Rishonim* use *hashgaḥa* in its neutral sense – God is keeping

His eye on a certain person, family, nation, or Land.[103] This monitoring can be for protection or for punishment – the result of this divine surveillance depends on the subject's moral station.

Here, once again, Amos uses the combination of A-D-N-Y + Tetragrammaton, which reassures that God's absolute might and judgment is accompanied by His abiding love for all His creations.

Are on the sinful kingdom, and I will destroy it from off the face of the earth

Most *Rishonim* read the "sinful kingdom" here as Samaria, Amos's target audience, but this approach depends on how the previous verse is read. If it is part of Amos's rebuke against his audience, then it stands to reason that they are the "sinful kingdom." If, however, we see the previous verse as preparing the ground for the affirmation of Israel's chosen status, we may read it differently.

Whichever approach we take must be sympathetic with the next phrase: "I will not destroy the house of Jacob."

Rashi identifies the sinful kingdom as the house of Yehu (Jeroboam) – to the exclusion of Judah. R. Joseph Kara agrees, but widens the meaning of "the sinful kingdom" to the northern monarchy overall, noting that, nonetheless, it will not be entirely destroyed.

Ibn Ezra, who also views the "sinful kingdom" as Israel, makes an astute distinction between Israel's sinful *monarchy* (a theme that permeates Amos) and the *people* of Israel: God will destroy the royal house, but not all of *Beit Yaakov*. Radak concurs.

R. Eliezer of Beaugency reads "sinful kingdom" as a general providential reality – God watches *every* sinful kingdom and will destroy them. However, whereas other sinful nations will be utterly destroyed, Israel will suffer exile and oppression – but never complete annihilation.

Similarly, Abravanel argues that the "sinful kingdom" is *not* Ephraim (= Israel). Rather, this verse expresses Israel's unique status: God will obliterate ("in an instant") any *other* nation that sins before Him. He draws on both biblical and post-biblical history to point out

103. See Deuteronomy 11:12.

how many once-mighty nations have passed from the world. This recalls Mark Twain's famous essay, "Concerning the Jews":

> The Egyptian, the Babylonian, and the Persian rose, filled the planet with sound and splendor, then faded to dream-stuff and passed away; the Greek and the Roman followed, and made a vast noise, and they are gone; other peoples have sprung up and held their torch high for a time, but it burned out, and they sit in twilight now, or have vanished.
>
> The Jew saw them all, beat them all, and is now what he always was, exhibiting no decadence, no infirmities of age, no weakening of his parts, no slowing of his energies, no dulling of his alert and aggressive mind. All things are mortal but the Jew; all other forces pass, but he remains. What is the secret of his immortality?

His secret, Amos would affirm, is his eternal covenant with God.

The previous verse, which equates Israel with other nations, seems to support R. Eliezer of Beaugency's view that this is a broad statement of how God's providence operates with all nations, without distinction. But Ibn Ezra's approach also bears repeating: Amos is presenting a powerful truth that is at once harsh and comforting. To equate a nation with its leadership – *l'etat c'est moi* – is pointedly refuted here. The kingdom may be destroyed, but the people will live on. Where the monarchy – especially the northern monarchy – has failed, the people will survive, because God's covenant is a bond with His *people.* They may be exiled – which marks the fall of their sovereignty – and they may be oppressed, but they will never be destroyed.

Yet I will not utterly destroy

In this context, the word *efes* (yet) signals a reservation or limitation on something said before. Amos uses this word to express that while all other sinning nations *will* be completely destroyed, this will not be true of the house of Jacob. The use of *efes* here supports Abravanel's view that the "sinful kingdom" refers to everyone *except* for Israel.

The subsequent combination of *ki* and the negative *lo* expresses the strongest possible emphasis: "I will *absolutely never* utterly destroy the house of Jacob." Here, it generates consolation and relief.

The house of Jacob

Amos uses this name for Israel twice: in his indictment against the altars at Beit El (3:13) and here. The use of *Beit Yaakov* should remind the people of two things. It recalls the national covenant forged at Sinai,[104] a covenant that is founded upon absolute loyalty to God, which was violated at Beit El. In addition, this name emphasizes the people's common history, lineage, and *family* connection. As part of the same family, Israel should show responsibility for each other, rather than the upper class's oppression of the poor that Amos has condemned throughout the book.

This penultimate prophecy, phrased to offer consolation and hope to the people, restores *Beit Yaakov* to its cherished place as a term of honor, a reminder of the people's commitment to their ancestors – and each other – and God's eternal covenant with Jacob.

Says the Lord

This mini-signature marks the end of an idea. Verses 7–8 have described God's providence and how it operates – all kingdoms are held accountable to God, but the *people* of Israel will outlive them all.

9: For, surely I will command

These next two verses explicate the previous statement. God has committed to destroy sinful kingdoms; on the other hand, *Beit Yaakov* will not be wiped out. We now hear how this tension will be resolved. Unlike other nations, whose success and survival are fully dependent on their sovereignty, Israel can withstand exile, dispersion, and even subjugation. That is why Amos began this prophecy by evoking the Exodus:

104. *Ko tomar leveit Yaakov* – Exodus 19:3.

though Israel were slaves in an alien land for centuries, they endured and achieved independence and sovereignty in the Land.

God has already "commanded" in this eschaton; He threatens to command the serpent to bite those who try to hide from Him at the bottom of the sea (9:3), and to command the sword to kill the captives "fleeing" His presence (v. 4).

God uses a range of intermediaries to fulfill His will – a wind, a fish, and a plant all act as God's agents in the Jonah story. What is God commanding here? This very ambiguity indicates that He will shape history to His will; this "command" may also extend to the next verse, again referring to the sword that will kill "all the sinners of My people."

And I will sift the house of Israel among all the nations

Harsher than mere exile, this is the threat of wandering. Israel will be thrust from nation to nation. The verb *noa'* here recalls the beginning of this eschaton, where people will "wander (*vena'u*) from sea to sea... to seek out the words of Hashem." This further contributes to the two visions' cohesion and may even be perceived as further explication of the "wandering" in the first: if the people abandon their search for God's word and return to their evil ways, they will be subjected to a more severe form of wandering with more disastrous consequences.

As one shakes with a sieve, but no pebble shall fall to the ground

There are various possible readings for this image. The question is whether remaining "in the sieve" represents safety or being trapped.

Radak explains that there are three groups among the people, symbolized by grain (the righteous), the dirt and detritus (the wicked, including the leaders), and the pebbles (those for whom there is still hope). He alternatively suggests that the purpose of the sieve here is to rid the collected grain of the bad seeds, which will fall out to the ground.

R. Eliezer of Beaugency, in contrast, reads the grain as the leadership – grain is sifted out of the sieve, while the "pebbles," the poorer and lesser people who will remain – not one will fall to the ground.

Abravanel interprets *tzeror* not as "pebble" rather as "bundle":[105] some members of the nation will be killed, but the *tzeror*, the collective people – *Beit Yaakov* – will not fall.

Hakham argues that the fine, edible part of the grain is sifted out and used, while the coarse pebbles and inedible parts remain in the sieve – symbolizing the wicked, who are trapped in the sieve and cannot escape punishment: "no pebble shall fall upon the earth" = no sinners will escape punishment.

10: All the sinners of my people shall die by the sword

The sword is a recurring motif in this eschaton. Amos mentions it three times (out of a total of eight in the book) in this chapter, always as God's agent of punishment.

This phrase – *hata'ei **ami*** – cannot be referring to any other nation.

These verses present how God gradually deals with His people: He will first exile them among the nations, sifting them out like grain from a sieve; then, those who are beyond hope of redemption will be killed outright by the sword. Who is beyond help? Those who deny that there is anything wrong, the obstinate and complacent. They refuse to admit their own sin or that there is anything wrong, thus making reflection and repentance impossible.[106]

Who say: "The evil will not overtake nor confront us"

This is denial of the principle of reward and punishment. In the absence of a moral compass, which Amos has bewailed throughout his oracles, the only hope for repentance and redemption is fear of punishment. If the people remain convinced that nothing bad will befall them, then how will they ever return? Given that they are beyond hope, the sword will catch up with them. The rest of the nation – perhaps the oppressed lower classes – will survive and ultimately return, as described in Amos's hopeful epilogue.

---

105. As in Deuteronomy 14:25.
106. See, for instance, Jeremiah 7 and Amos 6:1.

11: On that day

This phrase brings us back to the previous passage – and to even earlier ones that mention "day" or "days." Through "on *that* day," the prophet connects the following line to a "day" he has already mentioned. A biblical "day" may refer to a period of time, not an actual twenty-four-hour period.[107] This may refer back to *hayom hahu* (8:9), the day of terrible weeping and mourning, but it seems more likely that that passage, being the end of Amos's "present-time" oracles, is not connected to this prophecy. Another possibility is the beginning of Amos's eschaton: "Behold, the *days* are coming, says the Lord God, that I will send a famine in the land" (8:11). This marks the beginning of Amos's vision of the distant future, a time that will begin with a terrible famine and a thirst for God's word – but neither will be sated. God will command the shaking of "the building," which will lead to the death of all those who attempt to flee; finally, the kingdom will be destroyed, and the people exiled, sifting out those who are beyond rehabilitation. Then, on that day – at the end of that time – God will set the beginning of redemption into motion.

The phrases *hinei yamim ba'im* and *bayom hahu* form a classic chiastic structure:

8:11 *hinei yamim ba'im* (the famine)
    8:13 *bayom hahu* (the results of the famine)
        9:1–10 The final "vision" and judgment of all the nations, and Israel's special status
    9:11: *bayom hahu* (the beginning of restoration)
9:13: *hinei yamim ba'im* (complete restoration)

I will raise up David's fallen tabernacle

The meaning of the phrase *Sukkat David* has generated much scholarly debate. While we instinctively associate this term with the festival of Sukkot,[108] this limits our understanding of the verse.

107. Ibn Ezra makes that point here: "*yom* refers to a time period."

108. Tabernacles – see, *inter alia,* Leviticus 23:33–43.

The word *sukka/sukkot* appears thirty-three times in Tanakh;[109] seventeen instances refer to the holiday. Thirteen refer to temporary huts constructed for basic shade and shelter during travel, war, or harvest-time, or as a metaphor for protection – of clouds that cover and shield or of divine protection from enemies.

Considering these connotations of protection, two of the remaining instances are surprising: one describes how the wicked lie in wait for the innocent (Ps. 10:7–8):

> He sits in ambush in the villages; in hiding places he murders the innocent. His eyes stealthily watch for the hapless, he lurks in secret like a lion in his *sukka;* he lurks that he may seize the poor, he seizes the poor when he draws him into his net.

The other describes how the lion lies in wait for its prey (Job 38:39):

> Can you hunt the prey for the lion, or satisfy the appetite of the young lions, when they crouch in their dens, or lie in wait in their *sukka*?

This leaves the remaining instance of *sukka*: here, in Amos, "*Sukkat David.*" What is the significance of this famous phrase?

Rashi cites the Targum's explanation that this refers to David's royal line.

In his second commentary, R. Joseph Kara concurs: "After I destroy the wicked kingdom (v. 8), at that point I will restore the monarchy of the house of David." In his first commentary, however, he interprets *Sukkat David* as the Temple.

R. Yosef ibn Kaspi writes similarly:

> And the survivors will return to Jerusalem and will build the House, as it says: "On that day I will raise up the fallen *Sukka* of

109. I am not reckoning Job 40:31 which, according to most commentators, has a completely different meaning and root; nor the nineteen uses as a toponym, eighteen of which refer to the location identified as Deir 'Alla on the east bank of the Jordan.

David" and this was said about Zerubbabel who was from the Davidic line.

R. Eliezer of Beaugency explains that shepherds make huts so that they can sit in the shade as they watch over their flocks; since David was considered Israel's shepherd, the phrase *Sukkat David* likens Jerusalem and David's royal house to these shepherd huts.

Radak explains that the monarchy here is called *sukka* because it covers and protects the nation. Perhaps this concept also supports the above view that it refers to the Temple, which is perceived as a place of protection for Israel.

Reading *Sukkat David* as the Temple is also supported by use of the verb *hakeim*, which usually expresses the "fulfillment" of a promise or the "erection" of a structure,[110] and, most significantly, describes how the Tabernacle is erected in the wilderness.[111]

Drawing on all the above, I would like to suggest that *Sukkat David* indeed refers to the Davidic monarchy. As Radak points out, a king's role is to protect his subjects; moreover, the shepherd motif is inextricably linked to David's leadership.

Other motifs associated with the *sukka* also contribute to this reading.

First of all, as is clear from a ritual perspective and from its use during harvest-time, travel, or war, a *sukka* is, by definition, temporary (the Sages use the term *dirat arai* – a temporary dwelling).[112] Dwelling in such an insubstantial, temporary dwelling expresses certain dependence on God: the *sukka* is thus at once a symbol of divine protection and of instability.

---

110. Such as the stones at Gilgal in Joshua 4:20.

111. Exodus 40:2; Numbers 10:21.

112. This phrase was evidently coined by Rava – see, *inter alii,* Yoma 10b. See Rubenstein's article in Jeffrey L. Rubenstein, "The 'Sukka' as Temporary or Permanent Dwelling: Study in the Development of Talmudic Thought," *Hebrew Union College Annual* 64 (1993): 137–166. Nonetheless, the experience of *sukka* as temporary dwelling significantly predates Rava, and seems to be anchored in the nature and typical use of the structure itself.

This reading is further enriched by the two anomalous instances of the *sukka* referring to the lion's lair. Although David is romanticized as a gentle, caring shepherd and poet, he was also a mighty warrior and a scion of the tribe of Judah, the royal tribe compared to a lion (Gen. 49:9). The lion symbolizes David's power and military prowess.

Amos's use of *sukka* is thus a brilliant, complex metaphor for the royal house of David.

On one hand, the *sukka* is inherently temporary, an expression of ultimate dependence on God. Without God's support, monarchy is but a house of cards; it is inherently insubstantial and exists only for the people's protection. Leadership that focuses on its own gratification – especially at the people's expense – is doomed to failure. Amos has already warned of the fall of the northern monarchy while promising the return of the *people* of Israel. Here, the divorce between the people and their failed leadership comes to the fore: the house of Jacob will survive, but the *kingdom* will fall because it misunderstood its role. Its job was not to feed itself or to see its subjects as a means to its own self-gratification. Rather, its job is to protect its citizens (the *sukka* as protection), to exemplify the awareness that all protection comes from God (the *sukka* as temporary and flimsy cover), while also demonstrating tenacity and valor against the enemies, pouncing on them like a lion from its lair. The phrase *Sukkat David,* with its complex, multifaceted connotations, is an ingenious symbol for the restoration of the Davidic monarchy in its ideal form. Amos imagines a Davidic monarchy, mighty as a lion, bringing protection and security for the people – yet it will ever remain a *sukka,* an inherently insubstantial structure whose stability is entirely dependent on the extent of its loyalty to God and His divine truths of righteous justice: "David reigned over all of Israel, and David upheld justice and righteousness for all his people" (II Sam. 8:15).

And close up its breaches

The word *peretz* is profoundly associated with David. Not only is David descended from the Peretz clan of Judah, but the word also appears repeatedly throughout the David narrative cycle.[113] Thus, this verb is well-suited to the context of the royal house of David and is also linked to Jerusalem's security. The verb *gadarti* supports reading *Sukkat David* as the royal city, not the Temple.

And I will raise up his ruins

Hakeim appears twice in this verse – raising up *Sukkat David* and raising up the ruins of the city. Abravanel connects this to the tragic prophecy in 5:2:

> *Nafla lo tosif kum betulat Yisrael; nit'sha al admatah ein mekimah.*
>
> She has fallen and will never again *rise*, the maiden of Israel; she has been abandoned on her own land, there is no one to *raise her up*.

Abravanel sees our verse as "redeeming" the earlier one, and distinguishes between *betulat Yisrael* – a symbol of the northern monarchy (that will never rise again), and *Sukkat David,* which will reunite all the tribes under Davidic rule.

Here, too, Amos draws on his earlier material to reimagine Israel's glorious future.

And I will rebuild it as in the days of old

All the verbs in this verse are in the first person: at this point, the people are God's passive beneficiaries, but a fuller, more mutual partnership will emerge in the epilogue.

The phrase *kiymei olam* appears only three times in Tanakh, most famously in Malachi 3:4, with the promise that sacrificial delight will be restored *kiymei olam*. Micah's closing prophecy begins with this beautiful image (7:14–15):

113. See, for example, II Samuel 5:20; I Kings 11:27; II Kings 14:13.

> Shepherd your people with your shepherd's rod.... Allow them to graze in Bashan and Gilead, as they did in the old days (*kiymei olam*). As in the days when you departed (*kiymei tzeitkha*) from the land of Egypt, I will show you miraculous deeds.

The sense of nostalgia is palpable here; the phrase *kiymei tzeitkha* also evokes the Exodus, which the prophets paint as a time of deep romance between God and His people.[114]

Amos's image of a rebuilt Jerusalem also evokes a golden age – the "glory days" of the united monarchy in Jerusalem. Just as Malachi's *kiymei olam* anticipates return to the sweet offerings of the First Temple period, Amos's *kiymei olam* anticipates return to those halcyon days of Davidic rule.

12: That they may possess the remnant of Edom

The word *lema'an* can be understood in one of two ways: as defining the purpose of the previous clause, or as an independent statement. The former approach implies that the purpose of this restoration is to disinherit the remnants of Edom and complete the prophecy given to the pregnant Rebecca: "the younger shall the elder serve" (Gen. 25:23).

It is more likely that *lema'an* here describes the next step of the restored Davidic kingdom: to use the *sukka* as a lion's lair from which to pounce on Edom and defeat them – a metonymy of the expansion of Israel's borders.

And all the nations upon whom My name is called

Should this be read as "all the nations of the world (because they are all) called by My name"? Does this include *all* the nations, or does it refer to a specific group – and if so, how do we define this group? Are they nations that are somehow linked to the God of Israel, such as those descended from Abraham? Or does it mean all of the nations whom God's prophets have addressed?

114. See Hosea 2; Jeremiah 2:1–2.

Says the Lord who does this

This conclusion reiterates that this renewed, powerful monarchy is only as powerful as its connection with God, who will give the Davidic king and his flock the strength to realize this vision.

Chapter 12

Consolation and Restoration (9:13–15)

After the harrowing rises and falls of Amos's vision of the end of days, we are finally led home to still waters and serene pastures in his final words of consolation.

Biblical authors traditionally conclude their works with uplifting, hopeful messages.[1] This is especially salient after a work that is mostly reproach and dire warning; the two sharpest examples are probably Amos and Joel.[2]

Even so, Amos's sudden softening of mood and tone is surprising, leading some to suggest that these final three verses were added by a later author, perhaps even exilic or post-exilic, in order to make the book

1. This practice influenced R. Yehuda HaNasi, the editors of the Talmud Bavli, as well as medieval codifiers to follow suit.
2. See the illuminative comment in Midrash Tana'im, Deuteronomy 33:1.

palatable to a vanquished population.[3] I disagree not from a doctrinal perspective, but from a literary perspective: the language and imagery of this coda is clearly Amos's voice – loud, clear, and dulcet – echoing through the generations. Amos pieces these sweet lines together from images from the rest of his book – only this time, the images are colored in tones of light and redemption.

The Text

(יג) הִנֵּה יָמִים בָּאִים נְאֻם ה׳ וְנִגַּשׁ חוֹרֵשׁ בַּקֹּצֵר וְדֹרֵךְ עֲנָבִים בְּמֹשֵׁךְ הַזָּרַע
וְהִטִּיפוּ הֶהָרִים עָסִיס וְכָל הַגְּבָעוֹת תִּתְמוֹגַגְנָה: (יד) וְשַׁבְתִּי אֶת שְׁבוּת עַמִּי
יִשְׂרָאֵל וּבָנוּ עָרִים נְשַׁמּוֹת וְיָשָׁבוּ וְנָטְעוּ כְרָמִים וְשָׁתוּ אֶת יֵינָם וְעָשׂוּ גַנּוֹת
וְאָכְלוּ אֶת פְּרִיהֶם: (טו) וּנְטַעְתִּים עַל אַדְמָתָם וְלֹא יִנָּתְשׁוּ עוֹד מֵעַל אַדְמָתָם
אֲשֶׁר נָתַתִּי לָהֶם אָמַר ה׳ אֱלֹהֶיךָ:

13 Behold, the days come, says the Lord, that the plowman will overtake the reaper, and the treader of grapes him who sows seed. And the mountains shall drip sweet wine, and all the hills will melt. **14** And I will return the captivity of My people Israel, and they shall build the waste cities and inhabit them; and they shall plant vineyards and drink wine from them; they will also make gardens and eat fruit from them. **15** And I will plant them upon their Land, and they shall never again be plucked up from their Land which I have given them, says the Lord your God.

13: Behold, the days come

This *Hinei yamim ba'im* echoes the eschaton's opening (8:11), bringing this entire end-of-days sequence full circle.

The first *Hinei yamim ba'im* warned of a famine; this one heralds a time of plenty. The first warned of wandering from place to place, of

3. Oft-quoted in the literature is Wellhausen's observation that the final verses of Amos are "Rosen und Lavendel statt Blut und Eisen" (roses and lavender instead of blood and iron) – see *Die Kleinen Propheten* (Berlin, 1898), 96.

starving for sustenance and God's word. This, by contrast, promises stability, permanence, and deep roots in solid ground.

Says the Lord

In the previous section, God is entirely active, and the people entirely passive; this section presents a more even-handed relationship.

To maintain the constant awareness of the source of Israel's strength and blessing, the vision opens and closes with the divine signature.

That the plowman will overtake the reaper

The two planting cycles referenced here are wheat and grapes. In the Levant, wheat was planted in mid fall, after plowing the land. It was harvested in late spring – Shavuot is the wheat harvest festival. Grapes are typically planted in late winter/early spring, begin blossoming in early summer, and are harvested in late summer or early fall.[4] Along with olives, these are the Land's most famous crops; each has a planting-to-reaping cycle of approximately half a year.

For the "plowman to overtake the reaper" means that there is such an abundance of produce that the seasons are now running year-round; the wheat crop is thriving to the extent that the ground never lies fallow. Usually, this is neither feasible nor healthy for the ground: the wheat seeds need rain to germinate and soft spring rain and sunshine to sprout; moreover, crop rotation is an ancient wisdom that both preserves and revives the land.[5] Such year-round abundance is a special sign of divine favor.

And the treader of grapes him who sows seed

Though there is evidence of grape-pressing tools predating the monarchic era, the image of treading the grapes by foot is pastoral and romantic;

---

4. See Judges 21:19 – the grape harvest festival which was, per 4QMMT on Av 15 (mid-summer).
5. See, *inter alii*, Bava Batra 29a and *Mishneh Torah, Hilkhot To'en veNit'an* 12:4.

an expression of a personal connection with the Land and its soil. Boaz, for example, despite his wealth, spends the night on the threshing floor to guard the grain crop; this devotion characterizes him as a model of love for the Land and the honest physical labor involved in its harvest.

As in the previous clause, the person completing the harvest cycle overtakes the one who begins it. Note the chiastic structure, with the harvest at its center:

Plowman
    Reaper
    Grape-treader
Seed sower

The phrase *moshekh hazara* immediately evokes the famous "Song of Ascents" (Ps. 126), where the *moshekh hazara* carries a *meshekh hazara* – a sack of seed. The author of Psalm 126, likely post-exilic, intentionally draws on Amos's idyllic imagery to bolster the hope and faith of the returning exiles and to motivate their reconnection with the Land.[6]

Rashi and Ibn Ezra connect these phrases to the blessing at the end of Leviticus: "Your threshing shall reach to the vintage, and the vintage shall reach to the sowing time" (26:5).

R. Eliezer of Beaugency points out that Amos's vision surpasses that blessing: Leviticus promises agricultural seasons without a break; in Amos, they overlap each other. As Radak concurs: "similar to *vehisig lakhem*… but this one is greater."

R. Joseph Kara notes that this blessing redeems Amos's earlier curse (4:7):

> And I also withheld the rain from you when there were yet three months to the harvest; I would send rain upon one city and send no rain upon another city; one field would be rained upon, and the field on which it did not rain withered.

6. Yitzchak Etshalom, "*Al HaDimah ve'al haRinah* (The Tears and the Song): Analysis of Psalm 126" [Heb.], *Megadim* 42 (2005): 49–59.

This shows that this beautiful coda is an integral part of Amos's book; it closes circles and redeems his harsh warnings.

The mountains shall drip sweet wine

Whereas the previous line may be hyperbolic, this image is clearly exaggerated, though delightful: the hillside vineyards bloom with such abundant clusters of grapes that their fruit – far too much to harvest – bursts with sweet juice that runs down the hills.

This reading refers to grapes and their wine, but *asis*, which appears five times in Tanakh, can mean any kind of fruit juice.[7]

Indeed, both R. Eliezer of Beaugency and Radak translate it as "sweet juice." Radak explains its etymology:

> *Asis* is a general name for any liquid that comes out of grapes or other fruit... it is called *asis* because the liquid comes out of them via squeezing and crushing, per *va'asotem resha'im.*[8]

Expanding the meaning paints an even more fruitful landscape: the fertile hills will burgeon with wheat, grapes, and so much sweet ripe fruit that the mountains themselves will flow with their juices.

And all the hills will melt

Harim/geva'ot is a common biblical pair, usually translated as mountains/hills, though the distinction between them – like here – is not always significant:

> The *mountains* (*heharim*) will dance like rams,
> [The] *hills* (*geva'ot*) like young sheep. (Ps. 114:4)

Just a few verses earlier (9:5), Amos describes God's touch as melting the earth.

7. In Song of Songs (8:2), *asis* explicitly refers to pomegranate juice.
8. Malachi 3:21 – means "you will *crush* the wicked."

Here, this word appears in a positive sense: instead of the earth melting in fear, the hills are melting with sweet juices. Rather than the earth quaking out of fear of God's judgment, God's presence is manifest in bounty and blessing.

In this first verse, the people are active in response to God's abundance – there is so much blessing that they have no choice but to keep working. By the next verse, they will begin to take initiative and further develop their relationship with God.

14: And I will return the captivity (fortune) of My people Israel

Beginning with Moses's farewell speech (Deut. 30), Israel's redemption is often expressed using wordplay that combines two roots with a similar sound but different meanings.

The root *shuv* (*shin, vav, bet*) means "return." The root *shavo* (*shin, vav, hei*) means "capture." Both meanings are explicitly related to redemption, for example: "The Lord your God will return (*veshav*) your captives (*shvutkha*)."[9] God promises that He will bring the captives back to their Land.

This is an odd sequence: it seems as if the hills will be dripping juice *before* the farmers come back, and as if the Davidic monarchy will be restored *before* the people's return.

And they shall build the waste cities and inhabit them

Amos envisions that the newly redeemed people will not build *new* cities; rather, they will rebuild the ruins of old, and choose to live *there.* This itself is significant. A new generation often seeks to make their own mark, to build new cities and set off in directions that their forebears did not take. Alternatively, they may slip back completely into their ancestors' ways, even those that led to perdition. This vision presents a perfect balance: back from exile, the people do not choose to abandon the old cities, but to resettle them with a fresh spirit – not just *uvanu,* but also *vayashavu.*

---

9. Deuteronomy 30:3; see also Psalms 126:4.

They shall plant vineyards and drink wine from them

Are these the same vineyards as in the previous verse, or does it reflect a sequence?

One option is that first the land will begin producing in unprecedented abundance *in anticipation of its people's return*;[10] and then the people will rebuild cities and plant their own vineyards, desiring to have an active hand in the Land's restoration.

Another possibility is that v. 13 presents a general picture, and then our verse describes how the people themselves will bring the Land back to a place "flowing with milk and honey."

Notice that the first thing that the returnees plant is vineyards. Whereas the Midrash criticizes Noah for beginning the world's replanting with a vineyard,[11] here the people are praised for reintroducing viticulture into the Land.

They will also make gardens and eat the fruit from them

The people also plant gardens in addition to vineyards; note the subtle chiasm that this forms with Amos's description of the five disasters that have befallen the people: "I laid waste to your gardens and vineyards" (4:9) – once again, this promise gently redeems the curses Amos pronounces throughout his book.

As mentioned in that context, the biblical *gan*, like the Garden of Eden, is closer to what we might call an orchard.[12]

15: And I will plant them upon their Land

Note the beautiful symmetry here: the people will plant fruit in their Land; and God will plant *them* in their Land. It is not only a measure of poetic justice, but also an absolute affirmation of their acts. A farmer

---

10. See Ezekiel 36:8 and Sanhedrin 98a: "There is no clearer indication of the redemption..."
11. Genesis Rabba [Theodor-Albeck] 58:36.
12. The popular word for orchard, *pardes*, is a Persian word that comes in to Tanakh fairly late. It moves on to Greece, where it is a παραδεισον, and from there to the English "paradise."

lives a life of perennial doubt, always worrying about the crop, blight, infestation, and, more than anything else – rainfall. Yet, if God promises to "plant" His people in the Land, this serves as an anchor to the people and their relationship to what *they* plant – they will flourish and bloom, as will their crop.

And they shall never again be plucked up

The verb *natash* is the biblical opposite of *nata* – plant.[13]

Although the verb here – *natash* – is written with a *tav*, it is like the word *natash* with a *tet* – to abandon. Earlier, Amos gravely warns (5:2):

> The maiden of Israel has fallen and will never again rise; she has been *abandoned* (*nit'sha*) on her Land, there is no one to raise her up.

Here, too, this coda redeems the woes of his earlier pronouncements, lighting a small candle against the overwhelming darkness.

From their Land which I have given them

With all the people's initiative, their rebuilding and replanting, it is crucial to remember that the Land is theirs because God gave it to them. This takes us back to the *sukka*-image of the monarchy: the king's royal house will only endure if he remembers the source – and purpose – of his mandate.

Says the Lord your God

These three final words so beautifully sum up what Amos has been trying to communicate throughout. The Lord is, first of all, a God who *communicates* His will through the prophets. Second, He is *the Lord*, the God of compassion who desires to see the people's hearts and deeds turn

13. Jeremiah 1:10, 24:6.

toward each other. And, finally, He is *Elokekha* – in a constant relationship with you and with your kings.[14]

We study Amos with a threefold reverence. First, these are God's words: even Amaziah's dismissive words to Amos in chapter 7 are part of a context in which God's words are expressed; they lack full meaning without that context. Second, Amos's sheer brilliance casts a sense of awe over the sensitive reader: even the darkest of warnings is woven with elegant, intricate wordplay and rhetorical genius. Finally, we understand that Amos operated at the nexus of the national Israelite experience. Reading and experiencing his oratory as living words provides us with the opportunity and context to understand and (vicariously) re-experience key moments in Jewish history.

Amos's sweet epilogue, its sense of promise, and the integral role of the Land and its produce in defining the redemption certainly speak to us today. Though lilting and magnificent, it is not merely *descriptive*; the text also pulses with a subtle *prescriptive* rhythm. Beyond its promise of vineyards and gardens, of a Land overflowing with produce, of formerly abandoned towns being revived and rebuilt, these words also beat with the pounding heart of a nation who has finally found their way back home and its deep commitment to make those vineyards flourish, to make those gardens succeed – to become so anchored in the Land that they will never again become uprooted. Amos's epilogue is the epitome of the prophecy "needed for generations." And it is our generation of redemption whose ears are attuned to this prophecy and whose hearts are deeply stirred by its words.

THE EPILOGUE

The epilogue itself unfolds with a dramatic progression, beginning with God taking center stage with His passive people on the sidelines. In the first verse, there are only four people present – a plowman, a reaper, a grape-treader, and a seed-planter. Although they represent the population, this synecdoche and the singular form of the verb downplay the

14. A beautiful expression of this is found in Samuel's words to Saul at his final coronation – I Samuel 12:14.

people's role to a minimum; this is further achieved through the mountains' and hills' personification as parallel players, the active verb *vehitifu* implying that the hills are pouring out their juices as intentionally as the plowman is plowing the earth.

The next verse places the entire nation in the spotlight. Once God brings them home from their exile, they are fully active and fully committed: six verbs in third person plural in the second half of this verse express the nation's bustling activity. These verbs come in three pairs: a verb of industry followed by a verb of enjoying the fruits of that labor:

Building → dwelling; planting → drinking; making → eating

The final verse brings God back to center stage: instead of the people planting, He now plants the people upon their land; the one verb relating to the people is in the passive form. This verb describes not what they will do, nor even what will befall them, but rather what will *not* befall them (*velo yinatshu*) and their land: they will never again be uprooted from the Land "that I gave to them."

Once again, while any biblical prophecy can be viewed from the perspective of its original audience as well as from that of any reader over the generations, this epilogue perhaps resonates most powerfully with the readers of today, our own generation.

The significance of this prophecy "for the generations" is clear to us. We are a people who have lived on faith and hope for millennia. This epilogue provided a divine image of the landscape of our hopes and dreams, and inspired generations of those who longed to return to Zion.[15]

We can also try to picture the impact of these words on Amos's contemporary audience. Beneath their complacent façade, the Samarian audience who openly scorned the words of the Judean prophet may have still been moved by his eloquent visions and rebukes. Though the nation has not yet suffered exile or the captor's sword, these words still

15. For example, *Ḥovevei Tziyyon*, an affiliation of Orthodox rabbis in Eastern Europe who were supporters of the political movement (including the Netziv), were driven by these visions.

hark back to a simpler, sweeter time, an age more idyllic and tranquil. Perhaps they stir yearning, or imagined nostalgia, for a former era. Perhaps, beneath the surface, Amos's audience realizes that such an age of pure partnership with the Land can only be achieved through a long period – a crucible – of turmoil and oppression. Perhaps these words would inspire repentance and introspection to shorten that necessary, painful process. Perhaps.

In the end, we know just how tragic that long and winding road proved to be.

The Epilogue and Its Place Within Amos's Eschatology

We have defined Amos's eschatology as nineteen verses in four sections. The first is introduced with *Hinei yamim ba'im* and describes a terrible famine, both literal and theological – people wander from place to place to find both food and God's word, but find neither.

The epilogue redeems this image of famine and wandering with another *Hinei yamim ba'im,* introducing a vision of abundance and stability: the people are "planted" firmly upon the same earth that produces their bountiful harvest.

The second passage in the eschaton is a frightening vision of God threatening His own people with the sword, warning that He will hunt them down no matter where they attempt to escape His presence. The people will ultimately be taken into captivity and slaughtered there.

The epilogue redeems this vision as well, promising that these captives will come back home, rebuild their ruined cities, and never be threatened with displacement again.

Finally, the third section seems to equate Israel to other nations – "are you not like Cushites to Me?" – but ultimately highlights Israel's unique relationship with God. All sinful nations will be punished – even theirs – but while other nations will fade away, Israel alone will survive and be protected by *Sukkat David* – the royal house of David, risen anew.

This too is brought home in the last line of our epilogue, which concludes Amos's vision of the end of days and the end of his entire book with a poignant signature: *Amar Hashem Elokekha.* The Lord, who speaks to only you, is your God and will not abandon you.

Each step of this epilogue sweetens the dark, haunting phases and phrases of the eschatology, and replaces them with hopes and dreams of the end of days – a vision that has sustained Israel throughout thousands of years of homelessness, oppression, and genocide; a vision that inspires its people to ever strive for its realization.

Our generation, which is privileged to rebuild the very cities Amos spoke to and spoke of, has witnessed the beginning of its fulfillment. Many of our friends have this last verse engraved on the walls of the homes they have built upon this newly revived soil. This is a statement of realization as well as commitment; it demonstrates a keen awareness of the special times in which we live, and the powerful commitment and precious burden we are privileged to bear.

וּנְטַעְתִּים עַל־אַדְמָתָם
וְלֹא יִנָּתְשׁוּ עוֹד מֵעַל אַדְמָתָם אֲשֶׁר נָתַתִּי לָהֶם
אָמַר ה׳ אֱלֹהֶיךָ

And I will plant them upon their Land,
and they shall never again be plucked up from their Land
which I have given them,
says the Lord your God.